CW01475766

The Joan Palevsky Imprint in Classical Literature

In honor of beloved Virgil—

"O degli altri poeti onore e lume . . ."

—Dante, *Inferno*

The publisher gratefully acknowledges the
generous contribution to this book provided by
the Classical Literature Endowment Fund of
the University of California Press Foundation,
which is supported by a major gift
from Joan Palevsky.

Contested Triumphs

Contested Triumphs

Politics, Pageantry, and Performance in Livy's Republican Rome

Miriam R. Pelikan Pittenger

UNIVERSITY OF CALIFORNIA PRESS
Berkeley Los Angeles London

University of California Press, one of the most distinguished university presses in the United States, enriches lives around the world by advancing scholarship in the humanities, social sciences, and natural sciences. Its activities are supported by the UC Press Foundation and by philanthropic contributions from individuals and institutions. For more information, visit www.ucpress.edu.

University of California Press
Berkeley and Los Angeles, California

University of California Press, Ltd
London, England

Library of Congress Cataloging-in-Publication Data

Pittenger, Miriam R. Pelikan (Miriam Ruth Pelikan), 1967–.
Contested triumphs : politics, pageantry, and performance in Livy's Republican Rome / Miriam R. Pelikan Pittenger.
p. cm.
Includes bibliographical references and index.
ISBN 978-0-520-24139-8 (cloth : alk. paper)
1. Rome—History—Republic, 265–30 B.C. 2. Rome—Politics and government—265–30 B.C. 3. Political customs and rites—Rome—History. 4. Rites and ceremonies—Rome—History. 5. Livy. Ab urbe condita. I. Title.
DG241.2.P58 2008
937'.02—dc22 2008009086

Manufactured in the United States of America

16 15 14 13 12 11 10 09 08 07
10 9 8 7 6 5 4 3 2 1

This book is printed on Natures Book, which contains 50% post-consumer waste and meets the minimum requirements of ANSI/NISO Z39.48-1992 (R 1997) (*Permanence of Paper*).

In loving memory of my father,
Jaroslav Jan Pelikan, Jr.,
1923–2006

Was du ererbt von deinen Vätern hast,
Erwirb es, um es zu besitzen.

What you have as heritage, take now as task.
For thus you will make it your own.
GOETHE, *Faust* 683–84

CONTENTS

PREFACE

Livy's triumph debates may seem like a frightfully arcane topic even to some classicists, but my researches in connection with this project have in fact ranged rather widely through a number of diverse and well-documented subfields. I have labored in earnest to make myself accountable to specialists across the spectrum and to put my various arguments in all the right scholarly contexts, yet there are limits. So I apologize at the outset to anyone who might feel slighted by not finding his or her own name or favorite authority cited. In particular, because the final revisions of the manuscript (prior to copyediting) were interrupted by my father's death in May 2006, readers will notice a paucity of references to works published since then. Certain relevant items available earlier also came into my hands too late to receive more than a cursory notice. Among these, I am especially sorry that I was not able to make better use of Karl-Joachim Hölkeskamp's compelling *Rekonstruktionen einer Republik* (Munich, 2004) and the admirable collection of essays published under the title *Representations of War in Ancient Rome* (Cambridge, 2006). Tanja Itgenshorst's *Tota illa pompa* (Göttingen, 2005) shares some of my conclusions about the rules governing the *ius triumphandi* under the Republic, but I believe the author misrepresents the complex political dynamics between the magistrates, senate, and people of Rome. Beyond noting broad points of agreement and divergence, however, I have not addressed her arguments in detail. Last but not least, Mary Beard's much-anticipated *The Roman Triumph* (Cambridge, Mass., 2007) had been proclaimed with fanfare but was still outside the city gates when my book went to the copyeditor, and John Briscoe's brand-new commentary on Livy Books 38–40 (Oxford, 2008) came along later still. Quite frankly, though, these works little alter what I have to say. The ideas presented here are what they are, and at a certain point I simply had to stop endlessly updating footnotes so that I could finally get the manuscript off my desk. I will stand behind what I have written despite any errors of omission, commission, or transmission that may be found in these pages to keep me humble. *Dis manibus,* as the expression goes . . .

It has been a long road in more ways than one. My literal journeys brought me to libraries all over the map, including (in roughly chronological order) the Bancroft Library at the University of California, Berkeley, the Blegen Library at the American School of Classical Studies in Athens, the Byzantine Library at Dumbarton Oaks, the Library of Congress, the Robarts Library at the University of Toronto, the Ashmolean Library in Oxford, the Classics Library at the University of Illinois at Urbana-Champaign, the Yale University Classics Library, and the Blegen Library at the University of Cincinnati. Once upon a time I received funding from the Mellon Foundation and the Chancellor's Dissertation Fellowship at UC Berkeley, and later also from the Campus Research Board and the Center for Advanced Study at UIUC. Many individuals contributed as well to the "care and feeding" of this book and its author over the years. Among my professors at Berkeley, Charles Murgia, Thomas Habinek, and Andrew Stewart all had a formative influence. Graduate-school colleagues Eric Orlin and Sara Johnson took a sustaining interest in my work from the beginning and showed me how to think more like an ancient historian, while Andrew Riggsby, Matthew Roller, and Anthony Corbeill have always kept me kept me honest from the Latinist side, where my real roots lie. In the course of this project I have had the distinct honor of collaborating with a succession of remarkable women from the University of California Press. Kate Toll, onetime acquisitions editor, shepherded me through the early stages of revision and got me the publishing contract, with input from three shrewd anonymous readers, whose comments did much to point my efforts in the right direction. After Kate's departure, Lynne Withey, Director of the Press, did double duty in acquisitions for a time and helped me along, until Laura Cerruti took over. Without Laura's professionalism, good humor, and seemingly endless patience—not to mention the occasional well-timed ultimatum—I sincerely doubt whether this book would ever have made it into production. Her assistant Rachel Lochman proved invaluable too. Then, as the actual publication date began to draw near and only a few last hurdles remained, project editor Cindy Fulton was a treasure trove of knowledge and encouragement. I grew up with an inside view of academic publishing, since my father was not only a prolific author in his own right but also chaired the publication committee at a major university press for many years, but Cindy still taught me a great deal about how the production process works. Our phone conversations and e-mails were very reassuring, and at times downright hilarious. I owe further debts of gratitude to the keen instincts of copyeditor Paul Psoinos, who worked wonders to complete the transformation of my erstwhile doctoral thesis into a polished book accessible to a wider audience; to the painstaking efforts of the indexer, Roberta Engleman, who saved me from having to undertake that particularly thorny task myself; to the resourcefulness of Karen Dudas in the Classics Library at UIUC, who efficiently answered several of my urgent last-minute queries from hundreds of miles away, and to the brilliant suggestion of Ann Kuttner that led, somewhat circuitously, to the cover design.

In all likelihood, I would not have run across Livy's triumph debates in graduate school, much less ever contemplated eventually putting my ideas about them into print, without Erich Gruen, my mentor, taskmaster, advocate, and very dear friend. I wish that his beloved wife, Joan, were here to join in the celebration and the sense of relief that he will undoubtedly feel to witness this publication at last. Living with an author in the throes of her first book is clearly not for the faint of heart, but my husband, Laurence, has coped magnificently from start to finish. His love and our laughter keep me going, always. Finally, although it was my mother, Sylvia, who first inspired me to study classics at a very young age, I am dedicating this book to the blessed memory of my father, Jaroslav Pelikan, who on countless occasions ungrudgingly turned from pen or keyboard to lend me his tender support and sage advice on demand. He remained a tower of strength until his dying breath, and I can easily picture the fond grin that would have lit up his face to see a finished volume with my name on the dust jacket for once, rather than his own. The epigraph to this book, his favorite passage from Goethe's *Faust* with the elegant translation that I remember him first crafting and then often heard him quote, has something to say about what the accomplishment means to me as well.

Introduction
Livy's Republican Rome

VICTORS AND THEIR HISTORIES

The Roman triumph exists at a point of intersection between the art of war and the art of self-promotion. These are two areas where the Romans clearly excelled, and they mastered the further trick of doing both things at once.[1] Triumphal spectacles and the enduring victory monuments associated with them rank among the most recognizable and vivid icons from the Imperial period, and under the Republic the annual homecoming contest among magistrates returning from the provinces continually brought tales of accomplishments in warfare (*res bello gestae*) to the forefront of public attention. Commanders inevitably sought recognition at home (*domi*) for their successes at war (*militiae*), and so war stories became potent weapons in the political arena by appealing to a set of widely shared and highly prized ideals, such as courage (*virtus*), duty (*pietas*), loyalty (*fides*), and the like. The system favored soldiers who were also gifted speakers, storytellers, and performers, able to translate their victories abroad into power and prestige at home.[2]

1. For an excellent survey of both Roman militarism and Roman showmanship, as well as the abiding link between them, see recently Welch 2006c.

2. For a taxonomy of the process that transformed victory into power (albeit with more of an emphasis on material culture than on speechmaking and *res gestae* narratives), see Hölscher 2006.

This book contains a fair amount of Latin and some Greek as well. Every effort has been made to provide translations for passages quoted from ancient authors in the original languages and to gloss terms that appear in the text itself the first time that they are used. Quoted passages in Latin have been printed in roman type with quotation marks, whereas Latin terms elsewhere appear in italics. These typographical conventions may sometimes produce a rather odd visual effect when both occur side by side, but I hope the differentiation will be clear enough.

Over time something akin to a canonical history of Rome emerged, loosely stitched together from the variegated *res gestae* narratives of returning war heroes, year after year and generation after generation, and along with stories from the past came a habitual way of thinking about national values and exemplary characters. Livy's *Ab Urbe Condita* gives wide scope to the annual magisterial cycle under the Republic, including requests for triumphs, because therein lay the very origins of the very type of exemplary history that the author himself had set out to write, bound up for him as it was with the need to rediscover and reformulate Roman national identity after the Civil Wars.

STARTING POINT: TWIN *CERTAMINA*

Proconsul M. Fulvius Nobilior returned home in 187 B.C. from a successful stint in Aetolia that had begun with his consulship two years earlier, but before he could enjoy a triumph to mark his achievements he faced a major ordeal.[3] One of the consuls for that year, M. Aemilius Lepidus, bore a grudge against him and worked hard to lay stumbling blocks in his path from victory to glory. Nobilior fought back, though, and at length the senate voted in his favor and he set a date for the triumph with relief, since by now Lepidus's duties had carried him off to Liguria. Removal to the periphery should have ended the consul's involvement in the affair, but he managed to keep his hand in play, even at a distance, by suborning a loyal tribune to act against Nobilior on his behalf. Nor did he relent on learning that the senators had authorized the triumph over his objections. Instead he left his province and set out for Rome posthaste to stir up further trouble. What could he have done at this late stage? It is not inconceivable that he actually meant to disrupt the triumph itself somehow.[4] At any rate his efforts fell through, because a sudden illness detained him en route,

3. I have relied on the following Latin editions of Livy's history throughout: Ogilvie 1974 (Books 1–5), Walters and Conway 1919 (Books 6–10), Walters and Conway 1929 (Books 21–25), Johnson and Conway 1935 (Books 26–30), Briscoe 1991 (Books 31–40), Briscoe 1986 (Books 41–45). Packard 1968 also proved indispensable, even in this era of electronic resources. English translations are my own unless attributed otherwise. References to passages from Livy will be listed by book and section number only and embedded within the text itself wherever possible rather than being buried in the notes. All unlabeled dates are B.C.

4. Livy's precise wording (39.5.11: "ad impediendum triumphum," "in order to interfere with the triumph") certainly does not rule out the prospect of direct intervention. Walsh 1994, *ad loc.*, translates "to block the triumph." Yet for all the contentiousness of triumph debates, we rarely hear about riots, demonstrations, or other disruptions during the actual performance of the ritual. The murky affair of L. Postumius Megellus, consul in 294 (10.37), comes to mind as a possible exception, but even then concerted opposition could not stop a triumphal procession once in progress, because supporters of the *triumphator* barred the way against the protesters.

allowing Nobilior to seize the initiative. In fact, the relevant passage in Livy stresses not so much Lepidus's hasty departure from Liguria as its effect on the would-be *triumphator* in Rome: "*lest he face even more of a struggle over his triumph than he had in the war,*" we are told, "he moved up the date of his triumph" (39.5.11–12).[5]

With the expression italicized here Livy is making a grim pun, in that the phrase "plus . . . certaminum" ("more of a struggle") refers simultaneously to the clash of armies hand to hand in the field (Romans vs. outsiders) and to the rhetorical combat of political foes in the Forum and senate house (Romans vs. other Romans). Metaphors are not the same thing as reality, but even a notional blurring of the boundaries between battlefield and civic arena is usually no joke. Livy and his contemporaries knew all too well from their own painful experience what it meant for the closely guarded distinction between *domi* and *militiae* to break down, so that the two spheres long kept separate began to overlap, actually turning politics into warfare and fellow citizens into the enemy and Other.[6] In the clinical light of Augustan-era hindsight, the Nobilior-Lepidus débâcle might be seen as symptomatic of the same pathology that eventually led to the outbreak of civil war. Above all, it reveals the broad scope afforded to competition between members of the officeholding élite.[7]

Yet the trope of dual *certamina,* the pairing and intermingling of contests both military and rhetorical, at home and abroad, comes off here as more playful and ironic than genuinely frightening. In the second century, the threat of anything even approaching outright civil war remained quite remote, for one thing, so that no matter how far the rivalry between Lepidus and Nobilior might seem to escalate as the story progresses, a Roman audience would hardly need reassurance about the Republic's ability to weather the storm. Moreover, in the events leading up to Nobilior's triumph Livy

5. 39.5.11–12: "cum audisset consulem M. Aemilium, litteris M. Aburii tribuni plebis acceptis de remissa intercessione, ipsum ad impediendum triumphum Romam venientem aegrum in via substitisse, ne plus in triumpho certaminum quam in bello haberet, praetulit triumphi diem."

6. The crucial distinction is marked by the *pomerium* or sacred boundary dividing the city of Rome on the inside (*domi*), where a strict taboo forbade the carrying of arms, from the whole territory outside (*militiae*), where weapons and warfare were sanctioned. The threat of violence could then be properly channeled *outward* against the enemy and Other, rather than *inward* against the community of fellow citizens. See, e.g., Roller 1996, 322.

7. Note the dark assessment by Barton 2001, 97: "The imperial triumphs of the Roman Republic had been purchased with the attenuation or destruction of the codes that made these triumphs meaningful, the traditions by which these activities could be framed and interpreted." On the vast subject of aristocratic competition in Rome, see in particular Hölkeskamp 1987 and 1993; Rosenstein 1990a, 1990b, and 1995. On the failure of conventional safety valves in the Late Republic, Raaflaub 1974 is the place to start. Other references will appear at appropriate places below throughout.

has introduced another element, which works from the other side of the equation, to offset the supposed intensity of the political strife, and hence the potential menace to the order of things in the imbalance between the two *certamina:* to wit, the allegation that Nobilior had not fought a real war. Long before the commander's return, Lepidus engineered a senate decree to the effect that the stronghold of Ambracia, captured by Nobilior in 189 and a key to his triumph hopes, "did not seem to have been taken by force" (38.44.6).[8] With a charge of that nature hanging over a general's conduct in his province, the notion of his waging "even more of a struggle" in the senate house than on the battlefield need not actually amount to very much, relatively speaking. The whole long-drawn-out conflict between Lepidus and Nobilior, thoroughly bloodless as it was, thus emerges as a tempest in a teapot.

The fighting in Aetolia was long over and its outcome fixed by the time Nobilior came home to ask for a triumph, but the stature of his achievement would rest with the debate in the senate. As Livy's narrative unfolds, therefore, each new maneuver in the political struggle *domi* reflects on the senators' emerging judgment (and so on ours as well) of what had already happened *militiae.* With the declaration about Ambracia not having been taken by force, Lepidus sought to forestall the predictable course of the argument with a preemptive challenge to any assertion that Nobilior deserved a reward for his sack of the town. Yet by downplaying the war in Greece, the consul only added fuel to the political fire in Rome. Competing claims about the battlefield were now vying against one another in the senate. Once Nobilior arrived to make his case in person, the body of his peers concluded that he did deserve civic honors for his achievements. That verdict should have sufficed to put an end to controversy. The celebration would officially herald a job well done, forever sealing the general's good name as a conqueror of Rome's enemies. Up to the very eve of the triumph, however, the commander's Roman rival pursued the campaign against him on the home front so relentlessly that it now actually threatened, Livy tells us, to overshadow the original conflict abroad. Because the historical record bears witness to both *certamina,* foreign and domestic, on more or less equal terms, Livy enshrines them side by side and explicitly draws the comparison: "lest he face even more of a struggle over his triumph than he had in the war."

Lepidus's precipitous return from Liguria in 187 may represent the extreme lengths to which a vindictive *nobilis* might literally go, but M. Fulvius Nobilior was by no means the only victorious *imperator* under the Republic whose triumph bid ran into stiff opposition.[9] Throughout the

8. 38.44.6: "adiecit senatus consultum, Ambraciam vi captam esse non videri." The expression "urbs vi capta est" ("the city was captured by force") has a formulaic ring.

9. For a catalogue of the triumph debates attested in Livy 21–45, see appendix A below.

era of expansion, as the armies of the SPQR began to march steadily farther and farther afield, and Roman influence began to play itself out on an ever wider canvas, finally embracing the whole Mediterranean world, the fantastic influx of wealth and power, on a scale unheard of before, sparked increasingly fierce competition among Roman aristocrats vying for chances to lead lucrative campaigns abroad and so to enhance their prestige at home.[10] Nothing brought out the prevailing tensions within the Roman élite quite like the moment when one of their number came home victorious and asked for recognition. Livy has Scipio Africanus remark that "there is nothing more magnificent"—that is, no greater prize or more splendid badge of honor—"among the Romans than the triumph" (30.15.12).[11]

Triumphal processions helped to define the sacred topography of the city from a very ancient date.[12] Similarly, triumph debates—often angry ones—emerged early and remained for centuries as a prominent feature of the political landscape in Republican Rome. Like the ritual itself, the ability to grant or refuse access to the city's highest rewards helped to delineate the center of power. In the period of retrenchment after the Civil Wars, Augustus began to limit the award of triumphs to himself and other members of the imperial family.[13] Under the Republic, as we shall see, no easy rule of thumb determined who deserved the honor and who did not, which is one reason why triumph requests often became hotly contested. So Augustus was sending out a very clear signal: from now on, he alone would occupy the top step on the civic podium. Roman aristocrats might

10. For a reliable historical survey of the era of Roman expansion, see Astin 1989a, with Astin 1989b on the ancient sources. Roman imperialism as such is an enormous topic. For a concise summary of the main competing viewpoints, see Gruen 1984a, 5–7. With reference to previous scholarship, see also recently Brunt 2004; Crawford 2004; Eckstein 2006a and 2006b; Gruen 1984b; Harris 1985 (a highly provocative and seminal work) and 2004; Kallet-Marx 1995; North 1981; Raaflaub 1996; Rich 1993.

11. 30.15.12: "neque magnificentius quicquam triumpho apud Romanos." The word *magnificum* suggests aspects both of spectacle (as in "glorious to behold") and of status symbol (as in "enlarging the reputation"), but the two concepts naturally merge to a significant degree. Cf. Feldherr 1998.

12. See, for example, Edwards 1996, 21 and n. 56; Favro 1994; Hölkeskamp 2001 and 2006; Hölscher 2001; Stambaugh 1988, 7–47.

13. The final entry in the Fasti Triumphales belongs to proconsul L. Cornelius Balbus the Younger, who triumphed from Africa in 19 B.C. (Degrassi 1947, 86–87, 571). As others have often pointed out, Balbus, born in Gades in Spain, was the first *triumphator* of provincial (i.e., non-Italian) origins and also the last who was not a member of the imperial family. Flower 1996, 231 n. 31, adds that his theater was "the last public building erected in Rome by a general from his spoils." Clearly everything changed with the consolidation of the Principate. On Augustus's efforts to limit triumphs and thereby secure his own position, see also Eck 1984, 138–43; and 2003, 60–69; Hickson 1991; Miller 2000, especially 409–14; Syme 1939, 404.

still compete with each other for lesser prizes (e.g., *ornamenta triumphalia* or *insignia triumphi*) in the traditional way, but no one could hope to vie directly against the *Princeps* any longer.[14] Livy's history looks back on the *libera res publica* ("free Republic") from the vantage point of its greatest crisis, which eventually transformed it into something new and very different.

THEORETICAL FRAMEWORK

Both the title of this book and its subtitle were carefully chosen. The Roman triumph has often been an object of study in its own right, but in the present volume the focus lies less on the ritual itself than on the manner in which Roman aristocrats under the Republic competed for triumphs and argued over them among themselves: not just triumphs as such, then, but *contested* triumphs. The hunt for civic honors in fact formed part of a continuous power struggle both within the élite and between the various branches of the political order: magistrates, senate, and popular assembly. The alliterative triad of politics, pageantry, and performance captures the idea, familiar to any student of things Roman, that the key to success in this ongoing quest for praise and renown (*laus* and *gloria*) was public display in a variety of forms. That said, the phrase "Livy's Republican Rome" is unusual and probably calls for further explanation. "Livy" of course designates the author and his work, and "Republican Rome" refers to the historical period and political system of the SPQR; but what do these two elements signify when used together?

Quite a while ago, I began to wonder about the rules governing triumphal procedure under the Republic. How typical was the vehement opposition encountered by M. Fulvius Nobilior in his triumph bid? What exactly did it take for a commander like him to earn a triumph? What basic requirements, if any, had to be met? Who authorized triumphs to those who requested them, and if a question should arise in a given instance, how was a verdict reached? How many triumph requests succeeded, on average, and how many failed that we know about? Did some disputes become more heated and bitter than others, and if so, why? These inquiries arose from plain curiosity about a familiar aspect of the Roman world, and yet I soon found out how naive it would be to look for simple or straightforward answers. Triumphal decision making, like many aspects of civic procedure under the Republic, turns out to be a decidedly murky business. It lies, after all, within the broad compass of ancestral custom (*mos maiorum*), and therefore an element of indeterminacy persists, even with the best evi-

14. See, e.g., Dio Cass. 54.24.8, Suet. *Tib.* 9.2, Tac. *Ann.* 1.72.1. On *ornamenta triumphalia* in particular, see Boyce 1942 and Eck 1999.

dence available. Historical questions also inevitably lead to historiographical ones. Most of what we know about the award of civic honors under the Republic comes from Livy, who writes from a perspective centuries later than and at several removes distant from the events he describes. So try as we might, we cannot take the author out of the equation either.[15]

Only a tiny portion of Livy's vast history has survived.[16] To make matters worse, the so-called annalistic material in Books 21–45—where most of the triumph debates appear—has tended to fall through the cracks between ancient historians and Latinist literary critics, working at cross-purposes. Much depends on whether one views Livy's *magnum opus* primarily as a text or as a source. Historians routinely rely on later Livy for valuable evidence about the Middle Republic, but because of their predominantly legalistic and procedural approach to constitutional issues such as the *ius triumphandi* (i.e., the rules governing who should triumph and who should not), they often dwell on technical details and brief passages taken out of context.[17] Literary critics delight in unraveling complex narrative structures and might have valuable insights into the nature of Livy's annalistic project in the later books, but for reasons of their own they rarely stray beyond the First Decade (i.e., Books 1–10). So the later books have remained largely the preserve of the historians. Recent years have witnessed a resurgence of interest in Livy from the Latinist side. Literary monographs have appeared exploring themes such as time and space, monument and spectacle, memory and ideology in the *Ab Urbe Condita*.[18] These studies have done much to buoy Livy's reputation as an author worth reading closely, but they still focus disproportionately, if not overwhelmingly, on the First Decade,[19] despite a splendid new Teubner edition of Books 31–45 having

15. Anachronisms from the Late Republic are particularly evident in Livy's account of the Conflict of the Orders. See Oakley 1997–98, 1.86–89, for a brief discussion; and Mitchell 1990 for an extended treatment.

16. By all accounts the *Ab Urbe Condita* originally consisted of 142 books, which he must have written at an average rate of three books per year from perhaps the mid-30s B.C. until his death ca. A.D. 17 (Luce 1965, 231 and n. 61). From this massive corpus workable manuscripts exist for only thirty-five books in their entirety (1–10 and 21–45), along with a collection of brief ancient summaries (*Periochae*) covering each book in turn except 136 and 137. Comparison between the epitomes and the actual text of the extant books, however, casts considerable doubt on the reliability of the former as a means of reconstructing anything more than a sketchy outline for the missing material.

17. In a similar vein, Forsythe 1999, 133, voiced a "need to base major scholarly conclusions upon a careful consideration of Livy's entire text, not just a handful of selected passages which happen to conform to an author's preconceived notion."

18. Thus Chaplin 2000; Feldherr 1998; Jaeger 1997; Miles 1995.

19. In all fairness, it must be said that Jaeger 1997 includes one section on the Hannibalic War and another on the so-called trials of the Scipios. Moreover, Chaplin 2000 makes extensive use of Livy's later books and even deals with triumph debates as such. But these are exceptions to the persistent general rule.

been published not long before by one historian, followed by a series of student commentaries on Books 36–40 by another one.[20] In perpetuating the notion that the real Livy dwells in the First Decade, even the most thoughtful and well-meaning critic can harbor misleading assumptions about the author and his vast project.

Why have literary scholars shied away en masse from the annalistic books? Graduate reading lists are partly responsible, because they act like a genetic code for would-be classicists, imprinting them with what their teachers consider important.[21] Taste plays a role too: by comparison with foundation legends and primordial history, as found in the First Decade, the later material admittedly makes for a dry read with its mundane and repetitive cycle of elections, provincial assignments, armies, levies, portents, campaigns, embassies, triumph debates, triumphs, and so on, down to the next set of elections, where the sequence starts all over again.[22] But the prevailing bias also reflects the extent to which evocative, shadowy figures from the dim early days of Roman history make the best (i.e., the most transparent) foils for Augustus when one is seeking to expose the ideological underpinnings of the Livian narrative and catch the text off guard in its construction (or reconstruction) of reality. No one would deny that Romulus and Remus, the Tarquins, Lucretia, Brutus, Hortensius, Mucius Scaevola, Torquatus, Manlius Capitolinus, Camillus, and the like are properly the stuff of legend rather than of history. Reliable records from the formative period simply did not exist, even in Livy's time. What previous authors did not invent outright, they cobbled together piecemeal from the wayward chronicles of various noble families, full of pious praise for their illustrious ancestors but notoriously prone to self-aggrandizing

20. The Teubner edition is by J. Briscoe, with Books 41–45 appearing in 1986 and Books 31–40 in 1991. The series of commentaries on Books 36–40 was published in sequence by P. G. Walsh in 1990, 1992, 1993, 1994, and 1996, respectively.

21. An informal survey of Ph.D. reading lists among various major classics programs in the United States reveals a remarkable consistency: Books 1–5 of Livy are universally favored over all the rest, with the later portions represented occasionally (if at all) by Books 21–22. The inference is unavoidable that no one but a hard-core ancient historian would bother with Books 31–45.

22. For a convenient outline of the Roman annalistic schema, modeled on Livy's basic narrative pattern or patterns, see Lintott 1999, 9–15 ("A Roman Political Year"). On the tensions sometimes created by attempting to narrate extended episodes within the strictures imposed by the annalistic framework, and on the degree of flexibility and adaptability displayed by Livy in modifying the schema to suit his own purposes, see, e.g., Rich 1997, Warrior 1996 (with the review by McClain 1997); also Kraus 1994, 9–13. I strongly concur with Kraus and Woodman 1997, 62, however, that since the annual cycle "*is* a pattern . . . and one that Livy's readers come to expect to find, it provides a . . . kind of 'map' to [his] written city: as the elections, military assignments, and other such events formed the backbone of the state, so they form the backbone of Livy's narrative, assuring that it, like the state it describes and recreates, moves ahead in predictable, traditional fashion."

fiction.[23] So Livy borrowed what he could from the sources available to him, and then shaped and expanded the story as he saw fit, carefully crafting his account of the city's origins to suit his grand compositional scheme. Historians are understandably skeptical about the result of such a process: "the author takes leave of legend only to plunge into fiction."[24] From there it does not require much of a stretch on the literary side, especially with the rise of New Historicism and similar approaches, to begin viewing the entire *Ab Urbe Condita* as a vast creative construct, an artifact of the author's own time that may bear eloquent witness to the concerns and preoccupations of the Augustan era, but where one searches in vain for any reliable guide to Rome's actual past.[25]

Before long, the imagined past as such becomes just like any other fic-

23. The formation and growth of the Roman historical tradition—often loosely, if somewhat inaccurately, termed annalistic—is an extremely complex and controversial subject, most of which lies beyond the scope of the present investigation. The once widely accepted view of a monolithic development simply will not hold. As one recent book reviewer has stated: "It has become obvious that the origins and early phases of Roman historiography were determined by a variety of intellectual approaches, narrative patterns, and competing intentions of authors" (Beck 2005). Cf. also Cornell 1986b, 58, arguing that the annalistic tradition "was not an authenticated official record or an objective critical reconstruction; rather, it was an ideological construct designed to control, to justify, and to inspire." See also Brennan 2000, 6–8 and nn.; Bucher 1987; Cornell 1986a; Forsythe 2005, 59–77; Frier 1999, passim; Kierdorf 2002; Kraus 1994, 9–17, 27–29; Kraus and Woodman 1997, especially 1–9; Northwood 2000; Petzold 1993; Rawson 1971; Rüpke 1995; Ungern-Sternberg 1986; Wiseman 1986 (all with reference to previous scholarship). For ancient testimonia regarding the Annales Maximi, see Cato fr. 77 Peter (*apud* Gell. 2.28.6), Cic. *De Or.* 2.52, and Serv. Auct. *ad Aen.* 1.373; for the so-called *libri lintei* ("linen books"), see 4.7.11–12, 13.7, 20.8, and 23.1; on family chronicles, *stemmata,* and *laudationes,* see, e.g., 8.40.4–5, Dion. Hal. 12.20.17, Pliny *NH* 35.6–7, Cic. *Brut.* 62, Sen. *Ben.* 3.28.2 and *Ep.* 44.1, Mart. 4.40.1, Juv. 8.1, Suet. *Nero* 37.1.

24. Syme 1959, 27. Walsh 1961 put forward a broadly skeptical view of Livy's value as a historical source, throughout his work but particularly in the First Decade, and the same author's series of commentaries on Books 36–40 all follow suit (Walsh 1990, 1992, 1993, 1994, and 1996). The groundbreaking efforts of Burck 1964 paved the way for our understanding of Livy as a gifted narrator with his own agenda. For other, varying assessments of the special problems with using the First Decade as a historical source, see among others Badian 1966; Burck 1971; Lipovsky 1981; Luce 1977 and 1993; Miles 1995; Musti 1993; Oakley 1997–98, 1.3–151, 331–79; Phillips 1982; Walbank 1971; Wiseman 1979; Woodman 1988. Modern critical histories of early Rome continue to appear, and of course anyone writing such a work must decide what to do with the material from Livy: e.g., Cornell 1995; Forsythe 2005; Oakley 2004; Raaflaub 2006; R. Stewart 1998.

25. Note the colorful imagery invoked by Jaeger 1997, 8: "The image of Livy lost in the records of Roman history and dogging the tracks of the annalist Valerius Antias in one direction before turning aside to follow Claudius Quadrigarius in another has given way to one of Livy as a Roman Daedalus constructing a monument from the rubble of the ages and leaving broken edges visible as reminders that any coherent account of the past is, at best, contrived from ruins." For a longer and more detailed discussion, see Miles 1995, 8–74 (neatly summarized by Feldherr 1997b, 137 n. 5).

tion, despite its ostensible claims to represent something real and recoverable—and so much for the possibility of historical research based on literary sources. Anyone with an active interest in historiography as a genre, or who has ever taken (or taught) graduate-level history and literature courses side by side in the same semester, is familiar with the headaches produced by trying to reconcile the underlying assumptions from different disciplines about the nature of texts and their referents.[26] It therefore emerged as a central goal of this study to treat the *Ab Urbe Condita* both as a source of historical data relating to things outside itself and events that actually took place, and as an important text of the Augustan era, politically informed and ideologically implicated, and worthy of scrutiny and criticism in its own right. The triumphs and triumph debates in Livy's narrative clearly invite both approaches, as we shall see. The challenge was to explore what we can learn from the text about the workings of the Republic without ignoring the underlying assumptions and deep structures of the narrative itself.

Even apart from any discussion of Livy's own techniques and limitations,[27] he is at best only as good a factual historian as his sources will allow. For Books 21–45, he relied mainly on the Greek author Polybius and certain early Roman annalists, notably Valerius Antias and Claudius Quadrigarius. From annalistic sources Livy derived his basic narrative framework, along with lists of magistrates and their accomplishments, year by year.[28] Unfortunately, these writers do little to inspire confidence in other ways: their extant fragments display a hackneyed repertoire of stock motifs, a heavily pro-Roman bias, a tendency to sensationalize, and a dim understanding of events that took place anywhere far afield.[29] Polybius thankfully does a better job with Roman foreign affairs, especially in the

26. On the dilemma, see Kraus 1991: "if one does not separate the historian from the literary artist one can become immersed in an apparently endless—and at times epistemologically frightening—theoretical discussion about the nature and aims of history in general and of narrative history in particular." Cf. Frier 1999, x: "history and historiography are not the same thing, but rather complementary. If the two disciplines are to be good neighbors, they need some boundaries between them; they must not be merged or subordinated one to the other."

27. For broad discussions of Livy's habits as a writer, see especially Bispham 2006, 38–39 (a brief but lucid summary of the central issues); Burck 1964; Luce 1977, 185–229; Walsh 1961, 1966, and 1974; Woodman 1988, xv–xxvii.

28. Cf. Kraus 1994, 10, arguing that despite severe doubts about the extent to which early Roman historians relied on the Annales Maximi as such, the chronicle "gave the kind of historiography known as *annales* its distinctive formal structure: a chronological sequence of the eponymous magistrates by whom the Romans dated their year, with an accompanying record of state business."

29. On the techniques of the early Roman annalists and their limited reliability, see among others Badian 1966; Kraus 1994, 15–17; Luce 1977, 139–84; Oakley 1997–98, 1.72–108; Petzold 1993; Walsh 1961, 110–37. On patriotic history in particular, see also (variously) De Monte 1999; Feichtinger 1992; Polo 2004.

East, and where his account has survived, scholars have been able to trace Livy's abridgments and reworkings to good advantage.[30] Source criticism has its place, but when it becomes too much an end in itself, it quickly reduces the entire *Ab Urbe Condita* to a string of disjointed episodes mindlessly copied from the works of previous authors. Such a view does Livy a disservice as an interpreter of human events in his own right.[31] Nor, despite the well-justified criticisms often leveled against the early annalists, would historians agree to toss out everything that Livy may have derived from them. No one would question the immeasurable contribution to our understanding of the Republic made by the prosopographical and other factual data from Books 21–45.[32] Indeed even the most outspoken critic of Livy's shortcomings as a historian still acknowledges "the enormous historical value of the yearly catalogue of the election of officials, and of the other public business conducted in the senate and in the assembly."[33]

Within the predictable patterns of Livy's annalistic narrative, the notices of victory celebrations appear right alongside elections and provincial assignments, and appear to share the same reassuring look and feel of archival data.[34] Yet a healthy skepticism in particular instances comes well recommended, especially for the early centuries of the Republic. In a famous passage Cicero complains about noble families seeking to enhance the fame of their ancestors by fabricating honors for them.[35] That said, it always helps when Livy's account can be corroborated by the Capitoline Fasti (official epigraphic lists of *triumphatores* from Romulus to Augustus).

30. On Livy's use of Polybius, see, e.g., Briscoe 1973, 1–12; 1981, 1–3; and 1993; Luce 1977, 185–229, epecially 205–21; Tränkle 1977 (a landmark study); Walsh 1961, 110–90. Polybius is widely regarded as a reliable witness to the events he describes, but note the incisive remark of Kraus 1991: "Polybius was as much an interpreter as Livy, and it is dangerously misleading to imply that if we had his narrative we would have either the historical actors' *ipsissima verba* or the 'true facts' of any given incident."

31. On the limits of *Quellenforschung* both for historians and for interpreters of Latin literature, see the judicious comments of Oakley 1997–98, 1.16–18; and cf. Jaeger 1997, 8 and nn.

32. It is sobering to realize, for instance, just how much of Broughton 1951 comes from Livy and nowhere else.

33. Walsh 1996, 13.

34. Cf. Kraus et al. 1997, 7: "It is in these passages, with their often simple, list format and reporting of information basic to the functioning of the state, that the 'origins' of Latin historiography, the *Annales maximi*, make their spirit, if not their actual influence, felt." For a splendid taxonomy of the annalistic (and loosely archival) data found in Livy, see Oakley 1997–98, 1.38–72. In an odd extension of the rule of *lectio difficilior,* Itgenshorst 2005, 150–58, tries to argue that the formulaic nature of Livy's triumph notices marks them as timeless descriptors rather than historical data, whereas triumph debates exhibit more variation and can therefore be taken as truer reflections of reality; but I have to agree with Östenberg 2007 that "Livy's laconic standardized phrasings of the triumphal ritual reflect Republican annalistic sources."

35. Cic. *Brut.* 62. See Ridley 1983.

Triumphal celebrations also left an increasingly well-delineated and verifiable footprint as time went by. From the Hannibalic War onward Livy apparently had access to detailed descriptions of the booty displayed in triumphs, in addition to mere names and dates.[36] Far graver concerns arise, however, with regard to triumph debates and the arguments supposedly raised for and against individual triumph requests on the senate floor. The problem is that discussions within the senate did not customarily become public record, since the senators (*patres*) met behind closed doors and liked to keep their deliberations secret.[37]

Fortunately for our purposes, the competition for status among the élite hardly confined itself to the senate floor. Plenty of opportunities would have arisen for pertinent information to leak out or even to be broadcast on purpose. It would have been nearly impossible to conceal a triumph request; and what self-respecting Roman aristocrat with a substantial victory to his credit would want to keep it hidden? Commanders in the field routinely sent home official dispatches with news of their exploits, which would be read publicly at the wide-open meeting known as *contiones,* albeit after the senators had heard them in closed session first.[38] Personal correspondence circulated as well, and letters of either sort could easily become documentary evidence later on.[39] The returning victor also typically had his whole army camped right outside the city's ritual boundary (*pomerium*). Even if the veterans did not conspicuously gossip, joke, and argue about it, the outcome of their commander's dealings with the senate would hardly

36. As Oakley 1997–98, 1.57, remarks, "it was easier to invent triumphs for the period before 300."

37. On the secrecy of senate deliberations, see among others Brennan 2000, 9 nn. 23 and 24; Harris 1985, 6–7 and 255; Mommsen 1887, 3.942; Morstein-Marx 2004, especially 9–10 and 246–51.

38. For field dispatches read to the people after a closed senate hearing, see Livy's account of news reaching Rome from the disaster at Trasimene (22.7.6–8) and the victory at the Metaurus (27.50.4–11 and 51.5). The fact that these two narratives are highly embellished type-scenes does not compromise the evidence from them that such *contiones* were known and indeed expected to take place: "Livy's dramatic reconstructions of the arrival of the news . . . illuminate contemporary practices and assumptions even if they cannot be assumed to be accurate descriptions of the actual events of 217 and 207" (Morstein-Marx 2004, 247).

39. On letters from the field, see 5.28.13 and 45.1.7. Also cf. below, p. 128 n. 1. For an instance of private correspondence coming to bear on a triumph debate, note the case of L. Cornelius Merula in 189, where the receipt of certain "litteras . . . inter se pugnantes" ("letters conflicting among themselves," 35.8.4) helped to fuel the controversy. We also have real examples of letters, both official and private, pertaining to an incident from the Late Republic: Cic. *Fam.* 15.1 and 15.2 are his field dispatches to the senate concerning military operations in his province of Cappadocia, whereas 15.3, 15.4, 15.5, and 15.6 document a private exchange between Cicero and M. Cato in which the orator attempts (albeit without success) to influence the senate vote from behind the scenes. Also cf. Hickson-Hahn 2000, 246 and n. 12, for an interesting parallel from Pompey's career.

go unnoticed in town. He might celebrate a full triumph, or a lesser *ovatio,* or the smaller-scale triumph on the Alban mount, or even enter the city without any fanfare whatsoever—but no matter what happened, people would talk about it, and discuss why.

Roman aristocrats in particular must have avidly discussed the technicalities of the *ius triumphandi* among themselves, at dinner parties no less than in official meetings. The pursuit of *laus* and *gloria* mattered deeply and personally to them. Their social lives and their political lives were closely intertwined. Surely they kept track of the stipulations raised against would-be *triumphatores,* past and present alike, and enjoyed comparing notes with one another: for the rules of the game applied to each one of them no less than to their colleagues and rivals. The most sensitive conversations probably took place strictly within aristocratic circles and behind closed doors. But if the assembly became embroiled in a triumph debate (as happened on occasion), then the arguments on either side would likely be canvassed all over town, not only in more formal gatherings (*contiones*) but also simply by word of mouth. And after the fact, manubial temples and other monuments, public inscriptions, ancestor masks (*imagines*) on display in people's houses, the eulogies (*laudationes*) given at funerals—all helped to maintain the persistent hunt for civic honors as a going concern. The available evidence leaves no way of knowing whether Livy's information on triumph debates ultimately derives from the Annales Maximi, from family archives, from oral histories, or from some other source or sources, but perhaps it is not so far-fetched after all to assert, at least as a matter of general principle, that his sources must have got their information somewhere.

Triumph debates also occupy a special place in the internal logic of Livy's history. Passages throughout reflect the authentic conceptual vocabulary of triumphal discourse, and the work as a whole likewise could not have taken its present shape without centuries of Roman commanders coming home from their campaigns in search of honor and renown, and telling their stories accordingly. It seems a foregone conclusion that *res gestae* narratives originally spun in the course of the hunt for civic honors must have had a formative effect on the annalistic tradition as Livy inherited it. Granted, within the text we can catch only echoes of long-gone, distant voices. Nor could anyone now hope to trace the actual stages of transmission through so many intervening years and generations of lost evidence. Livy also undeniably reworked his source material. But the lineage reaching back in time remains visible at least in outline, because the same type of storytelling turns out to be fundamental both to the conduct of triumphal politics under the Republic and to the writing of the *Ab Urbe Condita.*

The rights and privileges of would-be *triumphatores* from the past plainly held more than merely idle antiquarian interest during Livy's lifetime, and at least one bygone incident apparently engaged the interest of the *Princeps* himself. The puzzling affair of A. Cornelius Cossus still draws attention because of the singular way in which Augustus intrudes into Livy's text.[40] According to tradition, if a Roman general killed the leader of the enemy in single combat, he could strip the armor from the corpse and dedicate it in the Temple of Jupiter Feretrius on the Capitol as *spolia opima* ("rich spoils"). As far as we know, only three such dedications were ever made: the first supposedly by Romulus (1.10.5–7; cf. 4.20.3), the second by Cossus in the late fifth century, and the last by M. Claudius Marcellus in 222.[41] In his account of the slaying by Cossus of Lars Tolumnius, a leader from Veii, in 437 (4.19), Livy consistently refers to the Roman warrior as a mere tribune of the soldiers (*tribunus militum*) serving under the dictator Mamercus Aemilius. He reports that Cossus stole the show at Aemilius's triumph by appearing with the *spolia opima* and being loudly compared to Romulus (4.20.1–2, 4).[42] Then, in an aside (4.20.5–11), the historian reveals that whereas he had followed the unanimous view of earlier authorities with regard to Cossus's rank, Augustus reportedly claimed to have seen the original dedicatory inscription in the Temple of Jupiter Feretrius, stating that Cossus won the *spolia opima* as consul.

Livy suddenly finds his narrative at odds with what the most powerful man in Rome has been telling people.[43] A passage from Dio has long

40. Among the recent treatments of this notorious episode, with reference to previous scholarship, see Badian 1993; Flower 2000; Hickson 1991; Jaeger 1997, 182; Kraus and Woodman 1997, 71–72; Miles 1995, 40–47; Rich 1996; Sailor 2006; R. Stewart 1998, 79–88; Wiedemann 1996. Also cf. Toher 1990.

41. Of the three attested *spolia opima* dedications, only Marcellus's appears in the extant portions of the Fasti: see Degrassi 1947, 78–79, 550. Val. Max. 3.4.2–5 lists all three examples. See also Prop. 4.10 (with the detailed literary discussion by Ingleheart 2007; cf. Harrison 1989) and Serv. *ad Aen.* 6.855–59. Other ancient testimonia can be found in Flower 2000 (arguing not uncompellingly that Marcellus was instrumental both in fashioning and in promulgating the two earlier exempla). For possible historical reasons why the *spolia opima* were so rare, see Ingleheart 2007, 124–25; Oakley 1985, 398.

42. 4.20.2–3: "longe maximum triumphi spectaculum fuit Cossus, spolia opima regis interfecti gerens; in eum milites carmina incondita aequantes eum Romulo canere. spolia in aede Iovis Feretri prope Romuli spolia quae, prima opima appellata, sola ea tempestate erant, cum sollemni dedicatione dono fixit; averteratque in se a curru dictatoris civium ora et celebretatis eius diei fructum prope solus tulerat" ("by far the greatest spectacle of the triumph was Cossus, carrying the *spolia opima* of the slain king. The soldiers sang rough songs comparing him to Romulus. With a solemn dedication he put up his spoils as a gift in the Temple of Jupiter Feretrius near the spoils of Romulus, which having first been called *opima* were the only such at that time; he had turned the faces of the citizens from the chariot of the dictator to himself and taken the fruit of that day's renown practically on his own").

43. Badian 1993, 14–16, points out that Livy's precise wording indicates some form of hearsay, rather than a direct confrontation, as the vehicle by which the historian learned of Augustus's alternative viewpoint.

been read in conjunction with Livy's editorial comments to suggest that Augustus's interest in the Cossus affair may have been sparked by wanting to prevent M. Licinius Crassus (son of the triumvir) from dedicating the *spolia opima* in 27. Crassus had killed the leader of the Bastarnae in battle while serving as proconsul in Macedonia, and Dio says that he would have made the dedication "if he had been a general with fully independent powers."[44] The contrary-to-fact condition implies that Crassus lacked the proper authority to claim the *spolia opima,* but Dio does not actually state that he ever tried to press the issue, or for that matter that Augustus intervened to block him on the grounds that he was not a consul in office. On the other hand, another commander conspicuously likening himself to Romulus via the *spolia opima* could have proved extremely embarrassing for the *Princeps,* and the alleged Cossus inscription provided a handy, not to say expedient, exemplum.[45] The whole episode thus ties in with the broader theme of Augustus's seeking to restrict access to civic honors, as already noted.

After convolutedly weighing both sides, Livy refuses to make a definitive judgment and leaves the question open for the reader to decide: "one may move about among all the opinions" ("versare in omnes opiniones licet," 4.20.11).[46] Modern scholars have found inventive ways to interpret this multilayered and ambiguous evidence. Some suggest that Livy is subtly criticizing or subverting the authority of the *Princeps* by presenting the issue as open to dispute, whereas others conclude that the historian agreed with the contrary testimonial but never got around to revising his earlier account in accordance with it, and still others see a balance carefully maintained between opposing perspectives, presumably for the benefit of the reader.[47] Livy's attitude toward Augustus and his program of broad-reaching political and social reforms has been a major scholarly preoccu-

44. Dio Cass. 51.24.4: καὶ τόν γε βασιλέα αὐτῶν Δέλδωνα αὐτὸς ὁ Κράσσος ἀπέκτεινε. κἂν τὰ σκῦλα αὐτοῦ τῷ Φερετρίῳ Διὶ ὡς καὶ ὀπῖμα ἀνέθηκεν, εἴπερ αὐτωκράτωρ στρατηγὸς ἐγεγόνει ("And Crassus himself killed their king Deldo. And he would have dedicated his spoils as *opima* to Jupiter Feretrius if he had been a general with fully independent powers").

45. Cassius Dio does claim (51.25.2) that Augustus took the title of *imperator* for Crassus's achievements, but note Flower 2000, 52 and nn., on the problems with this assertion. *Contra* see also Rich 1996.

46. Miles 1995, 40–47, attentively traces all the twists and turns in the Cossus digression (neatly paraphrased by Kraus and Woodman 1997, 72). In keeping with the confusion in Livy's text, later ancient authors predictably offer divergent accounts of Cossus's rank and qualifications: see Flower 2000, n. 58.

47. For an example of a subversive (i.e., anti-Augustan) reading, see recently Sailor 2006. For the pro-Augustan interpretation with an emphasis on Livy's carelessness in failing to revise his narrative, see, e.g., Luce 1965, 212–13; Ogilvie 1958; and 1974, 563–64. For a more neutral view, see, e.g., Fornara 1983, 74–75; Jaeger 1997, 182.

pation for a long time,[48] especially in light of the obvious parallels between the centralizing aims of the Principate and the historian's own vast project to create "a unified and comprehensive picture of the totality of the Roman state."[49] Livy's partisanship with regard to the new regime eludes capture, however, partly because the contemporary portions of his history have not survived, but mainly because he maintains a certain level of detachment: "a shared project does not necessarily mean a lack of independence."[50]

As fascinating as these various arguments undoubtedly are, it is important to remember that most of Livy's intended audience lived outside the imperial palace. Too narrow a fixation on Augustus can become a distraction from what Livy has to say to us—and more important, to show us—about the workings of the Republic. For although the lessons of history that he is trying to draw for his readers can be applied to the present and future, they must come from the past. The Cossus episode illustrates a significant pattern. When we first read Livy's account of a commander's exploits in the field, it seems fairly straightforward on its own terms. But then at a later point certain aspects of the preceding narrative become problematic, or at least worthy of reexamination, in light of questions raised by some authority other than the historian himself. Opposing viewpoints embedded within the text therefore help to bring out the hidden biases and possible political involvements of the author and the strand (or strands) from the historical tradition upon which he is drawing. Uniquely, with Cossus, we find Augustus himself telling an alternative version of the story, which abruptly pulls Livy's history into the sphere of current events. In triumph debates elsewhere throughout the *Ab Urbe Condita,* by contrast, the divergent voices come from the past, from the opponents of

48. As one noted authority has written, the question of Livy's attitude toward Augustus and the Principate "has attracted more attention than any other single issue" with regard to his history (Kraus 1994, 6). Just as with the Cossus episode (which is a microcosm for the broader issue), scholars' interpretations have varied so widely that by now almost every conceivable position has been taken by someone. See surveys by Deninger 1985; Phillips 1982. Over the years Livy has alternately emerged as Augustus's loyal "improving publicist" (thus famously Syme 1959, 76), as a skilled rhetorical encomiast for the new regime (e.g., Woodman 1988, 128–40; and cf. Cizek 1992), as a respectful but distant admirer of the *Princeps* (e.g., Burck 1991), and as a committed old-style Republican who set out to criticize the loss of freedom in Rome either overtly (e.g., Badian 1993) or subtly and indirectly (e.g., Miles 1995, with an emphasis on Livy's status as a relative outsider; also cf. Mette 1961 and Petersen 1961). The sheer breadth of learned opinion on this issue suggests forcibly that the evidence is ambiguous, to say the least, and that the conclusions reached by any particular scholar will probably reveal as much about him or her as about Livy's discernible political views. For a balanced account of the profound transformation in the nature of all Roman history writing that came with the arrival of the Principate, see recently Toher 1990.

49. Feldherr 1997b, 136.

50. Kraus 1994, 8. Cf. Kraus and Woodman 1997, 70–74.

the would-be *triumphator* speaking out against both him and his *res gestae*. The reader faced with disparate perspectives on the same events, no matter where they came from or how they arise, is compelled to take a second look at the stories Livy has been telling and to think about the implications of understanding history one way or another.

OUTLINE OF THE ARGUMENT

The body of the discussion to follow falls into two main parts, plus a conclusion. Part I offers a detailed treatment of the political process and standards of judgment by which triumphs were awarded to some and denied to others under the Republic. Along the way certain key historical figures and incidents, a number of important recurring themes, and elements of Livy's conceptual vocabulary will be introduced. This portion of the argument will also focus on constitutional issues, exposing the complex dynamics of the interaction between the senate, magistrates, and people of Rome. By locating the *ius triumphandi* and the criteria of assessment within the flexible framework of the *mos maiorum*, it will become readily apparent that we are not dealing with a rigid juridical system of rules after all, but rather with concepts bound to a traditional understanding yet also fluid, subject to political manipulation, and caught up in the delicate negotiations of status both for individual aristocrats and for the élite (*nobiles*) collectively within the broader social world of the SPQR. A word of warning: the material in Part I is often highly technical, by necessity, to avoid misconception. The only way to trace the working boundaries of inherently indeterminate rules is to encompass the full range of exceptions and counterexamples.

Despite the undeniable vehemence of so many triumph debates in the extant portions of Livy's history, it will emerge that the vast majority of victorious commanders who asked for triumphs during the period in question walked away with some type of reward in the end. So the odds are that those, like M. Aemilius Lepidus in 187, who objected to other people's triumph requests must have had some further motivation besides a simple desire to keep the triumph from happening, because that result was unlikely. What could this additional factor be? The answer lies in the realization that they stood to gain from the oppositional stance by itself, a benefit inherent in the *process* of debate, as opposed to the outcome. Much more than triumphs lay at stake in triumph debates. Thus begins an extended exploration, in Part II, of performative elements in the hunt for public honors, the continual self-fashioning by individuals and groups that contributed to the creation and ongoing maintenance of aristocratic and civic identity in Rome. Three case studies from the Hannibalic War and seven episodes from Livy 31–45—all briefly discussed in Part I under various headings—will now be reexamined from this other perspective.

These ten close readings, taken together, will uncover an intricate social and political structure at once mirrored, refracted, and reinforced by the debates over triumphs, both in their historical context and in the broad scope of Livy's work. Then, as seems only fitting at last after so much discussion of triumph debates, the concluding pages will focus on the ritual and symbolism of the Roman triumph itself, which was unmistakably the most powerful and iconic spectacle in the civic life of Republican Rome, not to mention its distinctive role in the sweeping pageant of Livy's narrative.

Nor are those two contexts—the historical and the literary—as distinct as they might first appear. When Roman generals came home victorious, they talked about their exploits in a characteristic way, clearly expressive of the aristocratic ethos. Their self-fashioning narratives were initially crafted for an audience of fellow *nobiles* in the senate, then sanctioned by vote of the *patres* with the award of civic honors, then splendidly paraded before the people in the celebration of triumphs, and finally put on permanent display both through the use of *imagines* in houses and funerals, and through various manubial dedications that lined the triumphal route. Each stage in the process served to foster, by means of continual repetition and reinforcement, a vision of Roman history as a digest of aristocratic *res gestae* in service to the state: Roman history, that is, precisely as it emerges from Books 21–45 of Livy.[51] Everyone who took part in triumph debates—the would-be *triumphator,* his supporters, and his critics alike—had a share in the public life and vital discourse from which all prestige flowed. Together they were hammering out and articulating their core values, shaping a definition of what it meant to be truly Roman, and determining what the official self-image of the Republic, its collective memory and sense of identity, should look like. Even more to the point, they were enacting those values and breathing life into that self-image through their political drama.

By reproducing that same drama on the stage of his history, then, Livy invites his audience to engage with it actively and thereby to join in the ongoing process of Roman self-definition, which will serve as the basis for the type of edifying moral awareness desperately needed in the aftermath of civil war (*Praef.* 10):[52]

51. Note Toher 1990, 147: "History was the forum for the display of aristocratic service in behalf of the community . . . the purpose of the genre was a function of the aristocratic struggle for honor and status in the community." Cf. Frier 1999, 205: "The annalistic tradition was thus, in essence, the history of the free and aristocratic government of Rome; it spoke for the endurance of an aristocratic ideal that was the essence of the Republic."

52. *Praef.* 10: "hoc illud est praecipue in cognitione rerum salubre ac frugiferum, omnis te exempli documenta in inlustri posita monumento intueri; inde tibi tuaeque rei publicae quod imitere capias, inde fodeum inceptu foedum exitu quod vites." For a recent careful reading of Livy's *Praefatio* in the context of contemporary ideology as well as the Roman historiographical tradition, see Feldherr 1998, 1–50. Also cf. Earl 1972; Gowing 2005, 17–27 (especially

> This is especially healthy and fruitful in the study of history, for you to look upon lessons of every type of behavior placed upon a well-lit pedestal; from there you may grasp for yourself and your commonwealth what you should imitate and what you should avoid as vile from start to finish.

Note the deliberate link being forged here between the individual's ethical consciousness and the interests of the community at large, as well as the pivotal role played by the reader's critical gaze in distinguishing good exempla from bad and applying those valuable lessons to the present day.[53] Livy's overall purpose is avowedly didactic and political, with a view toward transforming people's attitudes and character. He seems to assert that "his *History* can act autonomously as an instrument of social and political change."[54] And in order for that to happen, "reader and historian must cooperate: the latter serves as a guide and a teacher, the former not passively absorbing lessons but as an active learner."[55]

Throughout this discussion, in order to reconstruct how the would-be *triumphatores,* their supporters, and their critics behaved on the basis of Livy's testimony, we will need to look at what they did and at what they said, or rather at what the historian portrays them as having said, in particular situations. The precise content and wording of speeches will therefore count for a lot. Eyebrows will undoubtedly be raised at this in certain quarters—the problem dates back to Thucydides 1.21 and τὰ δέοντα[56]—but in spite of all the inherent difficulties I firmly believe that Livy's speeches do not need to be accurate, verbatim transcriptions of the speakers' ipsis-

21–24); Kraus and Woodman 1997, 51–81; Leeman 1967; Moles 1993; Oppermann 1967; Walsh 1955 and 1967.

53. On the second person singular in *Praef.* 10 as a direct appeal from Livy to each individual reader, see Feldherr 1998, 3 and n.4; Gowing 2005, 24; Kraus 1994, 13–14; Moles 1993, 152.

54. Feldherr 1997b, 137. Cf. Gowing 2005, 23: "The memory conveyed by [Livy's] history equips the reader with a sense of wrong and right as determined or exemplified by the actions of one's predecessors; it also equips us with the capacity to make sense of, and correct, the present. His history aims to accomplish, in short, precisely what gazing on the busts of one's ancestors is meant to accomplish. . . . History here is envisaged as a tomb which, as any Roman tomb, needs to be revered, cultivated, and respected; remembering the past, like remembering the dead, is seen as a process entirely central to the Roman aristocrat's sense of self-worth and identity."

55. Kraus and Woodman 1997, 56.

56. The speeches routinely used by ancient writers of history to dramatize certain critical moments in their narratives are usually discussed as examples of artistic rhetoric rather than as sources of reliable historical information. Yet as Oakley 1997–98, 1.11, remarks, "speeches were useful both for the analysis of a situation and for characterizing the speaker," which makes them part and parcel of the story. Cf. Kraus 1994, 12–13 and nn. For a fascinating recent treatment of the problem from a theoretical perspective, see Laird 1999, 116–52. Also see Briscoe 1973, 17–22; Brock 1995; Feldherr 1998, 60 n. 31; Luce 1993; Walsh 1961, 219–44; Woodman 1988, passim.

sima verba in order to present us with an authentic illustration of what a historical character might well have said under the circumstances. An acknowledged master of rhetorical *inventio,* Livy sought at all times to make his story and its characters plausible. Vocabulary, grammatical constructions, rhetorical devices—all convey shades of meaning and associations of ideas that would have been apparent to a Roman audience, and which it is our job as students of antiquity to discern as closely as possible. The *Ab Urbe Condita* allows us to watch historical figures in the act of transforming themselves into exempla before our very eyes. By their exemplary nature, the kinds of things these characters do and say have integrity as a source of information about Roman values (broadly termed), even if or when the author is only imagining them for us. Moreover, Livy continually invites us to reach back beyond his text to the foundations on which it rests, and ultimately to the performative gestures of the would-be *triumphatores* themselves.

This book is not an attempt at source criticism in anything like the conventional sense, but neither has there been any effort made to sever Livy's historical outlook from the tradition within which he plainly sought to locate his work. Indeed, far to the contrary, a complicity will emerge between Livy and the characters in his history. They tell their stories to their peers in the senate and to the Roman people at large, seeking to craft themselves into exempla for future generations. He then shines a historical spotlight on them, so that readers can observe them in action and learn important moral and political lessons. By thus carefully embedding their narratives inside his own, Livy offers models to help his contemporary Roman audience rebuild a meaningful national identity after the trauma of the Civil Wars and allows us, albeit centuries later, to look over the shoulders of his fellow citizens as they struggle to come to grips with the legacies of the past.

THE APPLICABILITY OF VARIOUS SOURCES

As already noted, Livy's narrative operates and must be interpreted within two distinct frames of reference: one relating to his subject matter from the heyday of the Republic and the other to his status as an Augustan author in the aftermath of the Civil Wars. Always bearing that duality in mind, it would be well here at the outset to distinguish the following seven clusters of ideas and related ancient sources, which intersect and overlap in a variety of ways to help place Livy's triumph debates into their proper historical and ideological context.

1. Livy's account itself follows a strict annalistic format (albeit with some minor variation), especially in Books 21–45. Notices for each year give

us the names and dates of would-be *triumphatores,* including their election to office and assignment to provinces, the progress of their military campaigns and possible extension of command in successive years, and their eventual return to Rome, followed in due course by the request for honors, the triumph debate, the verdict, the official celebration or lack thereof, the material commemoration of the victory through the dedication of temples or other monuments, and any significant political aftermath, before the whole cycle starts up again. Within this predictable and repetitive pattern, the historian creates variations from year to year and episode to episode by omitting expected details or placing a special emphasis here or there as warranted by the events themselves. The only reason we know that triumph debates must have occurred at all for most of these people is that Livy tells us so, often with explicit reference to the reasons cited for and against particular requests. From the collective evidence of many such passages, scholars have cobbled together a rough list of criteria that supposedly governed the award of triumphs under the Republic, including the four-part ritual formula *imperio auspicio ductu felicitate,* which will provide the starting point for our investigation.

2. The enormous twin inscriptions known as the Capitoline Fasti date, like Livy's history, to the Augustan period. Two comprehensive lists of names—one of kings and consuls (Fasti Consulares) and the other of those who celebrated triumphs (Fasti Triumphales), each proceeding year by year from Romulus onward—were carved on opposite sides of the central doorway of the triumphal arch built by Augustus in 19 B.C.[57] Sadly, the stones have survived only in fragments, with numerous gaps in various places. By comparing the Fasti with the annalistic material from Livy where both are extant, however, and by filling in lacunae in each one with information from the other wherever possible—sometimes both are missing—scholars have worked out a detailed prosopography of who did what, when, that is almost complete, especially for the period covered by Livy 21–45 (i.e., 218–167 B.C.). It is important to note that while the Fasti duly record election to the highest office and the celebration of triumphs, they say nothing whatever about triumph debates, or about the criteria used to accept some bids and reject others. There Livy stands alone, or almost. With the backbone from Livy and the Fasti, many other sources—inscriptions, historical accounts (Polybius, Plutarch, Diodorus, Valerius Maximus, etc.), fragments of

57. For the text of the Fasti inscriptions with historical commentary, see Degrassi 1947. On their discovery in the sixteenth century, see McCuarg 1991. For possible cross-links with Roman historiography, see among others Itgenshorst 2004; Rüpke 1995. Further bibliography appears below: p. 21 n. 7.

speeches (e.g., Cato the Elder), and so on—have helped to flesh out the details of particular military campaigns and other aspects of the political careers of famous individuals. Important as they are in their own right, for the sake of space these additional sources will be cited below only where they directly impinge on the discussion at hand.

3. A number of seminal texts and material remains provide evidence alongside Livy for the Roman aristocratic ethos under the Republic. The most important of these include the Scipionic epitaphs (*CIL* 1^2.6–15), the *laudatio* of L. Metellus and information on the use of *imagines* as recorded by Pliny the Elder (*NH* 7.139–40 and 37.6–8, respectively), Polybius's description of the aristocratic funeral (6.53.1–54.2), the *elogia* of the *summi viri* ("greatest men") from the Forum Augustum, Roman portrait sculpture especially of the veristic type, fragments of the early poets such as Ennius and Naevius, certain aspects of Plautine comedy and the historical drama known as *fabula praetexta,* the exempla tradition as reflected particularly in the writings of Valerius Maximus and Cicero, and descriptions of relevant monuments in various authors. From this body of evidence our fundamental understanding of the concept of *mos maiorum* has taken shape, with an emphasis on competition and the typical path of a political career (*cursus honorum*) and the traditional canon of aristocratic virtues, including *virtus, pietas,* and *fides,* as already glossed, along with the serious demeanor appropriate to participation in civic life (*gravitas*), a proper sense of one's status and worth within the community (*dignitas*), the ability to command respect and influence debate (*auctoritas*), and so on. Something very like a collective consciousness seems to operate among the members of the ruling élite.

4. When it comes to understanding the so-called constitution of the Roman Republic and the practical politics of the SPQR, the analytical discussion by Polybius (6.11–18, later imitated by Cicero in *De Re Publica*) has been hugely important, because in praising Rome's government as an example of a mixture between democratic, monarchical, and oligarchic elements, he introduces the seminal notion of a system of checks and balances. The aristocratic ethos took shape in a particular social and political environment, and an extremely complex, often highly contentious dynamic—which Livy's account amply illustrates—governed relations at any given moment between the senate, magistrates, and people of Rome. Long-standing traditions and prevailing cultural values were subject to broad historical developments, especially the continually expanding military horizons and the huge influx of wealth. These, coupled with internal tensions both within and among various groups within the society, created an ongoing continuity-in-change against which each new episode played itself out.

5. We know quite a bit about the Roman triumph as such, because the ritual inscribed itself so deeply and indelibly into the topography and monuments of the city, as perhaps best exemplified by the imperial arches still prominently visible today. On the literary side, triumphal ekphrasis became a stock-in-trade for historians and biographers, and sometimes even poets. Among such passages, Josephus's elaborate description of the Flavian celebration after the sack of Jerusalem in A.D. 70 (*BJ* 7.121–62) clearly has pride of place, although, since it belongs to the Empire rather than the Republic, it will not be cited very often in what follows. Antiquarian testimonia also bear witness to various technicalities.
6. Livy wrote in the traumatic aftermath of civil war and the final collapse of the Republic. Caesar and Cicero, among others, provide contemporary witness to those turbulent times. A crisis of values was clearly perceived, particularly in hindsight. Writers of history habitually return to the theme of moral decline. Sallust, for example, attributes the Catilinarian conspiracy to the spread of greed (*avaritia*) and political ambition (*ambitio*) "like a plague," whereas Livy in his preface first offers an elaborate architectural metaphor for the gradual decay of Roman order (*disciplina*) and customs (*mores*), and then switches rather suddenly to the language of disease and pathology with reference to his own day.[58] The opening of Tacitus's *Annales* likewise paints a grim picture of freedom (*libertas*) fleetingly enjoyed, only to be swept away by civil strife (*discordiae*) and the emergence of autocracy (*dominatio*).[59] And of course the Augustan poets, Vergil prime among them, repeatedly dwell on themes of pain and suffering, anger, loss, and disillusionment in the wake of the titanic internecine struggles of the Late Republic. Though attributable to individuals, according to Roman ideology the values most urgently called into question by civil war, such as *virtus, pietas, fides,* and the like, are all properly exercised in the civic sphere for the benefit of the whole community. So a crisis for these values has a traumatic effect on all of Rome, lending a special urgency to the need for history as exempla.
7. When the emperor Augustus came to power, first eliminating his rivals one by one and then finally putting an end to fratricidal strife, he pro-

58. Sall. *Cat.* 10: "contagio quasi pestilentia invasit" ("the contagion burst in like a plague"). Livy *Praef.* 9: "labante . . . paulatim disciplina velut dissidentes primo mores sequatur animo, deinde ut magis magisque lapsi sint, tum ire coeperint praecipites, donec ad haec tempora quibus nec vitia nostra nec remedia pati possumus perventum est." ("It followed that with discipline slipping bit by bit, customs, as if acting contrary to their original character, thereafter fell down more and more, then began to move headlong, until it came at length to these times, when we are able to endure neither our vices nor the remedies for them").

59. Tac. Ann. 1.1–2.

> ceeded to rebuild both the Roman political order and the material fabric of the city itself from the ground up, using his enormous personal *auctoritas* to anchor the government and a monumental building program to reshape the urban landscape. As the biographer Suetonius famously records, Augustus bragged that he had found Rome a city of bricks and left it a city of marble.[60] He did the same thing with aristocratic ideology. Major constructions such as the Forum Augustum with its *elogia* and statues of the *summi viri,* the triumphal arch bearing the huge Fasti inscription, and the mausoleum with Augustus's own *Res Gestae* on proud display—all incorporated images and texts together into impressive monumental spaces. Familiar paradigms systematically reappeared on a radical new footing. In response to the trauma of the Civil Wars, Augustus painstakingly set a whole new standard for what it meant to be a Roman in the traditional sense, with himself as the crowning exemplum, and Livy's account of the Roman national past grew up in that context, alongside the works of poets such as Vergil, Horace, and Ovid.

One may map these seven diverse fields of scholarly inquiry onto the prevailing theatrical metaphor by conceiving of the prosopography from Livy and the Fasti as the dramatis personae, the aristocratic ethos as the script (and to some extent also the lighting), the political dynamics of the Republic as the blocking and choreography, the triumphal ritual and urban topography as the stage and backdrop, respectively, and the Civil Wars and Augustan reconstruction of Roman identity as the dramaturgy for the ongoing theatrical display that was life under the Republic as the *Ab Urbe Condita* presents it. A proper reading of the text as a whole, and of the triumph debates embedded within it, must take all these elements into account. In what follows they will variously collide, intersect, and overlap to give us Livy's Republican Rome.

60. Suet. *Aug.* 28.3: "Urbem . . . excoluit adeo, ut iure sit gloriatus marmoream se relinquere, quam latericiam accepisset" ("He so tended the city that he boasted by right of having found it of bricks, and left it of marble").

PART I

Setting Standards

IMPERIO AUSPICIO DUCTU FELICITATE

Who deserved to triumph? The author of a magisterial work on triumphal ritual notes that "Rome would not have been Rome if it had not developed an elaborate casuistry in this field."[1] Triumph requests came up for discussion year after year throughout the long history of the Republic. When differences of opinion arose, as quite often they did, about the worthiness of a particular claim, detractors would seek to undermine a commander's triumph hopes—and champions to bolster them—by arguing along conventional lines, usually by appeal to precedent or some lack thereof. References to the *mos maiorum* loom very large in Roman accounts of triumph debates. Eventually the arguments would lead to a verdict. Triumphs were awarded to some and refused to others, and then a public victory celebration either would or would not take place, each new result adding a new layer of precedent for the next time around. Over centuries the "elaborate casuistry" evolved to which the noted scholar refers. Successful bids were all alike, inasmuch as they all adhered to the same fourfold ritual formula: a commander triumphed *imperio auspicio ductu felicitate*.[2] Yet despite learned opinion periodically expressed to the contrary, ample

1. Versnel 1970, 164.

2. The four-part expression actually appears only once in its complete form, in Livy's description of the inscribed *tabula* recording the dedication of a temple by victorious general L. Aemilius Regillus in 179 (40.52.5: "auspicio imperio felicitate ductuque eius"), but Versnel 1970, 176–77 and 356–71, especially 360, is clearly right to view this as the proper triumphal formula. Varying subsets of the four elements found scattered in appropriate contexts throughout Livy's history may therefore be read in synecdoche for the whole list.

evidence suggests that the Romans of the Republic never settled upon a foolproof set of positive criteria for the awarding of triumphs, which, once demonstrably met, or not, would automatically secure the outcome. Politics continually intervened. For the pursuit of civic honors in Rome, though undoubtedly constrained by tradition and authority, was subject at all times to the shifting tides of aristocratic competition.[3]

Still, the constraints were very real. The hunt for triumphs could not readily dissolve into a free-for-all, because each of the four terms in the aforementioned formula—*imperium, auspicium, ductus, felicitas*—had a well-established, technical, procedural definition.[4] *Imperium* originated as the supreme power of the kings in warfare and matters of law, up to and including administration of the death penalty.[5] Under the Republic it evolved into the right for certain high-ranking elected officials (consuls, *dictatores,* praetors, and later proconsuls and propraetors as well) to give orders and exact obedience (*imperare,* "to command") both at home within the city limits (*domi*) and in the field abroad (*militiae*).[6] Its visible symbols were the fasces and lictors, the "portable kit for flogging and decapitation" that set those invested with *imperium* apart from their fellow citizens by signaling their awesome right to take violent action, if need be, on behalf of the SPQR as a whole.[7] A commander's term of office, be that a regular magistracy, a *prorogatio,* or a special appointment, limited the extent of his

3. Itgenshorst 2005, 159–76, arrives independently at much the same conclusion based on a cursory survey of Livy's triumph debates but does little to situate her arguments within current scholarly discussions about the constitution of the Roman Republic. Note Hölkeskamp 1993, 37, on the Republic's habit of "establishing informal and flexible rules, rather than . . . fixing formal and inflexible constitutional enactments." Also cf. Brennan 1996, 316, on the "often-shifting and largely subjective prerequisites for receiving the proper Roman triumph."

4. The constitutional powers of Roman magistrates and especially the technicalities of *imperium* and *auspicium,* and the relation between the two, have fostered an enormous body of scholarly literature. Anyone who has ever delved into these issues at length can sympathize with the confession of Versnel 1970, 313, that "the writer of a book about the triumph, who finds the unavoidable complex of problems about *imperium auspiciumQUE* in his way, feels his heart sinking." The seminal work of Mommsen 1887, 1.22–24, 61–65, 76–116, still remains the chief starting point for any scholarly investigation. On the powers of magistrates generally, see the recent summaries by Lintott 1999, 94–120; and North 2006, 263–66; also Badian 1988. For work on *imperium* since Mommsen, see the important survey by Brennan 2000, 12–33, now reinforced by Brennan 2004, especially 36–42; also Combès 1966; Giovannini 1983 and 1988; Hölkeskamp 1993, 20–21; Jashemski 1950; Magdelain 1968 and 1977; Rüpke 1990, 41–50. On *auspicium* in particular, see Linderski 1986 and 1988; also Rüpke 1990, 129–30; R. Stewart 1998 (greatly exaggerating the role of the ritual allotment).

5. The noun *imperium* seems to derive from the verb *parare* ("to prepare, arrange, put in order"): so Brennan 2004, 37, following Bleicken 1981, 37 and n. 38.

6. On *imperium* as the ability to exact obedience, even when used in the broader sense of *imperium populi Romani,* see Kallet-Marx 1995, 24–29; cf. also J. S. Richardson 1991.

7. Marshall 1984, 131. Cf. Goltz 2000.

imperium in time; the allotment of a *provincia,* in space likewise. *Auspicium* went along with *imperium.*[8] Officials needed the right to consult the omens (*auspicia imperativa*) prior to the undertaking of public business, including both civic functions *domi,* like the census, elections, meetings of the senate, and so on, and operations *militiae,* especially if these involved the possibility of engaging the enemy. *Ductus,* the most tangible and least abstract of the four elements, was the physical act of leading troops into battle (*ducere,* "to lead") and directing their combat. A person showing *ductus* literally took command of his army in the field, thereby actively exercising the powers inherent in *imperium* and *auspicium. Felicitas,* finally, was the successful outcome of an endeavor, manifesting the favor of the gods.[9] It could adhere to an individual, but when that individual was acting on behalf of the *res publica,* carrying out his *imperium, auspicium,* and *ductus,* it did not belong to him alone, but, significantly, to the whole community. His success, and that of his army, was now bound up with the *fortuna populi Romani.*[10]

The decision about whether or not to award a triumph on any given occasion, then, broke down more or less as follows. Did the commander hold lawful *imperium* and *auspicium* at the time when and the place where his forces engaged the enemy? Did he himself lead his troops into battle? Was the outcome a success, and did it enhance the stature and good fortune of the Roman people? Because discernible patterns emerge in the available answers to these questions, the temptation to codify in retrospect has proven irresistible. First came such antiquarians as Dionysius of

8. The two powers operate so closely together in the activities of magistrates that Mommsen 1887, 1.90, wrote: "They express the same idea considered under different points of view."

9. See recently Hatscher 2000; Linderski 1996, 169–72; Wistrand 1987, especially 9–26; also Fears 1981.

10. Flower 2004a, 8, refers to the Roman aristocratic definition of success "based on material profits and on a religious concept of manifest destiny." The latter sums up *felicitas* in a nutshell. For Livy's use of "bene ac feliciter" ("with success and good fortune") to complement forms of *evenire* (hence literally "outcome"), see 21.17.4, 31.5.4, 31.7.15, 31.8.2. For the same expression with verbs like *rem gerere* ("to accomplish"), see 31.48.12, 38.48.15, 38.51.8, 39.4.2. For the augural "felix faustumque" or "faustum felixque" ("fortunate and blessed" or vice versa) with beneficiaries (individual and collective) in the dative case, see 1.17.10, 1.28.7, 2.49.7, 3.34.2, 3.54.8, 8.25.10, 10.8.12, 24.16.9, 26.18.8, 27.45.8, 42.30.10. Cf. also 7.13.5: "nobis deum benignitate, felicitate tua populique Romani, et res et gloria est integra" ("by the good will of the gods and the good fortune belonging to you and the Roman people, both the enterprise and our glory are complete"). This is the formulaic language of civic officials acting on public business, either to express the hope for success at the start of an enterprise or to make the happy announcement at the other end of the process. On Roman beliefs about the role of the gods in determining the outcome of battles, see Rosenstein 1990a, passim, with an important word about personal *fortuna* at 161–62 and n. 21. On the connection between benefits to individuals and the good of the Republic as a whole, see also *Praef.* 11, "tibi tuaeque rei publicae" ("for yourself and your commonwealth").

Halicarnassus, the elder Pliny, Valerius Maximus, and Aulus Gellius, all of whom devoted passages of varying length to aspects of the *ius triumphandi*.[11] Following systematically in their footsteps in the nineteenth century, with what must be termed monumental influence on everyone since, Theodor Mommsen combed through the ancient sources to compile an exhaustive inventory of arguments cited for and against various triumph requests. He then set forth a catalogue of rules that supposedly governed the award of triumphs under the Republic. All had a legalistic dimension and stemmed from the *imperium* of magisterial office.[12]

Yet even Mommsen had to admit that the triumphal code that he had derived existed on a level of rarefied abstraction untouched by historical contingencies, whereas real Roman decision making seems to have allowed for considerable leeway on a case-by-case basis. In practice, old rules had to bend when new demands arose. The technicalities of *imperium* and *auspicium* became increasingly intricate as Roman military operations expanded and the role of promagistrates grew.[13] And although *ductus* emerged straightforwardly from most battle narratives, *felicitas* was a different matter: What counted as credible evidence of divine favor toward the Roman commander and his army? How big a victory was required? When did the final success outweigh any risks or Roman losses incurred along the way? Such questions did not revolve on mere facts: they called for an act of assessment and evaluation (*existimatio*), which immediately brought subjective judgments and community values into play. Family connections, personal prestige, *gratia*, the *auctoritas* of the commander and his supporters (relatives, friends, associates)—all weighed in as well, and could swing the decision one way or the other.[14] Attention could be drawn away from technicalities, or toward them, and the outcome always reflected a mixture of procedural and political issues. Ideally, compromise led to consensus among those empowered to judge each case, but stalemates could and did

11. Non-Livian testimonia include Gell. 5.6.20–21 (on the *corona ovalis*); Dion. Hal. 5.47.4; Pliny *NH* 5.125; and Val. Max. 2.8 ("De Iure Triumphandi"). On the Valerius passage, see recently Itgenshorst 2005, 180–88.

12. Mommsen 1887, 1.126–36.

13. Mommsen 1887, 1.134–35 (my translation): "for these [rules] in themselves and even more in their application to the individual case . . . it was naturally of great importance on whom the decision over their application depended. . . . As the triumph celebrated during the magistracy took place less and less often, and even in the normal course of events became legally impossible (once Sulla had linked *imperium militiae* to the proconsulship and propraetorship), so the triumph developed—inasmuch as for the proconsular and propraetorian triumph, according to the aforementioned principles, it always required an exemption from the laws—from a magisterial privilege into a concession bestowed upon individual commanders through a special vote by the people, and later the senate."

14. Cf. Brennan 1996, 317.

occur as well. Each new verdict set a slightly altered precedent for future negotiations in turn, sparking a dialectic or creative tension between perceived norms and actual behavior.[15]

One historian has argued that efforts by the Roman senate, in the decades after the Second Punic War, to keep a sudden "flood of applications for triumphs" under control resulted in "a series of *ad hoc* compromises, the accumulation of which became elevated into a principle."[16] In reply, another scholar tackles both prongs of the assertion but in reverse order, first the constitutional or legalistic claim, and then the quantitative one: "There was not as much trial and error in the senate's handling of claims as [the author] believes. We should not think in terms of a 'rush for triumphs' in the period after the Hannibalic War." Instead, this writer insists that "there were in fact traditional concepts which could be used as the basis for dealing with new situations."[17] So the first argument emphasizes shifting patterns in the award of triumphs; the second, an underlying continuity. Yet these are really two aspects of the same phenomenon: a society faced with rapid change and desperately needing to innovate, but also struggling to work within certain acknowledged boundaries. Differing emphases aside, in a sense both claims hold equally true.

This exchange illustrates a (perhaps *the*) fundamental paradox about the nature of governmental practice under the Roman Republic. For inasmuch as the so-called constitution of the Republic ever existed as such, it rested on a largely unwritten code of traditional values, structures, and principles (*mos maiorum*) that at once never seemed to change, and yet also left room for innovation within the old familiar framework, through ad-hoc decisions in response to unforeseen circumstances or sudden crises. The author of a major work on the subject has phrased it this way:[18]

15. The Romans employed an empirical and inductive method of reasoning rather than a juristic and deductive one. Lintott 1999, 4, notes "an enormous spectrum ranging from basic unwritten laws—*ius*, even if not *scriptum*—to what one may term mere *mos*, the way things happened to be done at the time." Cf. Brennan 2004, passim, and especially 57–58. The theoretical observations of Geertz 1983b, 173, are also strikingly relevant here: "The realization that legal facts are made not born, are socially constructed . . . raises serious questions. . . . If the 'fact configurations' are not merely things found lying about in the world and carried bodily into court, show-and-tell style, but close-edited diagrams of reality the matching process itself produces, the whole thing looks a bit like sleight-of-hand. It is, of course, not sleight-of-hand, or anyway not usually, but a rather more fundamental phenomenon, the one in fact upon which all culture rests: namely, that of representation."

16. J. S. Richardson 1975, 62.

17. Both quotations are from Develin 1978, 436–37.

18. Lintott 1999, 5–7. In a similar vein Develin 1985, 37, writes that an "absence of enforceable rules is typical of the Roman constitution." Cf. also Barton 2001, 69–70; Blösel 2000.

> Roman *mos* was regarded as something in continuous development . . . the constitution of the Republic was not something fixed and clear-cut, but evolved according to the Romans' needs by more means than one. It was also inevitably controversial: there were frequently at least two positions which could be taken on major issues.

The same oddly flexible traditionalism described in this passage evinces itself in other aspects of Roman culture and society as well: their habit of adopting foreign cults by accretion, for instance, without allowing the worship of newly imported gods to supplant ancient local rites and customs.[19] Accordingly, although their judgments about who deserved to triumph were not entirely capricious or arbitrary, conditioned as they were by institutional structures and guided by a strong sense of principle and proportion as well—there were limits, in other words, beyond which they simply would not or could not go (*imperio auspicio ductu felicitate*)—still the Romans of the Republic did not blindly rely on a checklist of criteria, because such standards as they tried to keep never applied across the board in a simpleminded way.[20]

All the while, conventional wisdom prevailed about the sorts of things a would-be *triumphator* probably ought to have accomplished in the field in order to make himself worthy of recognition: "the enemy defeated, citizens rescued, calm restored, terms of peace finished, / war snuffed out, a job well done, the army and garrisons intact," as Plautus says in a comedy conveniently dated to the early second century—that is, right in the middle of the most intense period of triumph debates on record in Livy.[21] We must draw a firm distinction, however, between the obvious components of military success per se and the criteria of judgment by which the senate and people distributed civic honors among those who claimed to have achieved such success at any given moment. Whereas the former were easily articulated, as in the Plautus passage, and not much open to change or controversy, the latter gave play to a highly subjective, even quixotic understanding, in ways that tended to mirror power structures within the community.[22] In

19. Note Cicero's expression at *Leg. Man.* 60: "maiores nostros . . . semper ad novos casus temporum novorum consiliorum rationes accommodasse" ("our ancestors always adapted the reasoning behind their new plans to the new exigencies of new times"). The emperors showed themselves particularly adept at articulating this paradox: cf. Aug. *Res* Gestae 8.5; also Tac. *Ann.* 11.24 and *ILS* 212.

20. Cf. Brennan 1996, 317; Gruen 1995, 65; also Develin 1978, 438 n. 74, arguing from the opposite direction.

21. Plaut. *Per.* 753–54: "hostibu' victis, civibu' salvis, re placida, pacibu' perfectis, / bello extincto, re bene gesta, integro exercitu et praesidiis." See recently Itgenshorst 2005, 42–53.

22. Thus Brennan 1996, 317–18, writes: "Livy in Books 21–45 presents us with a coherent and essentially plausible picture of the Senate introducing additional minor rules for the

Republican Rome both the commanders asking for triumphs and those who guided the decision making belonged to the same aristocracy. As a group notoriously prone to infighting, they felt keenly aware of the need to maintain and continually renegotiate a balance of status and privilege within their own ranks.

Therefore although "perceived convention" always guided the conduct of triumph debates,[23] such perceptions did not remain entirely static, and under pressure from various quarters the so-called triumphal criteria gave ground one by one to a series of timely compromises and shrewdly calculated accommodations. Livy's history allows us to trace that process in some detail, and although the resulting analysis sometimes has the curious effect of placing exceptions before the rules, only thus, in an honest assessment of both patterns and variations, will the true dynamism and complexity of the situation become apparent.

---

triumph on an *ad hoc* (or better, *ad hominem*) basis, with commanders in the field struggling to conform with new stipulations as they emerged."

23. Develin 1978, 438.

CHAPTER 1

Triumphal Decision Making and the SPQR

Tacitus's *Annales* opens: "From the beginning kings held the city of Rome."[1] If indeed, as both Livy and the Fasti would have it, Romulus and his regal successors also celebrated the earliest triumphs,[2] then they did so presumably on their own merits and by their own sovereign proclamation, needing no further sanction from anyone else. But under the Republic the situation grew far more complex, as command of Roman armies, and hence the opportunity to become the focus of a victory celebration, passed from the kings to the consuls and *dictatores,* later joined also by promagistrates and eventually praetors too.[3] How then was it determined who deserved to triumph? The answer to this question turns out to be as subtle and multilayered as the Republican constitution itself.

For each recorded triumph, the Fasti Triumphales include the following: the name of the *triumphator* (including patronymics and cognomen); the office that he held at the time; a Roman numeral, where appropriate, to mark a second triumph (or third, or fourth, etc.) by the same individual; the name of the enemy over whom he celebrated his victory (marked by *de* plus the ablative case); and the year (from the founding of the city), the month, and the date when the triumph took place. Although a special

1. Tac. *Ann.* 1.1: "urbem Romam a principio reges habuere."

2. For the earliest entries in the Fasti, see Degrassi 1947, 64–65, 534–35. Livy describes Romulus's procession to the Capitoline with the spoils of his victory at 1.10.5 but does not call it a triumph. The word *triumphus* first appears at 1.38.3, for a celebration by Tarquinius Priscus over the Sabines.

3. Q. Publilius Philo became the first proconsul to celebrate a triumph, in 326, during the Samnite Wars (8.26.7 and Degrassi 1947, 70–71, 541), but no praetor triumphed until L. Furius Purpureo in 200 (31.49.2–3, with the Fasti not extant). Both these men clearly set important precedents.

note will also indicate an *ovatio* or naval triumph as opposed to the far more regular full type, the Fasti tend to efface distinctions between one triumph and another.[4] If controversy erupted over a general's triumph request at the time, it fades into silence here as long as the results came out in his favor, and triumph bids merely assayed only to be rejected or discarded for whatever reason leave no trace whatsoever. Conspicuously absent as well is any mention of the governing body or bodies involved. Entries in the Fasti therefore reveal almost nothing about the decision-making process leading up to any given award, and offer only indirect hints about the criteria that may have been used to distinguish valid claims from invalid ones.

Nor do the authors generally cited to corroborate or refute details from the early Fasti—Livy's First Decade mainly, supplemented by excerpts from Dionysius of Halicarnassus, the elder Pliny, Valerius Maximus, Eutropius, the anonymous *Liber de Viris Illustribus,* and others—offer very much help.[5] At one point Livy expresses surprise at the failure of his sources to explain why a particular triumph was not granted or even requested, suggesting that he may have looked for such information as a matter of course.[6] Given the pitiful state of the sources, though, triumphs (as opposed to triumph debates) dominate the available picture from the start of the Republic until the mid-third century at the earliest. With the loss of Livy's Second Decade, we do not have the full benefit of his account until the Hannibalic War. Triumphal rules and procedures from the early period must therefore be reconstructed, if not entirely from scratch, then all too often on the basis of late, highly unreliable evidence.

Laying criteria aside for the moment, we are on somewhat firmer ground

4. I.e., *ovans* or *navalem* [sc. *triumphum*] *egit.* The *spolia opima* awarded to Marcellus in 222 also receive conspicuous mention, although the first such, said to have been taken in the field by Romulus himself, do not appear. In the notorious case of A. Cornelius Cossus in 428, the stone is sadly missing. See Degrassi 1947, as follows: 64–65, 534 (Romulus); 538 (Cossus); 78–79, 550 (Marcellus).

5. Most of the triumph notices in Livy's First Decade simply state (Fasti-like) that X triumphed over Y: 2.7.4, 2.16.1, 2.16.9, 2.20.13; 4.10.7; 5.23.4, 5.49.7; 6.4.1, 6.16.5, 6.29.8; 7.11.9 (cf. 7.11.11), 7.15.8, 7.27.8; 9.15.10, 9.16.11, 9.43.22, 9.44.14, 9.45.18 (an anonymous celebration); 10.1.9, 10.5.13, 10.13.1, 10.30.8, 10.37.13, 10.46.13. Here and there, Livy mentions a senatorial decree: 2.47.10; 3.29.4, 3.70.14; 4.53.11; 8.12.10, 8.16.11; 9.40.20, 9.43.22; 10.37.6. Sometimes he uses a passive verb with no stated agent (3.10.4; 4.43.2; 5.31.4; 7.11.9; 8.13.9, 8.26.7; 10.36.19) or occasionally a formula more in keeping with the dual-sovereignty model of the SPQR (4.20.1, 6.42.8, 7.11.9; and cf. 10.46.2).

6. 3.70.14: "triumphum nec ipsos postulasse nec delatum iis ab senatu accipio, nec traditur causa spreti aut non sperati honoris" ("I have not learned either that they themselves sought a triumph or that it was granted to them by the senate, and the reason for the honor being turned down or not hoped for is not recorded").

with the question of who awarded triumphs. Here two important observations suggest themselves: first, the senate seems to have emerged as the chief arbiter of *triumphi spes* under the Republic from a very early date; but second, an *imperator* who met with intractable opposition in the *curia* might rescue his triumph bid, under the right circumstances, by recourse to the popular assembly or even to his own *imperium* by itself. All three elements from Polybius's famous excursus (6.11–18) on the nature of the Republican government as an example of what Aristotle had termed the "mixed constitution"—the senate representing oligarchy (τὸ ἀριστοκρατικόν), the Roman people representing democracy (τὸ δημοκρατικόν), and the magistrates, whose powers of *imperium* and *auspicium* derived from the sole rule of kings (τὸ μοναρχικὸν καὶ βασιλικόν)—were known to play a decisive part on occasion. Triumphal ritual uniquely brought the whole SPQR together, highlighting the paradigmatic entry of the commander into the *urbs* with the good fortune that his victory brought to all its inhabitants.[7] Triumph debates likewise reveal an intricate pattern of interactions between the different elements of Roman society and government. It would be well, following the Polybian schema, to examine the roles of the senate, the people, and the magistrates of Rome in determining who should triumph and who should not.[8]

SENATUS: THE SENATE

Among the various checks and balances within the governing structure of the *res publica,* Polybius singles out the power of the senate both to award triumphs and to allocate public funds to pay for them.[9] A commander came before his aristocratic peers first and foremost to narrate his *res gestae* and

7. The concept of εἰσήλασις or the ritual homecoming by a victorious hero forms the core of Versnel's understanding of the Roman triumph, neatly summarized in the closing pages of his book: Versnel 1970, 371–97.

8. Itgenshorst 2005, 189–218, points to certain prevailing tensions between the *triumphator* on the one hand and his soldiers, the people, and the senate on the other. The individual's quest for self-aggrandizement repeatedly runs up against the *patrum auctoritas* jealously guarding the right to triumph. Often stymied by their peers, aristocrats go out of their way to show themselves as successful commanders, and in their bid to retain their *dignitas* and a measure of independence from the tyranny of the senate, they emphasize their family lineage and make victory count for much more than triumphs. I believe that fairly sums up her argument. The problem is that most of the would-be *triumphatores* were themselves senators and the sons, grandsons, nephews, brothers, etc., of senators, which means that their personal and family interests were not as radically distinct from those of the senate as a body as Itgenshorst suggests. A more complex and nuanced model is called for that takes both the competition between members of the aristocracy and their solidarity into account. Cf., e.g., Hölkeskamp 1993.

9. Polyb. 6.15.7–8.

make his formal triumph request.[10] The process is well known and often described in the scholarly literature. A would-be *triumphator* met with the senate outside the *pomerium*—often in the Temple of Bellona or of Apollo Medicus nearby—because it was taboo (*nefas*) for anyone endowed with *imperium militiae* to cross the sacred boundary.[11] The *patres* would weigh his claim, and if they agreed, the triumph would go forward. Technically every *triumphator* may have required the consent of the people as well,[12] but regardless of how dual approval from the senate and people together may have been obtained in practice, the fact that the *patres* generally dominated

10. For a good example of the standard formulaic language, see 31.47.7: "senatum in aede Bellonae habuit expositisque rebus gestis ut triumphanti sibi in urbem inuehi liceret petit" ("he held a meeting of the senate in the Temple of Bellona, and having narrated his accomplishments he asked for permission to enter the city in triumph").

11. Gell. 15.27 writes: "centuriata comitia intra pomerium fieri nefas esse, quia exercitum extra urbem imperari oporteat, intra urbem imperari ius non sit" ("it is taboo [lit. 'unspeakable'] for a meeting of the centuriate assembly to be held inside the *pomerium,* since command over an army must be exercised outside the city limits, [and] there is no right for command to be exercised within the city limits"). A similar prohibition, as early as the XII Tables, governed the burial of the dead: Cic. *Leg.* 2.23.58, Dio 45.7.1 (cf. 53.2.4), Eutr. 8.5. On meeting places of the Roman senate, see Bonnefond-Coudry 1989, 25–198, with a careful discussion of the ideological reasons for holding triumph debates outside the *pomerium* at 137–60. On the archaeology of the temples of Bellona and Apollo Medicus in relation to the topography of the triumph, see Coarelli 1988, 395–99. Also note the clearly labeled plan in Künzl 1988, 33. Certain generals from the Late Republic waited outside the city literally for years in hopes of being allowed to celebrate the signal honor: L. Licinius Lucullus, Q. Caecilius Metellus Creticus, Q. Marcius Rex, and C. Pomptinus. Cf. Brennan 1996, 329.

12. Promagistrates apparently needed a special dispensation in order to triumph, because their original term of office had technically expired. Livy mentions a *relatio ad populum* for this purpose on two occasions: for the *ovatio* of M. Claudius Marcellus in 211 (26.21.5) and for the triumphs of L. Aemilius Paullus, Cn. Octavius, and L. Anicius Gallus in 167 (45.35.4). See Mommsen 1887, 1.132 and nn. More problematic for lack of evidence is the supposed extension of this practice to all *triumphatores,* including those currently in their year of office. Versnel 1970, 192, argues as follows: "The crossing of the *pomerium* forms the pivot around which all juridical usages connected with the triumph revolve. Within this *pomerium* only the *imperium domi* was operative. On the day of the triumph, however, the triumphator had, with the people's consent, the *imperium militiae.* This fact seems to me to be the central one, which requires an explanation." Farther down on the same page (in n. 3), he cites Mommsen as above, and then adds, "it is also possible, and in my view more probable, that the normal magistrate, too, needed the people's permission to retain his full military *imperium* in the city." Brennan 1996, 316, follows Versnel's lead, also citing Mommsen. If this model holds, we have to assume that Livy has compressed his description of the process more often than not, omitting reference to the popular vote in every instance but the two exceptional cases listed above. He certainly demonstrates elsewhere an inconsistency in the length at which he spells out such procedural details: Linderski 1993, 56–59, convincingly traces a similar phenomenon with regard to the haruspices. Also note the ever-present link between *imperium* and *auspicium:* Brennan 2004, 42, calls the Porta Triumphalis "a hole in augural space," because a commander "who properly entered through it was entitled to retain his military auspices in the city for a single day so as to make a formal procession to the Temple of Jupiter."

the proceedings is still beyond doubt. Every attested triumph debate began in the senate even if it did not end there, and all but one in Livy 21–45 take place entirely within the ranks of the *curia*.[13] Nevertheless the *patrum auctoritas* did not stand alone: both the Roman people at large, as those who bestowed *imperium*, and the magistrates themselves, as those who bore it, maintained a vital role in triumphal negotiations across the centuries; and because in practice the *mos maiorum* left room for strategic political realignments as events called for, either one or the other of two additional branches in the power triangle could on occasion go so far as to authorize a triumph on its own, without senatorial consent.

POPULUS ROMANUS: THE PEOPLE OF ROME

During the first several centuries of the Republic, a handful of generals apparently triumphed by order of the people alone: two together as early as 449, then one in 356, and another in 223. One more seems to have raised the same possibility in 294, before taking a different course of action. These four widely scattered incidents represent the only actual triumph *debates* in Livy's extant narrative before the Second Punic War.[14] Given the shortage of reliable evidence for Rome's early history, we must of course view them all with a healthy skepticism.[15] But taken together, especially in connection with an important parallel from the second century, they seem to reflect an ongoing or at least sporadically recurring power struggle between the senate and the people over control of the *ius triumphandi*.

According to Livy's by no means entirely trustworthy version of events, L. Valerius Poplicola and M. Horatius Barbatus, consuls in 449, ran afoul of the senate in the troubled aftermath of the Decemvirate.[16] The *patres*

13. The one glaring exception to the rule that triumph debates took place in the senate is the controversy over honors for L. Aemilius Paullus in 167 (45.35–39), where the senate voted overwhelmingly in the commander's favor and heated arguments broke out only in a later motion before the people. See chapter 14 below.

14. A single late source (Zonar. 7.19.5) reports finding evidence (λέγεται, "it is said") that none of the so-called *tribuni consulares* who led Roman armies into battle during the late fifth and early fourth centuries ever triumphed, although "many of [them] often won victories." Livy never raises the possibility of triumphs for these officials, and Zonaras's cryptic statement leaves a fair bit of room for interpretation, as we shall see in chapter 2 below.

15. J. S. Richardson 1975, 58, refers to the "somewhat doubtful early cases."

16. Livy's heavily dramatized account of the *decemviri* has been called into question many times, if not dismissed as an outright fabrication. For a balanced treatment, with a helpful summary of previous scholarship, see Ungern-Sternberg 1986. Perhaps the episode of the triumph debate, by itself, need not be tarred with the same brush as other elements of the story—Mitchell 1990, 193, guardedly refers to it—but the whole thing must remain dubious at best, even though Livy clearly regarded it as the first item in a series and a significant precedent. He even has one would-be *triumphator*, many years later, cite it as an exemplum to justify his claim amid opposition (10.37.10).

grudgingly voted a joint public thank-offering (*supplicatio*) for the consuls in honor of their impressive victories over the Aequi and the Sabines, only to deny them both the right to triumph, at which point a defiant tribune brought up a motion before the people (*rogatio populi*). Despite vigorous opposition from the senators this measure passed, and both consuls triumphed on the strength of the popular vote (3.63.8–11).[17] Livy for his part emphatically focuses attention on the prerogatives of the various governing bodies in Rome at the time, through the mouthpiece of the indignant senators: "never before had the issue of a triumph been argued before the people; the evaluation and judgment concerning this honor had always belonged to the senate. . . . The state would finally be freed, and the laws made just, only if each *ordo* retained its own rights and privileges" (3.63.9–10).[18] Enough questions have been raised about Livy's narrative throughout the period of the *decemviri* to render this episode decidedly suspect, and strong words like "never" and "always" (from the senators' complaint, cited just above) give pause in a context where the fledgling Republic has barely existed for fifty years. By the same token, the fact that it apparently took another century or more for history to repeat itself lends a measure of credence to the irregularity supposedly decried by the *patres*.

The next alleged episode came in 356, when C. Marcius Rutilus, notably the first plebeian to serve as *dictator*, threatened the status quo one step further by naming a fellow plebeian, C. Plautius, as his second in command (*magister equitum*, "master of the horse"). According to Livy's brief account, the outraged senate tried to keep Rutilus from going to war on Rome's behalf, but the *populus* indulgently gave him everything he wanted, up to and including a triumph at the end of his term. Without further elaboration about the triumph debate as such, except to tell us that among other things Rutilus could boast that he had seized control of the enemy camp and taken a number of prisoners, Livy just states that he triumphed "without the authority of the senate by order of the people" ("sine auctoritate patrum populi iussu," 7.17.6–9).[19]

The third affair revolves around C. Flaminius, one of the most controversial and enigmatic figures in late third-century Rome. His notoriety began as tribune of the people in 232, when he introduced a measure

17. Cf. Dion. Hal. 11.49.5 and 50.1. Also see Degrassi 1947, 66–67, 538. Signs of friction between the senate and people had apparently already manifested themselves over the *supplicatio* in honor of the consuls' victories (3.63.5).

18. 3.63.9–10: "nunquam ante de triumpho per populum actum; semper aestimationem arbitriumque eius honoris penes senatum fuisse . . . ita demum liberam civitatem fore, ita aequatas leges, si sua quisque iura ordo, suam maiestatem teneat."

19. See also Degrassi 1947, 68–69, 540; Hölkeskamp 1987, 89.

to distribute farmland in Picenum to Roman citizens.[20] Cato the Elder reports that this proposal was eventually carried out,[21] but at the time it ignited such explosive feelings among the senators that Flaminius was labeled forever after as a dangerous rabble-rouser. It also made him appear forcibly to later historians, from Polybius onward, as a precursor to the Gracchi, thereby permanently distorting any view that we might once have glimpsed of his actual goals and accomplishments.[22] Although he went on to be elected consul twice and even censor—giving his name to both the Via Flaminia and the Circus Flaminius—he was hounded by allegations of one scandal after another throughout the rest of his long career.[23] He died in the battle of Trasimene, in 217 (22.6).[24] From even this brief biography, there emerges a mixture of deeds and personality traits that ancient authors found alternately praiseworthy or dubious, or at times oddly both at once. The literary tradition is ambivalent to say the least.

As consul in 223, Flaminius and his colleague, P. Furius Philus, led the first Roman army across the Po to score an important victory over the Insubres in Gaul.[25] Meanwhile, at least according to one late and markedly hostile tradition, trouble was brewing at home. Plutarch and Zonaras tell us that on the eve of the decisive battle, the *patres* in Rome issued a dispatch citing some alleged irregularity with the auspices and the propitiation of omens and ordering Flaminius and Furius to relinquish their command and return at once. The consuls waited to open the summonses until after they had already engaged and defeated the enemy.[26] On one level, this undeniably risky political strategy appears to have worked: although the *Periocha*

20. Relevant sources listed by Broughton 1951, 225. See also Develin 1976.

21. Cato *apud* Varro *RR* 1.2.7.

22. According to Valerius Maximus, Flaminius's agrarian bill angered some senators so much that they actually considered enlisting an army to stop him. His own father then dragged him bodily off the Rostra (5.4.5). On the thematic connection with the Gracchi, see Polyb. 2.21.7–8. The hostile tradition about Flaminius may stem, at least in part, from his conflict with Q. Fabius Maximus (Cic. *Sen.* 11), which presumably caused Fabius Pictor to cast him in a negative light.

23. For Flaminius's censorship in 220, which may have involved registering freedmen into the four city tribes, see *Per.* 20. On the broader context of his career, especially the agrarian bill, as well as his central involvement in a later dispute over a law restricting the shipping rights of senators, see the engaging and thoughtful treatment by Feig Vishnia 1996, 11–48, with reference to earlier scholarship.

24. On Flaminius's death see also Polyb. 3.84.6.

25. For a narrative of the battle that follows a hostile tradition in attributing victory not to the consul but to his junior officers, see Polyb. 2.23–33. In defense of Flaminius, Staveley 1989, 435, writes: "he was given little credit either by his political opponents or by the tradition which they helped to mold, and it was left to the popular assembly, rather than to the senate, to vote him the triumph which he so richly deserved."

26. Plut. *Marc.* 4.3, 6.1; Zonar. 8.20.

for Livy's lost Book 20 describes only the victory in Gaul and nothing of its aftermath,[27] we know from elsewhere that both men celebrated triumphs. Not only do the Fasti attest this,[28] but some years later, during the post-Cannae crisis in 216, Livy reports that the *dictator* M. Iunius Pera equipped some of his emergency troops with a cache of Gallic weapons that had been carried in Flaminius's triumph (23.14.3–4). Furthermore, Livy intimates that Flaminius, elected consul again in 217, felt eager to set off for his province as quickly as possible, recalling all his earlier struggles with the senate, including the triumph debate (21.63.2). There is a sad irony in Flaminius's desire to set out so quickly, given what befell him at the end of his journey.

Thus extant Livy tells us only that Flaminius's triumph bid met with opposition in the senate, which was eventually overcome, but Plutarch implies and Zonaras actually states that both consuls in 223 owed their victory celebrations to a vote from the people.[29] It stands to reason therefore that Flaminius and Furius must have triumphed by a political procedure similar to that outlined above for the two earlier incidents. Plutarch goes on to add another twist to the story, suggesting that the senate may have retaliated against the consuls for having marched off into battle despite their recall notices, by later forcing them to lay down their office before the end of the year.[30] Whether the account of this supposed fallout is true or not, it serves to illustrate both the intense animosity felt by members of the senate toward defiant magistrates and the crossover between specifically triumphal politics and politics in general. Having incurred the wrath of the senate, Flaminius and Furius tried to evade the consequences by taking their cause to the people instead. In the process they may have gained the right to triumph, but then lost the elected office that had opened the whole opportunity for them in the first place.[31] Unless other similar incidents have simply vanished altogether from the historical record, no one ever triumphed again solely by a vote of the people.

Still, even long after, the popular assembly retained an important stake in triumphal negotiations. In 167 L. Aemilius Paullus, consul from the year before and victor at Pydna (44.33–46) over Perseus of Macedon—the last successor to the throne of Alexander the Great—sailed up the Tiber

27. *Per.* 20: "exercitibus Romanis tunc primum trans Padum ductis Galli Insubres aliquot proeliis fusi in deditionem venerunt" ("Roman armies were led across the Po then for the first time, and the Gauls called Insubres, being routed in several battles, came under submission").

28. See Degrassi 1947, 78–79, 550.

29. Plut. *Marc.* 4.3; Zonar. 8.20.

30. Eckstein 1987, 16, writes that Flaminius and Furius had "crossed the limit of magisterial behavior acceptable to the *patres.*"

31. But see Brennan 1996, 334 n. 52, for an innocent explanation that is far from implausible.

to Rome in a enormous royal barge heavily laden with spoils (45.35.3). A few days behind him came two other commanders who had aided in the campaign against the king and his allies: Cn. Octavius, propraetor in charge of the fleet, had captured Perseus alive at Samothrace and brought him bodily into Paullus's custody (45.5–6), while L. Anicius Gallus, also a propraetor, had led a successful campaign against the Illyrians and their king Gentius (44.21.4–10, 44.30–32.15, 45.3.1–2).[32] The senate voted full triumphs to all three men, without any trace of controversy or dispute in Livy's account, and then arranged for a motion to be put before the assembly granting each of them *imperium* on the day of the triumph, as required for promagistrates (45.35.4). So far, so good. But then Paullus's troops, apparently upset at having received a smaller share than they had expected from the extravagant royal plunder of Macedon, decided to use the popular vote as a venue to air their grievances.[33] Led by Ser. Sulpicius Galba, one of the military tribunes, they aimed their attack not at Octavius or Anicius, but only at the supreme commander, whom they held responsible for their supposed ill treatment (45.35.5–6).

Galba deliberately prolonged his harangue until sundown, so that the measure could not come to a vote until the following morning (45.36.2–5). At first light disgruntled soldiers thronged the Capitol, and with them in the front ranks of voters, the early returns went against Paullus. The naysayers might even have prevailed, Livy tells us, had not a group of civic leaders (*principes civitatis*) dramatically intervened at a critical moment to rescue Paullus's imperiled triumph bid. These high-ranking aristocrats stormed up the hill through the crowd in righteous indignation and pressured the tribunes in charge of the assembly to interrupt the proceedings, nullify any results from the voting so far, and start the whole process over again, having first given one of their number, the former consul and *magister equitum* M. Servilius, a chance to speak in defense of the would-be *triumphator* (45.36.6–10). Servilius hailed Paullus's achievements and his service to Rome at length, pointing out just how scandalous it would be for a commander's own troops to deprive him of a triumph after he had led them to so great a victory, especially when the war had previously dragged on for so long to no avail. Moreover, they were charging him not with any gross misconduct, but rather with upholding traditional Roman military discipline too strictly. Who could properly fault an *imperator* for that? Servilius's speech, as Livy presents it (45.37–39), gives ample testimony to the importance of triumphs in mediating between the senate, magistrates, and people on the one hand, and the civic gods on the other.

32. On the battle of Pydna see also Polyb. 29.14–18. Broughton 1951, 427 and 433–34, lists other sources for the campaign.

33. Also cf. Plut. *Aem.* 30–32.

At the climax of his speech, Servilius apparently wanted to make a bold gesture that would assert his *auctoritas* by offering tangible proof of devotion to the *res publica.* Lifting his toga to display an array of battle scars—all in front, of course—he accidentally uncovered rather more of his aged anatomy than he had intended. Nervous laughter erupted at that. It was an extremely awkward moment, and potentially disastrous for Paullus's triumph bid, but Servilius did not lose his cool. Instead, he brilliantly turned even the audience's ridicule to his own advantage, proclaiming loudly over the jeers of the crowd that, far from causing him any embarrassment as it stood revealed, the swelling in his groin actually made him proud, because it bore witness to many hard years in the saddle as a loyal soldier of the SPQR (45.39.16–19). All the ugly marks on his body, both those that he had meant to show off and those that a sense of decorum would normally have kept hidden, together became a text that he masterfully decoded—like a living veristic portrait-statue—to reveal a quality of character that he knew everyone present would instantly recognize and admire.[34] Not only did Servilius vindicate himself thereby, but the patent disloyalty of Paullus's troops to commander and country stood out all the more starkly in contrast. This clinched the argument.

Livy's narrative of the final vote has disappeared into one of many lacunae in the single damaged manuscript that preserves Books 41–45, but of the eventual outcome there can be no doubt: with the full consent of both senate and people, Paullus celebrated a magnificent triumph, richly adorned with booty from the royal palace at Pella and crowned with the piteous spectacle of the Macedonian king Philip himself, led as a prisoner in chains (45.40).[35] And whether the soldiers' complaints had any basis or not, a vast amount of wealth did eventually find its way into the treasury.

IMPERATORES: THE MAGISTRATES THEMSELVES

A clear pattern emerges. Although the vast majority of attested triumph debates showcase cooperation between the senate and the people, the latter could sometimes take independent, not to say subversive action, and a poorly attested episode from the third century suggests another, still more radical possibility. According to one of several conflicting accounts that Livy found in his sources, L. Postumius Megellus, consul in 294, celebrated a triumph not only against the wishes of the senate, but even

34. On the power of veristic sculpture to convey moral character (*auctoritas, gravitas, dignitas,* etc.) "warts and all," see especially Nodelman 1975; also Richter 1955, and more recently Tanner 2000.

35. Also cf. Plut. *Aem.* 32–34, especially 34.1–4.

without a popular vote.[36] Livy says that when the *patres* turned down his triumph request, Postumius proudly invoked his *imperium* as consul and walked out. Tribunes declared allegiances on either side. Later called upon by one of them to plead his cause before the Roman people, the commander brought attention to the powerful exempla from 449 and 356, duly naming Horatius, Valerius, and Rutilus (10.37.6–10). He nevertheless stopped short of putting the matter of his own triumph to a vote in the assembly, because he knew that certain hostile tribunes ("chattels of the *nobiles*") would block the measure. Instead he proclaimed that he would always rely on the "will and favor of the people in agreement with him," and the next day simply went ahead with his triumph in open defiance of all opposition.[37] Even the combined forces of the senate and seven of the ten tribunes proved powerless to halt a public celebration in progress, after the consul had set things in motion. Postumius's own three loyal tribunes stood nearby, ready to block any action by their colleagues (10.37.12).[38]

As far as we know Postumius's self-appointed full triumph had no precedent, and afterward the status quo in triumphal negotiations between the senate, magistrates, and people of Rome swiftly and powerfully reasserted itself. Triumph debates uniformly took place in the senate again, and in lieu of marching up to the Capitol without so much as a by-your-leave, as Postumius had done, the alternative triumph on the Alban mount (*in monte Albano*)—celebrated first in 231 and then three more times in the period 211–172—seems to have emerged for a while as the preferred recourse

36. The Fasti list triumphs in 294 for both Postumius and his colleague, M. Atilius Regulus (see Degrassi 1947, 72–73, 544), whereas Livy, after recounting first a victory by Atilius over the Samnites and then a raid with heavy Roman casualties, says that the triumph was denied because of excessive losses (10.36.19). Postumius supposedly remembered this incident when his own triumph came before the senate (10.37.7), but Livy later reports (at 10.37.13–14) that Claudius Quadrigarius and Fabius Pictor attributed different actions and outcomes to one or both consuls. To make matters worse, a fragment of Dionysius of Halicarnassus (17[18].5.3) places Postumius's contested triumph not in 294 but three years later, in 291, when neither Livy nor the Fasti are extant to confirm or deny the report. Surely the same individual could not have celebrated *two* such triumphs, especially within such a short interval. On this score Degrassi 1947, 544, expresses doubt, but understandably opts to withhold judgment.

37. 10.37.11: "adiciebat se quoque laturum fuisse ad populum, ni sciret mancipia nobilium, tribunos plebis, legem impedituros; voluntatem sibi ac favorem consentientis populi pro omnibus iussis esse ac futura" ("He added that he too would have put a motion before the people, if he did not know that the chattels of the *nobiles,* the tribunes of the plebs, would block the law; for him the will and favor of the people in agreement with him were and always would be as good as all [*sc.* other] demands").

38. Badian 1988, 459, comments wryly that this is "one of Livy's sedate little ironies, easily missed by those who merely check their references in his text. For it soon turns out that Postumius, a Patrician noble, himself 'owns' three tribunes whose support ensures his doubtfully legal triumph! Livy should be allowed his little joke."

of commanders who could not win adequate support among the *patres*. A recent study has traced the history of the Alban triumph in some detail, arguing that C. Papirius Maso, consul in 231, introduced the practice as a deliberate "act of protest against the arbitrary and uncertain process of receiving permission to triumph from the Senate."[39] The *patres* apparently refused him because his dubious victory over the Corsi had resulted in a considerable loss of Roman life.[40] So instead he went to the Alban Mount, site of the annual *feriae Latinae,* to celebrate his triumph. He could do this on his own authority because the place lay outside the city: he would not have to cross the *pomerium.*[41] He also scheduled his celebration to mark the anniversary of the first triumph by one of his ancestors nearly a century before, thereby manipulating both space and time with equal proficiency to enhance his public image.[42]

Note the interplay between center and periphery: as an alternative to the full triumph, the ceremony *in monte Albano* inevitably lacked the same prestige, not only because the commander who triumphed there did not have official sanction (or public funding) for what he was doing, but also because the whole thing took place far from the Capitol, the locus of power, where Jupiter reigned supreme over his people.[43] After refusing Papirius the honor of a triumph, the senate went on to deny him permission to build a temple within the city limits, thus reiterating their earlier vote, in effect, and therefore censuring his decision to hold a private celebration against their will, and also forever banishing even the memory of his *res gestae* to a place outside the *pomerium,* away from the public eye. Plainly grasping the import of the further slight to his *dignitas,* Papirius designed

39. Brennan 1996, 320; cf. Develin 1978, 437. For the notice in the Fasti that Papirius was the first to triumph *in monte Albano,* see Degrassi 1947, 78–79, 449.

40. Zonar. 8.18.14.

41. Livy marks triumphs *in monte Albano* as taking place "iure imperii consularis" ("by right of consular *imperium*") at 33.23.3 and "sine publica auctoritate" ("without the authority of the people") at 42.21.7. Ancient writers never describe the ritual performed *in monte Albano* in much detail, but it presumably mirrored the full triumph as closely as possible, differing in location only, as the notices in the Fasti would seem to indicate. Versnel 1970, 165–66, 279–82, and others have wanted to see the Alban ritual as a primitive form of the Roman ceremony, but this remains a matter of speculation, and the unmistakable perceived novelty of Papirius's celebration seems to argue against it. Cf. J. S. Richardson 1975, 55.

42. On these various significant connections, see Brennan 1996, 322 and nn.

43. Livy's remarks at 33.23.8 concerning the third triumph *in monte Albano* would have been true *a fortiori* the first time: "is triumphus ut loco et fama rerum gestarum et quod sumptum non erogatum ex aerario omnes sciebant inhonoratior fuit, ita signis carpentisque et spoliis ferme aequabat" ("Although everyone knew that this triumph was less prestigious in its location and the reputation of the accomplishments and because the cost was not paid for out of the treasury, nonetheless it was practically equal in [the number of] statues and two-wheeled carts and spoils"). On Gallic *carpenta* as a regular feature of triumphs, see Östenberg 2003, 30–36.

a countermeasure: in later years he always wore the myrtle crown of the *ovatio* while attending civic games, a defiantly pointed reminder of what he felt the ungrateful establishment owed him.[44] Yet although the open division between commander and senate over the issue of a triumph seems to have provoked some lingering ill will during Papirius's lifetime, his name still made it into the Fasti—albeit with a special notice of the variance from general practice—and set a useful, if somewhat limited, precedent.

Two decades passed, and then in 211 the senate granted only an *ovatio* and not a triumph to M. Claudius Marcellus, conqueror of Syracuse, on the grounds (previously unheard of, or at least unattested) that he had not brought back his army (26.21.1–12). That this was more a calculated political maneuver than the formulation of a new general rule will emerge from the discussion of the *deportatio* provision below in chapter 4. Here the incident deserves note for two other reasons. First, when Marcellus's *res gestae* proved too controversial to gain unanimous approval yet too impressive to ignore, the *patres* revived an ancient ritual (the *ovatio*), which no one had celebrated for at least eighty and probably more like a hundred and fifty years, as a means of rewarding success that would still fall short of a full triumph.[45] Second, when he found himself snubbed by his peers in this way, Marcellus followed Papirius's example to boost his public image and simultaneously register a complaint with the senate. He swallowed his pride and duly held the *ovatio,* but having triumphed *in monte Albano* first (26.21.6).[46] As far as we know, no one else under the Republic—either before or after—ever staged two such ceremonies to mark a single victory. It has been suggested that Marcellus's "acceptance of the *ovatio* shows that he thought the Alban triumph was not enough in itself."[47] But the argument would work just as well, if not better, the other way around: Marcellus held his triumph on the Alban Mount because he thought the *ovatio* inadequate.[48] He had already demonstrated a flair for attention-getting victory

44. Cf. Brennan 1996, 322–23 and nn.: "This ostentatious gesture—surely a protest measure—must have irritated many in the senatorial establishment." On the pointed symbolism of the myrtle crown, and Papirius's decision to wear it, see Gell. 5.6, Val. Max. 3.6.5, Pliny *NH* 15.126, Plut. *Marc.* 22. One should note that no *ovatio* had been celebrated in Rome for over a century before Papirius, and that the ceremony was not revived as a political compromise until M. Claudius Marcellus in 211. Only an antiquarian, or a high-minded Roman aristocrat, would have a long enough memory of past civic honors to catch the reference.

45. Cf. J. S. Richardson 1975, 54. The last well-attested *ovatio* before Marcellus marked the victory of consul M. Fabius Ambustus over the Hernici in 360. See Degrassi 1947, 540; and 7.11.9. M'. Curius Dentatus may have celebrated one over the Lucani in 290 or 289, but the sole reference is a dubious notice in *De Vir. Ill.* 33.4. See Brennan 1994; Degrassi 1947, 69–70, 545.

46. See also Degrassi 1947, 551.

47. Brennan 1996, 324.

48. See J. S. Richardson 1975, 55; Develin 1978, 432. The implication that Marcellus might have refused the *ovatio* seems out of place, given the evident astonishment with which

celebrations with his dedication of the *spolia opima* in 222, which earned him the single longest entry in the extant portions of the Fasti.[49]

The next incident did not take place until fifteen years after Marcellus. In 197, the consuls Q. Minucius Rufus and C. Cornelius Cethegus had both been allotted Italy as their province (32.28.3–9). Their combined strategy worked to secure a major victory for Cethegus against the Insubres and Cenomani (32.30.5–13), and successes for Minucius as well against the Ligures (32.29.5–30.4, 32.31.1–5). The senate voted a four-day *supplicatio* in honor of them both (32.31.6). But on their return, despite a concerted effort, their hopes of celebrating a joint triumph were thwarted by opposition from a pair of tribunes, who mounted such a vigorous and sustained protest to Minucius's bid, on a number of different grounds, that he finally had no option left except to abandon his request and save face with a triumph *in monte Albano,* while his colleague celebrated a full triumph with the overwhelming consent of the *patres* (33.22–23). The intensity and rancor of the debate suggest not only that Minucius's *res gestae* could not command enough attention to win him so much as an *ovatio,* no matter how hard he might press his claim (he was plainly no Marcellus), but also that his resolve to triumph alongside Cethegus, no matter what the cost, almost matched that of his opponents to stop him.[50] Livy says that in electing the Alban ceremony Minucius claimed to be following "the example of many illustrious men" (33.23.3), although we know of only two (Papirius and Marcellus) before him.[51] Of course, the greater a notional precedent he could invoke on his own behalf in the moment of backing down, the more he could legitimize his cause and cushion the disgrace of rejection.[52]

After this the Alban triumph fell into obscurity again for another quarter-century, until C. Cicereius, praetor and former scribe, found recourse to it in 173. Following his defeat of the rebellious Corsi, Cicereius exacted from them by way of *praeda* some two hundred thousand pounds of bees-

---

Livy writes of consul M. Fabius Vibulanus in 480 (2.47.10–11), the one commander ever said to have turned down civic honors granted by the senate. It should be added that Vibulanus acted out of *pietas* and grief, not indignation, both his colleague and his brother having died in the battle that brought him his victory.

49. Degrassi 1947, 78–79, 550.

50. Brennan 1996, 325–26, claims somewhat unconvincingly on the grounds that twenty-five years elapsed before the next such celebration that Minucius's Alban triumph "may have somewhat devalued the institution . . . for future commanders." It is a question of degree, but the interval seems roughly comparable to the prior twenty years between Papirius and Marcellus. The triumph *in monte Albano* never carried enough prestige to make it anything more than a rare occurrence.

51. 33.23.3: "in monte Albano se triumphaturum et iure imperii consularis et multorum clarorum virorum exemplo dixit" ("He said that he would triumph on the Alban mount both by right of his consular *imperium* and by the example of many illustrious men").

52. Cf. Chaplin 2000, 149–50.

wax, a prized local export (42.7.1).[53] His request for a triumph must have sounded very presumptuous, for the senate turned him down flat, as one scholar has put it, "in part because of his social status" and also "thinking he would just go quietly away."[54] After an apparent interval during which he must have sought an avenue for converting the wax into ready cash to pay for the ceremony—it probably found its way into candles for the upcoming Saturnalia, or perhaps into tablets indulgently purchased by his former colleagues in the *collegium* of scribes[55]—Cicereius took advantage of what had by now become accepted *mos* and triumphed *in monte Albano* instead (42.21.7). Do three previous incidents constitute the minimum critical mass required to establish a series of ad-hoc compromises as the authentic *mos maiorum?* That remains an open question, but by all accounts Cicereius was the last to invoke this particular custom. He may have effectively put an end to the whole thing by creating just the sort of *exemplum indignum* that status-conscious Roman aristocrats in future generations would hardly deign to follow. So the triumph *in monte Albano* faded into obscurity, just as it had come to light for a brief time, through the vagaries of élite competition.

The Fasti Triumphales are missing for 154–130,[56] and without Livy to help fill in the gaps, it is hard to develop a picture of triumph debates after 167—until the Late Republic, that is, when "triumph debate" could sadly become a historian's euphemism for civil war. Nevertheless, one reasonably well-attested incident from the second half of the second century demonstrates that the hunt for civic honors continued unabated whenever the opportunity arose.[57] It did not matter that the triumph *in monte Albano* had ceased to be a viable option after Cicereius, because, as L. Postumius Megellus had amply demonstrated as early as 293, there was never any real constitutional barrier against a full triumph on a magistrate's own authority. Nothing short of violence, if that, could hinder a lawful holder of *imperium* from celebrating a victory as he liked, provided only that he showed enough audacity or even just raw determination.

The sources show a decided ambivalence about the conduct of the commander in question. Ap. Claudius Pulcher, consul in 143, seems to have lost as many men as he killed of the enemy in a narrow defeat of the Gallic

53. Brennan 1996, 336 n. 76, cites a parallel at 40.34.12, where the Corsicans paid half that amount of wax (a mere 100,000 lbs.) to praetor M. Pinarius Rusca. Also cf. Diod. 5.13.4.

54. Brennan 1996, 327.

55. Brennan 1996, 336–37 nn. 75, 76, and 80. Pliny *NH* 21.84 suggests that Corsican wax may also have had medicinal properties.

56. See Degrassi 1947, 558.

57. This *pace* Brennan 1996, 328–29, who points to a marked downturn in triumphs in the late second century, perhaps because of lingering embarrassment over Cicereius and his beeswax.

Salassi.[58] On his return, he asked the senate for public funds to pay for a triumph, as if the honor itself had already been awarded.[59] The *patres* evidently refused him the money, because although the relevant chunk of the Fasti is missing, later authors attest that Claudius ultimately paid for the triumph himself, without approval from either the senate or the people.[60] His daughter, a Vestal Virgin and therefore inviolate, rode in the triumphal chariot alongside him. While this memorable family tableau may have won Claudius a certain notoriety, as witnessed by allegations in one source of a rapacious and arrogant desire to triumph at all costs, later generations hailed the young woman's *pietas* for having thrown herself between her father and his assailant, a tribune, who tried to drag him bodily from the car.[61] To be sure, any brief scandal that may have arisen over the triumph did not put an end to Claudius's illustrious political career. He went on to serve as censor in 136 and later as *princeps senatus*. Father-in-law to Ti. Gracchus, he also played a leading role on the famous land commission.[62] Modern scholars, faced with the almost bewildering mixture of praise and blame in the sources, have passed their own differing verdicts.[63]

Both halves of a paradox now stand clearly revealed. On the one hand, inasmuch as the senate and people exercised control over the right to triumph, they did so only on the strength of custom and tradition. Their authority rested de facto and not de iure. The triumphs of Postumius and Claudius, separated by a span of exactly a hundred and fifty years, make plain a simple truth that the celebrations in between held *in monte Albano* actually help to conceal, namely that no one and nothing could technically

58. It is in connection with Claudius's exploits against the Salassi that Valerius Maximus 2.8.1 mentions a law requiring a minimum of 5,000 enemy casualties in a battle to justify the award of a triumph.

59. Dio fr. 74 Boissevain.

60. Oros. 5.4.7 says that Claudius paid for the triumph with his own money ("usus privatis sumptibus," "using his private expenditures"), whereas Suet. *Tib.* 2.4 states that the celebration took place "iniussu populi" ("without the vote of the people").

61. Dio Cass. fr. 74 Boissevain says that Claudius's decision to attack the Salassi stemmed from overwhelming ambition and jealousy toward his colleague, M. Claudius Metellus. For a more positive rendition, see Cic. *Cael.* 34 and Val. Max. 5.4.6. Further references in Broughton 1951, 471.

62. On Claudius's censorship, see Dio Cass. fr. 81 Boissevain; Fest. 360L; Plut. *Ti. Gracch.* 4.1 ("princeps senatus"); *Per.* 56. On the Gracchan commission, see App. *BCiv.* 1.13 and 18–19; *CIL* 1^2.2.639–44, 719; Cic. *Leg. Agr.* 2.31; *Per.* 58; Val. Max. 7.2.6; Vell. Pat. 2.2.3; Plut. *Ti. Gracch.* 13.1.

63. On the presence of both pro- and anti-Claudian strands in the ancient tradition, see Wiseman 1979, 101–3. J. S. Richardson 1975, 58, singles out this incident as a "startling demonstration" of the "comparative impotence of the senate to stop a determined man from triumphing." Cf. also Brennan 1996, 319; Mitchell 1990, 107 n. 150.

stop a commander from staging his own triumph, even a full triumph on the Capitol, if he chose, though in the event he might rely on some form of symbolic shield (viz. Postumius's tribunes and Claudius's Vestal Virgin) to ward off opposition. Like the triumphal ritual itself, the unanswerable autonomy of one who holds *imperium* harks back to the legendary kings of Rome. But if custom and tradition did not exert the same binding constraints as formal rules might have done, they nevertheless counted for a very great deal. In practice, the overbearing self-will of individuals led to only two out of the many, many triumphs that took place on the Capitol over the centuries, demonstrating that under the Republic, as opposed to the monarchy, a would-be *triumphator* was certainly expected—and indeed perhaps all but legally required—to ask for permission first. Hence the standard formula for a triumph request in Livy's narrative (e.g., at 31.47.7): "that he might be allowed to enter the city in triumph" ("ut triumphanti sibi in urbem invehi liceret").

SUMMARY

How then did one go about obtaining the desired permission? Whenever the sources allude to the act of requesting a triumph as distinct from merely celebrating one, the procedure described invariably begins, and usually ends, with a meeting of the senate. Only a handful of victorious generals from the early years of the Republic are ever said to have turned to the assembly for redress after finding their triumph hopes rejected by the body of their peers, and no one, as far as we know, ever went straight to the people without at least putting in a perfunctory appearance before the *patres* first. Moreover, in the many triumph debates that Livy records in some detail from the Hannibalic War onward, the assembly fades deep into the background. With the exception of the Paullus controversy, as already noted, such episodes are staged *entirely* before the senators.

Even if the consistency of this behavior turned out to be a deeply embedded narrative pattern in later authors and not an accurate representation of standard practice under the Republic, it would still attest to a pervasive assumption on Livy's part about the way things worked in the past. Technically, at least, no one could triumph without the consent of the people, because the ritual demanded it. This accounts for the dual formulas in some of the early notices: proper triumphs took place with official sanction from the whole SPQR. All the same, there eventually came a time when the assembly as a body no longer became directly embroiled, or at most only rarely, in the contentious process of determining who should triumph and who should not. Either popular approval amounted to little more than the proverbial rubber stamp once the senate had reached a decision, with the result that many assembly votes often left no trace in the historical record,[64] or else the tribunes of the people effectively spoke for the *populus Romanus* at large whenever all of them gave their consent to a motion before the *patres.* In the latter case the absence, or even just the timely withdrawal, of a tribunician veto could be taken in lieu of a popular vote.[65] Tribunes obviously played an enormously important role in negotiations between the various parties involved, alternately appearing as mediators and as agents provocateurs within the political machinery.[66]

Far from occurring in a vacuum, this prevailing trend in triumph debates coincides with the emergence, by the late third century, "of the senate as the principal organ of government, and of the nobility as the controlling element within the senate."[67] The conquest and reorganization of Italy on the one hand, and heightened contact with the Hellenistic kingdoms of the Greek East on the other, both played key roles in helping to establish the Roman élite as an élite, with their base of power in the *curia.*[68] In certain arenas, most notably that of legislation, popular sovereignty remained very real, and one need look only to the Late Republic for evidence of serious, even violent challenges to the *patrum auctoritas* from that quarter.[69] Still, the conduct of triumph debates always led to the senate floor: in order for his bid to succeed, a would-be *triumphator* had no choice but to begin by striving to impress his aristocratic peers first and foremost. The "elabo-

64. Linderski 1993, 56–59, has traced a similar pattern in Livy's treatment of procedural details regarding the haruspices: various key facts tucked away in isolated passages, with the full picture accessible only through a patchwork of many instances taken together. Once again there is a striking parallel between historiography and visual art. Cf. Kuttner 2004, 311: "Roman artists had evolved graphically sophisticated visual codes for intensely detailed narratives . . . [such as] expressionistic abbreviation, enlargement, compositional repetition, and stylistic eclecticism from scene to scene."

65. Thus Mitchell 1990, 193.

66. Note the remark of Brennan 1996, 316, that tribunes acted "for reasons that appear to have ranged from high-minded protection of constitutional propriety to the playing out of personal *inimicitiae.*" Cf. also Badian 1996; Feig Vishnia 1996, 179–81; Hölkeskamp 1988; Lintott 1999, 121–28 and 202–32; Thommen 1995; P. Williams 2004.

67. Cornell 1995, 369. Cf. Feig Vishnia 1996, 114.

68. On the political developments that helped to shape the emerging aristocratic ideology, see Hölkeskamp 1987, especially 114–203; also Hölkeskamp 1993, with well-placed emphasis on the conquest of Italy as a watershed event. Fears 1981, 773–78, meanwhile traces the deliberate importation into Rome of explicitly Hellenistic concepts of victory and conquest during the same period. Heightened contact with the kingdoms of the East brought profound changes in the way Roman aristocrats understood their place in the world. Naturally triumphs and triumph debates reflect the transformation.

69. The provocative work of Millar (1984, 1986, and 1998) has sparked a lively scholarly debate about the role of the democratic element in the constitution of the Roman Republic as well as both the nature and degree of senatorial control over civic affairs. Millar has doggedly championed the case for popular sovereignty, but North 1990b, 285, sounds an important

rate casuistry" surrounding Roman triumphal criteria was hammered out mainly by aristocrats in arguments among themselves.[70]

EPILOGUE

Before turning now at length to the subject of criteria, one final observation is in order about the phenomenon of triumphs *sine auctoritate patrum populi iussu.* Perhaps the single most significant shared feature of the episodes that fall under this heading is their uncanny timing: although separated by many years, even centuries, they all coincide with moments of political unease in Rome. On the three occasions when sources tell us that the popular assembly went over the heads of the *patres* to award a triumph, we also hear that something else, outside the immediate sphere of the triumph debate itself, had already upset the tricky balance of power between the senate, magistrates, and the people of Rome. In 449, it was an uproar over the *decemviri* and the codification of laws; in 356, the appointment of the first plebeian *dictator;* in 223, the question of land reform and Roman settlements in the *ager Gallicus Picenus.* From the same perspective, it is probably no accident that the unprecedented display of consular bravado by L. Postumius Megellus in 294 occurred when it did, so soon after the climax of the brutal First Samnite War. The achievements of Q. Fabius Maximus Rullianus at Sentinum—not to mention the acclaimed *devotio* of his colleague, P. Decius Mus, in imitation of his father—must have eclipsed all other claims to fame for some time to come.[71] As to Ap. Claudius Pulcher in 143, we need point only to his intimate connection with the Gracchi, although the real explosion there admittedly came a decade *after* his triumph.

Several possible explanations suggest themselves for this apparent link between triumphs *populi iussu* and tales of other disruptions in the three-way balance between the senate, magistrates, and people of Rome. If it

cautionary note: "The popular will of the Roman people found expression in the context, and only in the context, of divisions within the oligarchy." Among others see also Brennan 2004; Harris 1990; Hölkeskamp 2000 and 2004a; Lintott 1999, especially 40–64, 121–28, 199–207; Morstein-Marx 2004; Mouritsen 2001; North 1990a, 1990b, and 2006; Williamson 1990; and Yakobson 2006 (all with reference to previous scholarship).

70. Versnel 1970, 164, as cited above, p. 25. Cf. North 1990b, 286: "we are prisoners of the image of constitutional stability propounded by Polybius and Cicero . . . [which] might be said to represent the political ideal of the governing classes: to fix the business of the Republic through deals and arrangements among themselves, without reference to the views of less important citizens."

71. On the battle of Sentinum as a turning point, see Cornell 1995, 359–63. Note that Livy attributes Postumius's decision to cross over with his army into Etruria to the fact that the Samnite theater held little promise of an opportunity to show his skill (10.37.1).

is not just a coincidence—and we cannot rule out that possibility altogether—then it might reflect a systematic bias in the literary sources, whose authors have either consciously or unconsciously projected their own contemporary values and assumptions onto the past and, worse, painted an anachronistic view of the social and political structures of archaic Rome. Someone who viewed the *patres* as heroic defenders and guardians of the *mos maiorum,* especially against threats from below within the social hierarchy, would have trouble believing that they could ever have allowed a *popularis* rabble-rouser to triumph. If a hypothetical early annalist with such a bias found evidence that certain men identified as *populares* had indeed triumphed, therefore, he would conclude that the brazen assembly must have overstepped traditional boundaries on those occasions and usurped the senate's lawful rights, and he would write his history accordingly.[72] From there, even if his works themselves may have since disappeared, through later writers like Livy and Dionysius of Halicarnassus, among others, his biased version of events found its way into and soon became an established part of the literary tradition. Fabrications of this nature are certainly well enough attested to make the scenario plausible.[73]

But there is another possibility, no less compelling. By this account, the senate from an early date took charge of distributing civic honors within the overarching framework of the *mos maiorum,* and most of the time the magistrates and people acquiesced. Yet senatorial supremacy did not go unchallenged. Custom and tradition, as opposed to strict, legalistic rules, governed day-to-day interactions between the various elements of the mixed constitution in Rome. Therefore Valerius and Horatius, Rutilus, and Flaminius were all able—in moments of friction—to capitalize on their intense popular support, and thus to overrule the *patres,* precisely because no rigid structures existed to prevent their doing so. An enterprising and ambitious commander like Postumius, or Claudius, could even seize matters entirely into his own hands, defying both the senate and the assembly at once.

As mentioned earlier, triumphal spectacle and triumphal politics go closely together. Since triumphs as civic ritual brought the various *ordines* together to celebrate the good fortune that victory bestowed on the state as a whole, they served as a powerful expression of unity and harmony within Roman society. For whatever differences the Romans might have among

72. Of course, in the same vein, anyone who openly defied the senate, or even questioned the judgment of the *patres,* would ipso facto have gained a reputation as a troublesome *popularis.* See Develin 1979b.

73. See Ungern-Sternberg 1986. The argument of Mitchell 1990 similarly rests on a pessimistic view of the degree to which Roman authors accurately understood the distant past, even apart from how they chose to portray it.

themselves, the dramatic spectacle of a non-Roman enemy in defeat—with their own army on the winning side, of course—immediately gave them all something in common, stirring a shared visceral pride in the community to which they collectively belonged.[74] Conversely, triumph *debates* exposed the underlying social and political tensions both between different groups and within them, and thereby became flash points for other pressing concerns that affected the balance of power. Incidents of extreme dissension over triumphs, to the point where the senate and people could no longer work in tandem to mark important Roman victories, were in fact relatively rare. This bespeaks the general stability of the Republic; that they happened at all, however, reflects a latent indeterminacy in the order of things. Therein may even lie the seeds of ruin, because of the lingering threat that aristocratic competition might someday spin out of control, as of course it eventually (some might even say inevitably) did. This interpretation not only fits the limited evidence for the earliest triumph debates discussed here so far: as we shall see, it has intriguing implications for the later ones as well.

74. Thus Östenberg 2003, 8: "the triumph had what many other civic parades lack—a pronounced other, whose presence served as an antipode of normative community and reinforced sense of oneness among all Roman participants, processional partakers and spectators alike."

CHAPTER 2

Consular Tribunes and *Privati cum Imperio*

Magistracy and Triumph

The most enduring triumphal rules under the Republic have to do with officeholding. Mommsen once wrote that "the triumph depends not on the fact of military success, but on the legal right of the office."[1] No commander could triumph at the close of his mission, that is, unless his *imperium* had originated with one of the regularly elected upper-level magistracies: consul, *dictator,* or praetor, and the last of these only from 200 onwards.[2] The pair of triumphs that Pompey celebrated in the decade before his first election to the consulship form the unique Late Republican exception that proves the far older rule. A highly charged political climate, coupled with the scale of his achievements at a very young age, enabled the "adulescentulus carnifex" ("teenage executioner") to defy centuries of earlier precedent and cross a clearly perceptible barrier, which no one before him had ever successfully breached.[3] Previous attempts to put the stipulation about officeholding to the test had simply failed. None of the *tribuni militum consulari potestate* who led Roman armies into battle during the late fifth and early fourth centuries ever triumphed, for instance, "although," as one source states, "many of them achieved victories on many occasions."[4] Likewise, when a series of commanders went to Spain as *privati cum imperio*

1. Mommsen 1887, 3.130.

2. Thus J. S. Richardson 1975, 50–51.

3. Brennan 1996, 317, writes: "the first triumph of Cn. Pompeius Magnus (in 81 or 80) demonstrates exactly how much more could be rationalized." Cicero expresses outright disbelief (*Leg. Man.* 61–62); cf. Plut. *Pomp.* 14 and 21–22, and Pliny *NH* 7.26. Pompey's colorful nickname ("adulescentulus carnifex," "the teenage executioner") appears at Val. Max. 6.2.8.

4. Zonar. 7.19.5: λέγεται δὲ ὅτι οὐδεὶς τῶν χιλιάρχων, καίτοι πολλῶν πολλάκις νικησάντων, ἐπινίκια ἔπεμψεν ("But it is said that none of the tribunes, although many achieved victories on many occasions, ever celebrated a triumph").

pro consule in the years 211–197, most of them brought home deeds worthy of note, and some even sought recognition. Yet none of them triumphed either. Despite the obvious differences between these two groups—the first widely scattered throughout a formative period of the Republic for which reliable direct evidence is extremely hard to come by, the second from a later stage both more localized and better documented—certain similarities make it possible to interpret them as pieces of the same puzzle, illustrating the traditional Roman understanding and the senate's manipulation of triumphal rules.

PRIVATI CUM IMPERIO

Enough difficulties surround the whole subject of the consular tribunes that it makes sense to deal with the *privati cum imperio* first, where a clearer picture emerges of the rationale behind the senate's triumphal decisions. The story begins with the ad-hoc response to a sudden emergency: in 211/210, the two commanders in Spain (brothers from the family of the Scipios) died one right after the other fighting the Carthaginians. Rome lost all territory south of the Ebro, and Italy faced the threat of another Hannibal-scale invasion (25.32–36, 26.2.5).[5] The *patres* dispatched C. Claudius Nero to Spain in haste, *pro praetore,* to cope with the crisis (26.17.1), but he did not fare as well as they had hoped.[6] Meanwhile, Livy says, they instructed the tribunes to hold an assembly of the people for the purpose of choosing a new commander, with more troops at his disposal and full consular (or proconsular) rank (26.2.5). They clearly saw this as a momentous decision (26.18.3–4), but when the day came no one stepped forward, until suddenly all eyes fell on young P. Cornelius Scipio, son of one of the generals who had been killed and nephew of the other. The voters chose him unanimously in a rush of enthusiasm, though at that time he had never held public office above the rank of aedile (26.18.7–9).[7]

Curiously, Livy's account seems to shift without warning from the senate asking the tribunes to convene the popular assembly (26.2.5) to a typical scene from the *comitia centuriata* (26.18.4–9). Does this reflect a discrepancy between conflicting sources, or indeed accurately depict a two-phase

5. Cf. also Polyb. 10.6.2 and 7.1; App. *Hisp.* 16. For a detailed account of the two elder Scipios and their Spanish campaign (including some notorious difficulties with geography and dates), see Hoyos 2001.

6. Nero had been elected praetor the year before (25.2.5, 25.3.1) and was available at the time, the siege of Capua having recently ended. No precedent existed for elevating someone already in the field from praetorian to consular rank. See Jashemski 1950, 28–29; Knapp 1975, 88–89.

7. Cf. App. *Hisp.* 18. On Scipio's election as aedile in 213, see 25.2.6–8, *CIL* 1^2.1, and other sources listed by Broughton 1951, 267.

political process?[8] Because Scipio is later said to have acted in Spain "sine magistratu" ("without a magistracy," 28.38.4), some have argued that his appointment must have been made by the *concilium plebis* or perhaps the tribal assembly, but at any rate not the *comitia centuriata,* which gathered every year in the Campus Martius to elect the regular magistrates. Others deny this, on the grounds that only the centuries could have endowed him with proper *imperium.* It may even be the case that the so-called tribal assembly did not exist as such.[9] A *lex curiata de imperio* may or may not have been passed in Scipio's name as well, and this may or may not have made all the difference.[10] The procedural technicalities must remain largely a matter of conjecture. Still, although Scipio possessed *imperium, auspicium, ductus,* and *felicitas*—all four, since otherwise he could not have functioned day to day as a commander in the Roman army, much less been so successful at it—his irregular appointment to Spain did not count as a proper *magistratus,* and everyone knew it.[11]

Scipio's anomalous status did not entail anything like a radical rethinking of the whole magisterial system, to be sure. This was incremental change, as opposed to revolution. A few years earlier, in the confusion after Cannae, when Rome desperately needed able commanders, M. Claudius Marcellus had been granted proconsular *imperium* by a vote of the people, though tech-

8. For the state of the question relating to Scipio's appointment, see Brennan 2000, 156–59. For a soldierly attempt to specify precisely wherein the innovation lay, see Develin 1980, 357–60. On the notion that the confusion stems from multiple sources, see Taylor 1966, 136–37 n. 64. Taylor follows Mommsen 1887, 3.659 n. 4, in preferring the "more reliable account," which places Scipio's appointment in the popular assembly and blames Polybius for the mistaken alternative version. But note the comments of Develin 1975, 325–26.

9. On the variety of Roman voting assemblies, Taylor 1966 draws a firm distinction between the *comitia tributa* (where patricians could vote) and the *concilium plebis* (where they could not), but this view has come under attack. See Sandberg 2000, following Develin 1975. Also note Mitchell 1990, 229.

10. Knapp 1975, 89, concludes that a "special *lex curiata de imperio*" must have existed to give Scipio full lawful command in his province, whereas Versnel 1970, 188–89 and 350–51, asserts that *privati cum imperio* differed from regular magistrates precisely in the absence of a *lex curiata* on their behalf. Cf. also J. S. Richardson 1975, 59 n. 73. The challenge with the *lex curiata* is figuring out how to reconstruct authentic historical practice under the Republic from the evidence of later antiquarians (notably Cic. *Rep.* Bk. 2). For a cogent summary of the important ideas, starting with Mommsen, see Brennan 2000, 12–20, summarized in Brennan 2004, 41. Also see Cornell 1995, 25, 115, 127, 143, and nn.; Develin 1977; Giovannini 1983; Rüpke 1990, 47–51. The *curiae* clearly represent a very ancient form of organization. Mitchell 1990, 145–50, offers a sweeping reinterpretation of the transition from *curia* to century to tribe.

11. This is the force of "constabat" at 28.38.4. See alternatively Develin 1978, 433; and Knapp 1975, 90. Underneath the apparent nicety of Knapp's distinction between "a magistrate *of* the State" and "a magistrate with a special job to do *for* the State" lies an important insight about how the traditional framework of Roman civic administration coped with unforeseen events. Cf. the comment of Badian 1988, 469, regarding the consular tribunes: "We must not obscure the difference that we cannot fully explain."

nically a *privatus* at the time.[12] Unlike Scipio, Marcellus had just completed a term as praetor and had already served as consul before, so his appointment could be seen as an emergency extension of an existing post rather than the creation of a new one, but by disconnecting the outset of a command from election to office, it set enough of a precedent that Scipio really did not have to break very much new ground. As the empire expanded, various such ad-hoc appointments and extensions (*prorogationes*) gradually allowed the system of annual magistracies to encompass longer and longer campaigns under a single command.[13] Yet despite the fact (or perhaps even oddly because of the fact) that Scipio was largely following in others' footsteps, circumstances made his midyear appointment to Spain a striking event, especially since Rome was also witnessing the dramatic debut of a brilliant and ambitious but unproven young man. Close family ties with the two dead generals only added to the aura, which he apparently did more to cultivate than to dispel, that Scipio had come out of nowhere to save the Republic (26.18.11).[14]

He returned in 206 proudly victorious, and the senators duly gathered in the Temple of Bellona to hear him narrate his exploits on behalf of the SPQR: pitched battles, captured towns, subjected tribes, defeated enemies, not a single Carthaginian left in the province. Scipio had fought off four advancing Punic armies and driven them into retreat, bringing the whole territory of Iberia under Roman sway once again—an unmistakably impressive achievement (28.38.2–3).[15] Yet although he asked for permission to triumph (with Marcellus in mind?),[16] we learn that he merely

12. As praetor in 216 Marcellus had been in command of the fleet at Ostia, but he came ashore after Cannae to face Hannibal at Nola, with some success (22.57.1–2 and 7–8; 23.14.10–17.3, 19.4; Plut. *Marc.* 9–11; further references in Broughton 1951, 248). On his special appointment for the following year, see 23.30.19, and cf. also 23.32.3 and 48.2. Meanwhile a unanimous election as *consul suffectus* for 215, further proof of the popular favor that Marcellus enjoyed, was declared invalid by the augurs, allowing Q. Fabius Maximus to take his place (23.31.12–14, Plut. *Marc.* 12.1).

13. Cf. Jashemski 1950, 29.

14. Scipio's appointment is memorably followed by Livy's reflections on the cult of personality that surrounded Scipio all his life. Note especially 26.19.3 on his self-fashioning before the public eye: "fuit enim Scipio non veris tantum virtutibus mirabilis, sed arte quoque quadam ab iuventa in ostentationem earum compositus" ("For Scipio was not only worthy of admiration for his genuine good qualities, but also endowed from his youth with a certain skill for putting them on display").

15. Strikingly, M. Iunius Silanus, the more experienced commander sent to Spain along with Scipio as *adiutor pro praetore* (26.19.11), no doubt in response to concerns about placing too much public trust in an untried youth, plays only a minor role in the account of the younger man's *res gestae*, and certainly did not request military honors on his own account when they both returned to Rome. See Knapp 1975, 90–91.

16. Marcellus's triumph request after the capture of Syracuse had sparked a major controversy in 211, the year of Scipio's appointment to Spain: 26.21.1–13; Plut. *Marc.* 22; Val. Max. 2.8.5. Also Degrassi 1947, 78–79, 550.

tested the waters and did not press his claim. Despite his formidable *res gestae,* Livy portrays Scipio as aware of his audience and their limits, since "everyone knew that up to that time no one had ever triumphed who had brought about deeds without a magistracy."[17] But of course no one until now had ever brought about such deeds at all without a magistracy under his belt. In fact, the conservative-sounding pronouncement that Scipio could not hope to qualify for a triumph—with no mention of the *ovatio* as a possible alternative, one might add—stems from, and only reinforces, the perceived novelty of his original ad-hoc assignment. The senate held back from voting him honors of any kind, not out of a reluctance to bend the rules, much less through any lack of respect for his talents, but rather because they had set a bold enough precedent with him once already and did not dare to single him out any further. That their reasoning must have run along these lines, or close to them, will emerge all the more starkly from the turn of later events.

The dazzling career of Scipio Africanus cast a very long shadow (cf.

17. 28.38.4: "ob has res gestas magis temptata est triumphi spes quam petita pertinaciter, quia neminem ad eam diem triumphasse qui sine magistratu res gessisset constabat" ("On account of these accomplishments his hope of a triumph was merely tested out rather than diligently sought after, since everyone knew that up to that day no one had triumphed whose accomplishments had come about without a magistracy"). We may safely assert that Scipio did not triumph on this occasion, although two passages seem to suggest that he did: Polyb. 11.33.7, κάλλιστον θρίαμβον καὶ καλλίστην νίκην τῇ πατρίδι κατάγων ("winning for his fatherland a splendid triumph and a splendid victory"), and App. *Hisp.* 38.156, Σκιπίων μὲν θαυμαζόμενος ἐθριάμβευεν ("Scipio, being admired, triumphed"). Val. Max. 2.8.5 and Dio Cass. frr. 56B and 57 Boissevain join Livy in saying that he did not triumph. Modern scholars do not speak with one voice either. Gruen 1995, 61 n. 3, labels the tradition preserved in Polybius and Appian "plainly mistaken." Degrassi (1947, 551) and Scullard (1951, 75 n. 2) seek a way out by postulating that Scipio might have triumphed *in monte Albano,* but as J. S. Richardson 1975, 52, rightly observes, this attempt to have it both ways "must be regarded purely as guesswork" in the absence of further evidence. The suggestion by Broughton 1951, 299, that Scipio celebrated an *ovatio* simply cannot hold, because that would have set a precedent for L. Cornelius Lentulus, one of his successors in Spain, who returned in 200. According to Livy (31.20.5), the tribune Ti. Sempronius Longus claimed then that no precedent existed for a *privatus cum imperio* to receive an *ovatio,* let alone a full triumph. Livy thus records the same stipulation against both Scipio and Lentulus, in different enough words to allay suspicion of contamination between the two passages. Although Develin 1978, 432 n. 29, predictably argues against the contention of Badian 1958, 117, that the senate denied Scipio a triumph in 206 "on dubious technical grounds," they both agree that no triumph took place. Cf. Knapp 1975, 91 and nn. In an effort to resolve the confusion by appeal to the *lectio difficilior,* J. S. Richardson 1975, 52, concludes that "a source which says that a triumph was *refused* for what was generally acknowledged to be a splendid victory is less likely to be distorted than a source which represents the triumph as an automatic reward." The close association between the words θρίαμβος and νίκη in Greek, which he also points out, might help to explain the alleged mistake in Polybius and perhaps in Appian as well, depending on the precise wording of his source or sources—especially given the summary nature of both passages.

38.51.4), and perhaps nowhere more visibly than in triumph debates. He handed over the Spanish command in 206 to two men specially appointed as *privati cum imperio* to succeed him: L. Cornelius Lentulus and L. Manlius Acidinus.[18] To their credit, although neither one qualified as a rising young star, both served the Republic in Spain for many years. When Lentulus came back in 200, he narrated his *res gestae* to the senate as Scipio had done, emphasizing his devotion and hard work, and again like Scipio he asked for permission to triumph (31.20.2). The *patres* refused, citing the identical rule that had forestalled Scipio's triumph request six years earlier—no magistracy—but very strikingly, things did not play themselves out the same way from that point onward. The senators openly acclaimed Lentulus's achievements as "worthy of a triumph" (31.20.3), even while acknowledging that they "had not received from the ancestors any precedent for someone to triumph who had brought about his deeds as neither *dictator* nor consul nor praetor."[19] Note the expression "res triumpho dignas" ("accomplishments worthy of a triumph") used here: Lentulus would ultimately not have to demur as Scipio before him had done.

In search of some way to reward a commendable job without technically violating the magistracy rule, instead of a triumph the senators voted Lentulus an *ovatio.* This ancient ceremony, once fallen into disuse, had emerged as a welcome compromise not long ago in the cause célèbre of Marcellus's return from Syracuse, but more recently the *patres* had offered no concession whatever to Scipio, Lentulus's immediate predecessor. The tribune Ti. Sempronius Longus tried to veto the whole idea on these very grounds: if no precedent existed for a triumph, his argument ran, then

18. Livy refers to Lentulus and Acidinus as propraetors in 206 (28.38.1), unfortunately without mentioning their original appointment. We may safely infer from the arguments against Lentulus's request for a triumph in 200, however, that they inherited from Scipio not only the command in Spain but also his rank as *privatus cum imperio* (*pro consule*). Both men had been elected as praetors before (Lentulus in 211 and Acidinus the following year), but the appointment to succeed Scipio had nothing to do with those prior magistracies. The senate prorogued their *imperium* in Spain four times—for 205 (28.45.10), 204 (29.13.7), 203 (30.2.7, where they are called "veteribus imperatoribus," "old commanders"), and 202 (30.27.9)—and Livy consistently lists their rank as *pro consulibus.* See Jashemski 1950, 30–31; and Knapp 1975, 92 (with a handy chronological chart). Even after the expansion of the praetorship in 197, which obviated the need to appoint *privati* as governors of Spain, some confusion persisted in Livy's sources over the titles of promagistrates. According to Walsh 1961, 133, Valerius Antias regularly used the term *proconsul* for former praetors with prorogued *imperium,* whereas Claudius Quadrigarius referred to them as *praetor* or *propraetor.* Although Broughton 1951 uses "proconsul" as the generic term for all such prorogued magistrates, an effort has been made in appendix A below to distinguish between former consuls and former praetors.

19. 31.20.3: "res triumpho dignas esse censebat senatus, sed exemplum a maioribus non accepisse ut qui neque dictator neque consul neque praetor res gessisset triumpharet."

there was clearly none for an *ovatio* either (31.20.5). Yet the tribune's apparent attempt to enforce a strict reading of the *mos maiorum* could not prevail in the senate against a united front in favor of seeing a way through toward compromise. So Sempronius bowed to the consensus of the *patres,* Livy says, and Lentulus got his *ovatio.*[20] The bald prohibition against a triumph *sine magistratu* gave way, if only a little, by common agreement among the governing élite to honor one of their own. Paradoxically, the fact that Lentulus had actually accomplished *less* in the province than Scipio had done probably made it easier for the senate to reward him more openly. Whereas heaping further accolades on Scipio might have upset the delicate balance of *dignitas* among the senators, they found room for public recognition of Lentulus, who posed no such threat.[21]

In the realm of triumphal requirements, the *patres* as a body could defy perceived convention to suit changing times and varied contingencies. No inflexible formula governed their decrees in this gray area at the boundary of the *sine magistratu* rule. When L. Manlius Acidinus returned to Rome in 199 after almost seven years in the province as *privatus cum imperio,* the senators sought an *ovatio* for him as they had done for his colleague Lentulus, but the tribune P. Porcius Laeca blocked the measure by a veto (32.7.4).[22] Success in the field thus held no guarantees when it came to a vote in the senate. C. Cornelius Cethegus, sent to Spain to take over for Lentulus in 200, apparently did not want to risk any embarrassment. Despite a victory over the Sedetani, he did not seek a triumph (31.50.6, 10–11).[23] Neither did his successor, L. Stertinius, in 196. Livy's explicit remark (33.27.3) that Stertinius "did not even broach the subject of a triumph" implies that most *imperatores* with victories to boast of would at least make a perfunctory request.[24] Scipio had gone that far in 206, even when "everyone knew" (28.38.4) that the *patres* would turn him down. Why did Stertinius not take the same path? He was definitely not ashamed of his *res gestae.* Far from it: he erected a pair of manubial *fornices,* topped with gilded statues, near the

20. 31.20.6: "postremo victus consensu patrum tribunus cessit" ("finally defeated by the unanimity of the senators, the tribune yielded"). See Degrassi 1947, 551; and note the procedural remarks of Briscoe 1973, *ad loc.*

21. Cf. Gruen 1995, 62.

22. Note Brennan 2000, 161: "L. Manlius evidently could not muster enough senatorial support to have the tribune back off. Connections were very much needed, especially at a time when the rules were so hazy."

23. Cethegus was elected curule aedile in absentia and returned from the province when that term began. For his victory over the Suditani, see 31.49.7. Also cf. Jashemski 1950, 32.

24. 33.27.3: "ne temptata quidem triumphi spe" ("without even making a test of his hope for a triumph"). Livy regularly records triumphs granted or denied, but this is the only place in Books 21–45 where he actually says a commander did not *request* a triumph. Also see appendix B below.

customary triumphal route, where everyone could see them: one in front of the temples of Fortuna and Mater Matuta, the other in the Circus Maximus (33.27.3). These showy monuments, ironically "the first 'triumphal' arches we hear of in Rome," loudly attest to the wealth of Stertinius's spoils and his characteristically Roman eagerness to put his achievements on public display.[25] Then, as if to point up the unaccountable element in Stertinius's failure to ask for a triumph, his colleague and fellow *privatus* Cn. Cornelius Blasio celebrated an *ovatio* the same year with the blessing of the *patres* (33.27.1–2).[26]

Over the period 206–196, then, the six *privati cum imperio* who returned from Spain saw no fewer than four different outcomes in the senate on the question of triumphs: Scipio asked, but did not press the issue, though he had arguably accomplished the most of the six by driving the Carthaginians at least temporarily out of the province; Lentulus and Blasio celebrated *ovationes* in spite of tribunician vetoes; Acidinus missed out on an *ovatio* because a veto stood; Cethegus and Stertinius did not so much as ask. Through all these test cases the *patres* never overtly broke the rule barring a triumph for a commander whose *imperium* had not come from a regular magistracy, but they did bend it more than once. The *ovatio* allowed them to negotiate compromises, if they wished, on an "*ad hoc* (or better, *ad hominem*)" basis.[27] Although the magistracy requirement may have precluded triumphs for every one of these men, merely invoking it on the senate floor did not magically put an end to controversy or forestall improvisation on the part of the *patres.*

Meanwhile, important constitutional changes, in the long-term aftermath of Hannibal's defeat, had already brought the brief era of the *privatus cum imperio* (*pro consule*) in Spain to a close. In 197 the total number of praetors elected was increased from four to six, and Spain divided into two separate provinces, Nearer and Farther.[28] Thenceforth the Spanish com-

25. Brennan 1996, 328; and cf. Welch 2006a, 505. On the development of triumphal arches in Rome, see Wallace-Hadrill 1990.

26. See Degrassi 1947, 78–79, 552. The manuscripts of Livy give the cognomen Blasio to the Cn. Cornelius who returned from Spain at approximately the same time as Stertinius in 196 (33.27.1), although the new governor in 200 appears there as Cn. Cornelius *Lentulus* (31.50.11). The latter is clearly a mix-up with the L. Cornelius Lentulus about to return from Spain at that time. So Broughton 1951, 329 n. 3; and Degrassi 1947, 552; *pace* Develin 1978, 362–63, who implausibly reconstructs a delegation of *imperium* to account for the two Cornelii in Livy's text. During this heyday of the gens Cornelia, with so many members of the clan holding public office, Livy or his copyists (or both) could easily have lost track of one stray cognomen. See also Jashemski 1950, 32–33.

27. Brennan 1996, 318.

28. Whereas Livy vaguely credits these events to Roman expansion in general (32.27.6 and 32.28.11), Appian (*Hisp.* 39) places them in a more immediate and pressing context: an

mand each year went to praetors, or a consul when need be, with the result that the senate never again had to face the question of a triumph for a *privatus cum imperio* from that quarter.[29] The development is revealing. The special appointment of *privati cum imperio* in Spain began as an emergency measure to cope with the crisis of 211, and continued only long enough to stabilize the situation there after the war. It was not allowed to become a permanent practice. The senate's reply to Lentulus in 200 pointed out the contradiction of *res gestae* worthy of a triumph coming from a commander whose status left him technically ineligible for one. Although the *ovatio* provided an interim solution, it did not and could not fully address the deeper problem. If governors from a province were going to keep producing deeds worthy of triumphs, but *privati cum imperio* could never triumph, then those governors had to cease being appointed as *privati cum imperio.* The absorption of Spain into the sphere of the regular magistracies corrected the imbalance and paved the way for future triumphs if the senate should see fit. Thus the magistracy rule remained unbroken still—but only because administrative adjustments rendered it functionally obsolete until the turbulence of the Late Republic brought it once again to the fore.[30]

CONSULAR TRIBUNES

So much, then, for the *privati cum imperio.* Similar interpretations have been put forward in connection with the consular tribunes, although the sparse available evidence barely supports the immense weight of learned argument, often highly speculative, that has grown up around these enig-

---

opportunistic revolt in Spain arising from Roman preoccupation with Philip on the one hand and the Gauls on the other. That crisis goes a long way toward explaining the renewed Roman attention to Spanish affairs during the 190s. Livy's later reference to Blasio and Stertinius as having served in Nearer and Farther Spain (33.27.1–5), despite the fact that there were not two separate Spanish *provinciae* when these men were first appointed, suggests that having prorogued their *imperium* for 198, the senate then sent them at the end of the year to meet C. Sempronius Tuditanus and M. Helvius, respectively, in the two newly designated regions without actually renewing their commands in the process. Since, as Appian says, the Spanish natives were restless to the point of revolution right at this time, the Romans would have wanted to keep their veteran generals there both to help the war effort and to ease the transition to the new system, rather than bring them home right away. See also Knapp 1975, 93–94. One should note that the designation of two separate *provinciae* did not bring about a formal administrative organization right away. Indeed the issues of provincial designation and succession from one commander to another in Spain during the immediately succeeding years are extremely complex, and commanders in the field seem to have moved around a good deal. For a general survey see Brennan 2000, 154–81; and Develin 1980; *contra* Sumner 1970 and 1977.

29. Accordingly M. Porcius Cato (the Elder), consul in 195, was sent to Hispania Citerior to quell a major revolt. He achieved victory and celebrated a triumph the following year (34.46.2; and cf. Degrassi 1947, 78–79, 553).

30. Mommsen 1887, 1.131–32.

matic officials from the Early Republic. It would lie well outside the scope of the present study to trace the history in any detail, but summarizing as briefly as possible, consular tribunes were elected in varying numbers, intermittently from 444 to 409 and almost without interruption from 408 to 367, then no longer. They functioned as an alternative to consuls and *dictatores*.[31] Scholars do not agree on the original purpose of the office, which may have been primarily social, political, military, or all three at once, but Livy's narrative makes it clear that they could at times lead armies into battle.[32] Specifically on the subject of their right to triumph or lack thereof, we have only the broad assertion from Zonaras (7.19.5), which he found in his sources (λέγεται, "it is said"), that none of them ever triumphed, "although many achieved victories on many occasions."[33]

From this slim attestation, no earlier than the twelfth century A.D., it is impossible to tell whether any of the tribunes actively sought honors that were refused on technical grounds, as with the *privati cum imperio*. The single word καίτοι ("although") might mask a long history of lost triumph debates, but then again it might easily not. Perhaps no tribune ever raised the issue of a triumph. Perhaps Zonaras's source, or even the source of his source, merely observed a pattern in triumphal celebrations remembered from the period and wondered about it.[34] Maddeningly, the portion of the Fasti that might have allowed us at least to verify that pattern has not survived.[35] Livy and Diodorus, for their part, do not record any triumphs celebrated, or even requested, in the era of the tribunes except by consuls and *dictatores*.[36] Zonaras's observation stands primarily in the absence of evidence to the contrary—and so calls for some explanation. Recent arguments over why the tribunes did not and possibly even could not triumph

31. On the consular tribunes generally (as opposed to the specific topic of their right to triumph), see Adcock 1957; Brennan 2000, 49–54; Bunse 1997; Cornell 1995, 333–40; Drummond 1980; Mitchell 1990; Pinsent 1975; Ridley 1986; Sealey 1959; Stavely 1953; R. Stewart 1998, 52–94.

32. The ancients themselves could not agree on the origin of the consular tribunes. Livy gives two alternative accounts, one sociopolitical, having to do with the Conflict of the Orders (4.1–6), the other military and administrative (4.7.1–2), having to do with Rome's territorial expansion. Modern scholars likewise take different sides. In defense of the military model, see, e.g., R. Stewart 1998, 66. *Contra* see Ridley 1986, 455–59, with a survey of all the battles fought by consular tribunes in Livy's narrative.

33. See p. 54 n. 4 above for the full text and translation of Zonaras's statement.

34. On the means available to confirm or deny Zonaras's claims, see the thoughtful comments of Richard 1992, 237–41.

35. See Degrassi 1947, 538–39.

36. Thus J. S. Richardson 1975, 50–51. Note also the resourceful if somewhat far-fetched attempt of Palmer 1970, 222, to attribute the apparent silence of the literary tradition on this score to deliberate efforts by the emperor Augustus to suppress evidence that might support Cossus's (and therefore, notoriously, Crassus's) claim to the *spolia opima*.

echo the debates in the senate that Livy records over honors for the *privati.* This should come as no surprise, given that scholars are trying to learn from the ancient Romans how to discuss these issues cogently. Fundamental structures of Roman triumphal discourse resurface in the modern exchange, when details from Livy's account of the *privati* are adduced, on the strength of supposed analogies between the two groups, to reconstruct what may have happened in the more mysterious case of the tribunes.[37]

First come the technicalities that define the rights and privileges of officeholders.[38] Since these two discreet sets of people were never allowed to triumph, it would be convenient if a single explanation could cover both: the absence of a *lex curiata,* for instance.[39] The tribunes clearly occupied a lower status than consuls or *dictatores*—in respect to *imperium, auspicium,* or both—but how exactly? One hesitates to extemporize too much over what must remain at bottom a murky facet of Roman thinking. The fact that the earliest tradition consistently calls them *tribuni militum consulari potestate* and not *tribuni militum consulari imperio* does suggest that in the albeit narrow and ill-defined gap between *potestas* and *imperium* lies a fundamental difference between the tribunes and those others—the consuls and *dictatores*—who by contrast had full *imperium iustum,* and who could most certainly triumph.[40] Although both patricians and plebeians held the office of consular tribune, ancestral patrician ownership of and control over the auspices may have been at issue here.[41] Common sense would seem to dictate that the Romans would not have bothered to designate these officials in opposition to others without some technical justification.

One notable study has gone in the opposite direction, by refusing to mark any distinction in power and authority between the tribunes and other officeholders, and instead impugning their *res gestae:*[42]

37. Thus, for instance, the treatment by R. Stewart 1998, 79–94, keeps slipping from one context (and one century) to another, on the grounds that institutional continuity and traditionalism justify a synchronic view.

38. Richard 1992, 245, refers to "une incapacité de droit" ("a legal hindrance").

39. So Versnel 1970, 186–89 and 350–51.

40. Thus Badian 1988, 469: "what they lacked was, precisely, *imperium:* the avoidance of that term must have been deliberate. We cannot specify in detail what the difference was: we simply do not know enough. . . . The 'magical and supernatural' powers . . . were deliberately left incomplete: they were not given *imperium.*"

41. For a table with the numbers of patricians and plebeians in the (somewhat insecurely) reconstructed Fasti of the consular tribunes, see Cornell 1995, 336. On *auspicium,* see Linderski 1988, 41. Note, however, from Linderski's discussion, that the sacral rules governing auspices had a direct bearing on questions of *imperium* as well, so that *imperium* and *auspicium* cannot ever be completely disentangled. More recently, cf. also Brennan 2004, 38–39.

42. Ridley 1986, 459. He then offers a detailed survey of the various military engagements in which tribunes are said to have been involved with little more than indifferent success.

> As elected magistrates with consular power, able to name a dictator who could triumph, there is no reason why the tribunes could not also. It seems, however, that they did not, and the reason is made all too clear by Livy. No tribune won a victory worthy of a triumph.

This argument—laying technicalities aside in a clear echo of the stipulation cited against Lentulus in 200—calls attention to the central act of subjective assessment by the *patres* in assigning triumphal honors. The question of merit is precisely the elusive, slippery factor that mitigates against the strict application of juridical rules in triumph debates, because with the *dignitatis contentio* politics always enters the equation. It fell to a commander's peers in the senate, after all, to interpret the *mos maiorum* and decide how to apply traditional rules to the present case. Thus, although Zonaras says that "many of the tribunes won many victories," the scale of their accomplishments in the field may not have been enough to overcome institutional strictures. Pompey would then stand alone in that regard. During the period when the tribunes were active, the Romans seem to have elected consuls or appointed a *dictator* in moments of genuine military crisis, which would imply that the tribunes were not entrusted with the most dangerous commands. Then again, as another scholar has written: "Did all the triumphators win victories worthy of a triumph? Fair play is all too often a misleading guide to history."[43]

Like the *privati cum imperio,* though after a much longer interval, consular tribunes were eventually replaced within the governmental machinery by regular magistrates. Whatever original purpose the anomalous office may have served, and whatever broader social and political aims the Licinian-Sextian legislation of 366 may have had, the latter certainly put an end to the former by restoring the dual consulship, and thus ushering in the era of the patricio-plebeian aristocracy.[44] Under the Republic, impulses toward experiment and change in response to new challenges always coexisted with equal and opposite trends toward consolidation and regularity once events simmered down. New officials alternately appeared and disappeared again as the empire continued to grow. We return to the paradox of *mos maiorum.* A recent study of constitutional developments from the fifth through the third centuries has stressed the role of religious and political institutions in articulating a developing relationship between the individual and the *res publica,* most notably in the case of aristocrats who ran for public office. Consular tribunes came to prominence, therefore, during an important formative phase of the Republic, in which lasting structures evolved that

43. Linderski 1988, 45 n. 36.

44. For recent treatments of the Licinian-Sextian laws, with references to earlier scholarship, see Cornell 1995, 328–40; Ridley 1988; R. Stewart 1998, 95–136.

would govern the complex interaction between the senate, magistrates, and people of Rome—including triumph debates—for centuries to come.[45] As we shall see, subsequent history certainly bears this out.

SUMMARY

Neither the consular tribunes nor the *privati cum imperio* ever triumphed, for reasons both institutional and political. In order to triumph, a commander needed the senate to vote in his favor, with qualifications subject to the *patrum auctoritas,* but always under the rubric of *imperio auspicio ductu felicitate.* Pompey's eventual success proves that *ductus* and *felicitas* between them, at the right time and of sufficient magnitude, could indeed garner so much support (*gratia*) as to outweigh any technicalities in the realm of *imperium* and *auspicium.* However, the fact that it was not until the Late Republic that someone celebrated a triumph without ever having been a magistrate first should demonstrate that *imperium* and *auspicium* not only mattered to some degree, but indeed remained crucial factors all along. When civic honors lay at stake, therefore, the senate was engaged in a balancing act between principle and politics.

45. R. Stewart 1998, 56–57, asserts: "The office of *tribuni militum consulari potestate* formed part of a process of innovation, experiment, and transition in articulating and identifying communal authority."

CHAPTER 3

Crossing Provincial Boundaries

Joint Campaigns and Overlapping Jurisdictions

As mentioned right at the outset, the mandate of a military commander under the Republic had its limits both in time and in space, through a regulated system of annual elections and the assignment of *provinciae,* usually by lot. It required a special dispensation known as *prorogatio imperii* for a general to stay on with his army for another year after the next set of duly elected magistrates took office.[1] Yet depending on circumstances, any given territory might easily play host to more than one commander at a time. Unless defined by some unmistakably prominent feature such as a river or a mountain range, the precise geographical boundaries between allotted *provinciae* often remained somewhat fuzzy. Even within a single area the sojourns of one governor and the next could overlap, usually more by accident than by design, before the first returned to Rome. In a crisis, the senate could deliberately dispatch two *imperatores* to the same place—two praetors, one of the consuls and a praetor, or both consuls—until the hot spot cooled down enough for a single official to take sole command. Sudden opportunities could also allow generals from technically separate *provinciae* to join forces, or sudden dangers could compel one to come to another's rescue. Amid all these contingencies, the senate did its best to respond and to guide matters if it could, but difficulties in communication across long distances meant that commanders in the field had broad discretion, especially in deciding when, where, and how to engage enemy forces.[2]

1. Sometime in the early second century, the senate appears to have taken sole control of this function, no longer putting the extension of commands to a popular vote. Cf. Brennan 2004, 45.

2. Cf. Eckstein 1987, xii: "the senate tended to rely heavily on ad hoc decisions already made by Roman commanders in the field (men who were usually the elected magistrates of

Battles also tend to follow their own unpredictable timetable, as Livy plainly understood (see, for instance, 31.48.10). The triumphal formula *imperio auspicio ductu felicitate* left room for considerable interplay between technicalities and politics even with only one commander involved. With two or more at once, the number of variables dramatically increased. Whenever the question of a triumph arose amid complications of any kind, it fell to the *patres* to determine after the fact who should get credit for what. They did not even try to establish an immutable pattern.

M. LIVIUS SALINATOR AND C. CLAUDIUS NERO, 207

In 207, during the midst of the Second Punic War but after a period of tentative calm in the region, Hasdrubal Barca, Hannibal's younger brother, invaded the Po Valley from the north across the Alps, suddenly posing a considerable threat to Roman security. The senate decided to send one of the consuls and a praetor to Ariminum together to deal with Hasdrubal, while the other consul went to face Hannibal in the south (27.35.10–12). These lots fell to consul M. Livius Salinator with praetor L. Porcius Licinus, and to consul C. Claudius Nero, respectively (27.36.10).[3] Emotions in Rome ran very high indeed as the consuls set off for two different theaters of war, both alarmingly close to home. Then Hasdrubal arrived even faster than anyone had expected, having crossed the Alps with surprising speed, and soon laid siege to Placentia (27.39–40).

A Roman foraging party near Tarentum, meanwhile, intercepted a pair of Numidian messengers en route to Hannibal from his brother. The letter they carried, once opened and translated, revealed a plan for the two Carthaginian armies to join forces somewhere in Umbria (27.43). As soon as Nero got hold of this intelligence, he duly forwarded it to the *patres* in Rome, but instead of waiting for their instructions, which might have cost him a valuable opportunity, he set off at once with a picked legion under his own initiative, in hopes of reaching Salinator and Licinus in time to help them block Hasdrubal and prevent the worst. The bulk of his troops, who of course still had Hannibal to contend with, he left behind in the camp with one of his *legati* in charge. Nero's move seemed bold to the point of rashness and risky in the extreme, and the news sparked an understandable uproar in the senate. One Hannibal in Italy was dangerous enough, Livy says. The Roman leadership had no idea how to handle two of them.[4]

---

the Roman people). Indeed, those decisions often formed the *basis* of Roman foreign policy, especially in regions beyond the shores of Italy."

3. The whole Metaurus campaign is deftly handled by Eckstein 1987, 43–47.

4. 27.44.5: "veteres eius belli clades, duo consules proximo anno interfecti terrebant: et ea omnia accidisse cum unus imperator, unus exercitus hostium in Italia esset: nunc duo bella

With events already in motion and beyond their control, however, the *patres* in Rome could do nothing but sit still and, as one scholar has put it, "await the outcome of a decision most of them opposed."[5]

Thankfully, for all the tremendous anxiety that attended the campaign, the plan succeeded. Nero and his men arrived at Salinator's camp by night, and a careful stratagem kept Hasdrubal unaware of their presence until it was already too late (27.45.12). In a fierce pitched battle near the Metaurus River, where the combined Roman and allied forces probably outnumbered their enemies by almost two to one, the consuls crushed the Carthaginian army. Hasdrubal, his elephants, and most of his men were killed.[6] Nero also made it safely back to his own camp in the south only six days later, to find that Hannibal had not attacked in the interim (27.50.1). When the longed-for victory was first rumored, and then at last officially announced in Rome—after an agony of anticipation and dread felt, Livy says, in every quarter of the city—it brought such an overwhelming surge of relief that the senate joyously decreed a three-day *supplicatio* in honor of the two commanders (27.50.4–5).[7] Livy describes women giving thanks to the gods "released from all their fear, just as if the war were about to be over" (27.51.9).[8] With security thus restored on the northern frontier, the *patres* ordered both consuls to return home at the end of the year, although they kept Nero's legions on guard against Hannibal while allowing Salinator to bring back his army. The two men contrived among themselves to reach the city at the same time. They came before the senate together in the Temple of Bellona, thronged with well-wishers, to make their formal triumph request, and the *patres* voted triumphs to both of them in solemn public thanksgiving for their victory (28.9.4–9). A certain bitterness that flared up between them both before and after their year as consuls makes the unanimity of their homecoming even more remarkable.[9]

Punica facta, duos ingentes exercitus, duos prope Hannibales in Italia esse" ("The earlier disasters of that war, the two consuls killed the previous year, were still terrifying, and all of those had taken place when there was one commander, one army of the enemy in Italy. Now there were two Carthaginian wars in progress, two huge armies, practically two Hannibals in Italy").

5. So Eckstein 1987, 47. Cf. 27.44.1, and note the remark of Lazenby 1978, 186: "we can well believe [Livy's description here], for this was the last great crisis of the war."

6. 27.48–49; cf. Polyb. 11.1.2–3.6. Walsh 1961, 144–45, cites this as the locus classicus for distortion of casualty statistics by the Roman annalists (Livy's 57,000 Carthaginians killed vs. Polybius's 10,000). For a detailed discussion of the battle, including an estimate of the numbers of soldiers (and casualties) involved on either side, see Lazenby 1978, 187–90.

7. Burck 1971, 39, singles out the Metaurus campaign as an "excellent example" of emphasis on the mood swings of Rome's inhabitants as a feature of Livy's narrative style.

8. 27.51.8: "perinde ac si debellatum foret omni solutae metu deis immortalibus grates agerent."

9. On the earlier *inimicitiae* between Livius and Nero, and their public reconciliation (under political pressure for unity) prior to the start of the consular year, see 27.35.5–9. The

Livy does not record any doubt or controversy over the award of this triumph to both consuls. In fact there is no triumph *debate* whatsoever, just an enthusiastic outpouring of positive feeling toward the victors, commensurate with earlier fear while the outcome still hung in the balance. But then Nero and Salinator announced that they had agreed between themselves (again) not to hold two separate triumphs, or even a single triumph side by side as equals, but rather a special joint celebration designed to reflect the unusual circumstances. According to Livy they did so for several reasons: the decisive battle took place in Salinator's *provincia;* his auspices happened to be in force on that day (i.e., when both consuls worked together they took turns); and he, unlike Nero, had brought his army home. The *imperium* and *auspicium* for the victory were Salinator's, in other words, although the *ductus* and especially the *felicitas* clearly belonged to his colleague. Nor for all his stunning leadership and initiative had Nero managed to do anything about Hannibal, who still remained a terrible threat in the south even after the death of his brother, so that Salinator's designated enemy target had been eliminated but Nero's had not. Therefore the place of honor and full status as *triumphator* would go to Salinator: he would ride in the triumphal chariot with his legions on foot behind, whereas Nero would enter the city on horseback (28.9.9–11).

This account raises questions for scholars, because it does not seem to fit any of the usual patterns. Above all, what exactly did the *patres* decree, and how much initiative did Nero and Salinator subsequently take on their own? The relevant chunk of the Fasti is sadly missing. Weighing the evidence, Mommsen concluded that the technicalities would not make sense unless the senate had in fact voted an *ovatio* to Nero, as they had done with Marcellus a few years before.[10] Tellingly, the *deportatio exercitus* argument had surfaced there too, indeed played a decisive role.[11] Yet several times Livy specifically calls the award to Nero a triumph, not an *ovatio,* and he generally distinguishes very carefully between the two.[12] The magnitude

concordia between them did not last: they quarreled again during their joint censorship in 204 (29.37). See Epstein 1987, 13, 17–18, 45, 47, 70, and 94; and (especially on their divisive censorship) Feig Vishnia 1996, 81–82.

10. Mommsen 1887, 1.126. Degrassi 1947, 551, followed suit when reconstructing the missing passage from the Fasti.

11. R. Stewart 1998, 89–90 n. 103. Cf. Develin 1978, 433; Eckstein 1987, 47–48 n. 95; J. S. Richardson 1975, 54–55.

12. Only once to my knowledge does Livy ever use the word "triumph" in loose reference to what was by other accounts technically an *ovatio,* and the passage in question is ambiguous. In the year 503, the Fasti record a full triumph for one consul (Agrippa Menenius Lanatus) and an *ovatio*—the first ever—for the other (P. Postumius Tubertus). See Degrassi 1947, 64–65, 536, and note that a single letter *O* next to a break in the stone is all that actually marks the *ovatio* as such. Livy meanwhile makes the perfunctory remark (2.16.9) that "et hoc anno

of the victory, especially after the extremity of perceived danger to the Republic, had led to a joint *supplicatio,* and it is not inconceivable that something similar may have happened on the question of a triumph as well, only to be dramatically upstaged by a gesture of scrupulous adherence to the rules of *imperium* and *auspicium* on the part of the consuls themselves. Perhaps they came up with the idea of combining elements of the triumph and the *ovatio* into a spectacle all their own.[13] The example of C. Claudius Pulcher in 143 certainly points to the wide degree of latitude that an *imperator* enjoyed in that regard.

Moreover, there is something unmistakably self-conscious and stagy about the consuls' response to the award, as if the *patres*' earlier stipulation that Nero must leave his army in the province while Salinator brought his troops home had signaled an implicit difference in status between them, which they were now publicly demonstrating that they understood and acknowledged. Perhaps their solution helped to restore a procedural balance that the exuberance of the *patres*' vote might have threatened to upset. One thing it emphatically did not do, however, despite any intuitive surface appearances to the contrary, was to diminish the heroic status of Nero's starring role in the Metaurus campaign. If anything, in fact, the joint celebration had the effect of bringing even greater *gloria* to both men, and especially to the one who ceded the primacy of honor to his colleague although he himself deserved greater credit for the victory (28.9.15).[14]

CHAINS OF SUCCESSION, BROKEN AND OTHERWISE

Nero and Salinator, two officers of equal rank, thus apparently came up with a unique way to memorialize their victory when circumstances led one of them to cross into the other's *provincia.* But if a junior commander happened to win a battle in the territory of a superior, that raised other concerns. No one expected praetor L. Furius Purpureo in 200 to see much

Romae triumphatum" ("this year also there were triumphs [or: "there was a triumph"] in Rome"). The impersonal form could be taken to cover both celebrations under a single notice but may just as easily be construed to omit mention of the *ovatio* altogether in favor of the larger honor. Cf. also Dion. Hal. 5.47; and Pliny *NH* 15.125 (using both *triumphans* and *ovans* in reference to the same person or event).

13. J. S. Richardson 1975, 55, remarks: "If this was an *ovatio,* it was an extremely odd one . . . it is clear that Nero was making a special effort to honor Salinator." Chaplin 2000, 145, offers a very telling paradox: "The consuls find themselves in an unprecedented situation and devise the essentially conservative plan of adapting the triumph as they know it to that situation." Also see R. Stewart 1998, 89.

14. On the greater glory that comes from turning down public honors once duly conferred, cf. 2.47.10–11, not to mention the obvious parallels from Aug. *Res Gestae* (4.1; 5.1, 5.3; 6.1; 10.2).

action in Cisalpine Gaul, despite signs of restlessness there among tribes who had formerly sided with the Carthaginians (31.2.5–11). Attention in Rome focused elsewhere. For that same year, though still nursing its wounds at home from the Hannibalic War, the Republic had just launched itself, reluctantly, on an enormous campaign in the Greek East.[15] The *patres* needed to marshal everything they could of strained resources against Philip of Macedon, which meant that on their orders Furius had discharged the bulk of his predecessor's army, keeping with him at Ariminum only a small garrison of five thousand Latin allies (31.8.7). A surprise attack by three local tribes, the Insubres, Cenomani, and Boii, then left Placentia in ruins and Cremona under siege, and at a desperate plea from the colonists for help, the praetor found himself vastly outnumbered (31.10.5–7).[16] Roused into action by this sudden emergency, the senate charged consul C. Aurelius Cotta with providing reinforcements to save the colony (31.11.1–3). He sent troops right away but himself did not get there in time. In the interim Furius seized his chance to score a major victory at Cremona: Livy says that more than thirty-five thousand Gauls were killed or captured in the rout, leaving fewer than six thousand of them alive (31.21.15–18).

The joyful *patres* proclaimed a three-day *supplicatio* in Rome to celebrate the victory (31.22.1), but Cotta did not share in their pleasure when he reached the province only to discover that a battle had been fought and won without him. Making no secret of his anger against the praetor for having tackled the enemy on his own, Cotta took command of the victorious army, though not much fighting remained to be done any longer, and packed Furius off to Etruria (31.22.3, echoed later in 31.47.4–5). Then, while Cotta was still busy in Gaul, Furius hurried back to Rome as quickly as possible to claim a triumph for his victory without the angry consul there to challenge him. This sparked a heated exchange in the senate (31.47.4–7).[17] Technically, Furius's praetorian rank probably put both him and his army under the higher command of the consul, especially once the *patres* had intervened to send Cotta to his aid. Technically. But in their original decree, not knowing what would happen, the senators had given Cotta freedom to decide whether the affairs of state would permit him

15. Thus 31.10.1: "omnium animis in bellum Macedonicum versis repente, nihil minus eo tempore timentibus, Gallici tumultus fama exorta" ("With the minds of all turned to the Macedonian War, suddenly, at a time when there was nothing they feared less, the rumor arose of a Gallic uprising"). The senators pushing for a declaration of war against Philip in 200 faced very stiff opposition even from the army. In fact almost all the centuries in the *comitia* voted against the motion the first time (31.6.3).

16. On the strategic reduction of forces in Gaul in this year, and possible reasons for the uprising, see Eckstein 1987, 55–56; McDonald 1974, 47–48.

17. See the concise discussion by Eckstein 1987, 57–58.

to lead an assault on Cremona right away himself. If not, they authorized him to stay behind in Rome for as long as he needed, leaving the praetor in charge of the army meanwhile, until he should arrive. Cotta clearly did not expect matters to come to a head as fast as they did, and he opted not to set out until after tying up some loose ends.[18] Thus the suddenness of the decisive engagement and the open-endedness of the original *senatus consultum* both helped to fuel the triumph debate after the fact. Had the praetor done the right thing? Furius's opponents accused him of having gone into battle "alieno exercitu" ("with another's army"), whereas his supporters took the opposite tack, arguing from the acknowledged *imperium* and *auspicium* of a praetor in his own province (31.48.2 vs. 31.48.8–9).[19]

As with the *privatus cum imperio* L. Cornelius Lentulus, who returned from Spain to an *ovatio* the same year, this struggle pitted the glory of a commander's *res gestae* against the force of tradition, albeit arguably to a lesser degree. For although Furius, unlike Lentulus, did hold a regular magistracy, no nonconsular praetor during his term of office had ever triumphed before.[20] A small group of elder statesmen, particularly from

18. Indeed based on the wording of the senate's instructions (31.11.1–3; and cf. 31.48.4), Cotta may not have imagined that it would come down to a pitched battle at all if a show of force by the praetor could intimidate the Gauls into relinquishing the colony—whereupon he would arrive himself to finish things off.

19. The phrase "alieno exercitu" is especially interesting (31.48.2), because one usually sees "aliena provincia" or "alieno auspicio," as with Nero in Salinator's province at the Metaurus. Furius, by contrast, fought in his own province and under his own auspices as praetor—and that is precisely the point that his supporters used to carry the day and win him his triumph. Cf. R. Stewart 1998, 90–92, on the role of the ritual allotment in designating *provincia* and *auspicium*. Army assignments, of course, came from the senate.

20. J. S. Richardson 1975, 52–53, asserted that "at the outbreak of the second Punic War the triumph was firmly established in Roman thinking as a consular preserve. . . . Thus Furius became the first non-consular praetor with an independent military command to celebrate a triumph." In 241, however, while exercising a command in Sicily prorogued from his praetorship the previous year, Q. Valerius Falto was awarded a naval triumph, the only exception to the previous consular monopoly. His name appears in the Fasti, at any rate (see Degrassi 1947, 76–77, 549). The *Periochae* are silent, but then Val. Max. 2.8.2 records a *sponsio* or primitive lawsuit brought by Falto against the consul C. Lutatius Catulus, land commander in Sicily, where the naval battle took place. Falto had apparently taken charge over the battle because Catulus lay wounded on a litter at the time, and according to Valerius the judge ruled in favor of the consul. How then did Falto triumph? Brennan 1996, 330 n. 10, suggests that he "must have received the Senate's dispensation or—less likely—triumphed by vote of the People or Plebs alone." The latter seems highly unlikely indeed. It is far easier to conceive that Valerius Maximus misconstrued the final outcome, as J. S. Richardson 1975, 51, suggests. Perhaps more pertinently, Develin 1978, 431, notes that Falto triumphed only after a dispute over his status: "It was decided that the *imperium* and *auspicium* under which the battle was fought belonged to the *consul*, but the *ductus* and *felicitas* could be seen as Falto's." The pattern adduced fits nicely with the outcome in Furius's case as well. To wit, consuls outranked praetors when the two came together, but if a praetor scored a victory—even with a consul

among the *consulares,* who as a constituency within the senate would presumably have had some interest in preserving the privilege of their own status, insisted that Furius should have held off on any decisive action until the consul arrived.[21] Instead he had marched straight into battle with an army already under someone else's command and had then made matters worse by abandoning his post in Etruria, where his superior officer had sent him, and rushing back to Rome with his brazen triumph request. They saw no precedent to sanction this behavior (31.48.3).[22] The *consulares* urged the senate not to repeat Furius's mistake but to postpone any judgment until hearing the other side of the story from the consul himself (31.48.5). A majority of the *patres,* however, sided with Furius because of the scope of his accomplishments (31.48.1). He had exercised the *imperium* lawfully conferred by the office of praetor to lead the army into battle and had won a clear-cut victory (31.48.6).[23] The catalogue of his *res gestae* should speak for itself: the enemy routed, their camp destroyed, one colony rescued from a siege, the citizens of another freed from bondage, and all by a single battle. And what is more, the senate had not hesitated at the time to vote a *supplicatio* to thank the gods for his achievement (31.48.10–12).

In the end these arguments from Furius and his *amici* outweighed the minority appeal to a strict reading of the *mos maiorum;* the full senate voted him his triumph after all (31.49.1).[24] It is crucial to recognize that the

technically in the vicinity—the senate enjoyed some discretion in sorting out the technicalities and adjudicating disputes over triumphal eligibility. In an attempt to downplay the novelty of praetorian triumphs as a matter of principle, Develin 1978, 431, says that although praetors had the requisite *imperium* and *auspicium,* it was simply "unlikely in the third century that a *praetor* would be in a position to request a triumph." Fair enough, as far as the history of Roman provincial administration is concerned, but a de facto consular monopoly or near monopoly may be every bit as staunchly defended as a de iure one. Oddly enough, though, after calling attention to the issue of Falto's status, Develin later proceeds to flatten out the Furius debate as if *his* status were never an issue, when the fact remains that something new did happen in 200. Indeed both Falto and Furius should be seen as stages in the same incremental exercise of the *patrum auctoritas* in the awarding of triumphs. Cf. Gruen 1995, 62: "Furius became the first praetor to enjoy the distinction of a triumph." In line with this, I like very much the suggestion of J. S. Richardson 1975, 53 n. 28, that Furius may have taken on the cognomen Purpureo at this time, to reflect the signal honor he had received in donning the obviously purple *vestis triumphalis.*

21. Livy pointedly marks the opposition as "elders" ("maiores natu," 31.48.2). On the generation gap within the senate at this point, see Feig Vishnia 1996, 182, and cf. 101–4.

22. Apparently Furius's critics believed that Etruria had somehow become his province de facto as soon as his superior officer sent him there. Yet he had left Gallia, the province allotted to him by the senate, at a direct order from the consul, and not to seek a triumph (31.47.5). Cf. Briscoe 1973, *ad loc.*

23. Citing this passage, Brennan 1996, 317, remarks that the "generally accepted criteria for the regular triumph" during this period "probably were no more detailed than what Livy reports (in *oratio obliqua*) in his account of L. Furius Purpureo's bid for a triumph in 200."

24. The relevant chunk of the Fasti is missing: see Degrassi 1947, 551.

two sides in this struggle were not appealing to a single code of triumph requirements. Instead, the argument is framed as a choice between two different paradigms of what the criteria ought to be, with one finally winning out over the other.[25] Cogent reasoning justifies Furius's claim in terms of his *imperium* and *auspicium,* but Livy also calls attention to the political element: *gratia* ("favor") toward the praetor, who was on hand for the debate, overcame the *maiestas* ("grandeur") of the absent consul (31.49.1).[26] Although left with command of the army and all the spoils of war, Cotta had forfeited whatever added influence he might have enjoyed from his status as consul by not being present to argue his case. This allowed the praetor to cash in on the one thing he indisputably had in his possession, namely the victory at Cremona, to gain for himself the further honor of a triumph.[27] When Cotta came back to Rome to hold the elections, he spoke out against the senate, but only to decry a verdict that by this time he no longer had any power to change (31.49.8–11).[28] The *consulares* had already made a bid to uphold strict precedent on his behalf, and they had failed. Like the compromise for Lentulus, also in 200, Furius's triumph confirms that if enough of them agreed to it, the *patres* could defy tradition in rewarding success.

But they could also stipulate against a commander if opinion should swing the other way. In 195 they denied a triumph to praetor M. Helvius returning from Farther Spain, on the grounds that he had fought "alieno auspicio et in aliena provincia" ("under another's auspices and in another's province") when he met and defeated a huge force of Celtiberi on his way back to Rome (34.10.5). Confusion surrounds both the local geography and the precise chain of command and succession in Spain at the time,[29] but according to Livy, Helvius had arrived in the newly designated province of Hispania Ulterior as praetor in 197.[30] After his term ran out, an illness

25. Note in particular the rhetoric of the pro-Furius contingent, asserting their view of what should count in a triumph debate: 31.48.6, "nihil praeter res gestas et an in magistratu suisque auspiciis gessisset censebant spectare senatum debere" ("They argued that the senate should not look to anything else except his *res gestae,* and whether he had acted while in office and under his own auspices"). And again 31.48.11: "pugnam ipsam eventumque pugnae spectari debere" ("The battle itself and the outcome of the battle should be looked to").

26. The relevant passage (31.49.1) is cited below, p. 176 and n. 23.

27. Livy expresses the same idea the other way around at 31.49.3 (cited below, p. 177 and n. 24), to the effect that Cotta seemingly had everything to his credit except the actual victory. The economic metaphor emerges as particularly apt.

28. Cf. Dio Cass. 18.57.81.

29. See Develin 1980; *contra* Sumner 1970 and 1977. More recently, see R. Stewart 1998, 90–93.

30. Helvius had been elected praetor for 197, the year of the electoral and provincial reforms that transformed the Spanish provinces forever (see above, pp. 61–62 and n. 28). As one of six praetors, then, he then took command in the newly designated province of Hispania Ulterior (32.27.6, 28.2, 28.11; App. *Hisp.* 39). His colleague in Nearer Spain, C. Sempronius Tuditanus,

detained him there for over a year, and so the army he led in 195 had been sent by then-praetor Ap. Claudius (his successor's successor) to escort him home. As if to complicate matters further, the battle itself appears to have taken place in Hispania Citerior, which in 195 had fallen to consul M. Porcius Cato (the Elder).[31] If this is correct, then the designation "alieno auspicio et in aliena provincia" actually involves three different people, because Helvius would have fought commanding Claudius's soldiers in Cato's territory. He must have had valid *imperium* and *auspicium* of his own in order to command the troops at all, but the technicalities are enough to give anyone pause: the senate awarded Helvius an *ovatio* (34.10.1–6).[32]

Meanwhile, his successor, praetor Q. Minucius Thermus, arrived in Rome a mere two months later in 195 on the heels of another Spanish victory. He had won a pitched battle at the town of Turda, with twelve thousand Spaniards killed, their leader Budares taken prisoner, and the rest put to flight, fostering an unexpected peace (33.44.4). Although control of his army had already passed to someone else, Thermus had at least fought during his term of office, and so the *patres* voted him a triumph apparently without a qualm (34.10.7).[33] The presence of a consular army in Hispania Citerior at the time meant of course that war in Spain was still ongoing, but that did not seem to enter into the calculations either for Helvius or for his successor.

ENFORCED INEQUALITY?

As a throwback to the monarchy, the Roman triumph focused attention on the achievements of a single individual in service to the community at large. Despite the value placed under the Republic on collegiality and shared power—whence the success of Salinator and Nero in a united front before the *patres*—combined efforts often led to one commander's winning a triumph at the other's expense. Once again, it is best to focus on evidence

---

died from battle wounds (33.25.8–9), and new praetors for 196, Q. Fabius Buteo and Q. Minucius Thermus, were sent to replace both of them (33.26.3–4). So presumably Thermus had already arrived when the illness struck that detained Helvius in the province for so long.

31. Thus after the battle Helvius and his troops made their way to Cato's camp (34.10.3). On the geography, see Develin 1980, 366–67, with references to previous scholarship.

32. See Degrassi 1947, 78–79, 552. There is sense in the suggestion of Develin 1980, 367, that it was Cato's consular *potestas* (and his presence in the province, unlike the situation with Cotta and Furius in 200) that effectively ruled out a triumph for ex-praetor Helvius, although some aspect of his *auspicium* may also technically have lapsed (R. Stewart 1998, 91 and nn.). Cf. Brennan 2000, 166–67, for a different angle, remarking that "Helvius is the only man from an obscure *gens* to celebrate an ovation or a triumph from Spain in the period 197–166." Also note Brennan 2004, 44.

33. Also see Degrassi 1947, 78–79, 552–53.

from Livy 21–45.[34] The consuls for 197, for instance, C. Cornelius Cethegus and Q. Minucius Rufus, had been allotted the province of Italy together to fight the Gauls, as we have already seen. Their joint appointment had itself come about through a political compromise: they had been about to cast lots separately for Italy and Macedonia when two tribunes intervened to prorogue *imperium* in the East for T. Quinctius Flamininus, now on the brink of victory over Philip (32.28).[35] Sent thus to Italy, the consuls coordinated their strategies in the province, with Cethegus marching against the Insubres and Cenomani while Minucius took on the Ligures and Boii. Largely because Minucius managed to keep the Boii from joining forces with them, Cethegus crushed both his tribes in a single pitched battle, in which Livy says that thirty-five thousand of the enemy were killed and another fifty-two hundred captured. Word of the slaughter sent both the Boii and the Ligures scattering homeward without a further fight, and letters from the two commanders prompted the decree of a four-day *supplicatio* in Rome. At the end of the year, Cethegus and Minucius went before the *patres* in the Temple of Bellona to request a triumph together (33.22.1).[36]

Tribunes C. Atinius Labeo and C. Afranius stepped in to block the joint request, refusing to stand by and let the senate bestow equal honor on deeds of unequal worth. Cethegus had accomplished glorious feats in battle to earn himself a triumph, they said; Minucius, plainly not.[37] Glossing over the *supplicatio* decreed on receipt of letters from both consuls, the tribunes argued that the public thanksgiving belonged, in effect, to Cethegus rather than to his colleague. Minucius tried to stress that they had worked together with a single strategy, and Cethegus himself spoke up on his behalf, but the tribunes still pushed their challenge to Minucius's right to triumph. They insisted (33.22.7–9) that he had won

34. There are two salient examples from the fourth century. The consuls for 392, L. Valerius Potitus and M. Manlius Capitolinus, fought against the Aequi together. Valerius triumphed, "quod perseverantior caedem iis in fuga fecit" ("because he more steadfastly carried out a slaughter among those in flight"), whereas Manlius celebrated an *ovatio* (5.31.4). The consuls in 360, C. Poetilius Libo and M. Fabius Ambustus, fought in separate provinces. Poetilius triumphed, and Fabius had an *ovatio,* apparently also because of a perceived difference in the scale of their achievements (7.11.9).

35. Hölkeskamp 1993, 24–25, observes: "By means of *prorogatio,* the uninterrupted continuity of command under a consul in a given theatre, with experience and expert knowledge of local conditions and the actual situation, could be guaranteed in order to bring a campaign to a successful end." So ran the theory. Yet the unsteady ad-hoc politics of prorogation in practice have been amply documented by Gruen 1984a, 204–19. See also Gruen 1995, 66–70.

36. For the campaign, see 32.29–31, with the *supplicatio* decree at 32.31.6. On their strategy and its mixed results, see McDonald 1974, 48.

37. For the names of the tribunes who opposed Minucius and the grounds of their complaints, see 33.22.2–9. For the political background to the attack on Minucius, see Brennan 1996, 324–26.

merely trivial battles, lost many men, and trumped up false numbers of surrendered cities to exaggerate his exploits. The allegation of excessive Roman casualties deserves special notice. Not even Cethegus could exert enough political clout to win his colleague a triumph that outspoken critics felt he simply had not earned (33.22.6).[38] The debate wore on for two full days before the consuls at last backed down and made separate triumph requests (33.22.10).[39] A full consensus of the *patres* first awarded Cethegus a triumph and then lined up against Minucius (33.23.1).[40] He could not afford to press the issue any further. To save face, and with only the barest gesture toward seeking the senate's approval, Minucius announced that he would hold a triumph under his own authority *in monte Albano* (33.23.3).[41]

Thus no matter how hard Cethegus and Minucius strove to keep up a united front before the body of their peers, political pressure eventually drove the *patres* to choose between them, and the same thing happened again the following year. Like their predecessors, M. Claudius Marcellus (whose father had famously laid siege to Syracuse) and L. Furius Purpureo, consuls for 196, would never have shared command at all, except that a tribunician veto once more kept Macedonia from being named as a consular province, this time allowing T. Quinctius Flamininus to work out the details of his peace with Philip (33.25.5–11).[42] Marcellus and Furius thus went together to northern Italy against the Gauls, as Cethegus and Minucius had done (33.25.10). Corolamus, chief of the Boii, took Marcellus by sur-

38. The passage referred to (33.22.6) marks a pointed contrast between Cethegus's "meritum triumphum" and the "honorem immeritum" that Minucius sought "impudenter." Note also "levia proelia" at 33.22.7, which Dorey and Lydall 1972, *ad loc.*, gloss to mean that unlike Cethegus, Minucius "had not fought a pitched battle." Develin 1985, 210, writes: "What is indicated is precisely the assessment of deserts. . . . It was better not to ask for a triumph which seemed likely to be refused." But as we shall see, that was not necessarily true amid the vagaries of the Roman political game.

39. Only two other triumph debates in Livy 21–45 are said to have run on into a second day: the struggle in the senate over the triumph of Cn. Manlius Vulso in 187 (38.50.1–3) and the arguments before the people in the case of L. Aemilius Paullus in 167 (45.36.1–2). For other political deliberations interrupted by nightfall, see, e.g., 3.17.9, 8.33.2; also cf. 26.17.10, 34.33.3. Of course the coming of night is often mentioned in battle narratives as being fraught with both opportunities and dangers. For changes of fortune explicitly said to have been brought about by the arrival of darkness, see 4.41.5, 5.41.4, 21.59.8, 25.34.14. Also see 4.39.5, 6.8.8, 7.8.6, 7.33.15, 9.23.4, 9.39.3, 10.12.5, 10.35.3, 10.42.1, 24.32.9, 27.2.9, 27.12.10, 31.17.10, 44.42.9; cf. 35.21.8.

40. For Cethegus's triumph (presumed to be from a missing chunk of the Fasti), see Degrassi 1947, 551.

41. See Degrassi 1947, 78–79, 552. The triumph *in monte Albano* had of course been celebrated only twice before.

42. In the previous year the senate had prorogued Flamininus's *imperium* until they should name a successor (32.28.9), so this time, deeming the earlier decree sufficient, they did not do so again.

prise and inflicted serious losses on his army, but the Romans held on to their camp, and the Boii war band scattered. Marcellus then won a decisive battle against the Insubres at Comum, where Livy reports more than forty thousand of the enemy killed and the Gallic camp destroyed (33.36.4–14). Later the two consuls joined forces against the Boii, and, though assaulted in mid-march, fought all the more fiercely and slaughtered them almost to a man (33.37).[43] At letters from them both the senate decreed a three-day *supplicatio,* and when Marcellus arrived himself shortly thereafter, they unanimously voted him a triumph. Marcellus triumphed over the Insubres and Comenses, whom he had defeated by himself. Livy says that he "left hope of a triumph over the Boii to his colleague," though, because that tribe had bested him on his own, only falling at length to the two of them together (33.37.9–10).[44] Nevertheless, whether or not Furius ever genuinely entertained such a hope, no record exists that he even asked for a triumph in 196, let alone received one. Perhaps he heeded the warning of what had happened to Minucius the year before and did not want to press his luck. Perhaps he did not want a repeat of the fight over his triumph as praetor in 200.[45] At any rate, merely assisting a colleague to win a battle—no matter how instrumental the aid in ensuring a Roman victory—left an *imperator* open to attack for not having acted independently enough. Salinator and Nero in 207 remain the exception that proves the rule.

Conversely, however, in 191 it was actually charged as a liability against the consul P. Cornelius Scipio Nasica that he *failed* to join forces with another commander. The *patres* had declared a *supplicatio* to mark Nasica's signal victory over the Boii (36.38.5–7),[46] and so he confidently sent his troops away with orders to appear in Rome on the day of his triumph. Clearly he did not anticipate any opposition (36.39.3–4).[47] But when he

43. On confusion in Livy's sources for this campaign, with a careful reading of the topography and local conditions, see McDonald 1974, 48–50.

44. See Degrassi 1947, 78–79, 552; and note the remarks of Dorey et al. 1972, *ad loc.*: "The basis of Marcellus' claim was rather weak, and he probably owed his triumph to his father's reputation."

45. Livy never mentions the prospect of a triumph for Furius in 196 again, leaving scholars to argue from silence. Münzer (1912) saw Livy's account of Furius's accomplishments in Gaul in 200 as a doublet for those of C. Cornelius Cethegus in 197, and on those grounds wanted to move the triumph attested for Furius in 200 to his consulship in 196. Both Broughton 1951, 326, and Degrassi 1947, 551, argue against this interpretation, which certainly complicates matters more than it clarifies them. It makes much better sense to assume that Furius not only did not receive a triumph in 196 but indeed never asked for one.

46. On the battle, see McDonald 1974, 51–52. Livy openly doubts the inflated casualty figures cited by Valerius Antias but attests that "it appears to have been a great victory nonetheless" ("magnam tamen victoriam fuisse apparet") because Scipio captured the enemy camp and obtained their surrender.

47. Note the remark of Briscoe 1981, *ad loc.*: "it seems that Nasica not only assumed that he would be granted a triumph, but decided on its date as well."

arrived to make his formal triumph request, the tribune P. Sempronius Blaesus objected. Instead of rushing back, Blaesus said, he should have led his victorious army to the aid of Q. Minucius Thermus, consul from 193, who had been fighting the Ligures for over two years already with no end in sight. Blaesus's argument, as Livy records it, runs as follows: the two commanders together (Nasica and Thermus) could have driven both tribes (the Boii and the Ligures) into submission at once and stopped them from helping each other against the Romans, but in his precipitous and self-seeking chase after a triumph Nasica had left poor Thermus to his own devices and thereby jeopardized any such hope for a lasting peace in the region.[48] This argument has the ring of special pleading on Thermus's behalf: one thinks of the tribunes' repeated intervention to secure *prorogationes* for Flamininus year after year. Curiously too Blaesus did not go so far as to call on the senators to deny Scipio his triumph outright: he asked them merely to delay it by sending the commander back into the field to finish what he had started. Once having secured the defeat of the Ligures, in other words, proconsul Nasica might claim his well-earned triumph with no lack of precedent behind him (36.39.5–10).

Even this guarded challenge demanded a response. Nasica began by pointing out that his allotted province had not given him any mandate to fight the Ligures (36.40.1).[49] Thermus, to whom the war in Liguria did belong, would most likely earn a triumph in his own right. Meanwhile Nasica himself had landed a resounding victory over the Boii and taken hostages from them to cement peace. Why should he not expect to triumph and bring his army home sooner rather than later? The turning point in his argument came when he reminded the *patres* of their unanimous favor toward him once before, on the day when they had named him as the *vir optimus* to welcome the Magna Mater into the city. According to Livy that reminder enabled Nasica to forge a new consensus now, strong enough to overpower the tribune and win the honor of a triumph for himself right away (36.40.2–10).[50] So ran the vagaries of triumphal politics. Ironically the following year, in 190, when Thermus sent word that he had forced the surrender of the Ligures at last, the senate ordered him to hand over command of his army to Nasica, back in his former province after all, now confiscating land from the defeated Boii (37.2.5). And the irony deepens.

48. Also note the comment of Walsh 1990, *ad loc.*: "In fact Celts and Ligurians were traditionally hostile to each other, and Livy offers no evidence of such cooperation between Rome's diverse enemies." Blaesus's argument sounds more and more like something concocted on the spur of the moment just to bring Thermus's (otherwise irrelevant) name into the discussion so as to air his apparent grievance at having been left without reinforcements.

49. For the original provincial assignments to Nasica and his colleague, see 36.1.1–2.1. At 36.1.9 the Boii are singled out as the designated enemy in the province of Italia.

50. See Degrassi 1947, 78–79, 553.

For although the tribune had forced Nasica to defend himself for not helping against the Ligures in 191, now, when Thermus returned victorious all by himself, far from recognizing that independent achievement the senate flatly refused him a triumph (37.46.1–2).

Based on these examples, one would conclude that joint campaigns held little promise of reward for both commanders. Yet plenty of pairs who fought together also triumphed together. Indeed that is what happened as often as not.[51] In 185, after the winter ending their year as praetors in the two Spains, C. Calpurnius Piso and L. Quinctius Crispinus coalesced their armies in Baeturia to fight with a single strategy. By throwing themselves bodily into the fray at a crucial moment, Livy says, they inspired their troops to an overwhelming victory, leaving no more than four thousand Spaniards alive out of over thirty-five thousand who had fought that day (39.30–31). News of the rout prompted the senate to decree a two-day *supplicatio* in Rome, and on their return each of the praetors triumphed over the Lusitani and Celtiberi by full consensus, Piso first and Crispinus a few days later (39.42.2–4).[52]

In 180 two proconsuls not only triumphed from the same province: they triumphed, Livy says, "without [even] having waged a war" (40.38.8).[53] P. Cornelius Cethegus and M. Baebius Tamphilus were allotted Liguria together as consuls for 181 (40.18.1, 3). A virulent plague at first hampered their levy and kept them from getting there in time to help the proconsul L. Aemilius Paullus fight his way out from under a sudden siege by a wayward tribe (40.24–6).[54] Paullus eventually triumphed, with quite a few prisoners of war. Other Ligurians sent envoys to Rome to sue for peace at the

51. From the earlier period (i.e., before Livy 21–45) note the following examples. The consuls of 505 both triumphed over the Sabines (see 2.16.1; and Degrassi 1947, 64–65, 535–36). The consuls of 459 both triumphed over the Volsci (3.24.8; and Degrassi 1947, 66–67, 537). In 361, 360, and 358 one consul triumphed over the Hernici, and the other over the Gauls (7.11.9, 7.15.5; and Degrassi 1947, 68–69, 540). The consuls of 343 both triumphed over the Samnites (7.38 3; and Degrassi 1947, 68–69, 541), as did the consuls of 322 (8.39.15; and Degrassi 1947, 70–71, 542). The consuls of 311 and 309 triumphed, one over the Samnites and the other over the Etruscans (9.31.16, 9.39.9, 9.40.15, 9.40.20; and Degrassi 1947, 70–71, 542). The consuls of 293, 291, and 290 all triumphed over the Samnites (Degrassi 1947, 72–73, 544–45, with reference to other sources in the absence of Livy's Second Decade), as did the consuls of 275 and 272, though with slightly varying designations (Degrassi 1947, 74–75, 546). The consuls of 268 both triumphed over the Peicentes (Degrassi 1947, 74–75, 547). The consuls of 267 and 266 all triumphed over the Sallentini (Degrassi 1947, 74–75, 547). The consuls of 258, 257, 254, and 241 all triumphed over the Carthaginians (Degrassi 1947, 76–77, 548–49), and the consuls of 219 both triumphed over the Illyrians (Degrassi 1947, 550).

52. The relevant chunk of the Fasti is missing: see Degrassi 1947, 554.

53. 40.38.9: "nullo bello gesto."

54. The comedy (or perhaps rather tragedy) of errors that prevented any help at all from reaching Paullus in time deserves separate treatment at some point, if only because it makes such a wonderful story.

same time but were spurned by the senate, who did not trust their promises (40.34.8–12). Thereafter Cornelius and Baebius enjoyed a calm year in the province (40.35.1; cf. 40.37.9). The senate prorogued their *imperium* for 180, with orders to stay put until their successors should arrive and then to dismiss their troops and return to Rome (40.36.7).[55] During the suspension of public business after the plague claimed the life of C. Calpurnius Piso, one of the new consuls, Cornelius and Baebius apparently took it upon themselves to march against the Apuani. Or so Livy implies: in the aftermath of Piso's death he does not mention any new instructions from the *patres* authorizing this attack.

Caught thus by surprise, the Apuani surrendered on the spot (40.37.1–38.1). With permission from the senate and at sizable public expense, as part of the arrangements following this *deditio* the proconsuls then brought thousands of men with their wives and children down from the mountains and settled them in former Samnite territory, now *ager publicus,* where they would pose less of an ongoing threat to the security of the Republic (40.38.2–7).[56] When the two commanders returned to Rome, the senate voted both of them a triumph, without even the slightest trace of controversy in Livy's account. Over the course of the next several years, consuls assigned to the region continued the policy of deportation, moving sizable populations of Ligures to colonies in central Italy (Luca, 40.43.1; Luna, 41.13.5). After generations of sporadic unrest, the SPQR had had enough.[57] Thus Cornelius and Baebius might arguably have helped to secure lasting peace in a long-troubled province, but they themselves had not fought a war, and they brought back neither captives nor booty. Such a triumph could never have come about either if a joint command caused problems per se or if technicalities and procedural rules about the scale of the victory always had the last word (40.38.8–9).[58]

In 178 another pair of ex-praetors, Ti. Sempronius Gracchus and

55. The successors had been allotted Liguria as well, to make war on the Apuani (40.35.8, 36.7).

56. These transplanted Ligures were later called Corneliani and Baebiani (Plin. *NH* 3.105). Note the remark of Walsh 1996, *ad loc.*, that the forced resettlement was "a more drastic solution than that in the case of the Boii in 191 (36.39.2)."

57. Note the comment of Harris 1989, 118, that "Luca, Luna and the land of the Statellates were the latest, and as it turned out almost the last, places in Italy which the Romans and Latins settled before the Social War . . . the wars against the Gauls and Ligurians were the first important step in the Romanization and Italianization of a large section of the peninsula."

58. J. S. Richardson 1975, 62, conspicuously labels this triumph as a "travesty," whereas Brennan 1996, 318 n. 19, more understatedly calls it "rather different from securing through special influence a triumph for a bloodless victory" and cites 38.47.5 and 40.59.1 as comparanda. Walsh 1996, *ad loc.*, sees 40.38.1 as evidence of "limited military activity" on the part of Cornelius and Baebius, and notes that "Aemilius Paullus' large-scale victory over the Ingauni in the previous year . . . may have weakened Ligurian resistance."

L. Postumius Albinus, celebrated triumphs back to back from the two Spains. They had set up a pincer movement into Celtiberia, with Albinus coming through Lusitania from the west and Gracchus from the east. Having brought the Spanish tribes under submission, they arrived in Rome together, and together they went before the senate in the Temple of Bellona to narrate their *res gestae.* In granting their triumph requests the senate distributed the credit between them just as they had divided command: Gracchus triumphed over the Celtiberi and their allies; Albinus, the next day, over the Lusitani and other tribes in the region (41.7.1–3). Last, when M. Aemilius Lepidus and P. Mucius Scaevola, the consuls for 175, mounted a joint offensive against a number of rebellious Ligurian tribes in Cisalpine Gaul, the *patres* decreed a three-day *supplicatio* for victories by both consuls (41.19.1), and on their return simply granted each of them a triumph over the Ligures.[59]

SUMMARY

When applying the broad traditional template of *imperio auspicio ductu felicitate* to the special problems posed by overlapping jurisdictions and joint campaigns, the senate clearly arrived at individual judgments on a case-by-case basis, with a wide range of possible outcomes. Claudius Nero and M. Livius Salinator in 207 fought a battle together that would turn the tide in the most deadly war the Republic had ever faced, and then instead of a dual triumph decided to mark it with a relatively austere victory celebration, oddly enough to the greater glory of them both. For having secured a major victory on a smaller scale, L. Furius Purpureo won an unprecedented triumph as praetor in 200 despite opposition from a senior official, but apparently he did not even try to press his luck again when his turn as consul arrived four years later. Q. Minucius Thermus in 197 was forced by political opponents to relinquish his *triumphi spes* in favor of his colleague. M. Helvius in 195 had to content himself with an *ovatio,* but plenty of others who had fought in joint campaigns triumphed by full consent of the *patres:* Q. Minucius Rufus in 197, M. Claudius Marcellus in 196, P. Cornelius Scipio Nasica in 191, Ti. Sempronius Gracchus and L. Postumius Albinus in 178, M. Aemilius Lepidus and P. Mucius Scaevola in 175, L. Aemilius Paullus, Cn. Octavius, and L. Anicius Gallus in 167. All these examples defy easy generalization, and the joint triumph of P. Cornelius Cethegus and M. Baebius Tamphilus in 180 without even having fought a proper war stands as a final testament to the inherent flexibility of triumphal criteria.

59. The entire first quaternion of the single manuscript that preserves Books 41–45 of Livy is sadly missing, and notice of these triumphs has disappeared in the resulting large lacuna; but see Degrassi 1947, 80–81, 555–56.

CHAPTER 4

The Importance of Closure

At the core of any triumph request lay the commander's claim to have done the job the senate and people had given him to do, and done it well: *res bene ac feliciter e re publica gesta* ("a thing accomplished with success and good fortune for the sake of the Republic"). His case would clearly benefit from his having won a decisive victory—that is, having dealt Rome's enemies the kind of crushing blow that would signal an end to the conflict. Ideally, he should be able to write home declaring "the war is over" (*debellatum est*), bring his troops back safely, and celebrate a triumph to mark the mission as officially completed.[1] As we have seen, Plautus outlines the best-case scenario thus: "the enemy defeated, citizens rescued, calm restored, terms of peace concluded, / war snuffed out, a job well done, the army and garrisons intact."[2] Yet with so many perennial battlegrounds and long-term struggles across a growing empire, especially during the war-torn years 218–167, it was awfully hard to say at what precise point some conflicts ever truly ended. So another broad avenue for the subjective play of political forces within the senate opened up over the question of when a war could be considered won, if not once and for all, then at least convincingly enough for the time being to justify a triumph. Once again the attested outcomes cover a wide range of possibilities. The *patres* were making ad-hoc

1. Hence the emotional impact of the prayers after the battle of the Metaurus in 207: "perinde ac si debellatum foret" ("almost as if the war were about to be fought to the finish," 27.51.8). Another speaker in Livy's history likewise refers to the triumph as the "decus perfecti belli" ("ornament of a war brought to a close," 45.38.4). Vergil's famous "debellare superbos" ("to fight the arrogant to the finish," *Aen.* 6.853) inevitably comes to mind as well.

2. Plaut. *Per.* 753–54: "hostibu' victis, civibu' salvis, re placida, pacibu' perfectis, / bello extincto, re bene gesta, integro exercitu et praesidiis." Cf. above, p. 30 and n. 21.

judgments in individual cases and did not even try to arrive at a single rigorous policy.

M. CLAUDIUS MARCELLUS, 211

In 214 consul M. Claudius Marcellus went to Sicily and launched siege operations against Syracuse.[3] When the city succumbed at last, some two years later, the senate prorogued Marcellus's *imperium* one last time so that he could make final arrangements prior to coming home, yet flatly refused him permission to bring back his veterans (26.1.6–8). The war was still ongoing (25.40.5). Praetor M. Cornelius Cethegus soon took command of Marcellus's legions and continued military operations on the island.[4] Nor did he really finish the job, for Sicily went on to become a consular province again the following year. Obviously the main reason why the senate voted to keep Marcellus's troops in place after his return was the continuing threat from the Carthaginians and their supporters in the region, made all the more alarming by the fact that right at that moment Rome was facing the most acute manpower shortages of the entire war.[5] But the denial of a commander's reasonable request must also reflect some hearty lobbying by his political foes.[6] Certainly Marcellus's veterans did not relish having their tour of duty extended, and the *imperator* himself must have felt a deliberate affront to his *dignitas*. According to Livy, he judged the matter worthy of complaint when he came before the *patres* in the Temple

3. The siege of Syracuse notably led to the death of the famed Greek mathematician and engineer Archimedes, who had been helping to build defense engines for the city (24.32–35, 25.23–26; cf. Polyb. 8.3–9, 37; Plut. *Marc.* 13–19).

4. When first listing the provincial assignments for the praetors in 211, Livy states that C. Sulpicius and M. Cornelius Cethegus received Sicily and Apulia, respectively (25.41.12–13), but then it is Cethegus who takes over on Marcellus's departure, with no further reference to Sulpicius's activities. As Broughton 1951, 277 n. 5, remarks, there are considerable "discrepancies in the accounts of the actions of the military leaders during Hannibal's march on Rome." For Cethegus's campaign in Sicily, see 26.21.13–17, 28.10.

5. See Brunt 1971, 66–67: "If the annalistic evidence is sound, the peak year for men under arms is 212 . . . [when] perhaps half the free able-bodied young men were with the armies and fleets." On trends and fluctuations in Roman war commitments across the history of the Republic, see also Rich 1993, 44–48.

6. The verb "negasset" at 26.1.8 implies both request and denial (i.e., voices raised alternately for and against the soldiers' return). Cf. "non licuisset" at 26.21.2 and "iussissent . . . decerneretur" at 26.21.4, all referring to the same action by the senate in response to Marcellus's request. His supporters plainly tried to bring a motion on his behalf, and failed. That the outcome did not rest merely on policy should be clear enough. After all, it is not outside the realm of possibility to imagine that the *patres,* though beset by chronic manpower shortages, might have chosen to make an exception for the conqueror of Syracuse had his political clout and that of his *amici* proven sufficient to quell opposition.

of Bellona to make his triumph request, boasting that he had completed his allotted task (26.21.1–2).[7]

A discussion ensued: Had that task been merely to reduce Syracuse, or in fact to pacify all of Sicily?[8] The resulting disagreement cost Marcellus his triumph, and the arguments on either side reveal both the wide extent and the appreciable limits of laissez-faire in relations between senate and general. It turns out that the SPQR had never formally declared war against the Syracusans: the impetus to attack had come entirely from the commander in the field, responding to local developments within his *provincia.*[9] Far from ordering him to desist, moreover, as they certainly might have done had they disapproved of his actions, the *patres* voted more than once to keep Marcellus in Sicily so that he could pursue the ongoing siege. The final victory belonged to this extended term as proconsul, but that in itself would hardly have made a triumph illegal, only unusual at the time. At least he began with a regular consulship.[10] Still, confusion lingered about the extent of his original mandate, or rather, more accurately, his mandate had remained open-ended all along, with the result that those who had perhaps been waiting a long time for a chance to take him down a peg or two—driven by φθόνος (i.e., *invidia,* "resentment"), as Plutarch says[11]—were able on his return to invoke a conveniently broad understanding of the job supposedly before him. On that basis they could claim that he had not finished what he started. The argument struck home, too, because by then he had already laid down his command, and with it any hope of further accomplishments.

Notice that Marcellus's detractors could not fault him directly for arriving in Rome unaccompanied by his army, for in that he had only been following orders.[12] By Livy's description the indignant commander brought up the *deportatio* question himself with his open criticism of the way the

7. On the lingering ill will among Marcellus's former troops, see 26.21.16–17.

8. Compare Marcellus's claim of having achieved "provincia confecta" (26.21.2) with the wording of the senate's instructions to him at 26.1.6–8.

9. Note Eckstein 1987, 154: "the new war in Sicily . . . began without a formal vote for war by the senate and the *populus* in Rome . . . simply because Marcellus, faced with what he considered to be an emergency, concluded that forceful military action was the best way to guarantee the safety of his *provincia* from elements he felt had proven themselves *hostes,* and dangerous."

10. So Develin 1978, 432. Yet cf. Eckstein 1987, 170: "not for eighty-nine years had a general received a triumph for success won during a promagistracy."

11. Plut. *Marc.* 22.1; also cf. Eckstein 1987, 170 n. 58.

12. This contrasts with the experience of praetor L. Furius Purpureo in 200, who met with harsh criticism in the senate (31.48.2–3) for having allegedly abandoned his post. Furius left his soldiers behind under another's command and came back to Rome by himself out of eagerness to celebrate a triumph, which he eventually did, opposition notwithstanding (31.49.2; and see Degrassi 1947, 551).

senate had treated his veterans. Nor did the opposition try to shirk responsibility for their earlier decisions.[13] Rather they turned their focus to the distressing fact that a state of war persisted despite the fall of the island's major city. This did not reflect well on Marcellus: How could he claim to have gotten the job done? From there they merely seized the advantage, arguing that no one should be allowed to triumph merely "quasi debellato" ("as if the war were over") in the absence of the real thing. By their view only an official declaration to the effect that *exercitum deportari licet* ("it is allowed for the army to be brought back"), coming from the *patres,* could truly and authoritatively signify *debellatum est* ("the war is over"). They thus championed the rights of the senate, as opposed to the commander in the field, to decide when a conflict was finished.[14]

The thought patterns embedded here reveal an important point about the system of rules and regulations that supposedly governed the *ius triumphandi* under the Republic. For if *deportatio exercitus* had indeed always constituted a notional requirement for the award of a triumph, the issue had apparently never arisen in a triumph debate before Marcellus. Perhaps the stipulation against a commander who did not meet this particular criterion had never even been put into words. Soldiers had always joined in the triumphal ritual, from its earliest foundations, and indeed for centuries their presence could be taken completely for granted, because the victorious army customarily returned home along with their commander after the successful close of a campaign. Tacit understanding would not give way to active concern on the senate floor until the *patres* found themselves faced with the new and unforeseen possibility that an *imperator* might be victorious in battle, as Marcellus had been, and still leave his veterans behind. *Mos* as perceived convention differs in precisely this way from a

13. Note the exact wording at 26.21.4 (cited in the next note). The reference to Marcellus's successor also subtly puts the commander in his place as only one in the continual series of annual appointees, all of whom serve their time in the province and then move on, while the senate remains.

14. To illustrate the precise wording on both sides of the argument, the relevant passage will be cited here in full. 26.21.3–4: "cum multis verbis actum esset utrum minus conveniret cuius nomine absentis ob res prospere ductu eius gestas supplicatio decreta foret et dis immortalibus habitus honos ei praesenti negare triumphum, an quem tradere exercitum successori iussissent—quod nisi manente in provincia bello non decerneretur—eum quasi debellato triumphare cum exercitus testis meriti atque immeriti triumphi abesset, medium visum ut ovans urbem iniret" ("When it had been argued with many words whether it was less appropriate, after a *supplicatio* had been decreed in someone's name on account of successes accomplished under his leadership, and honor paid to the immortal gods, to deny him a triumph to his face, or for someone whom they had ordered to hand over his army to his successor—which would never have been decreed unless a state of war still existed in the province—to triumph as if the war were over, when the army would not be present as a witness of a well-deserved triumph or its opposite, it emerged as the middle ground for him to enter the city in an *ovatio*").

straightforward checklist of preexisting requirements.[15] The sudden invocation of the rule in 211 was also pointedly aimed against Marcellus and his supporters. Even when triumphal decision making rested on legitimate procedural technicalities, the final verdict always emerged right in the thick of unavoidably subjective political considerations.

After all, why did the presence of the army even matter? A valid triumph could still take place in the absence of soldiers to follow the chariot. Based on what Livy says in the present instance it was not a precondition for the triumph in any strict legalistic sense but only a way of assuring that the senators could call upon reliable witnesses to the all-too-easily disputed (i.e., subjective) value of a commander's achievements.[16] If the *patres* as a body saw fit, they could easily dispense with the whole *deportatio* issue at will, simply by concluding that their assessments of the *imperator* and his *res gestae* needed no corroboration from the army.[17] Those arguing on Marcellus's behalf were quick to assert as much, but again indirectly (26.21.3–4). Without even mentioning the absence of the troops, much less assigning praise or blame for it, Marcellus's *amici* called the senators' attention to a different previous ruling instead, which made it highly inappropriate to deny the triumph. As soon as the long-awaited word arrived in Rome via messenger that the city of Syracuse had fallen, the *patres* had taken the good news on faith, even at that distance and (more tellingly still) in Marcellus's absence declaring a period of official thanksgiving or *supplicatio,* which was then duly offered to the immortal gods in his name at altars throughout the city. The reminder that "res prospere . . . gestas" ("a successful campaign") had come about "ductu eius" ("under his leadership") served to trigger the idea that in addition to *ductus* he also possessed *imperium, auspicium,* and *felicitas,* filling out the triumphal formula.

The problem was that the *patres* themselves had set opposing precedents while Marcellus was away, and now that it came time for a final assessment,

15. Lintott 1999, 4, notes "an enormous spectrum ranging from basic unwritten laws—*ius,* even if not *scriptum*—to what one may term mere *mos,* the way things happened to be done at the time." Cf. Geertz 1983b, 173: "the 'law' side of things is not a bounded set of norms, rules, principles, values, or whatever from which jural responses to distilled events can be drawn, but part of a distinctive manner of imagining the real. At base, it is not what happened, but what happens, that law sees."

16. The same holds true for the ritual performed before the community at large: a perfectly valid triumph could still take place in the absence of soldiers to march in the procession, but the resulting spectacle would be obviously missing something and would therefore fail to impress. The triumphs of L. Furius Purpureo in 200 (31.49.2–3) and M'. Acilius Glabrio in 190 (37.46.6) both notably suffered from this memorable defect. See below, pp. 92 and n. 29, 251 and n. 13, 288 and n. 54; also cf. Itgenshorst 2005, 203–6.

17. Cf. 31.49.9–10. For an idealized description of soldiers reacting to the spectacle of their commander's triumph, in which they themselves played an integral part, see 45.38.11–13.

his *res gestae* proved far too controversial to gain unanimous approval, yet far too impressive to ignore—a genuine impasse.[18] And the longer dissent was allowed to persist within their ranks, the less comfortably it sat with them. Only at the end of the day did they manage to salvage a measure of decorum when someone finally lit upon a clever compromise (26.21.5: "medium visum") in the form of the *ovatio*. Here at last they could agree, because this offered them a means of rewarding success that still fell somewhat short of a full triumph. The same overriding concerns are paralleled on the senate floor in one triumph debate after another throughout Livy's history: to give recognition where it was due while maintaining an atmosphere, whenever possible, of unity and cooperation among the *patres* themselves.[19] Plutarch reports that Marcellus saved face by publicly agreeing to the outcome, and therefore bowing to the *auctoritas patrum*,[20] but we have already seen that he expressed his pique at being snubbed by prefacing the *ovatio* with a self-congratulatory triumph *in monte Albano* first (26.21.6). His spectacular display of booty from Syracuse (26.21.7–10) could later be singled out as a significant moment in the dangerous influx of foreign *luxuria* to Rome. Livy has Cato the Elder make direct reference to Marcellus's famous spoils in his speech in support of the sumptuary *lex Oppia* in 184 (34.4.1–3).[21]

It would seem then that his peers as a body really did not know quite what to make of Marcellus, and indeed through the rest of his career, positive assessments continued to alternate with negative ones. He man-

18. Modern scholars cannot help unmistakably echoing the fundamental ambivalence from Livy's account when issuing their own summative pronouncements. Thus J. S. Richardson 1975, 54, asserts that "the magnitude of his achievement was not in question. The argument which caused Marcellus' case to founder . . . has the air of a technicality introduced for the purpose." Then Develin 1978, 432, counters: "we can see the senate's point of view. The possibility of an army being unrepresented at its commander's triumph had not arisen before; Marcellus' words, as reported by Livy . . . indicate that he knew this was an obstacle to the granting of his request. The *ovatio* was allowed as a compromise to reward genuine (and at this time rare) success without disregarding a condition for the full triumph." And Eckstein 1987, 170, tries to balance both sides: "Yet, admitting that Marcellus' enemies had legitimate arguments at their disposal, their political success in blocking the award of a triumph for one of the greatest feats of arms in antiquity is still striking."

19. Cf. Eckstein 1987, 170–71: "In Livy's carefully constructed narrative here, the *ovatio* appears as a compromise solution (26.21.4). There seems no reason to doubt this: no *ovatio* had been granted by the senate for 150 years; someone must suddenly have come up with the idea . . . a majority of the senate were moved by the sheer fact of Marcellus' victory at Syracuse—and perhaps also sought a way to avoid further dissension."

20. Plut. *Marc.* 22.1, where the mention of a third triumph is plainly mistaken. Marcellus triumphed only twice.

21. On the evils of *luxuria* as a prominent theme in Livy's history generally, cf. *Praef.* 11–12, 39.6.7–9. Also note Plut. *Marc.* 21.1–2. Plutarch claims that the sack of Syracuse yielded as much plunder as that of Carthage (*Marc.* 19.3).

aged to win another consulship for 210, in an election marred by political maneuvering (26.22.2–15). Then Sicily was declared a consular province again, effectively ratifying the argument used to deny his triumph request: the war would continue. On top of that the arrival of a Sicilian delegation with complaints about ill treatment at his hands actually forced Marcellus to switch provinces with his colleague, giving up an opportunity to place a final seal on his victory at Syracuse (26.26.5–9, 28–29).[22] He accused his immediate successor in the province, praetor M. Cornelius Cethegus, of having engineered this further embarrassment. Another bitter and protracted dispute followed, over whether or not to ratify his *acta* and the terms of peace that he had negotiated with various cities (26.31.11–32.5). Marcellus vigorously defended the rights of a commander in the field to follow his own judgments for the good of the *res publica* (26.31.10), and this time his supporters eventually prevailed, so that despite all the lingering controversy, his decisions about how to bring the war to a close were allowed to stand, as indeed his continued conduct of the war itself had been during his extended term as proconsul.[23] According to Livy, the Sicilian envoys even issued Marcellus a very public apology and staged an elaborate reconciliation with him as their patron before going home (26.32.8).[24]

What does all this mean? Structurally, the *deportatio* question mirrored the triumph request in advance, and foreshadowed the result, thereby situating the triumph debate proper within a much broader context of push and pull between commander and senate. Marcellus himself seems to have aroused equally strong feelings of partisanship and enmity throughout his long career. Among the shifting alignments of senatorial politics, the unpredictable play of events, such as a war that dragged on longer than anyone had expected, inevitably led to compromise and innovation within the traditional framework. Marcellus's *ovatio* brings us back yet again to the paradox of the *mos maiorum*. And the story's final twist is perhaps the most telling of all: having denied him a triumph, the senate nevertheless later voted to ratify his *acta*, substantively a far more weighty decision, having a much greater impact on many people's lives and bestowing deeper and lon-

22. See also Plut. *Marc.* 23.1; and cf. Eckstein 1987, 171–73.

23. Note the remark of Eckstein 1987, 175, that "the ancient sources are unanimous in viewing the senatorial decision as a vindication of Marcellus: so Plutarch, Valerius Maximus, Cassius Dio, and the Syracusans themselves in Livy." The senate's instructions to M. Valerius Laevinus, consul in 210, that he should look after the well-being of Syracuse (26.32.6) thus reflect not a denunciation of Marcellus but respectful courtesy to the provincials, who had traveled a long way to plead their cause.

24. Cf. Plut. *Marc.* 23.6 and Val. Max. 4.1.7. Eckstein 1987, 176, concludes: "Whatever loss of *dignitas* Marcellus had suffered in the previous proceedings must have been more than balanced by this public abasement of the Syracusans before him."

ger-lasting honor. Equestrian statues of the esteemed *imperator* and patron could still be seen in city squares throughout Sicily in Cicero's time.[25] Yet in Roman terms that ultimate vindication came at a price that his rivals exacted from the general at every step of the way.

PERMUTATIONS AND LIMITS

To qualify for a triumph, a commander not only had to return home victorious but also bring back his army with him as a sign that his work in the province was complete: this stipulation arose for the first time in the heat of a political struggle ending in compromise. Although Marcellus's *ovatio* set a useful precedent for future negotiations, the senate did not make any particular effort to apply it consistently.[26] For instance, two years after taking command in Nearer Spain as praetor in 188 (38.35.2, 35.10) and following the death of his colleague in battle, L. Manlius Acidinus Fulvianus routed the Celtiberi at last near the town of Calagurris, allegedly killing twelve thousand and seizing another two thousand prisoners (39.21.6–9). He returned to Rome in 185 and went before the senate in the Temple of Bellona to request a triumph. The *patres* acknowledged the merit of his achievements, Livy says, but found no example of anyone who had triumphed without having brought back his army with him—unless, that is, he had fully pacified the province and quelled all resistance before leaving it to his successor (39.29.4). Linked explicitly to the *mos maiorum,* the *deportatio* injunction here does not appear as a hard-and-fast rule. Rather, the qualifying clause beginning with "unless" points to certain contingencies at stake in many a triumph debate, and yet again highlights the role of the senate in picking out those individual victories that were deemed final and decisive enough at the time to warrant the public attention. In a ruling very reminiscent of previous compromises, they chose to award Manlius an *ovatio* as a "middle-grade honor."[27]

After Marcellus, a would-be *triumphator* clearly felt pressure to show that he had brought the fighting in his province to an end, especially if his troops remained behind on his return. L. Furius Purpureo clinched his controversial triumph as praetor in 200 in a speech quoted earlier, in which he emphasized to the *patres* that he had put the enemy to flight, seized their camp, lifted a siege from one Roman colony, and restored freedom to

25. Cic. *Verr.* 2.4.86 (as cited by Eckstein 1987, 177).

26. As J. S. Richardson 1975, 55, observes, "there is some evidence . . . to show that this requirement . . . was neglected until it again became useful in the 180's."

27. Livy 39.29.5: "medius tamen honos, Manlio habitus ut ovans urbem iniret" ("As a middle-grade honor it was granted to Manlius to enter the city in an *ovatio*"). Cf. Degrassi 1947, 554: the notice is missing in a lacuna in the Fasti.

the citizens of another, all by winning a single battle (31.48.10–11). The senate granted Furius's request despite the fact that he had handed over command of his army to the consul Cotta, so that no soldiers returned to Rome with him (31.49.3). When Cotta himself arrived, too late to stop the triumph, he chided the *patres* for their break with precedent: they should never have put the question to a vote without the army present to vouch for what Furius had said about his victory (31.49.10). But Furius and his friends had already undermined the consul's objections by claiming that the praetor had brought peace to the province, whether the army came home with him or not. So politics and persuasion could overcome concerns about the *deportatio exercitus*.[28] In what looks implicitly like a variation on the same theme, Q. Minucius Thermus apparently met with no objections to his triumph request in 195 even though he had turned over his army in Spain to the new praetor, P. Manlius (34.10.6–7, 17.1).[29] Moreover, Thermus had left the province behind him far from pacified, even on the brink of an escalation in the war.[30]

M'. Acilius Glabrio likewise had transferred his troops to the command of L. Scipio at Ephesus in 190 (37.7.7), and the war in Asia went on for some time thereafter, to be sure, but even so Glabrio triumphed over the Aetolians and Antiochus by full consensus (37.46.2).[31] No soldiers adorned Glabrio's "otherwise splendid" triumph ("alioqui magnificus," 37.46.6). Livy's wording reveals that this celebration was missing something: for all its magnificent spectacle, it lacked the special badge of honor bestowed on the *triumphator* whose army marched behind the triumphal chariot. Soldiers who came home with their commander signaled that he had brought genuine closure to the conflict, that he could risk withdrawing his forces from the province.[32] That was why the *deportatio* argument worked against Marcellus in 211: he could not convince anyone that his *provincia* was truly *confecta*. Glabrio had apparently not encountered opposition to his triumph from the senate as Marcellus had done, but people in Rome,

28. Livy couches the result in undeniably political terms: "gratia" vs. "maiestas" (31.49.1; cited below, p. 176 n. 23).

29. Cf. Degrassi 1947, 78–79, 552–53.

30. P. Manlius was sent to Spain as *adiutor* to the consul M. Porcius Cato for the deepening conflict (33.43.5, with troop designations at 43.8).

31. Cf. Degrassi 1947, 553 (another lacuna in the fragmentary stone).

32. This calculation of risk came into play even when only the commander himself needed to leave the province, whether to preside over the elections back in Rome or to come to the aid of a colleague in trouble somewhere else. In 193, Q. Minucius Thermus informed the senate that he did not think he could afford to leave Liguria to hold the elections with the outcome of his war still in doubt (35.6.2). Cf. the senate's instructions to consuls M. Valerius Laevinus in 210 (26.32.6; cited below, p. 156 and n. 26) and C. Aurelius Cotta in 200 (31.11.2; cited below, p. 168 and n. 1).

ordinary citizens who viewed the procession, might still use the presence or absence of the army in a triumph—even one voted unanimously by the *patres*—to gauge the real success of the campaign. This could not help but reflect badly on the *triumphator.* When Cornelius and Baebius triumphed in 180 "nullo bello gesto" ("without [even] having waged a war, 40.38.9), they did at least bring their army back with them from Liguria, albeit unbloodied: the fact that they could boast of having left a *provincia pacata* behind them must have helped their triumph bid (40.38.8). A lacuna in Livy makes certainty impossible, but something akin may also have happened to M. Titinius Curvus, who triumphed from Nearer Spain in 175 although the province was reportedly at peace under his governorship (41.26.1).[33]

A commander's rivals could turn this same reasoning on its head as well: if he had left the war unfinished, they could indict his judgment in deciding to bring the army home. In his attack on Scipio Nasica in 191, treated already at some length in chapter 3, the tribune P. Sempronius Blaesus criticized the consul for having brought soldiers to Rome to grace his triumph when they should have stayed in the province. Nasica may have defeated the Boii soundly enough, but Blaesus pleaded that he should have marched straight on from his victory to help Q. Minucius Thermus wrap up the continuing struggle in Liguria (36.39.6–9). In order to press this charge, the tribune had to argue that the two conflicts were effectively one, on the apparently quite specious grounds that the Boii and the Ligures often rose to each other's defense.[34] He claimed that the fighting would not truly come to an end until both tribes surrendered together. Later, when Thermus came back to announce that he had pacified the province by himself, the senate ordered him to hand over his troops to Nasica rather than the other way around (37.2.5). Nasica triumphed (36.39.5–40.10); Thermus did not (37.46.1–2). The *deportatio* provision could thus be used against a would-be *triumphator,* or alternatively ignored, belying the notion of any rigid formula at work in triumph debates.[35]

We saw with Marcellus that the *deportatio* question also became inexorably tangled up with the problem of succession between one governor in a province and the next. As the political body charged with making the annual troop assignments, the *patres* acted as intermediaries in such

33. The notice in Livy for Curvus's actual triumph seems to have disappeared in the substantial lacuna at the beginning of Book 41; but see Degrassi 1947, 80–81, 555.

34. On the lack of cooperation between the Boii and the Ligures, see Walsh 1990, *ad loc.* (cited above, p. 80 n. 48).

35. J. S. Richardson 1975, 62, asserts: "The history of the *deportatio* provision, then, shows how it developed from what was probably its first use by Marcellus' enemies to refuse him a triumph, through a period in which it seems to have been disregarded if not ignored, and finally its resuscitation, no doubt once again to control men whom the senate thought were getting triumphs too easily."

disputes. In 184, not at all accidentally only a year after the failed triumph request of L. Manlius Acidinus, a bitter argument erupted in the senate between returning generals and newly elected magistrates over the discharge of veterans. In chapter 3 the twin triumphs of C. Calpurnius Piso and L. Quinctius Crispinus from Spain were pointed out as exceptions to the general tendency of joint campaigns to yield unequal honors (39.42.2–4). Yet even though both of them triumphed by full consensus, Piso and Crispinus still did not escape their share of controversy. The *legati* who first announced their Spanish victory in Rome asked for two things at once on their behalf: that the gods be duly thanked, and that the senate allow the army to return home. Both would signify a job well done.[36] The senate voted a two-day *supplicatio* right away, lest they disrupt the *pax deum,* but they postponed any ruling about the army for several days more, until the time should come to assign legions for the commanders newly appointed (39.38.4–6). They could probably see trouble brewing.

According to Livy the two praetors on their way to Spain, A. Terentius Varro and P. Sempronius Longus, raised a large and effective protest (39.38.8). They lobbied to keep the veteran army in the province in lieu of having to recruit whole legions from scratch.[37] Friends and family meanwhile rose in support of Piso and Crispinus. Tribunes and a consul lined up on both sides. Veto threats flew. Public business momentarily ground to a halt (39.38.9). As it turned out, backers of the absent *imperatores* simply could not prevail (39.38.10), any more than the elders had succeeded in blocking Furius's triumph in 200 without the consul Cotta there to argue his side in person (31.49.1). The senate decreed that Varro and Longus should recruit just enough reinforcements for the army to allow the discharge of only the most seasoned veterans from Spain. In a small concession to the returning commanders after what must have been a bruising political defeat, the *patres* included any soldiers who had distinguished themselves in battle among those allowed to come home (39.38.10–12). Then somehow, despite its acrimony, not to mention its obvious link to the *deportatio* provision, this dispute did not affect the unanimous vote of triumphs to both Piso and Crispinus shortly thereafter (39.42.1–4).[38]

36. Livy 39.38.5: "postularunt simul ut pro rebus tam prospere gestis dis immortalibus haberetur honos, et ut praetoribus exercitum deportare liceret" ("They asked at the same time that honor be paid to the immortal gods for a campaign greeted with such success and that the praetors be allowed to bring their army home").

37. On the periodic difficulties faced by legionary recruiters in the decades immediately following the Hannibalic War, punctuated also by episodes of plague, see Brunt 1971, 61–90, especially 73–74.

38. Nor did victory in this debate carry over into further rewards for the new praetors: Longus died in the province after a long illness (40.20.5), and Varro celebrated only an *ovatio,* not a triumph, on his return in 183 (40.16.11).

Marcellus's mercurial career has already amply demonstrated that triumph debates took place in an extremely volatile political context, amid many subtle negotiations of status among aristocrats.

A strikingly similar confrontation broke out again in 180, when we learn more about the arguments used on both sides. Q. Fulvius Flaccus sent word from Nearer Spain of a decisive pair of victories over the rebellious Celtiberi, at whose surrender he claimed to have accomplished his allotted task in the province. Invoking the familiar formulas, the *legati* from Flaccus, like those sent by Piso and Crispinus in 184, asked the senate to offer thanks to the gods for victory and to allow the *imperator* to bring his army home after many long years of service, not only to him but also to his predecessors (40.35.4–7). To this request, Livy says, they added the very real threat of mutiny among the soldiers if the veterans were not to be discharged. Then Ti. Sempronius Gracchus, the praetor newly appointed to Nearer Spain, objected that he needed experienced troops to help keep the peace that Flaccus had won. Some of the Celtiberi may have surrendered, but no one could trust them not to rebel again, especially in outlying areas of the province; once they realized that unseasoned recruits stood guard over them (40.35.10–14). In reply, the spokesmen for Flaccus declared that whatever the Celtiberi might or might not do to a successor, the soldiers had openly vowed in a *contio* with their general either to detain him in the province by force or to return with him to Italy (40.36.4–7).

By Livy's account this altercation between the incoming praetor and the *legati* from the commander in the field did not escalate, as the earlier one had done, with tribunes threatening vetoes on either side. Instead, a motion from the consuls asking the *patres* to deal first with armies for them diffused the debate by interrupting it. When the question came up again, the senate ordered Gracchus to enroll a new army and authorized the returning commander to discharge the long-term veterans and surplus troops as he had requested. They set the consulship of Sp. Postumius and Q. Marcius, in 186, as a cutoff point: any soldiers taken to Spain before that time would now be allowed to come home. Of troops recruited after 186, only those needed to fill out the number of the freshly enlisted legions would have to remain in the province (40.36.8–11). The verdict itself achieved a compromise not unlike the one from four years before, but nevertheless it struck a very different tone. As in 184, the senators again singled out the veterans of distinguished service, but this came as an honor rather than merely a concession to Flaccus (40.36.11). The *supplicatio* decreed at the same time gave further sanction to his success (40.36.12), whereas by granting one to Piso and Crispinus in 184 the *patres* had barely cushioned the blow that lay in store.

But before the commanders of 180 could put the senate's plan for their armies into practice, Flaccus met and defeated the enemy a third time.

While waiting for his successor to arrive, he led his legions out of winter quarters against the more remote Celtiberi who had not yet surrendered (40.39.1).[39] On his way from there to meet Gracchus at Tarraco, designated as the place for the discharge of veterans, the Spanish rebels assaulted his army in a narrow pass (40.39.2–6). As Livy would have it, Flaccus rallied his men against an enemy they had crushed twice already, urging them on to add further glory to the triumph that lay ahead for them in Rome (40.39.9). In a picturesque touch, Livy adds that at a crisis in the battle, the Celtiberi all but broke through the Roman line, but Flaccus's leadership saved the day. The troops openly deferred to his command and begged him to tell them what to do, behaving not at all like soldiers on the brink of mutiny (40.40.2–10). Livy's reliability has been called into question for episodes like this, emotionally moving images of loyalty and morale among Roman troops in dangerous situations.[40] But rather than automatically impugning the historian for a lapse in judgment, why not see in these elements instead the distant traces of Flaccus's own self-congratulatory narrative? When at last they reached Tarraco, Livy says, Gracchus came out to greet them and congratulated Flaccus on all his exploits. And then the two commanders, old and new, proceeded harmoniously to name the soldiers who should stay in the province and those who could now return home (40.40.14). They apparently parted in good order, with no trace of their former animosity (another motif redolent of senatorial politics), and Flaccus came back to Rome to win not only a triumph but also election as consul for the following year, no doubt largely on the strength of his *res gestae* narrative (40.40.15, 43.4–7).[41]

The same apparent caprice-within-limits that sometimes marked the outcome of triumph debates carried over to these *deportatio* battles too, ancillary though they clearly were to the triumph discussions proper, even in Marcellus's case. In 176, having taken command in Sardinia as consul the year before, Ti. Sempronius Gracchus won a series of battles in which Livy says that fifteen thousand of the enemy were killed and the rest forced to surrender. The commander sent *legati* to the senate with two by-now familiar requests: that honor be paid to the gods for his success in war, and that he be allowed to bring his army home. Meeting in the Temple of Apollo Sosianus, the *patres* declared a two-day *supplicatio* to give thanks for Gracchus's victory, but they ordered him to stay in the province with his troops for another year (41.17.1–4). We do not hear specifically how or why they came to this decision, but earlier in 176 the praetor M. Popillius

39. Gracchus of course had used these still rebellious tribes of the hinterland to warn the senate of continued danger in his speech against Flaccus (40.35.10–14).

40. See for example the scathing criticisms leveled by Walsh 1961, 157–63.

41. On Flaccus's triumph, cf. Degrassi 1947, 555.

Laenas had declined an appointment to Sardinia, on the grounds that a change of command would jeopardize the campaign already in progress there. The senate had granted Laenas's request to let Gracchus finish what he had begun (41.15.7–9). Emphasis fell upon the danger of delay from a novice commander's need to learn his way around before he could act decisively. Gracchus himself had used a related argument as praetor in 180 to justify keeping Flaccus's veteran army in Spain, lest the enemy take advantage of vulnerable new recruits (40.35.10–14).

Oddly enough, the blunt insistence that Gracchus stay in Sardinia through 176 appears to have had no ill effect on his triumph request at the end of the year.[42] Livy gives a marvelous description of the inscribed *tabula triumphalis,* in the shape of the island of Sardinia, that was set up in the Temple of Mater Matuta in 174 to commemorate Gracchus's achievement (41.28.8–10). Nor did Gracchus's colleague, C. Claudius Pulcher, face any repercussions for his triumph from the bitter and unusual dispute that broke out with his predecessors. The consuls from the year before, M. Iunius Brutus and A. Manlius Vulso, who had had their *imperium* prorogued to remain in Istria for the winter (41.6.2), scored a sudden victory in the spring, by Livy's account killing some four thousand Istrians and compelling the rest to sue for peace (41.10.1–4). Pulcher had also been assigned to Istria for 177 (41.9.8). Fearing that the other commanders might pacify the province without him, he set off at top speed in the middle of the night, with no lictors in uniform, and informing only Gracchus of his plans. When he ordered Brutus and Vulso *in contione* to leave the province at once, they refused to heed his stern rebukes, on the grounds that he had departed from Rome in an inappropriate way (41.10.5–9). Livy evokes a dramatic scene in which the furious consul had to turn back amid the jeers and laughter of the soldiers. He returned very soon, though, this time with lictors in the proper dress and legionary reinforcements behind him, and now Brutus and Vulso obeyed his command, even leaving him to take over a siege that they had begun (41.10.10–11). He went on from there to subdue not only the Istrians (41.11.3–9) but the Ligures as well (41.12.1–9).[43] His triumph (41.13.6–7)[44] celebrated the rare victory over two tribes in a single year (41.12.10).

By now it should be amply clear that many vagaries emerged in deciding what gave a commander the right to claim that he had discharged his

42. Once again notice of the triumph itself has disappeared in the lacuna at the beginning of Livy 41; but Degrassi 1947, 80–81, 555, has restored it in the text of the Fasti.

43. For his further victories in Istria, see 41.11.3–9. He wrote to the senate for permission to cross over to Liguria (41.12.1–3, 7), where victory in a major pitched battle sent the enemy fleeing to their homes (41.12.8–9).

44. Cf. Degrassi 1947, 80–81, 555.

duty and done enough to earn a triumph, particularly as Rome's military involvements spread farther and farther afield, leading to more extended engagements that did not readily admit of definitive closure. Sometimes we also hear of charges that an *imperator* went too far. When Cn. Manlius Vulso came back from Asia with eager triumph hopes in 187, two spokesmen for the *decem legati* who had worked with him on the Apamea settlement, L. Furius Purpureo and L. Aemilius Paullus, apparently tried to label his Galatian campaign as dangerous and unsanctioned by the senate and Roman people. Instead of pursuing peace with Antiochus, they said, Vulso had eagerly sought an excuse from the beginning to cross the Taurus in arms. They claimed he had acted purely out of self-interest, far overstepped the bounds of his lawful *imperium,* and set off without the proper fetial procedures on what amounted to a personal, undeclared, and opportunistic war (38.45.1–7).[45] These charges against Vulso sparked a confrontation so heated that it lasted into a second day, one of only three instances from Books 21–45 where Livy mentions the arrival of nightfall as a significant factor in a triumph debate.[46] In this case the historian actually credits the eventual outcome to the fact that the senators went home overnight and had a chance to mull things over before the final vote (38.50.1–3). Several factors meanwhile helped to fuel the peculiar vehemence of the dispute, including a personal grievance apparently felt by Furius and Paullus against the commander for the death of their colleague Q. Minucius Thermus (38.46.7), which shall gain further significance in chapter 5 from the discussion of Roman casualties as a recurring element in triumph debates.

Vulso also lay somewhat vulnerable to political attack because of the way he had come to acquire his province in the first place. The *patres* had originally meant for one of the consuls in 189 to take over L. Scipio's army in Asia and carry on with the war against Antiochus, already in progress. That lot fell to Vulso (37.50.2–3).[47] Then suddenly word reached Rome

45. The rhetorical embellishments are clearly Livy's own, and a number of the specific allegations against Vulso cited in this passage have been dismissed as "annalistic fiction" (Walsh 1993, *ad loc.*), but the central crux of the argument about the justification for the war against the Galatians cannot be dismissed quite so easily: "Clearly a majority of the ten commissioners . . . favored a more conciliatory approach to Antiochus' former allies; Volso on the other hand emerges as a hawk eager to impose a settlement through military prowess and martial glory" (ibid.).

46. The other two triumph debates where Livy says that the arguments dragged on into a second day involve C. Cornelius Cethegus and Q. Minucius Rufus in 197 (33.22.10) and L. Aemilius Paullus in 167 (45.36.1–2).

47. Note the comments of Walsh 1992, *ad loc.*: "While anti-Scipionic sentiment may have played its part in the replacement of the commander, the ambition for military glory of the new officials must also have been important." Both *invidia* and *ambitio* (to use the Latin terms for Walsh's characterization of the two sides of this story) fall under the purview of *existimatio,* for the *patres* were always faced with a balancing act between various factions and interests.

that Asiaticus had crushed the king's forces in the battle at Magnesia (37.51.8–52.2). Scipio might well have hoped that the senate would now allow him to stay in the province and hammer out a peace settlement pursuant on his victory, as T. Quinctius Flamininus had done after Cynoscephalae in 196, but instead they recalled him at once and put Vulso in charge of the negotiations—another prime example of their recurring anxiety over giving too much headway to the Scipios. Meanwhile they also kept the new consul in command of the veteran army, citing fear of the Galatians, who had backed the Seleucid cause (37.51.10).[48]

That opened the door to Vulso, and of course he immediately leaped at the chance to test himself on the battlefield. Since Livy's narrative pointedly skips from broad hints of a possible conflict ahead in the region (37.60.2) to the scene of the consul enthusiastically rousing his troops for battle (38.12.3), there is no record that the senate and people ever did officially vote to authorize the Galatian campaign. Then again, one would do well here to draw another lesson here from Marcellus at Syracuse: a commander in the field, especially someplace far from Rome as Asia most certainly was, had a very wide berth to pursue any *hostes* whom he himself could identify within his *provincia*.[49] In a largely ad-hoc political maneuver against L. Scipio, the senate had shipped Vulso off to Asia fully armed but with only a vague and general mandate. He would naturally try to capitalize on any opportunity to make a name for himself, but when he eventually came back full of proud stories about his *res gestae,* his political enemies could seek to turn the supposed terms of the original provincial assignment against him.

The parallel with Marcellus in 211 is again revealing: whereas Marcellus's critics had tried to broaden the notional boundaries of his *provincia* in order to prove that he had not completed his assigned task, Vulso's adversaries did exactly the opposite, hoping by a more restrictive definition of his powers to prove that he had overstepped his bounds.[50] A question of mandate in different circumstances during the Gallic emergency of

48. Walsh 1992, *ad loc.*, calls Livy's attribution of motive in this passage "*post hoc* reasoning," because the senate could not have anticipated a threat from the Galatians before Antiochus had even surrendered. On Flamininus put in charge of peace negotiations with Philip of Macedon (by direct intervention of tribunes on his behalf), see 33.25.5–8. For the anti-Scipionic bias of the senate's decision in 189, note also Gruen 1995, 69.

49. Eckstein 1987 obviously does not carry his argument forward into the 180s, but it certainly applies to Vulso every bit as much as to Marcellus three decades before. Cf. Rich 1993, 56: "War decisions which were reached when a Roman army was already in the field were generally taken by the army commander."

50. Cf. Rich 1993, 57: "Some commanders were criticized at the time for beginning war without due cause and the fiction that wars required the consent of the people was sometimes exploited to add to their discomfiture." He then cites Vulso as a prime example of this latter phenomenon.

200 had almost scuttled the triumph hopes of then-praetor L. Furius Purpureo—ironically the same Furius who years later would stand up against Vulso from the other side. Defending his triumph bid, according to Livy, Vulso claimed that the Galatians had actually declared war on Rome, rather than the other way around, when they had chosen to fight against L. Scipio in the army of Antiochus. In other words, he merely finished what Asiaticus had begun (38.48.6–10).

Having made this point, Livy says, Vulso then effectively shifted the grounds of the discussion, exactly as Furius had also done and Marcellus likewise had tried to do, toward the indisputable outcome of his *res gestae:* with the surrender of the Galatians, the whole region west of the Taurus now lay more at peace than Italy itself (38.47.6). His supporters followed through on this line of argument, as the second day of deliberations wore on, to win him a triumph in the end, over the objections of the *decem legati* (38.50.1–3).[51] Insisting that Rome would have beaten Antiochus in vain without the overthrow of the Galatians as well (38.47.13), Vulso echoed what the tribune Blaesus had said in opposition to Scipio Nasica in 191 about the Boii and the Ligures (36.39.6–9). The question of mandate loomed large for Nasica too. Nor apparently did the idea that one conflict followed the other spring up suddenly during the triumph debate. According to Livy, Vulso first announced the Galatian campaign to his troops specifically as an outgrowth of the war against Antiochus. When he took command at Ephesus, the soldiers gladly embraced their next mission at word that the conquest of the Galatians would allow them now to seal their hard-won success (38.12.4–5). Such reasoning would never have helped Vulso on the senate floor in 187 if the *patres* felt genuinely bound by a narrow code of triumph requirements, because two years before they had already awarded Asiaticus a triumph for the decisive defeat of Antiochus *and all his forces in Asia* (37.59.1). The war could hardly have been both finished and unfinished at the same time.

The complaints of the *decem legati* did not ultimately cost Vulso his triumph. His mandate was judged sufficient so that in the end the results could speak for themselves. Yet a magistrate who took it upon himself to wage war without appropriately pausing to consult the common interest might upset the whole fragile balance of power between the Roman state and commanders in the field. A pivotal moment in the career of Scipio Africanus provides an interesting example. After Scipio's overwhelming success in driving the Carthaginians out of Spain, he was elected consul for 205 to finish the war against Hannibal. The people were pinning all their hopes for an end to that dreadful conflict on him (28.38.7–10), and

51. Cf. Degrassi 1947, 80–81, 554.

Scipio vowed that he would push the fighting out of Italy onto African soil by popular mandate even over the wishes of the senate (28.40.1). Always a voice for caution and restraint, his bitter rival Q. Fabius Maximus rallied the elder senators against the consul with the allegation that Scipio would sacrifice the public good in pursuit of his own private ends (28.42.22). The senators preferred Fabius's long-acknowledged *auctoritas* and *prudentia* to the *animus ferox* ("savage mind") of the brazen youth Scipio (28.43.1). When asked point-blank by the prominent senator Q. Fulvius Flaccus whether he would abide by the senate's designation of his province or put a motion before the assembly, Scipio refused to back down and answered merely that he would do what was best for Rome (28.45.2–3).

His reply spoke to the public interest, but nevertheless he remained in defiance of the senate. One is reminded again of Marcellus's triumph *in monte Albano* in 211. At this point Flaccus announced that he would withhold his vote, with the threat of a tribunician veto behind him, until the consul should publicly defer to the will of the *patres* (28.45.4–7). Matters stood thus at an impasse after the first day, just as in the debate over Vulso's triumph. It was only the next day, after conferring with his colleague, that Scipio agreed at last to bow to the senate's decree. The senators in turn authorized him to cross over from Sicily to Africa if the interests of the Republic should demand it (28.45.8), and when the time for the crossing eventually came, in 203, they called for a *supplicatio* that all might go well for the Roman people, the commander, and his army (30.1.11). In 190 likewise, since the successor to M'. Acilius Glabrio in Greece would have to pursue Antiochus farther east, the senate scrupulously gave L. Scipio, brother of Africanus, the right to cross the Hellespont into Asia should he see fit (37.2.3). Then at news that the *imperator* had passed that fabled threshold, the first Roman commander ever to do so, the *patres* again decreed a day of *supplicatio* in Rome (37.47.4–5).

Unlike Vulso, both Scipio brothers set off on their campaigns with explicit orders from the senate, but the contrast does not mean that an ironclad procedure was somehow mysteriously overlooked in the allotment of provinces for 189. The new election of magistrates for each new year meant a full-scale review of provincial assignments every single time. Sometimes the *patres* chose to designate specific *hostes;* sometimes not. Africanus obviously won his mandate in 205 only through a political showdown; he first had to negotiate a settlement, publicly, with Fabius and the elder senators. He also secured the assignment to Greece for L. Scipio over C. Laelius in 190 by promising to serve as his brother's *legatus* if the senate would grant the province to him rather than to his colleague (37.1.7–10).[52] Permission

52. Livy is quite explicit about the key role played by L. Scipio's famous (or infamous) elder brother in getting him elected in the first place: "elections were held in Rome, in which

to cross the Hellespont did not come automatically to Asiaticus either, but as an afterthought to the original appointment (37.2.3).[53] Moreover, despite the fact that Vulso's opponents were able score political points against him with allegations that he had acted on his own, open senate approval at the start certainly did not spare either Publius or Lucius from later controversies, as the famous, albeit mysterious, so-called trials of the Scipios make abundantly clear.

SUMMARY

The *patres* had control over authorizing the return of veterans as well as the recruitment of new legionaries. Manpower issues played a role, but so did political considerations. Reference to the *deportatio exercitus* is inevitably tied to the question of mandate. Partly on account of practical concerns such as the difficulty of rapid communication across long distances, an *imperator* had broad authority within his *provincia* to conduct operations where, when, and even against whom he should see fit. On his return, however, he was subject to the approval or disapproval of his peers in the senate, both on the question of civic honors and for the ratification of his *acta.* Either of these could arouse dissension and debate, and provide an opportunity for a commander's *inimici* to attack his *dignitas.* Marcellus in 211 stands as a fascinating example, because he came up short in the first struggle, over his triumph, only to win the second and more important one, over his *acta.* These debates had as much to do with the status and prestige of individual aristocrats as they did with rules and technicalities.

EPILOGUE

In the early second century T. Quinctius Flamininus, M'. Acilius Glabrio, L. Cornelius Scipio Asiaticus, and Cn. Manlius Vulso all waged extravagantly lucrative campaigns in the Greek East, one after the other. Yet although all four of these illustrious commanders celebrated fabulous triumphs, still none of them could escape the political backlash: Flamininus over his prorogations from 197 to 195, Glabrio from Cato in the censorial elections for 189, Asiaticus on public trial in 187, and Vulso with the *decem legati* the

L. Cornelius Scipo and C. Laelius were made consuls—with everyone looking to Africanus to finish the war with Antiochus" ("comitia Romae habita, quibus creati sunt consules L. Cornelius Scipio et C. Laelius—Africanum intuentibus cunctis—ad finiendum cum Antiocho bellum," 36.45.9). Note also the remarks of Walsh 1992, *ad loc.*

53. As Walsh 1992, *ad loc.*, is quick to remark, Livy's wording "suggests that there was no definite strategy for an offensive in Asia; the senate's overriding concern was to secure Greece against the Aetolia-Antiochus alliance."

same year.[54] The issues that keep recurring in these triumph debates—the chain of command, the scope of the conflict, the number of Roman casualties compared to those suffered by the enemy, the extent of control each commander should have in the field over how, when, and with whom to fight, and the definition of closure for an extended military engagement—reflect the intensity of aristocratic competition in Rome. Even in the heady aftermath of Zama, we can see a degree of indeterminacy in the modus operandi between senate and general as the Republic began to take an ever more prominent role in the larger Mediterranean world. Eckstein speaks thus of an earlier phase of Roman history, although the observation remains equally valid later on: "Not only does much Roman decision making in foreign relations . . . appear ad hoc and improvised, but the institutional structures producing such decisions seem to have been remarkably diffuse and decentralized, even primitive. In other words, Roman senatorial government, and the Roman people with it, simply 'muddled through.'"[55]

This observation about the nature of the *res publica* as a political system, harking back to everything already said about the informal, unwritten rules enshrined as *mos maiorum*, has obvious and profound repercussions for the interpretation of Livy's triumph debates. Conquest held the promise of inestimable wealth as well as military glory for individual commanders and for the state as a whole. It also meant terrible risks, not only with the loss of Roman lives on battlefields abroad but in the threat that the achievements of great individuals posed at home to the balance of status and *auctoritas* within the ranks of the ruling élite. Above all, amid uncertainty the *patres* took it as their collective task to keep the rewards of excellence in well-regulated but continual circulation.[56]

54. For the struggle to keep Flamininus in the East year after year, see 32.28.3–9, 33.25.11, and 33.43.6, as well as Polyb. 18.18–27 and Plut. *Flam.* 7.1–2. On Flamininus's family and political connections, see Badian 1971. For Cato's allegations that Glabrio had withheld booty from his triumph, see 37.57.9–58.1, with the comments of Walsh 1992, *ad loc.* Also note Shatzman 1972. On the trial of L. Scipio and related events, see Gruen 1995, with ample citation of primary sources; and for an analysis of all these disputes in a broad historical context, see Gruen 1984a, 203–49.

55. Eckstein 1987, xxii.

56. Gruen 1995, 65, writes that they were "apparently groping for ways to control the hunt for martial honors without discouraging the hunt itself—a quest in which every individual *nobilis* had a stake."

CHAPTER 5

Body Counts; or, Who Killed Whom

Throughout the previous pages, any casualty statistics cited from the *Ab Urbe Condita* have appeared carefully qualified with phrases such as "according to Livy" or "Livy says." Such tallies obviously enjoy a prominent place in debates over triumphs and the victory announcements leading up to them, yet they are notoriously unreliable. Numerals suffer disproportionately from textual corruption.[1] Ancient authors also tend to report large numbers in conventionally imprecise forms such as powers of ten or multiples of three, forty, and so forth.[2] Worst of all, Livy repeatedly complains about the wildly exaggerated figures given by his sources—especially Valerius Antias—for the number of enemies slain in battle. Modern scholars justifiably blame the early annalists for committing such errors, and Livy as well, for perpetuating them.[3] Writers of history fall prone to flights of fancy, overactive imaginations, national bias or chauvinism, and stylistic concerns like a desire to heighten drama. Yet the urge to make Roman victories look as grand and impressive as possible surely predates even the earliest

1. Reynolds and Wilson 1974, 201, 203. On confusion caused by the abbreviated numerals typically used in manuscripts, see Thompson 1966, 104–6; and Ullman 1980, 189–95.

2. Thus Scheidel 1996.

3. On exaggerations perpetrated by Valerius Antias, see, e.g., 3.5.11–13, 26.49, 30.19.11, 33.10.7–10, 36.38.6–7, 38.23.8 (where Livy implies that he does not trust Claudius Quadrigarius much either). For a typically sweeping modern indictment, see Walsh 1990, 8: "the accounts of the late annalists . . . [represent] a combination of patriotic bias and moralising distortion, compounded by errors of chronology and above all irresponsible fabrication of battle figures." The same author's commentaries on Livy 36–40 (Walsh 1990, 1992, 1993, 1994, 1996) are full of similarly derogative observations about virtually every battle report. Cf. also Walsh 1961, 120–21, 144–45; and note the pointed comments of Brunt 1971, 695, with reference to "the enormity and precision of [Antias's] inventions."

written histories: we must ultimately look to the habits of the would-be *triumphatores* themselves.[4]

Roman generals admittedly never had access to reliable figures in the first place. Before a battle, scouts could only estimate the numerical strength of the enemy; nor did the chaos afterwards lend itself to the compilation of accurate body counts on either side. To make matters worse, as one scholar has written, "because Saul slew his thousands and David his tens of thousands, David was the better man."[5] Returning commanders, needing to impress a difficult audience in the senate, would enumerate their achievements at length and no doubt stretched the truth sometimes. Their goal was to make *dignitas,* otherwise a slippery concept, quantifiable. That was how the system worked, and the fact that everyone knew it did nothing to stifle the impulse to exaggerate. Often enough the bragging paid off, and blatantly self-aggrandizing reports gained a measure of public sanction through triumphs celebrated in their honor. By the same token, statistics could illustrate failure as well as success: critics often cited numbers to deflate puffed-up claims or to offset the tallies of enemy dead by focusing attention on Roman casualties instead. Even today, the public welcomes news of victory with muted enthusiasm when it comes at too high a price. Narratives marked by all these familiar patterns of distortion helped to shape collective memory and eventually filtered their way into the historical record.

Military historians must proceed with extreme caution when dealing with Livy's casualty figures, then, but in the present discussion the unreliability of the numbers can paradoxically help to prove the point. When viewed as a political and cultural artifact rather than as a guide for reconstructing how a battle was actually fought, even the most wildly exaggerated historical account reveals characteristically Roman ways of thinking. Quantitative assessments of commanders and their *res gestae* are never disinterested and bear unmistakable signs, albeit at many removes, of aristocratic competition at work.

BLOOD TELLS, FOR OR AGAINST

When announcing his victory to the people at home, every would-be *triumphator* sought to maximize the impact of what he had done. Such

4. Thus Hoyos 2001, 90: "The battle-report was a favourite fantasy ground for Roman annalists who . . . could multiply losses and claim earth-shattering significance over and over. Yet several battles . . . look not like pure inventions but like fights of one kind or other that have been magnified into major coups of glory for one or both *imperatores.*" Cf. Oakley 1997–98, 2.189–90.

5. So Brunt 1971, 694, adding that "a general was always inclined to magnify the slaughter he had inflicted."

self-congratulatory stories simultaneously enhanced the reputations of generals in the field and inspired patriotism in their Roman audience. To choose an illustration, when *legati* from L. Aemilius Paullus arrived in Rome with official news of the battle at Pydna in 167, the final crushing defeat of the dreaded Macedonian phalanx, their ceremonious and long-awaited proclamation, made first in the senate and then *in contione* to the assembled citizens, dwelt on the sheer scope of the victory: "how great in number the forces of the king had been, foot soldiers and cavalry, how many thousands of these had been killed, how many captured, with the loss of how few [Roman] soldiers so great a slaughter of the enemy had been accomplished, with how few followers the king had fled."[6] The form of this announcement gives expression to a basic human understanding central to all triumph debates, and one that is inherently quantitative: *magnitudo rerum gestarum* ("the scale of the accomplishments").[7] An exuberant outpouring of joy and civic pride naturally followed, as the whole city eagerly awaited Paullus's triumphant return (45.2.6–7).

Statistics deftly deployed could easily turn the tide in a triumph debate, either in the general's favor or against him. The extant portions of Livy's history are full of examples.[8] Notably, as already discussed, the praetor L. Furius Purpureo encapsulated the tale of his exploits in order to vouch for the caliber of his Gallic victory in 200 (31.48.11). Likewise, even when he knew he could not entertain any hope of a triumph award, Scipio (later Africanus) in 206 still catalogued for the *patres* how many pitched battles he had fought, how many towns he had captured, how many tribes had surrendered, how many Carthaginian leaders he had defeated (28.38.2–3). His kinsman Scipio Nasica justified a triumph request in 191 under political fire by claiming to have fought and killed more Gauls in a single battle than any *imperator* in history (36.40.4.) So too in 189 the praetor L. Aemilius Regillus, in charge of the navy for the war against Antiochus, gave the senate an account of the total number of ships in the enemy fleet, the number sunk, and the number captured, before being awarded a naval triumph by full consensus (37.58.3).[9] Cn. Manlius Vulso proudly stated in

6. 45.2.4–5: "tantum temporis retenti dum exponerent, quantae regiae <copiae> peditum equitumque fuissent, quot milia ex his caesa quot capta forent, quam paucorum militum iactura tanta hostium strages facta, †quam pauci† rex fugisset." This passage is also cited below, p. 248 and n. 6. I have done my best when translating to cope with the impossible crux in the manuscript text. On the phrase "paucorum militum iactura" and others like it, see below, p. 111 n. 20.

7. Any reference in Livy or elsewhere to *magna* or *levia proelia* or a *magna victoria* (or the like) points in the same direction.

8. Traces of triumphal discourse in the form of battle statistics may be found throughout extant Livy, of course, not only in the later books. Among triumph notices from the First Decade, note, e.g., 2.16.9, 3.8.10, 6.47.7, 7.17.8, 9.45.17, and 10.37.3.

9. Note the remark by Walsh 1992, *ad loc.*, that Regillus's "record was hardly deserving of a triumph."

187 that he had fought pitched battles with hosts of Galatians several times, had captured or killed thousands of them, seized two camps, and left the entire province at peace (38.47.6).

According to Livy the opponents of L. Cornelius Scipio Asiaticus in 189 labeled the war he had fought as far more serious in reputation than in reality: a single pitched battle, they said, little more than an afterthought to the greater victory of M'. Acilius Glabrio at Thermopylae the year before. To fend off this attack, Africanus's brother had to assert the magnitude of his achievements by reminding the senate of the total forces Antiochus had amassed from all of Asia against his army (37.58.7–8).[10] In 188 the praetor Q. Fabius Labeo, commanding ships off the island of Crete, apparently heard allegations from his rivals that he had never even encountered the enemy. The arguments from this debate have survived in Livy only as an exemplum in a speech of Cn. Manlius Vulso defending his own triumph request in 187 (38.47.5–6). Labeo's supporters rallied to his defense, no doubt with ample testimonials to the scale of his achievements, and in the end the *patres* united as a body to outweigh a tribunician veto and voted him a naval triumph after all (37.60.6). Similarly, in 187, when the consul M. Aemilius Lepidus wanted to scuttle hopes of an Aetolian triumph for M. Fulvius Nobilior, he passed his decree through the senate to the effect that Ambracia had not been taken by force (38.44.6). For all his perseverance, as we know, Lepidus did not manage to block Nobilior's triumph either. As proof that he had in fact fought his way into Ambracia, Nobilior sketched the story of the siege, culminating in a sizable Aetolian death toll (39.4.9–10).

The consul Q. Minucius Rufus in 197 had to settle for a triumph *in monte Albano,* as we have seen, because two tribunes charged him with having fought only minor skirmishes against the Ligures (33.22.7),[11] and with having concocted false tales of surrendered towns to better his hopes for a triumph that he did not deserve (33.22.9). The tribunes seem to have based their strategy on the knowledge that generals often used the sheer number of enemy dead to awe the senate into awarding a triumph, rightfully earned or not. In addition, losses inflicted on the enemies of the Republic had to be

10. Note the historian's partisan contrast between the allegations against L. Scipio ("erant qui . . . interpretarentur," "there were those who understood," 37.58.7) and the arguments cited in his defense ("ceterum vere aestimanti," "but to someone making an accurate assessment," 37.58.8). Walsh 1992, *ad loc.*, calls this "one of his rare personal observations to challenge the criticism of the anti-Scipionic faction." Yet the fact that Livy makes his bias plain does not mean that he necessarily invented the allegation and counterargument, both of which fit so comfortably into their context as to suggest that they may well date back to the triumph debate itself or to contemporary discussions about it (or both).

11. Livy's "levia proelia, vix digna dictu" ("lightweight battles, hardly worth mentioning") at 33.22.7 must be where Dorey et al. 1972, *ad loc.* (as cited above, p. 78 n. 38), got their idea that Minucius's triumph was denied mainly because "he had not won a pitched battle."

balanced against deaths on the Roman side of the ledger. While belittling his accomplishments, the tribunes simultaneously condemned Minucius for having killed many of his own soldiers in the process (33.22.7). Two factors, minor victories coupled with major Roman casualties, compounded against Minucius's claim to a triumph.[12] As a poignant reminder of the individuals behind all the anonymous casualty figures, we learn the names of the military tribunes T. Iuventius and Cn. Ligurius from the Fourth Legion, who died "in the defeat with many other brave men, citizens and allies" under Minucius's command (33.22.8).[13] Livy clearly did not make up these names: he found them in his sources, piously preserved as they had been recited on the senate floor. Not even his colleague could salvage a triumph for Minucius under such pressure. The *patres* united against him, and he triumphed only *in monte Albano* (33.23.3).

In 193, during the war of conquest in Cisalpine Gaul, the consul L. Cornelius Merula vanquished the Boii in a major pitched battle near Mutina, which by Livy's statistics left fourteen thousand Boii dead and another 1,092 captured alive (35.4.5–5.13). His letter proclaiming the victory sparked a controversy among the *patres,* because the *legatus* M. Claudius Marcellus had also written privately to a number of senators with a much less rosy version of events (35.6.1). He declared that this success against the Boii belonged to the fortune of the Roman people and to the bravery of the soldiers, not to the consul, whose bungling had needlessly cost many Roman lives and allowed the enemy to escape as well (35.6.9–10). More than five thousand Romans and allies had perished in Merula's far from bloodless victory, including twenty-three centurions, four *praefecti socium,* and the military tribunes Q. and M. Marcius and M. Genucius, singled out by name among the victims (35.5.14). Once again the names ring poignantly true. Why would Livy invent them? The senate, faced with such conflicting reports, did not vote a *supplicatio* for the battle, but postponed debate on the subject (35.7.1), until at the end of the year the consul left his army under the charge of the very same *legatus* who was working against him, and returned himself to Rome to hold the elections (35.8.1–3).[14]

Merula first recounted his deeds of valor, which had brought peace

12. Labeo and Afranius were arguing essentially that Minucius should never have requested a triumph at all. Compare the case of C. Flaminius from Nearer Spain in 193. He certainly never approached the senate in hopes of a reward, because he knew that he had fought minor skirmishes with major losses as well (35.7.7).

13. 33.22.8: "adversa pugna cum multis aliis viris fortibus, civibus ac sociis, cecidisse."

14. The other consul, Q. Minucius Thermus, in command against the Ligures (34.55.5), was originally supposed to hold the elections, but when the time drew near he wrote back to the *patres* that he could not afford to leave his province with the outcome of his war still in doubt. He asked the senate to send for his colleague in his stead, and Merula agreed (35.6.2–7).

to the province, and chided the *patres* for their failure to thank the gods at the first news of so great a victory. Then he asked them in person to decree both a *supplicatio* and a triumph at once. They did not. Before the matter even came to a vote, Livy says, the prominent senator Q. Caecilius Metellus stood up and explained to the consul that his *legatus* had written to tell them a very different story (35.8.3–4). Knowing this, he should have brought Marcellus back to Rome with him so that the senate could hear both sides before making a decision; by coming alone he appeared to be hiding from the truth. Besides, he should have left someone with *imperium* in command of the army rather than Marcellus, who had none (35.8.5–7).[15] Metellus urged the senators to deny the consul's requests. When Merula continued to press both his demands, for a *supplicatio* and a triumph, the tribunes M. and C. Titinius announced that they would veto any decree from the senate, and the matter was dropped (35.8.8–9). No one tried to override the veto. By Livy's account the hostile Marcellus had succeeded in dividing the senators against his rival. Having defeated the Boii at arms, then, Merula still lost the political battle in Rome, proving that an *imperator* seeking a triumph could meet with trouble if his victory came at too high a price in Roman blood.

In 187 the triumph request by Cn. Manlius Vulso for his victory over the Galatians in Asia ran into stiff opposition from L. Furius Purpureo and L. Aemilius Paullus, spokesmen for the *decem legati* who had worked with him on the Peace of Apamea (38.44.10–11). Some of their arguments echo complaints raised against Merula five years before. Vulso, they said, owed victory in his reckless campaign far more to luck than to skill (38.46.4). Indeed he had almost lost everything in a surprise assault by the Thracians. Many brave men had fallen there on the Roman side, including one of their number, Q. Minucius Thermus (38.46.7). The far from subtle implication that Vulso had put Furius and Paullus at grave peril themselves surely lent added weight to their arguments (38.46.6). Apparently the Thracians had reduced the Roman army (and the *legati* along with them) to confusion and flight, common markers in Livy's narrative for ignominious defeat. These allegations sparked a long and heated dispute, in which the *imperator* claimed that he deserved to triumph precisely because he had taken bold risks against overwhelming odds and succeeded.[16] He could never have stopped Thracian brigands from lying

15. One is reminded of similar risks taken by C. Claudius Nero in 207, who left his camp under the control of a mere *legatus* so that he could travel north to help his colleague meet Hasdrubal's onslaught.

16. Brunt 1971, 695, remarks: "Romans were proud of their heroism in retrieving disasters; the greater the disasters, the more admirable was their recovery; '*tantae molis erat* . . .'" The last three words are, of course, a quotation from Vergil's *Aeneid* (1.33).

in ambush for his troops, any more than he could have saved the life of the wounded Thermus (38.49.7–8). As regrettable as the loss of such a noble and stalwart citizen must certainly be, Vulso urged the senate not to let it overshadow the joyous victory under his command (38.49.9–12). The *patres* did not vote for the triumph until the second day of deliberations, as remarked in the previous chapter, and then only under intense pressure from the *imperator*'s friends and relatives (38.50.1–3). Politics, not rigid policy, allowed Vulso to do what Merula had not.

In one of the many ironies that seem to typify triumphal politics, there is reason to believe that the same L. Aemilius Paullus who helped to launch the attack against Vulso's bid in 187 may have missed out on a triumph of his own two years before. In 189 Paullus, a prorogued praetor on his way back from Nearer Spain, scored a major victory in a pitched battle with the Lusitani, where Livy reports eighteen thousand killed, twenty-three hundred captured, and the enemy camp destroyed (37.57.5–6). The *patres* in Rome decreed a *supplicatio* to give thanks for Paullus's victory, almost always a harbinger of *triumphi spes* (37.58.5). Yet then the narrative falls silent about any award of honors. An alternative tradition does imply that Paullus triumphed three times (i.e., 189, 181, 167), but the Fasti contradict this. It seems more likely that he was proclaimed *imperator* three times but did not triumph in 189.[17] If Livy's silence implies that in fact he did not even make the request, one wonders whether perhaps he chose not to pursue civic honors because of the political fallout from another engagement with the same tribe the previous year, when six thousand had been killed on the Roman side, his own camp barely defended, and his army forced to beat a retreat (37.45.7–9).

Right at the center of these controversies often echo the portentous words at 35.5.14: "nec Romanis incruenta victoria fuit" ("nor for the Romans was it a bloodless victory"). Variations of this formula appear a total of sixteen times in the extant portions of Livy's history, always referring to casualties on the Roman side, often marked by "Romanis" in the dative case, and almost exclusively in litotes with "non," "nec," or "haud" alongside enemy death tolls after a battle to mark the high price of conquest.[18] Livy uses the

17. The *elogia* from the Fornix Fabianus state that Paullus "ter triumphavit" ("triumphed three times"): see Degrassi 1937, n. 71; and cf. Vell. Pat. 1.9.3. However, the word *ter* ("three times") appearing over a trophy on certain of Paullus's coins suggests the *imperatoris appellatio* instead. There is a lacuna in the Fasti where a triumph by Paullus in 181 would have appeared, but space is limited, and more significantly the extant notice for his triumph in 167 clearly calls that celebration his second, making the triumph in 181 (also attested at 40.34.7) his first. For a full discussion, see Degrassi 1947, 553–54, 556; and cf. Broughton 1951, 362. Note also the remark of Reiter 1988, 147 n. 15, that the notices of Paullus's supposed Spanish triumph "are quite late and just as false."

18. The formula appears at 2.31.6, 4.17.8, 7.8.7, 9.12.3, 10.29.18, 21.29.4, 27.14.14, 27.49.7, 30.18.14, 35.5.14, 37.16.12, 40.32.7, 42.7.10, and 42.66.10. Note also "minus cruenta

phrase more than any other ancient author, but he clearly did not invent it. Nor, more than likely, did the earlier historians on whom he relied, although he may indeed have learned it from them: the assessment of gains and losses encapsulated within this formula ties its probable origins to real triumph debates.[19] Commenting on a victory by Q. Fulvius Flaccus in 180, Livy remarks (40.32.7): "magna victoria, non tamen incruenta fuit" ("it was a great victory, but still not a bloodless one"). He thus draws a striking contrast between the kind of resounding success on the one hand ("magna victoria") that the *patres* customarily rewarded with the vote of a *supplicatio* (e.g., 30.22.1, referring to the battle won by L. Furius Purpureo) and on the other hand the doubts immediately raised in everyone's mind by heavy Roman casualties ("non tamen incruenta"). Sometimes Livy also uses the phrase *iactura militum* ("the loss [literally, "throwing away"] of soldiers") in similar contexts.[20] Further, we have seen more than once already in this

---

victoria fuisset" ("the victory would have been less bloody") at 28.34.2, and *cruenta victoria* by itself at 39.31.16, a clear indictment of the commander with reference to his public image. Also cf. *Per.* 38.11.

19. To label expressions like this as "staple clichés" of Roman annalistic writing without further comment (see, e.g., Walsh 1992 on 37.16.12) not only implies that any passage where such elements appear is both unreliable and uninteresting but also misses the point about where the repertoire of stock phrases probably came from and how (or why) it developed. Clichés usually have recognizable historical origins that can help to reveal the mindset of the people who use them. The earliest example of the litotes *nec incruenta victoria* that I can find is Sall. *Cat.* 61.7: "neque tamen exercitus populi Romani laetam aut incruentam victoriam adeptus erat" ("yet the army of the Roman people obtained a victory neither joyous nor bloodless"). The phrase also appears in Tac. *Agr.* 17.2; *Hist.* 2.15, 2.44, 3.8; *Ann.* 2.18; Gell. 5.6.22; Curt. 4.6.30; Flor. 1.12, 1.41; Fronto 2.3; Quint. *Decl. Min.* 272.12.4, 348.7.3. For *incruenta* ("bloodless") meaning "peaceful" without the double negative, see Tac. *Hist.* 1.29, 3.66; *Ann.* 2.46, 12.46, 13.37; Col. 9.9.7; Flor. 2.11. 2.13; Fronto 2.15; Sen. *Clem.* 1.11.3. Also note the chilling reference to *pax cruenta* ("blood-soaked peace") at Tac. *Ann.* 1.10.

20. For the phrase *iactura militum* or *militum iactura* on its own, referring to significant Roman losses, see 35.51.5, 37.12.7; cf. 22.8.2 ("equitum iacturam," "the loss of horsemen"), 22.61.3 ("tot iactura civium," "the loss of so many citizens"). Minimal casualties are often noted thus: "parva iactura" ("a small loss"), 4.32.2; "minus centum militum iactura" ("the loss of fewer than a hundred soldiers"), 23.36.1; "sine ulla militum iactura" ("without any loss of soldiers"), 38.48.15; "paucorum militum iactura" ("with the loss of [*sc.* only] a few soldiers"), 45.2.5. Cf. "unius iactura civis" ("the loss of one citizen"), 6.19.2. Double negatives occur as well: "proelia . . . nec sine iactura militum facta" ("battles . . . brought about not without a loss of soldiers "), 35.7.7; "victoria non sine iactura militum fuit" ("the victory was not without the loss of soldiers"), 40.40.12. Further examples of cost-benefit analysis can be found at 7.8.7 ("haud minus iacturae," "no less a loss"), 10.45.10 ("cum maiore sua quam hostium iactura," "with a greater loss to himself than to the enemy"), 21.59.9 ("maior Romanis quam pro numero iactura fuit," "it was a greater loss for the Romans than according to the number"), 25.1.4 ("minimum iacturae," "a minimal loss"), and 30.25.8 ("navis tantum iactura," "the loss of a ship only," balanced against the lives of the sailors, who survived the wreck). Finally, note the analogous phrases "iactura rei publicae" ("damage to the Republic"), 26.32.6; "temporis iactura" ("loss of time"), 5.5.8, 39.4.4 (cf. below, p. 204 and n. 23).

chapter that individual names, standing out like honorific epitaphs from among the numbers of Roman dead, could furnish additional weapons for a political attack against the commander.

Yet as so often with triumphal criteria, no absolute standards applied. Recriminations did not cloud the Gallic triumph of M. Claudius Marcellus in 196, for instance, although Livy dutifully preserves the names of military tribunes M. Ogulnius and P. Claudius, and the *praefecti socium* T. Sempronius Gracchus and M. Iunius Silanus, among those killed in a sudden attack by the Boii. Fortunately, Marcellus and his surviving troops managed to defend their camp that day, and later, after joining forces with the other consul, L. Furius Purpureo, caught the Boii by surprise in turn and utterly defeated them (33.36.5–33.37). Furius of course did not triumph in 196, but Marcellus did, and apparently without having to justify the heavy losses suffered earlier. Decisive victories could speak for themselves as *res triumpho dignae* ("deeds worthy of a triumph"). When the same Furius had celebrated a triumph as praetor in 200, amid the challenges no one took him to task for the more than two thousand casualties on the right wing of his army (31.22.2). No one brought C. Calpurnius Piso to account on this score either in 184, and yet his victory in Farther Spain had cost the lives of no fewer than five military tribunes (39.31.16). The senate voted him a triumph by full consensus (39.42.2). So also Q. Fulvius Flaccus triumphed in 180 despite the deaths (as Livy reports them) of over 200 Romans, 830 of the allies, and 2,400 auxiliaries in one battle, and another 472 Romans, 1,019 allies, and 300 auxiliaries in his final rout of the Celtiberi (40.32.7, 40.12–13).

LEGISLATIVE RECOURSE

How carefully, then, were the *patres* trying to regulate triumphs based on casualty figures? Evidence does exist for recourse to actual legal statutes. Valerius Maximus cites a law (unfortunately, without naming the author or authors or giving any specific date) that stipulated that an *imperator* had to have killed at least five thousand of the enemy in a single battle before he could ask for a triumph. "Certain commanders," he says, "wanted triumphs to be declared to themselves on account of insignificant battles," and so the law was passed, obviously in an effort to define just how great a war a commander had to wage, and win, in order to make the grade.[21] It is tempting to believe, with Richardson, that Valerius has Cornelius and Baebius from

21. Val. Max. 2.8.1: "Ob levia proelia quidam imperatores triumphos sibi decerni desiderabant. Quibus ut occurreretur, lege cautum est ne quis triumpharet, nisi qui V milia hostium una acie cecidisset." Cf. 33.22.7, as well as Cato *ORF* 58, 94, 97.

180 specifically in mind here.[22] That notorious incident of a triumph without a war ("nullo bello gesto," 40.38.9) would certainly form a convenient terminus post quem for the law, especially since Orosius (5.4.7) gives it a terminus ante quem of 143, the year when Ap. Claudius Pulcher killed five thousand of the enemy but the senate refused him a triumph because an equal number of Romans also fell in that battle. Almost a century later, in 63, tribunes L. Marcius and M. Cato passed another law, threatening punishment for those who dared to doctor the figures they gave to the senate either by inflating the number of enemy casualties or else by underreporting the extent of Roman losses.[23]

Several caveats need to be made, however, before regarding this legislation as evidence of firm and established rules. Valerius attributes the original law of five thousand to an overriding concern among the *maiores* for the enduring reputation of the city at large, as reflected in the triumphs celebrated there.[24] It would debase the coinage in *gloria* for all of Rome should civic honors start to flow too freely. No one can really put a number on the value of intangibles like status and fame, but this law, as Valerius describes it, represents a step in that direction. We see from Orosius that in 143 the *patres* were still weighing Roman casualties into the equation as well, regardless of the death toll inflicted on the enemy. Even then, that is, having killed at least five thousand of the enemy had become only a necessary condition for the award of a triumph, not a sufficient one. The law as such merely denied triumphs to generals who had not met the requirement; it held no guarantee that those who did meet it could count on any reward.

The senate still had to decide ad hoc, nonetheless, whether to grant or refuse any particular triumph request. The passages in Valerius Maximus and Orosius both serve to reinforce the idea, already amply shown from the debates in Livy, that the *patres* were constantly having to rearticulate what they meant by "deeds worthy of a triumph." Roman aristocrats turned to casualty figures as a ready means to quantify success and failure precisely in the absence of precise definitions, because the traditional framework of *imperio, auspicio, ductu, felicitate* had notoriously wide and often indeterminate boundaries.[25] The original law certainly did not do much to curb

22. So J. S. Richardson 1975, 62, following Rotondi 1912, 279. See also Combès 1966, 81 n. 25; Harris 1985, 26 n. 2, and recently Feig Vishnia 1996, 178 and nn.

23. Val. Max. 2.8.1. For strikingly similar allegations raised already in 197, apparently before the original law was passed, see again the case of Q. Minucius Rufus (33.22.7–9).

24. Val. Max. 2.8.1: "Non enim numero, sed gloria triumphorum excelsius Urbis nostrae futurum decus maiores existimabant" ("For the ancestors judged that the splendor of our City would be more exalted not by the number of triumphs, but by their glory").

25. See Develin 1985, 257: "We have seen already a number of areas where behavior was not all it might be. Triumphs were a matter of concern and rules developed to cope with problems."

the ambition of would-be *triumphatores,* who were still finding ways around it as late as 63. Valerius says that the new statute came about lest the old one fall into oblivion, "erased by the desire for laurels."[26] The history of the Republic shows a recurring theme: commanders all too eager for triumphs and a senate all too likely to grant them frivolously without a periodic call to restraint. One must agree with the following remark, a bit cynical perhaps, but probably not far from the truth: "It is doubtful, however, that any regulation would have restrained an ambitious Roman general."[27]

SUMMARY

The conventional presence of casualty statistics and other quantitative elements in battle descriptions may be traced to the rhetorical context of triumph debates. Commanders sought to magnify their achievements by tallying the number of enemies confronted, killed, and captured, whereas their opponents tried to downplay them either by deflating those figures or by calling attention to losses sustained on the Roman side, which could be seen to offset the gains and diminish the victory. Both sides sought to make as strong an impression as possible on their audience. Far from indicating a fixed and straightforward set of triumphal criteria, such painstaking attention to the *magnitudo rerum gestarum*—even when put into law—indicates a desire to quantify the essentially unquantifiable, and to create an objective standard for largely subjective judgments.

26. Val. Max. 2.8.1: "ne tam praeclara lex cupiditate laureae oblitteraretur."
27. Feig Vishnia 1996, 180.

CHAPTER 6

Patterns of Success

The fierceness of triumphal controversies in the late third and early second centuries reinforces the idea that certain mechanisms within the political structure of the SPQR gave free rein to a commander's critics to challenge his triumph request. Yet a countervailing impulse toward unanimity and consensus came to bear as well, often winning out in the end on behalf of the would-be *triumphator.*[1] What happens, then, when we try to gauge the actual extent to which the *patres* exercised control over the *ius triumphandi?* Were they more interested in maintaining open access or in restricting it?

This question brings the discussion around full-circle, back to a scholarly exchange cited at the very beginning. Responding to a prior claim that there was a "flood of triumphs"[2] in the early second century, a noted scholar resorts to manipulating the numbers in a fashion apropos to the present context:[3]

> Even if we adopt [the] period 200–170, thirty-six celebrations is not a startling number, even less so if we remove two triumphs on the Alban Mount and seven ovations: twenty-seven full triumphs in thirty years is not much greater proportionately than fifty (omitting Papirius in 231) in the sixty years 282–222. Quite simply, triumphal celebrations correspond with military activity and success.

The author seems to find the idea of rampant change unsettling, determined as he is to uphold the staunch traditionalism of the Roman Republic

1. See recently Hölkeskamp 2004a, 85–92.
2. J. S. Richardson 1975, 62.
3. Develin 1978, 436.

as a system of government. Yet despite what he says, it is not quite that simple: triumph *requests,* not triumphs, "correspond with military activity and success." Roman expansion after the Hannibalic War did mean more and greater opportunities for magistrates to distinguish themselves abroad, and this did lead, in the atmosphere of intense aristocratic competition, to an increase in triumph requests. By removing *ovationes* and triumphs *in monte Albano* from the calculation, one merely shows that the senate did not authorize many more full triumphs in the later period than before. The author claims "no reason to suppose anything like a senatorial desire to control those who seemed to be securing triumphs too easily,"[4] but since the lesser celebrations belong to those very cases where the *patres* refused to grant a full triumph for some reason, they indicate precisely the exercise of senatorial control.[5]

That having been said, though, how often did the *patres* really say no? Up to this point, in order to get at the full range of arguments used and criteria cited in Livy's triumph debates, the various episodes have been treated thematically, with an intentional blurring of the distinction between objections merely raised before the senators and later refuted, and those actually sustained in a vote against the would-be *triumphator.* In fact, one of the most glaring features of these political struggles as Livy describes them is the dizzying variety of possible outcomes: some requests not even mooted; some triumphs granted without apparent difficulty, and others highly controversial; some refused outright; some awarded *ovationes* instead; some triumphs celebrated *in monte Albano.* Before proceeding any further to look for patterns of success and failure in triumph debates, therefore, one must finally sort out all these procedural categories for the period covered by Livy 21–45 (i.e., 218–167).[6]

MISSING REQUESTS

A handful of people boasted victories that they might conceivably have tried to parlay into triumphs and yet, as far as we know, never did so. Only once does Livy actually state explicitly that a commander failed to seek civic honors: when *privatus cum imperio* L. Stertinius returned from Spain in 196 (33.27.3). The historian offers no explanation for the noted lapse, and does not even pause to narrate Stertinius's *res gestae,* leaving readers to speculate. In the same year consul M. Claudius Marcellus is further said to

4. Develin 1978, 435.

5. Cf. the similar calculations (with lovely bar graphs to show trends over time) by Rich 1993, 49–51, where *ovationes* and full triumphs are only notionally differentiated.

6. See also appendix B below, with a detailed discussion of several different ways to break down the same numbers, yielding wildly divergent results.

have deliberately left room for the *triumphi spes* of his colleague, L. Furius Purpureo, and yet Furius apparently did not pursue the matter, despite his almost total slaughter of the Boii in a huge pitched battle and a *supplicatio* decreed jointly in both consuls' names (33.37.6–12). Both consuls in 182 had earned a *supplicatio* for their joint successes as well, this time in Liguria (40.16.4): one of them, Cn. Baebius Tamphilus, was ordered home immediately to hold elections and apparently never heard from again, while his colleague, L. Aemilius Paullus, had his *imperium* prorogued for the following year and eventually went on to triumph (40.34.7–8).[7] Ironically, earlier in his career the senate had announced another *supplicatio* for the same L. Aemilius Paullus, because as proconsul (ex-praetor) in Spain he had bounced back after initial reverses to rout the Lusitani and destroy their camp. It would appear, however, that on his return in 189 he avoided the limelight and did not demand further recognition.[8]

All this talk of the *supplicatio* as an indication of possible *triumphi spes* is no mere idle conjecture. Across the board we can see a demonstrably close link between days of thanksgiving proclaimed at the first news of victory and a triumph or *ovatio* later awarded to the commander on his return. Indeed, in the period under consideration, a *supplicatio* fails to presage a larger victory celebration only five times, including just two commanders among the great many whom the historian describes as having asked for triumphs, as well as the three mentioned here, who seem not to have bothered. The two who asked for triumphs and did not receive them despite earlier *supplicationes* decreed in their names were P. Cornelius Scipio in 206 and Q. Minucius Rufus in 197. In either case, as we shall see, there were clearly mitigating circumstances, procedural, political, or both, preventing the award.

Two more commanders may have lacked a *supplicatio* to their credit, but still produced deeds worthy of note, yet both look like nonstarters in the triumph department. In 199 C. Cornelius Cethegus, one of the *privati cum imperio* sent to Spain, had won a battle over the Sedetani, in which Livy reports fifteen thousand enemy killed and seventy-eight military standards captured (31.49.7). As we have seen, the use of numbers in such contexts is suggestive. Similarly, when M. Claudius Marcellus, also ex-praetor, returned from Spain in 168, he had captured Margolica, which Livy calls a "noble city" ("nobili urbe capta," 45.4.1), in a passing remark that would seem gratuitous were it not tellingly redolent of *magnitudo rerum gestarum.*

7. Cf. Degrassi 1947, 554.

8. On the earlier defeat, see 37.46.7–9. For the subsequent victory, which happened just prior to the arrival of his successor, see 37.57.5–6. For the *supplicatio,* see 37.58.5. Degrassi 1947, 553, concludes that no triumph request was made in 189, despite a mistaken notice to the opposite effect in Vell. Pat. 1.9.3 (easily accounted for by the future course of Paullus's illustrious career).

These indications suggest that both victors must have found ways to make their achievements known down the ages, but there is no talk in Livy or anywhere else of either one's having cherished *triumphi spes.*

Of course the writers of history in antiquity missed many things that we now wish they had included and passed by many more such in knowing silence, but it still seems likely, especially given what Livy says openly about Stertinius and Furius, that some or even all of the commanders listed here had opportunities to pursue civic honors and really did not take advantage of them. If that is true, in the absence of further testimonia we can only speculate as to why. Some, despite their successes, may have thought that their *res gestae* would not measure up to the accepted standards because of mitigating factors. Paullus in 189, for instance, might have felt too embarrassed over the defeat and near disaster that he had suffered before fighting back from the brink. Others perhaps did some preliminary canvassing to weigh the degree of political support that they could count on in the senate and found it wanting. Both Furius and Baebius participated in joint campaigns where the honor fell to the other *imperator.* Noteworthy accomplishments did tend to gain the recognition they deserved, one way or another, but there was only so much *laus* and *gloria* to go around, particularly when two commanders came before the *patres* at the same time. Recent triumph debates, be they successes or failures, could also indicate prevailing moods among the *patres* at any given moment, which might well have proved discouraging to the next potential contender.[9] At any rate, if even those commanders with substantial victories to their names nevertheless sometimes took themselves out of the running on purpose for fear of rejection at the hands of the *patres*—whether because of technicalities, politics, or a mixture of the two—it would certainly bespeak the acknowledged power of that body to regulate triumph requests.

Stertinius's decision not to ask for a triumph in 196 may mean simply that he took his status as *privatus cum imperio* to heart, but all the same he was anything but shy in proclaiming his achievements: he deposited no less than fifteen thousand pounds of silver into the treasury, and that apart from the two manubial *fornices* that he built in the Forum Boarium area, both topped with flashy gilded statues (33.27.3–5). Marcellus in 168 likewise deposited a million sesterces' worth of gold and silver into the treasury (45.4.1). In 196 L. Furius Purpureo dedicated a temple to Veiiovis on the Capitol, apparently from a vow he made as consul (35.41.8). Even without the approbation of the senate or any kind of public victory celebration, in other words, proud servants of the Republic always had avenues open to put themselves on display.

9. Livy himself acknowledges as much, in his remarks at 3.70.14–15 on the consuls of 446 (shortly after the first alleged example of triumph *sine auctoritate populi iussu* in 449).

OUTRIGHT REJECTIONS

Very few of those who requested triumphs came away totally empty-handed. As we have seen, the brilliant young P. Scipio (later Africanus) did not press his claim when he returned from Spain as *privatus cum imperio* in 206, because notwithstanding his obvious success in the field, he had never held a proper magistracy (28.38.4). But the senate's refusal of a triumph hardly disgraced Scipio. Indeed far from it: before his arrival in Rome the *patres* had decreed a *supplicatio* to mark his victory (27.7.4), and immediately after the supposed failure of his triumph request, Scipio was able to cash in on the fame and glory of his military achievements in Spain to secure an easy victory in the consular elections for the following year. Livy's narrative in fact so closely associates his return with his election to the consulship that one almost imagines Scipio entering the city, depositing the spoils of his victory into the treasury, and marching directly from there to a resounding success at the *comitia*—all in a single sweeping motion northward through the city (28.38.6–7). Whatever factors may have led to this chain of events, the final result can hardly be called a crushing political defeat.

There was another close call in 199, when a tribunician veto suddenly blocked the *ovatio* that would otherwise have been granted to L. Manlius Acidinus, one of the *privati cum imperio* returning from Spain (32.7.4). Then in 193 the consul L. Cornelius Merula simply could not forge a consensus among his peers in the senate. He fell victim to the alternative, hostile version of his *res gestae* circulated in letters by a *legatus* (35.6.8–8.9). Q. Minucius Thermus might have expected a reward for his victory in 190, especially since Scipio Nasica had brought him to the attention of the *patres* the year before, highlighting his worthiness (36.40.2), but he did not triumph. Livy says nothing directly about why not, but perhaps whatever Thermus had accomplished in Liguria was simply eclipsed by the triumphant homecoming of M'. Acilius Glabrio, at about the same time, with a resounding victory over Antiochus at Thermopylae (37.46.1–2).

The remaining two rejections really belong in a separate category, for Livy does not actually record a formal triumph request in either case. The notorious affair of the brothers M. and C. Popillius Laenas in 173–172 pitted the senate against both *imperatores* in a challenge to public authority that Livy recounts as a grim parody of a triumph debate, a travesty that should never have taken place.[10] It all began in 173, when the outraged senate first issued and later upheld a decree restoring freedom to the Statellates, whom the consul M. Laenas had sold into slavery after their surrender (42.8–9).

10. Scholarly treatments of this curious episode are few and far between, but see Feig Vishnia 1996, 132–34; and Rich 1993, 57–59.

Laenas not only demanded the repeal of that decree but even went so far as to request a *supplicatio* for his victory (42.9.4–6). We have already had reason to notice the connection between days of public thanksgiving and triumphs. So when the consul went before the senate in the Temple of Bellona, scene of many a triumph debate, to ask that a *supplicatio* be decreed in his name, the action bore the semblance if not the reality of a triumph request—and the senators flatly rebuffed his brazen move. Recriminations were still flying when his brother served as consul the following year. Livy says that C. Laenas accomplished "nothing noteworthy" in Liguria (42.26.1). On his return, however, he narrated his *res gestae,* such as they were (a key ingredient in any triumph request), although once again the word "triumph" does not appear. He was shouted down by enemies of his brother, and the matter was dropped (42.28.2–3). This episode hardly fits alongside other, more straightforward triumph debates, but we will return to it at length in due time, because Livy's account is riddled with triumphal language—or at least mock-triumphal language—from start to finish.

OVATIONES AND TRIUMPHS *IN MONTE ALBANO*

We have already traced the encapsulated history of triumphs *in monte Albano,* which took place three times during the period covered by Livy 21–45. For Marcellus in 211 it was clearly an act of defiance against those who had denied him his request for a triumph on the Capitol and fobbed him off with an *ovatio* (26.21.1–12). Senatorial politics claimed Q. Minucius Rufus as the last casualty of his joint campaign when he found it impossible to take equal credit in 197 with his colleague, C. Cornelius Cethegus, for their work together in Cisalpine Gaul (33.22–23). The case of C. Cicereius and his Corsican beeswax in 172 mainly reflects the obscurity of the commander, but arguably also has something to do with the irritability of a senate still caught up in the ongoing Laenas fiasco (42.21.7). Thus the private triumphs of Minucius and Cicereius count as political failures, inasmuch as the senate deemed their *res gestae* unworthy of public recognition, whereas Marcellus falls into an intermediate category because of the *ovatio.* In comparison with the *fornices* built by L. Stertinius, as mentioned above, it is interesting to see that Cicereius vowed a temple to Juno Moneta in battle (42.7.1), which was dedicated five years later (45.14.10). He too despite his failure to win a triumph still left a conspicuous mark on the urban landscape with his name attached.

Notably, the noun *ovatio* does not occur in extant Livy: he uses only the participle *ovans,* and always in the formula *ovans urbem inire.*[11] If a com-

11. See Packard 1968 s.v. *ovans* (*vel sim.*) for details; and cf. Phillips 1974a, 270–71.

mander came before the senate to narrate his *res gestae,* in other words, Livy says that he cherished *triumphi spes.* There were no *ovatio* requests.[12] When the senate granted an *ovatio,* it meant that they were denying a triumph but still wanted to make their approbation known in some guise. Thus although they awarded full triumphs to both consuls in 207, as discussed earlier, C. Claudius Nero apparently took on the trappings of an *ovatio* to put himself deliberately in second place, so that he could participate in the triumph of his colleague M. Livius Salinator to mark their joint campaign rather than stage two separate ceremonies (28.9.9–18).

For four of the eight *ovationes* in this period (not counting Nero), Livy reveals the line of argument that led to an *ovatio* as a compromise between supporters and critics of the would-be *triumphator.* These passages stand as signposts for several important so-called requirements for the full triumph, because they indicate at least ostensible grounds for the senate's decisions. Thus the triumph hopes of Marcellus in 211 (26.21.1–12) and L. Manlius Acidinus in 185 (39.29.4–5) fell prey to the *deportatio* provision. The *privatus cum imperio* L. Cornelius Lentulus in 200 was told that he could not triumph for lack of a magistracy, despite the openly acknowledged worth of his accomplishments (31.20.3–4). The *patres* denied a triumph in 195 to M. Helvius because his victory on the way home after a long illness had occurred with his successor's army and in a third commander's province (34.10.3–5). We do not know much about the arguments raised in the cases of Cn. Cornelius Blasio in 196 (33.27.1), M. Fulvius Nobilior in 191 (36.21.10–11), A. Terentius Varro in 182 (40.16.11), or Ap. Claudius Centho in 174 (41.28.3). The senate must have voted *ovatio* for each of them, although Livy explicitly mentions a decree only for Blasio and Centho.

At any rate, these decisions clearly hinged as much on political considerations as on procedural technicalities, if not even more so. All but one of the eight *ovationes* under discussion here came out of Spain, a province that generally drew men of lesser rank and *auctoritas* to govern it.[13]

THE BROADER ARENA

We should remind ourselves amid all this talk of controversy and compromise that the senators had it in their power to award triumphs as well

12. This *pace* Briscoe 1973, *ad loc.*, who seems to believe that an *ovatio* request was at least prima facie possible, given his remark that "Stertinius did not try for an *ovatio* either." There is ample evidence of the *privati cum imperio* asking for triumphs, and perhaps indeed they hoped to come away with at least an *ovatio* to show for themselves, but no self-respecting Roman aristocrat would actively seek a lesser honor, especially amid so much flexibility in the criteria.

13. Spain remained almost exclusively a nonconsular, praetorian preserve long after the era of *privati cum imperio,* except for M. Porcius Cato (the Elder) who triumphed from there as consul in 194. So J. S. Richardson 1975, 56–57.

as deny them. In the course of Rome's conquest of the Mediterranean, a few men brought home achievements so manifestly splendid, contributing so much to the long-term prosperity and well-being of the *res publica,* so easily seen as the embodiment of all the highest ideals of *imperium, auspicium, ductus,* and *felicitas* in action, that the very thought of denying a triumph must have been almost impossible for the *patres* to imagine. Three individuals stand out above all the rest in Livy's account as having waltzed through the senate vote without a whisper of trouble: Scipio Africanus in 201 (30.45.1–2), T. Quinctius Flamininus in 194 (34.52.23), and L. Aemilius Paullus in 167 (45.35.3–4). The outcome on the senate floor was not at issue if the *magnitudo rerum gestarum* could not possibly be gainsaid. In fact Livy makes these three homecomings look like triumphs already, with crowds of people spontaneously flooding the streets to welcome their victorious leaders back from the fray.

If we broaden the field of vision even slightly beyond the compass of the triumph debate proper, however, none of these men emerged entirely unscathed. Flamininus apparently did the best of anyone in avoiding *invidia,* but Livy still records arguments over whether or not to prorogue his *imperium* in three successive years, 197–195 (32.28.9, 33.25.11, 33.43.6). Not only could these disputes easily have swung the other way and deprived Flamininus of the opportunity to do what he did, but they also affected the new commanders going into the field, since there were only so many major theaters of operation to go around. The so-called trials of the Scipios implicated both Africanus and his brother Asiaticus in 187 (or was it 184?) over allegations of funds misappropriated from the latter's campaign against Antiochus (38.50.4–60.10).[14] And Paullus nearly did not triumph at all, because after the unanimous vote in the senate his own soldiers, upset at the share of the royal booty they had received, tried to block the motion that went before the people to give him *imperium* on the day of his triumph (45.35.4–39.20). Aristocratic competition under the Republic worked toward two very different goals: individuals gained recognition who were perceived as worthy of praise, and simultaneously the political process served as a great equalizer, smoothing out distinctions that might threaten the balance within the ranks of the élite. As Livy says of Paullus at 45.3.5, "the middle heights are not touched by *invidia:* it reaches toward the top."[15]

Similarly, M'. Acilius Glabrio went on trial in 190 for withholding booty

14. Scholarly attempts to untangle the notorious crux surrounding these events have spilled more than their share of ink. From the history side, see Gruen 1995, with reference to earlier work (including Bandelli 1972 and 1974–75; Fraccaro 1956, 263–415; Luce 1977, 92–104; Mommsen 1879, 2.417–510; Scullard 1951, 290–303). Cf. Gruen 1984a, 229 n. 118; and more recently Feig Vishnia 1996, 129–32. Also note Jaeger 1997, 132–76, with a distinctly literary and historiographical approach.

15. 45.35.5: "intacta invidia media sunt: ad summa ferme tendit."

from his triumph the year before (37.57.9–58.1). We also learn of various quarrels that pitted C. Calpurnius Piso and L. Quinctius Crispinus against the new praetors in 185 (39.38.8–12), Q. Fulvius Flaccus against his successor in 180 (40.35.10–36.4), and C. Claudius Pulcher in 177 against his predecessors (41.10–11). Just like challenges within the triumph debate proper, all these ancillary *certamina* represent efforts by a commander's jealous rivals to diminish the worth of his *res gestae* for their own political ends. Some erupted before the triumph debate and then had no lasting effect, as if the fury were already spent; others broke out only after the triumph, as if the *inimici* of the *imperator* were looking for another way to get at him. None escaped controversy at some stage, in other words, yet every single one of these men—Flamininus (34.52.4–12), both Scipios (30.45.2–5, 37.59.2–6), Paullus (45.40.1–4, despite a lacuna), Piso (39.42.3), Crispinus (39.42.4), Flaccus (40.49.1), and Pulcher (41.13.6–7)—triumphed by the resounding consensus of the *patres.* Not much really separates them, then, from other would-be *triumphatores* during the same period who met with horribly stiff opposition when they first made their requests only to overcome it and win full accolades in the end, such as L. Furius Purpureo in 200 (31.48–49.3), P. Cornelius Scipio Nasica in 191 (36.39.5–40.10), Q. Fabius Labeo in 188 (mentioned in passing at 38.47.5 as an exemplum in a later debate), M. Fulvius Nobilior in 187 (39.4.2–5.17), and Nobilior's colleague Cn. Manlius Vulso (38.44.9–50.3).[16] Debates notwithstanding, most requests documented by Livy 21–45 yielded full triumphs, indeed roughly two out of three.[17] That fact must remain at or near the bottom line in any discussion.

SUCCESS RATES?

It turns out that the same raw data from Livy 21–45 can lead to two diametrically opposite conclusions about the success rate of triumph requests, depending on how the calculations are handled. If we first treat the different categories of celebration separately as gradations of honor in descending order from full triumphs to naval triumphs, *ovationes,* and triumphs *in monte Albano,* next count as failures those who might have made requests but apparently did not, and, last, correspondingly whittle down the number of successes until it includes only those *triumphatores* who appear to have met with little or no opposition along the way, then we see that less than half of victorious generals walked an unobstructed path from victory in the field to glory at home. Senatorial control of the *ius triumphandi* could not be more glaringly obvious. But if on the other hand we first group all the various types of public ceremony together as badges

16. Also see Degrassi 1947, 78–81, 551–55.
17. See appendix B below.

of honor among Roman citizens (since, after all, the Fasti enshrine them all side by side), next restrict ourselves only to documented requests that Livy actually says came before the senate (rather than speculating about *triumphi spes* that may have fizzled too early to leave any trace), and, last, disregard controversy (no matter how fierce or how long-lasting, provided that the final result turned out in the commander's favor), then suddenly it appears, by stark contrast, that the SPQR granted civic honors in nearly nine out of ten cases.[18]

EPILOGUE: BEYOND CRITERIA

The conclusion is inescapable: triumphs were by no means the only thing at stake in triumph debates. P. Scipio (later Africanus) did not force the issue of a triumph in 206, when "everyone knew" (28.38.4: "constabat") that he had no right to expect one—and yet he still made the request. Why? Did he harbor some genuine hopes, deep down, despite the well-established convention? Certainly the *patres* could bend the rules, if enough of them agreed to it: witness the *ovatio* for Lentulus six short years later (31.20.3–6). All things being equal, Scipio might have imagined that the senate could break with tradition for him. But things were not equal between Scipio and Lentulus in the eyes of their fellow aristocrats. The senators could afford to recognize Lentulus for his lesser success without fear of making him stand out too far, especially with Scipio towering behind him. In 206, by contrast, even apart from his remarkable achievements in Spain, Scipio already enjoyed the unique honor of *imperium* bestowed outside a regular magistracy. He could not expect to triumph too.

So why did Scipio bother to make a triumph request that he must have known the *patres* would reject? His behavior appears counterintuitive. To save face, it would make more sense "not to ask for a triumph which seemed likely to be refused."[19] Yet Scipio's immediate election to the consulship (28.38.6) reflects the widespread political favor that he enjoyed even without a triumph to crown his Spanish victories. It may be a mistake to think of that second, popular vote as a success-in-failure or a consolation prize after his rejection by the *patres*. Instead perhaps he had everything to gain in his exalted position, and little to lose, from openly asserting that he had done deeds worthy of a triumph, provided solely that he could find a way not to offend the authority of the senate in the process.

Just how light a touch he needed appears from the feud that quickly erupted after the election over who should assign the consular provinces. Scipio wanted to cross into Africa, and seems to have been prepared to

18. See appendix B below for details.
19. Thus Develin 1985, 210.

seize his own initiative no matter what, but the elder senators forced him in public to yield that authority to the senate as a body rather than either taking it upon himself or offering it to the popular assembly. Only then did they accede to his ambitions (28.45.2–8).[20] Scipio clearly knew how to stage dramatic public performances at crucial moments. Two famous scenes from the later part of his career further illustrate the point: his Day of Zama speech served as a powerful reminder of his status in the community and record of distinguished service to the *res publica,* with its symbolic reenactment of his triumphal procession through the city and up to the Capitol (38.51), and likewise the openly defiant act of ripping up the account books from Lucius's Asian campaign in front of his fellow senators dared them to demand a reckoning from him, of all people (38.55.10–13).[21]

These latter episodes also point out deep associations between triumphal ritual, the public image of the *triumphator,* and the deposit of money into the treasury—all of which, taken together, may help identify what Scipio possibly had to gain in 206 by asking for a triumph that he could not hope to receive. This must come under the heading of what French social theorist Pierre Bourdieu has termed "symbolic capital": an intangible but highly sought-after commodity, measured in terms of status and prestige, that generates a whole symbolic economy analogous to but also distinct from the commerce in material goods.[22] Between the wealth of booty and the quasi deification of the *triumphator,* triumphs put both economies on conspicuous display. Likewise, triumph debates not only provided a broad stage for the *dignitatis contentio* but involved a monetary transaction as well, since of course one of the distinguishing features of the triumph *in monte Albano* was that the commander had to pay for it out of his own money rather than having it come out of public funds by authorization of the *patres.* The dynamic interplay between the twin economies, symbolic and material, charged every exchange in the quest for civic honors with intense, vital energy. In Part II we will turn to the conceptual vocabulary and performative grammar of that crucial and ongoing discourse from Republican Rome, which is so central to Livy's history.

20. See also Feig Vishnia 1996, 107–8.

21. Also note the remarks by Lendon 1997, 82: "A city could be in debt to a man for a benefaction, and could feel that debt vividly. Thus the odd triumph of Scipio Africanus the Elder, victor in the second war against Carthage, under tribunician prosecution at Rome . . . and then he simply walked out of the court to sacrifice on the Capitoline followed by the whole assembly, leaving the thwarted tribunes gnashing their teeth. Such was the debt of gratitude owed to Scipio by Rome that the very bringing of a prosecution against him was widely thought disgraceful."

22. Bourdieu 1977, 171–83. On symbolic capital with specific reference to the aristocrats of the Middle Republic, see Hölkeskamp 2004a;and 2006, 490.

PART II

The Performance of Politics and the Politics of Performance

The play's the thing . . .

RES GESTAE: TRIUMPHAL PROCEDURE REEXAMINED

The relative flexibility of the criteria cited in Livy's triumph debates, by now amply demonstrated, should serve to highlight the act of judgment by the senate each and every time a would-be *triumphator* came before them. Of course he might opt, if met with rebuff, to triumph by his own authority *in monte Albano,* following the precedent set by C. Papirius Maso in 231, but a private ceremony lacked both the official stamp of approval and the benefit of public funding, and so did not come with anywhere near the same prestige. Such celebrations are rare with good reason. The victorious general stood before his peers knowing that they held the keys to a prize dearly sought. Yet although every triumph debate began with the same question, and must lead to one of only a limited number of eventual answers, the elaborate speechmaking and political posturing that went on in between had a deeper significance beyond its merely functional aspect. Even within the framework of conventional arguments and predictable outcomes, each new rhetorical context called for a new act of persuasion, challenging speakers to make their hearers listen. Moreover, the stately, ceremonial process of asking for triumphs, arguing over them, celebrating them, and later commemorating them in monumental form was all part and parcel of a much larger, never-ending performative display—*Romanitas* in action—that was crucial to the public identity of individual aristocrats and of the whole political class.

Having first cleared the way by establishing in Part I that triumphal decision-making involved subtle calculations and ad-hoc judgments rather than the simpleminded application of an objective standard, and that a complex dynamic governed the relations, anything but fixed or static, between the magistrates, senate, and people of Rome, let us now return to procedural questions by a different approach aimed at placing Livy's triumph debates in their proper aristocratic context.

Long before he came home in person, indeed practically before the dust had a chance to settle on the battlefield, the victorious commander already began to cultivate his *triumphi spes* from a distance, by sending a letter, crowned with laurel leaves, to the senate in Rome.[1] With this dispatch he proudly offered the firstfruits of his accomplishments, in official, narrative form, to the Republic for whose sake he and his soldiers had fought. He also spread the word on his own behalf. Ideally, the senate would respond by voting to ratify the victory as soon as the news arrived, designating a period of solemn thanksgiving in his name at shrines throughout the city (e.g., 27.51.8). The offering of a *supplicatio* meant in effect that the success of the *imperator* and his army in the field belonged collectively to all Romans, and had come as a gift from the civic gods.[2] Further, it showcased the role of the *patres* as overseers of the *pax deum,* ensuring that the gods always received due thanks for Roman victories, lest their indignant wrath endanger future commanders and their legions, or jeopardize future campaigns.[3]

This preliminary exchange over the *supplicatio,* though clearly distinct from the triumph debate proper, nonetheless foreshadows it both in structure and in ideological import.[4] Only five times in the years 218–167, by the previous tally, do Livy and the Fasti record that a victorious general failed to win a triumph or *ovatio* after the senate had voted a *supplicatio* in his name, three of these in joint campaigns where we know that the other

1. On laureate letters from the field announcing victory, see 5.28.13, 45.1.7. For triumphant laurels generally, see 2.47.10, 7.13.10, 10.7.9, 45.38.12; cf. Pliny *NH* 15.133. Also see above, p. 12 n. 39.

2. The formula for a *supplicatio* decree was "ut dis immortalibus habeatur honos" ("that honor might be paid to the immortal gods"): cf. 26.21.3, 28.9.7, 31.48.12, 35.8.3, 37.59.1, 38.44.10, 38.48.16, 39.4.2, 39.38.5, 40.35.5, 42.9.3, and cf. 33.22.5, showing close link with triumph. Reasons given for such celebrations include the following variations on the theme of success: (1) "quod bene ac feliciter . . . res publica gesta esset" ("because the business of the Republic was carried out with success and good fortune") at 31.48.12 or "quod rem publicam bene ac feliciter administrarit" ("because he carried out the business of the Republic with success and good fortune") at 38.48.15, both passages specifically naming the officials involved (also cf. 41.28.1); (2) "ob res prospere gestas" ("on account of a successful campaign") at 26.21.3, 33.24.4, and 40.35.5, or "quia prospere res gesserunt" at 40.16.5; (3) "victoriae causa" ("because of victory") at 36.38.7 or "victoriae ergo" (again, "because of victory") at 37.47.4.

3. Barton 2001, 55–56, ties the *supplicatio* to a group of related strategies designed to thank the gods for victory and keep them from getting angry. See also Lake 1937. Hickson-Hahn 2000 examines innovations in the Late Republic. For an adept analysis, from a somewhat different angle, of the abiding political link between war and religion at Rome, see Rosenstein 1990a, 54–91, and cf. Linke 2000.

4. One scholar even labels the "sententious" request for a *supplicatio* as an obvious "front for the request of a triumph" (Walsh 1994, commenting on 39.4.2 and 39.38.5, respectively).

general did triumph, apparently at his colleague's expense.[5] So tightly, in fact, were the two ceremonies bound up together in Roman understanding, that a would-be *triumphator* could even clinch his case by reminding the senate of a public thanksgiving earlier decreed in his honor. Confronted with such a reminder, the *patres* tended to acquiesce, because the *supplicatio* made it plain that they themselves had already given substance, officially and irrevocably, to the idea that the commander's *felicitas* was real and that therefore his handiwork, with the aid and blessing of Rome's tutelary deities, had brought benefits, both tangible and intangible, to the SPQR as a whole (e.g., 31.48.12). While that recognition in itself did not actually oblige them to follow through with the award of further honors, in the event they very often did. For a compelling logic led from the one to the other.

First during the *supplicatio* vote, and then with increasing intensity as the triumph itself approached, the exploits of Roman commanders and soldiers on campaign in the provinces came to be discussed and to win acclaim at home, chiefly among the aristocrats in the senate, of course, but presumably also, as the news of victory spread, from the Roman people at large. Narrative is the key to the whole process: deeds of valor in the field (*militiae*) emerged through repeated storytelling as powerful tokens of symbolic value within the civic sphere (*domi*). One scholar comments thus on a striking pattern in Livy:[6]

> We are rewarded for turning our attention . . . not to the facts behind tradition and the ways in which they might be retrieved, but rather toward thematic patterns that contribute to a portrait of Roman identity. . . . [Livy's] effective concern is less with the facts (the *res gestae*) that lie behind Roman tradition than with the tradition itself (*memoria rerum gestarum*).

The author rightly draws attention to the central role played by collective memory and conceptions of national identity, as opposed to strictly analytical and factual truth, in shaping Livy's history.[7] Yet whereas *res gestae* shows up somewhat casually, even offhand, in the passage cited, as a neutral term

5. Again the five exceptions during the period in question to the rule of thumb that a *supplicatio* equals success (and therefore heralds a triumph- or *ovatio*-to-be) were: (1) *privatus cum imperio* P. Cornelius Scipio in 206, who made a cursory triumph request but did not press the issue, being *sine magistratu* (28.38.2–5), (2) consul Q. Minucius Rufus in 197, who had to settle for a triumph *in monte Albano* after a nasty dispute, whereas his colleague received the full honor (33.22–23), (3) consul L. Furius Purpureo in 196, also apparently ceding the honor to his colleague (33.37.10), (4) proconsul and ex-praetor L. Aemilius Paullus in 189, who seems to have had his own reasons not to raise the issue (37.57.5–6), and (5) consul Cn. Baebius Tamphilus in 182, who likewise left things alone, whereas his colleague eventually triumphed (40.17.6–8).

6. Miles 1995, 68.

7. On collective memory and the formation of historical consciousness among the Roman patricio-plebeian élite, see Hölkeskamp 1996, especially 302–5; Timpe 1996.

to denote unvarnished historical fact, the raw material for subsequent political and ideological construction of the past, the all-pervasive idiom actually belongs on the far side of that dichotomy.

By the time facts have become *res gestae,* in other words, a carefully crafted story is already being told; ideology has already entered in. *Res gestae* narratives crossed the threshold from battlefield to *curia,* at the node in Roman discourse where the conduct of warfare abroad and politics at home effectively coalesced. To capture its full force, we might want to render *rem gerere* as not merely "to accomplish a task," but rather "to accomplish a task worthy of writing home about it."[8] Like the proverbial tree that falls in a forest, a general off in his province could win the most brilliant strategic victory in the history of Rome and still gain nothing by it if no one ever found out. His success did not become a genuine accomplishment until word of it got back to the people whose judgment mattered, by whom it, and he, would be remembered.[9] One of the things that indelibly marked the city of Rome itself as the conceptual center of the empire, with everything else on its periphery, was the reality that commanders and their armies set out from there every year to do battle and returned there again when the fighting was over, laden with spoils of victory and tales of valor.[10] The *supplicatio* vote, based on receipt by the senate of news from the front, accordingly reveals a reciprocal flow of information and esteem, from officers in the field to the senate in Rome to the whole SPQR and back.

Roman aristocratic culture placed an overwhelming emphasis, almost to the point of obsession, on gaining recognition for service to the state.[11] This prevailing ethos arose in response to the historical development that had led by the end of the third century to the consolidation of the emerging senatorial (i.e., patricio-plebeian) élite at the political helm of a rapidly expanding empire.[12] Annual elections kept the aristocracy—whether

8. On the concept of *res gestae* in precisely this narrative context, cf. Hölkeskamp 1996, 308–12.

9. Note the formulation used by Laird 1999, 151: "An event becomes a fact when it is constructed in discourse . . . because what was done can only be apprehended through what was said."

10. Cf. Favro 1994, 152: "The triumph was trenchantly bound to the city as a cosmological and political necessity. No matter how far Roman authority extended, the city on the Tiber remained the focal point of power. Rome was the wellspring of *romanitas* and the home of Jupiter Optimus Maximus."

11. Thus Barton 2001, 58: "For the Romans, being was being seen." There is a vast and continually growing body of scholarly literature on the Roman aristocratic ethos. Among notable treatments, see the important series of articles by Lind (1989, 1992, 1994); also Earl 1961, 18–27; Gruen 1996; Habinek 1998; Harris 1985, 10–41; Hölkeskamp 1987, 204–40; Minyard 1985; Rosenstein 2006, (with suggestions for further reading at 381–82); R.E. Smith 1976.

12. Flower 2004b, 325, comments: "once elite status was no longer defined purely in terms of birth and family, as it had been for the patricians in the earlier Republic, new modes of self-

potential candidates, those running for office, current officeholders, or former magistrates who had joined the ranks of the senate—continually beholden to the voting citizenry, and highly cognizant of the need to make themselves conspicuous as pillars of the broader community.[13] Their individual and corporate identity became thoroughly enmeshed in civic identity, and could not be disentangled. Cicero says that "glory is the praise of things well done and of great services to the Republic, which is given jointly not only by all the best men, but also by the testimony of the populace."[14] So the accolades (*laus* and *gloria*) for a *triumphator* spread outward in concentric circles: first the proud and patriotic narrative from his own lips, then an endorsement from his peers in the senate ("all the best men"), and finally the shouts of praise from the whole Roman people on the day of his triumph.

The multileveled exchange that Cicero describes actually forms part of an ongoing cycle, based on the system of annual magistracies. It began with the individual's candidacy, election to higher office, and investment with *imperium* on behalf of the whole SPQR. In his province, while exercising his command, the aspiring aristocrat strove to achieve *res gestae* worthy of note, so that on his return he could offer proof of his success to those who had sent him out in the first place to defend the common interests of all Romans. If and when he earned a triumph, the entire *civitas* joined in the celebration, which would lend distinction to him and his family for generations to come. The concept of *honos*—at once the active engagement in civic affairs, a precious virtual commodity, the mark of prestige, and ultimately a whole way of life—became the linchpin of personal identity for the *nobiles*, or in the words of one recent study, "the sum of the great algebraic system of counterforces on which Roman Republican society was maintained."[15] The quest for ever more widespread recognition naturally led to heavy trafficking in symbolic goods by Roman aristocrats at all times and in all places, as signaled by the pairing of *laus* and *gloria* in the Cicero passage

---

definition were needed by what represented itself as an aristocracy of merit and achievement." On the broad political developments that shaped the emerging aristocratic ideology, see Hölkeskamp 1987, especially 114–203, and more recently Hölkeskamp 1993, with well-placed emphasis, as already noted, on the conquest and colonization of Italy as a watershed event.

13. Note significantly Hölkeskamp 2006, 490: "Membership and rank within Rome's meritocracy depended entirely on public elections, and only the greatest 'honor,' the consulship, offered its incumbent as holder of *imperium* a realistic chance to scale the last and highest level of Roman *gloria:* the triumph, an achievement that in turn allowed the *triumphator* to inscribe himself permanently in Rome's memorial topography and public memory."

14. Cic. *Phil.* 1.29: "est autem gloria laus recte factorum magnorumque in rem publicam fama meritorum, quae cum optimi cuiusque, tum etiam multitudinis testimonio comprobatur."

15. So Barton 2001, 288. Whereas Barton deals more with personal emotions, Lendon 1997 focuses on the civic and administrative context in which the aristocratic honor code held sway.

cited above. Both these familiar terms refer to the social value placed on an individual and his *res gestae* by the judgment of an external audience.[16]

Polybius identifies the main driving force behind Roman public life as a desire "to gain a reputation in the fatherland for valor [in the field]."[17] According to his famous description of the aristocratic funeral, participants chosen for their physical similarity to the dead man's ancestors would appear wearing the *imagines* in a solemn public procession to the Rostra, where they would gather around the bier, each dressed in appropriate garb and bearing the insignia of the highest public office he had attained.[18] Any *triumphatores* among them were always singled out by their splendid regalia of gold and purple.[19] A young man, usually the son or another close relative, customarily gave a speech before this combined audience of the living and the dead, praising the "virtues and accomplishments" of the deceased,[20] as well as those of his illustrious ancestors one by

16. The decision by Moore 1989, 1 n. 2, to omit such words from his canon of Roman virtues reflects their socially determined aspect: "Not included are words which reflect more one's influence on others than any inherent quality (*auctoritas,* for example, and *gloria*)." Romans conceived of a person's identity so heavily in terms of what others saw in his or her character, however, that the effort to enforce such a distinction creates real problems. Note the Scipionic epitaph (*CIL* 1^2.2.7) that reads "consol, censor, aidilis apud vos" ("consul, censor, aedile among you") in a direct address to the audience, i.e., the Roman people, who were in a unique position to judge this man in their midst, and whose presence in turn as a significant constituency made each of the offices he had held really mean something. Similarly, the Metellus *laudatio* from Pliny *NH* 7.139–40 (cited in full below, p. 133 n. 21) lists "summum senatorem haberi" ("to be considered the highest-ranking senator") alongside other aspirations with "esse" ("to be"): a Roman aristocrat was what those whose opinion he valued *took him to be.* See, compellingly, Hölkeskamp 1987, 225–26.

17. Polyb. 6.52.11: χάριν τοῦ τυχεῖν ἐν τῇ πάτριδι τῆς ἐπ' ἀρετῇ φήμης. Note Lendon 1997, 73: "Honour was a filter through which the whole world was viewed, a deep structure of the Greco-Roman mind, perhaps the ruling metaphor of ancient society." Among the countless other ancient testimonia, see by way of example Cic. *Off.* 1.65, *Arch.* 14; Lucian *Pereg.* 38; J. Chrys. *Inan. Glor.* 4–14. On honor operative at a very early age, Mart. 6.38. Cicero wrote two books on *gloria,* now lost (*Off.* 2.31).

18. Polyb. 6.53.1–54.2. On the cultural significance of aristocratic funeral rites and the *laudatio funebris,* see among others Bell 2004, 204–8; Flower 1996, 16–59, 91–158; and 2004b, 331–37; Habinek 1998, 51–54; Hölkeskamp 1987, 222–26; 1996, 305–8; and 2006, 483, 493 (with additional bibliography); Kierdorf 1980; Nicolet 1980, 346–52; Walter 2004, 89–108. For a provocative reassessment, see recently Rüpke 2006b; and cf. below, p. 276 n. 4.

19. Polyb. 6.53.7: οὗτοι δὲ προσαναλαμβάνουσιν ἐσθῆτας, ἐὰν μὲν ὕπατος ἢ στρατηγὸς ᾖ γεγονώς, περιπορφύρους, ἐὰν δὲ τιμητής, πορφυρᾶς, ἐὰν δὲ καὶ τεθριαμβευκὼς ἤ τι τοιοῦτον, κατειργασμένος, διαχρύσους ("These men also put on garments [i.e., togas], with a purple border if he was a consul or praetor, all purple if a censor, and if he was also a *triumphator* or had achieved something similar, embroidered with gold").

20. Polyb. 6.53.2: λέγει περὶ τοῦ τετελευτηκότος τὰς ἀρετὰς καὶ τὰς ἐπιτετευγμένας ἐν τῷ ζῆν πράξεις ("he speaks of the virtues of the man who has died and the accomplishments during his life"). The Greek expression τὰς ἐπιτετευγμένας πράξεις is an unmistakably literal rendering of Latin *res gestae.*

one, beginning with the oldest and working his way forward generation by generation.[21] Thus enshrined with his *res gestae* into the grand noble lineage of his family, the newly departed officially joined the ranks of the *maiores.* He would appear right alongside them at the next family funeral, and continue to do so forever after. Strikingly, the occasion as well often marked the political debut of the young man who so prominently displayed his own ongoing assimilation into the collective values and aspirations of the clan. By publicly assuming the mantle, as it were, he made it clear that he hoped one day to be the next in line.

In this context, the so-called intrinsic merit of persons or deeds had no real substance, until or unless it was deliberately brought into the civic sphere and validated there by a discerning audience: what Roman aristocrats craved above all was the stamp of approval from others, and especially from members of their peer group.[22] So when the senators arrived at a consensus about whether or not to award a triumph, they collectively placed a more or less arbitrary value on the commander's performances *domi militiaeque.* The Latin verb for this judgmental activity is *aestimare* or *existimare;* the noun, *aestimatio* or *existimatio.* Both appear prominently in Livy's triumph debates: for example, at 3.63.9, where *aestimatio* is used to sum up the whole process of awarding civic honors or denying them, and 31.48.6, emphasizing the role of the senate as the arbitrating body for triumphal disputes openly discussed. The verb *existimare* originated strictly as a monetary term, "to set a price [*aes*] on" something, but then gravitated

21. Pliny *NH* 7.139–40 records just such a *laudatio* from father to son. It is rather long, but all the same deserves to be quoted in full: "Q. Metellus in ea oratione quam habuit supremis laudibus patris sui L. Metelli pontificis, bis consulis, dictatoris, magistri equitum, xvviri agris dandis, qui primus elephantos ex primo Punico bello duxit in triumpho, scriptum reliquit decem maximas res optumasque in quibus quaerendis sapientes aetatem exigerent consumasse eum: voluisse enim primarium bellatorem esse, optimum oratorem, fortissimum imperatorem, auspicio suo maximas res geri, maximo honore uti, summa sapientia esse, summum senatorem haberi, pecuniam magnam bono modo invenire, multos liberos relinquere et clarissimum in civitate esse: haec contigisse ei nec ulli alii post Roman conditam" ("Q. Metellus left it in writing in the speech that he gave with the highest praise for his father L. Metellus—who had served as pontifex, consul twice, *dictator,* master of the horse, a member of the fifteen-member panel for the distribution of lands, who first led elephants in triumph from the First Punic War—that ten things had consumed [his father], in pursuit of which wise men spend their time. For he wanted to be a warrior in the first rank, the greatest public speaker, bravest general, to achieve the greatest accomplishments under his auspices, to enjoy the highest honor, to be of the greatest wisdom, to be considered the highest-ranking senator, to accumulate great wealth by honorable means, to leave behind many children, and to be the most famous man in the state. [The son said] that these things had accrued to [his father] and not to any other man since the founding of the city").

22. Thus Lendon 1997, 37: "To be an aristocrat . . . was essentially to be thought well of by other aristocrats. It was not an objective quality, it was membership in a co-opting club." Cf. David 2006, especially 425–26.

into the social and ethical realm, where it came to signify the specifically aristocratic preoccupation with judging and being judged by one's peers on a scale of culturally embedded standards and expectations. As one scholar has written, this single word stands for the entire "aristocratic program of acculturation and ongoing evaluation of character and behavior" in Rome.[23] Because their whole lives were subject to *existimatio,* Roman aristocrats became preternaturally aware of hypothetical judges watching their every move. Indeed they saw the world fundamentally in terms of praise and blame within the civic sphere: their political discourse always carried an ethical dimension, and vice versa.[24] The *dignitas* ("worthiness") of accomplishments and of the individual who produced them likewise was seen to reside in the positive evaluation where it first became manifest. By reference to an earlier constitutive assessment, then, one could later remind a new audience that *dignitas* "always already" existed, so that once conferred it remained a permanent or at least an easily renewable indicator of enduring status.[25]

From the same root as *existimare* also comes the ubiquitous concept of an exemplum or paradigm: those under scrutiny, which is to say all Roman aristocrats at any given moment, strove not only to live up to the highest-water mark established by the great figures of the past, but also to set a new standard of their own by which others thereafter should be evaluated in turn. As Augustus writes in his *Res Gestae:* "I revived many exempla of our ancestors that had become obsolete in our era, and I myself passed on exempla of many things to posterity for imitation."[26] Not surprisingly, such precedents play a conspicuous role in triumph debates (e.g., 31.20.3–5). Because *existimatio* never ceased, exempla were not immovably fixed either, but instead found themselves continually being reconstituted and reconfigured by each successive act of open judgment. They helped

23. Habinek 1998, 57. See also Yavetz 1974.

24. Thus Lind 1989, 16: "the Roman virtues are most often demonstrated in political activity since on the highest moral level the state itself both provided and required the broadest scope for the greatest virtues. . . . Indeed, the distinction between moral and political in the realm of Roman ideas is difficult, if not impossible, to maintain." Also cf. Roller 2001, 126.

25. At both 7.11.11 ("rem triumpho dignam") and 31.20.3 ("res triumpho dignas"), for instance, the coveted label of an achievement or achievements "worthy of a triumph" results from an assessment issued by a group of judges on the spot. The episode of Scipio Nasica (36.40.8–11) also clearly demonstrates the enormous usefulness of reminding your audience of past honors in order to reconfirm your present and future status. Cf. Barton 2001, 218, on the potentiality for expansion inherent in *dignitas.*

26. Aug. *Res Gestae* 8.5: "multa exempla maiorum exolescentia iam ex nostro saeculo reduxi et ipse multarum rerum exempla imitanda posteris tradidi." For the full text of the massive inscription, see Brunt and Moore 1967. Note also the extremely lucid discussion of this particular passage and its connection to Livy's historical project by Feldherr 1998, 35–38.

to mediate between tradition and change.[27] The same applies of course to invocations of the *mos maiorum:* rhetorically one sculpted oneself in the image of one's ancestors, but in fact the patterning tended to work rather the other way.[28] That enabled the Romans to adapt their understanding of traditional values to the evolving needs and perceptions of new and unprecedented circumstances. Past actions, present stature, and future aspirations—whether we are talking about individuals, the family, or the whole *res publica*—all merged together under the far-seeing, reciprocal gaze of *existimatio.*[29]

The *supplicatio* vote brought elements of performance and evaluation into play, and in subsequent stages of the triumph debate the scope of their operation was amplified and enlarged, first within the élite inner circle and then also in the broader arena between the élite and the rest of the sociopolitical hierarchy. After the *supplicatio,* the next significant moment came when the victorious general arrived home to make his formal triumph request. Livy's notices on such occasions are highly formulaic and typically fall into two parts: first the commander narrated his *res gestae* to the assembled *patres,* and then he asked their permission to enter the city in triumph.[30] These two ceremonial gestures—battle narrative and by-your-leave, *res gestae* and *ut liceret*—not only complement one another in an emblematic way but also encapsulate between them the whole ideology of the triumph debate. Earlier the senators had joyfully greeted the first news of victory, sight unseen, with a vote for a *supplicatio.* Now the *imperator* stood before them in person to render an account of what he had done for the Republic.

A clue to the nature of the next proceedings lies in an obvious fact, but one easily overlooked: the would-be *triumphator* did not give this speech by way of debriefing. His audience already knew what had gone on in the province from the field dispatches he had sent them, so that this first-person monologue on his return to the city brought little news. Its content must therefore have mattered far less than its symbolic value, through the

27. On the significance of exempla both within Livy's history and as a typically Augustan preoccupation, see Chaplin 2000, especially 140–56, with a discussion of triumph debates in particular. Cf. Kraus and Woodman 1997, 73–74, on the balance and tension between old and new embodied in Livy's exempla. For broader themes, also cf. Bloomer 1992; Dueck 2000; Gleason 1995; Hölkeskamp 1996; Maslakov 1984; M. Stemmler 2000.

28. Habinek 1998, 53, writes: "There is no reason to think that the *mos maiorum* had a real, historical force independent of that ascribed to it by its contemporary promoters." Also note Chaplin 2000, 149: "The more novel something is, the more it requires precedents."

29. See Morgan 2000; Treggiari 2003.

30. Perhaps the most succinct example is found at 31.47.7: "expositisque rebus gestis ut triumphanti sibi in urbem invehi liceret petit" ("Having narrated his *res gestae,* he asked that it might be allowed for him to be carried into the city in triumph").

performative quality of the solemn occasion. His catalogue of accomplishments aimed not to inform the *patres* but to impress them.[31] He sought to appear in both word and deed as the incarnation of Roman aristocratic ideals.[32] His speech generally adhered to a fairly strict conventional pattern, outlined by the familiar triumphal formula *imperio auspicio ductu felicitate.* Accordingly, he would encapsulate the narrative of all the battles he had fought, all the enemies he had defeated, all the towns, encampments, prisoners, and booty he had captured, and he would embellish his account with names, numbers, and any other trimmings that could act as indicators of *magnitudo rerum gestarum,* as discussed in Part I.[33] Those same recurring elements in Livy's own battle narratives, then, which have been much maligned as indicators of a hackneyed imagination,[34] can testify to his faithful participation in a long-standing tradition with its roots in the self-fashioning of the commanders themselves.

The occasion of asking for a triumph set the stage for a very demanding performance by the would-be *triumphator* as he attempted to meet two diametrically opposite expectations. On the one hand, he needed to draw attention to himself in the boldest and stagiest possible way. His narrative was in the first person; the *res gestae* that he sought to build up in the eyes of his peers were the *res a se gestae.* Standing before the gaze of the *patres* on that day was a crowning moment in a Roman's career, second only to the triumph itself. Yet paradoxically, in order for his bid to succeed, he also had to craft his tale of glory with considerable care lest he vaunt himself overmuch. For the model Roman citizen in whose image he strove to sculpt his self-portrait lived above all to serve the state.[35] Of course ambition had its rightful place, and we must never retroject any quasi-Christian notion of abject selflessness onto the ethos of the *res publica.* Rather, the *nobiles* saw nothing wrong with reaping huge symbolic profits from conspicuous service, or even with serving conspicuously in order to reap huge symbolic profits. That was how the system worked: do all the right things, display all

31. Note that *expono,* which marks a commander's narrative in the passage just cited (31.47.7: "expositisque rebus gestis"), is unambiguously a verb of public display, literally "to lay out in the open[or: "in full view"]".

32. Cf. Phillips 1974a.

33. Gagé 1939 gives a succinct two-page note on conventional elements in *res gestae* narratives.

34. Thus H. Nissen, as cited by Walsh 1961, 158–59: "All the battle accounts are frighteningly dull variations on an identical theme. First the Romans, through the enemy's numerical superiority or through surprise, fall into difficulties; then, through the extraordinary bravery or cleverness of their leaders, they gain the upper hand, and finally kill 40,000 or 35,000 of the enemy, or occasionally fewer."

35. As Rich 1993, 58, pithily states: "simple triumph-hunting was politically risky." Cf. Bell 2004, 11. The perceived tension between self-promotion and service to the *res publica* could all too easily lend ammunition to the opponents and rivals of a would-be *triumphator.*

the right virtues in all the right times and places, get oneself noticed by the right people in the right way, and then riches in the coin of *laus, fama, gloria,* and *auctoritas* would (to borrow a salient expression) triumphantly follow.[36]

Aristocrats competed with extraordinary fierceness to outdo one another on behalf of the Republic. But elevate yourself too far above everyone else, especially those in your peer group, and at once you ran the terrible risk of *invidia.* An invisible boundary existed, usually apparent only when someone was believed to have crossed it, where pursuit of self-interest found itself at odds with maintaining the public interest. For anyone at or near that line, the quest for further *laus* and *gloria* brought only scandal and resentment.[37] However broadly a commander might boast of his achievements, then, the *ut liceret* half of the formula required him to yield in his triumph request to the higher authority of the senate. He must bow to the collective judgment of his peers (*existimatio*) to keep his self-congratulatory song in proper tune. From the careers of Scipio Africanus and others we have already seen the importance in Roman civic life of proper deference by magistrates in office to the *patres* as a body (e.g., the discussion of Scipio's crossing to Africa at 28.40–45.9). The senate stood in synecdoche for the Republic as a whole (*l'état, c'est nous*) and could demand gestures of respect from one of their own—whether spoken or unspoken—as tokens of appropriate submission to the public good and therefore as ample insurance against the ever-present threat of *invidia.*[38]

36. Sall. *Cat.* 7.6–7 is directly relevant, and the passage deserves to be quoted in full despite its length, because of all the significant notes sounded in it: "gloriae maxumum certamen inter ipsos erat: se quisque hostem ferire, murum ascendere, conspici, dum tale facinus faceret, properabat. eas divitias, eam bonam famam magnamque nobilitatem putabant. laudis avidi, pecuniae liberales erant; gloriam ingentem, divitias honestas volebant. memorare possum, quibus in locis maxumas hostium copias populus Romanus parva manu fuderit, quas urbis natura munitas pugnando ceperit, ni ea res longius nos ab incepto traheret" ("there was the greatest competition for glory among themselves: each one kept hastening to strike an enemy or climb a wall, and to be seen while he did a thing of this sort. They thought that these were riches, this was a good name and great social standing. They were greedy for praise, generous with their money; they wanted enormous glory, upstanding riches. I can remind you in what places the Roman people with a small band of men put the greatest forces of the enemy to flight, what naturally fortified cities it seized by fighting, [but I will not] lest those things take us too far from the point of origin"). Note Sallust's allusion at the end to the ability of numbers to make a battle sound more impressive. Also cf. Lendon 1997, 69.

37. Note the telling remark of Barton 2001, 54: "Victory was deliriously festive but also momentary, conditional, and dangerous." One immediately thinks of the charges leveled against Scipio Africanus and his brother: "regnum in senatu Scipionum accusabant" ("They accused the Scipios of reigning like kings in the senate," 38.54.6). The reference to the dreaded anti-Republican concept of kingship in this passage is hardly accidental: see Schlag 1968.

38. Develin 1985, 40, writes: "magistrates were either actual or potential members of the [senate] and would have to operate within the peer group. . . . the senate as a whole could act

Between the initial triumph request and the final verdict, the senate deliberated over how to apply the traditional parameters *imperio, auspicio, ductu, felicitate* to the case at hand. As we have repeatedly seen, situations varied widely. Commanders came from different family backgrounds and had different personal ties, both friendships and enmities. They arrived home asking for triumphs at different stages in their careers, with military exploits of every conceivable different character to their credit, large and small, having secured victories against different enemies in different provinces with different degrees of finality, and so on. It is clear that in the midst of all these many variables, a great deal of political maneuvering went into maintaining an equilibrium between the public status of individual aristocrats and the collective interests of the state they always claimed to serve. A victorious general's friends and supporters would work to back up his pious and patriotic assertions that everything he did, he did for Rome, while his critics took aim at him, and at them, in the very same terms. As a result, perhaps the most striking syntactical feature in Livy's account of triumph debates is the proliferation of normative expressions such as passive periphrastics and *oportet-* or *debeo-*plus-infinitive constructions: the correct interpretation of dearly held Roman values lay at stake.[39]

Nor did the would-be *triumphator* perform before a disinterested audience: the senators charged with weighing his merits had a vested stake in demonstrating their collective right to define Roman values on behalf of all Romans, as well as their power to grant or withhold the Republic's most highly prized civic honors. To them belonged the firstfruits of victory, in exchange for the personal status that only their *licet* could confer. Every time a victorious general openly sought the approval of the *patres* before celebrating a triumph, they too went on display, no less than he did, in their capacity as the rightful arbiters of *Romanitas*-in-action. Thus triumphal politics and triumphal ritual helped to define the status of the whole Roman élite within the *res publica*.[40] As seen in the earlier discussion of C. Claudius Pulcher in 143, among others, there was little to restrain a determined commander, who did not mind paying for the festivities himself,

---

to impose proper behavior on magistrates who were not following its lead." Cf. David 2006, 425–26: "Each senator . . . had to choose the words and arguments that corresponded to his position, striking a balance among assurance, audacity, and conformity to adapt his proposal precisely to the *auctoritas* that he was acknowledged to hold." Cf. also Bell 2004, 15; Harris 1985, 34.

39. Thus, e.g., in the Furius Purpureo episode Livy gives two alternative models, one from either side of a triumph debate, for what the senate should consider in making an informed judgment (31.48.6 vs. 48.10). Whoever managed to produce an account of the commander's *res gestae* that fit most convincingly with the senate's collective understanding of Roman values and ideals at that particular juncture would win the day.

40. Cf. Flower 2004b, 327–28.

from staging his own triumph without their leave if he chose. Yet as far as we know only a very small handful in the whole history of the Republic ever ventured to do so. The financial aspect naturally must have had something to do with this, but the willingness of would-be *triumphatores* to submit themselves to the *auctoritas patrum* also says a great deal about the commonality of interest between individual aristocrats and the senate as a body. When all of them authorized one of them to put on a grand show before the *populus* at large, both he and they drew tremendous prestige from the ritualized process of bringing the story of victory home.

Although the triumph debate focused primarily on the status of the commander as an individual within the élite, and of the élite as a whole within the wider social hierarchy, the would-be *triumphator* was not alone in shaping his personal identity through this process. Any senator could show himself to advantage before his peers as an upholder of traditional Roman values merely by taking the podium to speak out in a triumph debate, no matter which side of the argument he joined. This idea has serious and far-reaching consequences: no public appearance by a Roman aristocrat or speech on the senate floor was ever without an element of self-fashioning, even when someone else's triumph lay at stake. Everyone in the room simultaneously functioned as both performer and judge: through *existimatio* they always held each other accountable to the standards of aristocratic conduct. It pays to recall too that the senate at any given time was composed of two interwoven age-groups: up-and-coming young aristocrats hoping for a chance to seek the highest magistracies and most illustrious honors for themselves someday as well as senior officials who had already held office and sought triumphs in the past, and whose sons and protégés were making their way up through the ranks, even if they themselves would most likely not run again any more. Old or young, in other words, they were all very much in this process together.[41]

Pierre Bourdieu has observed that many societies carry out their most subtle and delicate negotiations of status within a closely guarded sequence and at a regulated pace:[42]

> When the unfolding of the action is heavily ritualized, as in the dialectic of offense and vengeance, there is still room for strategies which consist of playing on the time, or rather the tempo, of the action . . . holding back or putting off, maintaining suspense or expectation, or on the other hand, hurrying, hustling, surprising, and stealing a march, not to mention the art of ostentatiously giving time ("devoting one's time to someone") or withholding it ("no time to spare").

41. Ryan 1998 argues that junior senators under the Republic enjoyed a broader latitude to speak their opinions than previously believed. Cf. David 2006, 425–26.

42. Bourdieu 1977, 7.

Here and elsewhere, Bourdieu dwells rather heavily on the elaborate and often duplicitous schemes by which individuals and whole social classes are continually seeking to stake out an advantage for themselves *over someone else* at any given moment. We should bear in mind, however, that the ordered procedure of a triumph debate created an interval between the commander's proclamation of his own success and the public acknowledgment or reward for a job well done, which allowed many different actors to parade across the public stage, and many different voices to make themselves heard. Because simply having air time in the debate meant the opportunity to perform, to win the appreciative gaze of an audience, one senator's gain did not come *entirely* at another's expense. So the variations in tempo that Bourdieu describes—especially the ability to prolong a discussion even after the issue itself was no longer in doubt—subtly brought about a distribution of symbolic capital among all the various participants, irrespective of the final outcome.[43]

By no means did the performances cease either, once the *patres* had cast their final vote. For if the triumph debate put the commander and his accomplishments on meaningful display before his peers in the senate, then obviously the triumph itself—the most magnificent public spectacle in Rome (30.15.12)—did so all the more, and in the sight not only of the *patres* but of the whole Roman people who had invested him with *imperium* as their magistrate in the first place. In retrospect, performances in the *curia* emerged as a dress rehearsal for the bigger show. Narratives of *res gestae* took on a splendidly tangible form in the ritual of the triumphal procession, which epitomized and consummated the same act of bringing the fruits of victory home that had begun with the first laureate letter from the field. Not surprisingly, then, the politics of the debate often shaped the behavior of the *imperator* on the day of his triumph. This might include ceremonies held as the army gathered outside the city, where the general *in contione* would praise his troops for a job well done, and reward them with gifts of money, the amounts carefully keyed to rank and status (a fixed sum to all the soldiers, with double for centurions and triple for cavalry), and special recognition also for those who had distinguished themselves in battle and thereby contributed more than their share to the communal success being celebrated by all.[44]

43. Geertz 1983b, 211, writes tellingly of the Indonesian *adat:* "What matters finally is that unity of mind is demonstrated, not so much in the verdict itself, which is mere denouement, the afterclap of accord, but in the *public process* by which it has been generated. Propriety to be preserved must be seen being preserved" (my italics).

44. For money distributed to the army, usually on the day before a triumph, with a designated sum for infantry, double for centurions, and triple for cavalry, see the following: C. Cornelius Cethegus in 197 from Cisalpine Gaul (33.23.7), T. Quinctius Flamininus in 194 from Macedonia (34.52.11), P. Cornelius Scipio Nasica in 191 from Cisalpine Gaul (36.40.13),

Since the ritual of the triumph itself culminated in a sacrifice on the Capitol and the deposit of occasionally astronomical sums of money into the public treasury, we must never lose sight of the fact that the symbolic riches so ostentatiously circulated among all the participants in civic triumphal discourse had their distinctly material counterparts: the twin economies in fact were thoroughly intertwined.[45] Bourdieu himself quickly points out, after all, that the most complex symbolic economies tend to grow in precisely those areas where one segment of a society (viz. here the Roman élite) wishes to mask its control over the fundamentally monetary and material transactions that he claims, in true Marxist fashion, underlie all human social relations.[46] It is no accident therefore that the *aerarium* or public treasury becomes an important focal point for triumphal politics in the push and pull between the senate, magistrates, and *populus Romanus*. Hence, among other things, the famous show trials of M'. Acilius Glabrio (37.57.9–58.1) and L. Scipio Asiaticus (38.50.4–60.10) over the disposition of booty.[47] When publicly distributing largesse to his troops, not to mention parading the spoils from his conquests before the assembled multitudes in Rome, a *triumphator* was still every bit as hard at work on his public image as he had been when first appearing before his peers in the senate.

From start to finish he labored painstakingly to fashion the performative gestures and memorable spectacles that would inscribe his deeds into the collective civic memory, alongside the exploits of all the *triumphatores* who had traced the amburbial route before him. Every action and reac-

---

L. Cornelius Scipio Asiaticus in 189 from Asia (37.59.6, including double pay), M. Fulvius Nobilior in 187 from Aetolia (39.5.17), Cn. Manlius Vulso in 187 from Asia (39.7.2–3, including double pay), Q. Fulvius Flaccus in 180 from Nearer Spain (40.43.7), Ti. Sempronius Gracchus in 178 from Nearer Spain (41.7.3), L. Postumius Albinus in 178 from Farther Spain (41.7.3). Note the special *dona militaria* for acts of signal valor distributed by M. Fulvius Nobilior in 189 (39.5.17), discussed below in the context of the self-fashioning of the commander because of charges raised against him during the triumph debate (see below, p. 207 and n. 28). Also note 24.16.8. On the amounts of such gifts as recorded by Livy, see below, pp. 254–55 and nn. 22–24. See Östenberg 2003, 61–65; Rüpke 1990, 204–6; and (on military *contiones*) Morstein-Marx 2004, 34–35 n. 1; Polo 1995, especially 213–16. Last, cf. 45.38.12; and see below, p. 264.

45. Thus when Sall. *Cat.* 7.6 (cited above, p. 137 n. 36) tries to mark a distinction between the two economies, redolent of what Roman aristocrats would have you believe, he only demonstrates how intermingled wealth and status really were. The remarks of Harris 1985, 55–56, are telling: "What counts as an economic motive? If a Roman aristocrat sought to accumulate wealth for its own sake, or for consumption, his motives were obviously 'economic.' But what if he sought to enrich himself for the sake of prestige, to be gained by judicious distribution of the profits of war? Or if he did so in order to strengthen his political position? In practice such distinctions are seldom possible." Cf. Gruen 1984a, 289–95.

46. Bourdieu 1977, 172.

47. Cf. Grainger 1995, 41–42.

tion in the political sphere in Rome, at least where the aristocrats were concerned, belonged to this one central drama. Thus by a curious alchemy a commander's *res gestae*—mandated by his *imperium;* dutifully performed; proudly narrated, proclaimed, and put on display, first before his peers and then, with their approval, before the whole Roman people on the day of his triumph—went on to become part of his durable property and identity, *res* (*publica*) in precisely the etymological sense. Indeed, as already revealed in the picturesque funeral customs that Polybius so compellingly describes (6.53.1–54.2), the *res gestae* of Roman aristocrats lived on long after their deaths. It was actually illegal for home buyers to remove any old manubial dedications that might be affixed to the doorway, so that, in the words of Pliny the Elder, "even with a change of ownership the houses continued to celebrate triumphs forever."[48]

In addition there were epitaphs, such as those of the Scipio family, and other public *elogia* carved in stone, including the tributes to Rome's *summi viri* in the Forum of Augustus (nearly all of whom celebrated triumphs), not to mention the *imagines* on display in the atria of family houses, honorific paintings and statues, whether of veristic or idealizing type, erected in various places around the city, and manubial monuments, especially triumphal arches and temples to the gods, with displays of booty and proud inscriptions naming the *imperator* who dedicated them. Roman *nobiles* were literally surrounded by permanent, tangible reminders of what their ancestors had done for the *res publica*.[49] Constant psychological pressure from this material nexus on all sides, coupled with the performative demands

48. Pliny *NH* 35.7: "aliae foris et circa limina animorum ingentium imagines erant adfixis hostium spoliis, quae nec emptori refigere liceret, triumphabantque etiam dominis mutatis aeternae domus." On houses as loci for the display of *spolia* by victorious commanders, see now the masterful treatment by Welch 2006b.

49. The Scipionic epitaphs were published together in *CIL* 1^2.6–15. There is a helpful commentary to be found in Ernout 1973, 12–21. See also Hölkeskamp 1987, 225–27; Van Sickle 1987. The material nexus of Roman aristocratic ideology covers an enormously wide swath of scholarship. For a useful summary, see Hölkeskamp 1993, 26–29. Note what Kuttner 2004, 301, has to say about the social function of a *monumentum:* "Romans wished to be moved by their images. . . . And images let them imagine that representations were reacting to *them*" in turn. Also cf. Alcock 2002, 1–35, with a useful interpretive framework based on the need for collective memory. On the *elogia* from Augustus's Forum, see Luce 1990 and Chaplin 2000, 168–96. For a comprehensive study of aristocratic *imagines,* see Flower 1996 (with copious reference to previous scholarship). On honorific statues, see Sehlmeyer 1999. On verism and its expression of aristocratic virtues such as *gravitas, dignitas, auctoritas,* etc., see Kuttner 2004, 318; Nodelman 1975; Richter 1955; Tanner 2000; Welch 2006a, 532–37. On triumphal arches and *fornices,* see Wallace-Hadrill 1990; Welch 2006a, 505–6. On manubial temples, see Patterson 2006, 347; and especially Orlin 1997 (followed by Orlin 2000). On houses as significant repositories for memory and memorialization, see Bergmann 1994; Hölkeskamp 2004b; Welch 2006b.

of their daily lives in and about the city, inspired each new generation of *nobiles*—or shamed them (it is often very hard to tell the difference)[50]—to pursue political and military careers of their own, where they aimed at rivaling, if not eventually surpassing, the earlier benchmarks set by their ancestors and role models.[51] Hence the Scipionic epitaph that reads, after the man's name and a catalogue of the various public offices he had held: "I added to the virtues of my clan with my moral character and habits; I brought forth offspring; I sought after the achievements of my father. I have obtained the praise of my ancestors, so that they might rejoice at my having been born of them: my public service has ennobled my lineage."[52] A citizen could hardly ask for more.

Res gestae narratives in various forms thus helped in meaningful ways first to establish and then to propagate the personal identity of the *nobiles* in service to the state. The process began with a commander's own efforts during his lifetime and continued right on into Livy's history.

LIVY'S LANGUAGE OF HEROES

The heading just above—drawn of course from Richard Martin's masterful study of performance and tradition in the *Iliad*—is intentionally provocative. Those in search of Homeric comparisons from the Roman world generally turn to Vergil or his poetic predecessors, Livius Andronicus, Naevius, or Ennius, not to Livy, of all people. Nor would anyone ever try to claim that we should seriously view the *Ab Urbe Condita* as an oral-formulaic

50. Thus Barton 2001, passim (a difficult book but visionary in scope and well worth the effort). Cf. also Kaster 1997.

51. David 2000, 36, calls attention to the constant reminders of a family's success that served as "reproductive strategies" across the generations to shore up the fragile "consciousness of a legitimate right to govern the city" among Roman aristocrats. Note the wrongheaded attempt by Itgenshorst 2005, 112–25 (also discussed below, p. 307 n. 7), to demonstrate on the basis of the wide variety of attested victory monuments, many of which bear no explicit reference to triumphs as such, that the importance of the triumph has somehow been exaggerated. What then are we to make of passages like 30.15.12, which extol the supreme status conferred by Rome's highest civic honor? Besides, if the inscription on a monument does not directly link it to the celebration of a triumph (i.e., if the word "triumph" does not appear on it in some form), it may still be a "triumphal" monument in the broader sense. To understand triumphs within the cultural context of Roman militarism and aristocratic self-fashioning, both of which expressed themselves on many levels and in many different ways, does nothing to diminish their unique character.

52. *CIL* 1^2.15 (dated to the mid-second century B.C. with its appropriately archaic Latin): "virtutes generis mieis moribus accumulavi, / progeniem genui, facta patris petiei. / Maiorum optenui laudem, ut sibei me esse creatum / Laetentur: stirpem nobilitavit honor." The same passage is cited by Barton 2001, 84–85, as an example of how family as the "most closely bound unit . . . was also, necessarily, the focus of competition."

composition.[53] Nevertheless, in the course of his work on Homer, Martin sets forth a conceptual framework for the interpretation of speech acts that applies remarkably well to Livy's triumph debates. He writes:[54]

> Time and again the observer of performances can note that timing, gesture, voice inflection, tempo, proximity to the audience, the past of a particular performer with his or her audience, the setting, the season, the time of day—are factors that determine the meaning of the actual words spoken by a performer as much as if not more so than the literal meaning of the words themselves. This is to say that it is the performance, not the text, which counts.

The whole notion of performative rhetoric rests on an understanding that what some people might be tempted to call mere stagecraft can in fact prove itself a dynamic field of social and political interaction. In a formalized public context a speaker and his addressees exchange far more than words and glances: they are enacting significant identities and relationships. Furthermore, debate within an aristocratic peer group ensures solidarity among them, even between those who speak out on opposite sides, because despite minor differences in status within their ranks, they still have more in common with each other as members of an acknowledged *ordo* than with those below them who have no real voice in the political arena.[55]

Martin has convincingly shown that Homeric warriors actually contribute, through their *mythoi,* to the very process of shaping their identity as epic heroes. The way that they talk to each other about themselves matters as much for who they are—or at least for who the evaluating audience perceives them to be, which is effectively the same thing—as their deeds of valor on the battlefield: they strive μύθων τε ῥητῆρ ἔμεναι πρηκτῆρά τε ἔργων ("to be both a public speaker of words and a doer of deeds").[56] "Not only are heroic performers their own 'authors,' then," Martin goes on to assert, "but they fill the role of 'critic' as well, since all speech in Homer takes place in an agonistic context."[57] Homer's audience learns how to understand the heroic code by watching the way audiences respond to speech acts by

53. D. C. Young gave a talk at the 1971 annual meeting of the American Philological Association with the intriguing title "Statistical Light from Livy on Formulas in Homer" but apparently never published it. I have only seen the conference program, which a thoughtful colleague brought to my attention.

54. Martin 1989, 7.

55. On the theatricality of Roman public life under the Republic, in the interaction between *nobiles* and the populace at large, see recently Morstein-Marx 2004, especially 64–65, 242–46. For the same phenomenon under the early Empire, with its new distribution of power with the emperor on one side and everyone else (*nobiles* and commoners alike) on the other, see Bartsch 1994, passim, especially 10–12.

56. *Il.* 9.443, cited by Martin 1989, 26.

57. Martin 1989, 95.

heroes *within the poem*. A breathtakingly similar structure of embedded judgment and audience response has emerged by now also in Livy's account. For the historian makes it abundantly clear that in order to win a triumph, a victorious commander likewise needed words and performative gestures as well as deeds. So he writes concerning Romulus at the moment of celebrating the first, spontaneous but iconic, triumph: "cum factis vir magnificus tum factorum ostentator haud minor" ("both a man great in deeds and no less a displayer of them," 1.10.5). The would-be *triumphator* became his own author, just as Martin describes, deliberately fashioning an idealized portrait of himself before the eyes of *patres* and populace alike, in a context every bit as highly charged and overtly competitive as the Homeric one.[58]

For the commanders and their critics, the shared project of telling their stories to each other and then transmitting their consensus to the rest of the community served a vital function. In it they found the best of what it meant to be a Roman, to live up to the highest expectations and ideals of their society; and through it they also secured a position for themselves, collectively, as the body within their society empowered to set those very same expectations in line with their own needs and ambitions.[59] The *nobiles* of the Republic, magistrates and senators alike, took it as their task at the time to define what not only their own *imagines* but indeed the corporate civic identity of their entire culture should look like, and Livy carefully aligns himself—and his historical project—with their goals and general outlook. Indeed he puts the generative process of their self-fashioning on display for his readers, and gives it center stage: the characters in his history actively and self-consciously transform themselves into exempla right before our very eyes. Such models of conduct, good and bad, obviously provided the raw material for his account, grounded in the work of earlier historians and stitched together from the famous stories of what great men such as these had done to serve the *res publica* in ages past. Through the repeated cycle of narrative and embedded judgment, year after year, therefore, Livy gradually trains his readers to participate in the value-laden discourse that had been the lifeblood of the Republic before the outbreak of civil war.[60]

Note that by the time he gets around to describing the triumph debate,

58. Note Parker 1999, 168: "For the elite Roman . . . [the] goal was always to be in control of his self-presentation and reception, to make himself subject to none but *self*-presentation. . . . He must be the giver of images, never the object of others' interpretations."

59. Cf. David 2006, 433: "oratory was not just an instrument of political action. . . . It was the means by which the orator constructed a public image for himself. . . . Eloquence thus became a source of charisma, and brought the orator who demonstrated it to the peak of the city's hierarchy." Hadas 1940, 455, described the cosmic aspect of Livy's narrative thus: "The Romans are . . . children of destiny, lords of creation, fated to prevail over all other peoples."

60. Kraus 1994, 13–17, emphasizes the active participation of Livy's readers in constructing a meaningful past through engagement with the text. See also Vasaly 1987, 225, on Livy's

within the rhythm of the annalistic schema, Livy has already given his own version of the commander's exploits in the field. Comparison between the two reveals a tremendous complicity again and again, analogous to what Martin has found with Homer and Achilles, between the voice of the historian in those battle sequences as he narrates them in the third person and the self-fashioning of the aristocrats themselves in indirect discourse as they narrate the same events again and argue with each other. When staging the triumph debate for his readers, Livy places them on a footing similar to where the senators found themselves at the time. His earlier account of the battle functions for them like the field dispatches from commander to senate. Before the debate ever happens, in other words, all the pertinent information has already changed hands, so that all four parties involved—the would-be *triumphator* and his audience within the text, the historian and his audience on the outside—share both a common understanding of what took place *militiae* and a common set of expectations about how the argument *domi* should now proceed. In this regard, the political drama of the triumph debate is not very different from the spectacle of the triumph itself.[61]

There is an added twist, however, because one person in the fourfold structure outlined above knows more than all the others. He sees exactly how the story ends, *and has seen it all along*. In retrospect, Livy's seemingly innocent battle narratives often show telltale signs of issues and concerns that will arise later in contention during the triumph debate. When that happens, the author usually cannot resist taking sides in advance, or at least tipping his hand as to what shape the arguments will eventually take. Then the metanarrative threatens to lead in endless circles from battlefield to *curia* and back again, turned in on itself like a Möbius strip. Still, it is always possible to trace the various structural elements of the stories Livy tells, and the judgments he records, back to their formative source on the floor of the senate, at least insofar as the limits of imagination (ours and his), not to say the available evidence, will allow. A compelling picture should emerge by the end.

One last observation about triumphal criteria before moving on to the next phase of the discussion: it might almost appear that we have just come completely full circle, that the model presented here has done little more than substitute the standard canon of Roman aristocratic virtues, such as

exempla as "unchanging variables within a changing political universe," although the analysis could benefit from recognizing the formative and discursive processes that lead to the creation of exempla, which are therefore not actually static but continually open to renegotiation.

61. Cf. Kuttner 1999, 97: "each time a spectacle text was read or heard, the encounter could engender a spectacle reenactment in the hearer's mind. Thus, later readers would share at least some of the reactions of an original actor or viewer."

virtus, pietas, fortitudo, and so on, for the list of juridical rules so elaborately discarded earlier on. But that is quite simply not the case, because none of those labels, however deeply hallowed by centuries of aristocratic tradition, represents a fixed quantity in any way. They all depend, radically, on the ad-hoc, ephemeral judgment (*existimatio*) of a critical audience. Every supposed instantiation of the ancestral values had to be proven as such before gaining wide acceptance, and the *patres* worked by striving to achieve consensus. Thus the conventional elements of a *res gestae* narrative derived their persuasive power from the shifting dynamics of peer evaluation and a collective understanding that continually evolved—not by appeal to any rigid or permanent scale of values. In short, the application of the triumphal formula *imperio auspicio felicitate ductu* to any given case did not happen automatically or by some unthinking, mechanical fiat. Both the commander who came home in search of reward and the senators who judged his case were actively engaged, all the while, in sculpting the endlessly malleable stuff of personal and civic identity, hoping thereby to create lasting monuments for themselves. Much, much more than triumphs lay at stake in triumph debates.

POLITICS AND PERFORMANCE: CASE STUDIES

From here on, the longest and most intricately crafted triumph debates in Livy's history will take center stage in an exploration of their performative elements. A series of episodes drawn from Books 21–45 will appear in chronological order: first the few rare triumphs from the period of the Hannibalic War, which set the scene for everything that came after them in a number of important ways; then the paradigmatic Gallic triumph of L. Furius Purpureo in 200, awarded over the vehement objection of a superior officer; then the triumph bid by L. Cornelius Merula in 193, a spectacular failure exemplary in its own way; then the triumph of L. Cornelius Scipio Nasica from Italy in 191, voted unanimously despite the revealing ill effects of an all-too-prominent surname; then the successful efforts of M. Fulvius Nobilior to secure a triumph from Aetolia in 187, when a political rival did everything in his power to keep it from happening; then the triumph of his colleague, Cn. Manlius Vulso, from Asia, also in 187, and if anything even more of a close call for the would-be *triumphator;* then the outrageous behavior of M. Popilius Laenas among the Ligures in 173, which hardly led to civic honors but did provoke a sharp response from the *patres* intelligible only in terms of triumphal politics and triumphal discourse; and finally the triumph of L. Aemilius Paullus, victor at Pydna, which enjoys the distinction, unique in extant Livy, of having been argued before the people, not the senate, allowing it to reveal an important and otherwise hidden dimension of triumphal politics under the Republic.

CHAPTER 7

Prologue

The Triumphs of the Second Punic War

The title of this chapter should give pause. For although the Roman Republic did emerge from the Second Punic War victorious in the end, it was a long and dreadful fight (cf. 21.1.2). Many people endured physical, economic, emotional, even spiritual trauma.[1] The cry *Hannibal at the gates!* became a watchword for sudden terror (e.g., 23.16.2).[2] Property was devastated, farms laid waste, and a sizable percentage of a whole generation of fighting men in Italy wiped out.[3] It was rough going too for the workings of the symbolic economy among the Roman élite. The period 218–201 saw not only few signal victories and even fewer triumphs,[4] but also a crescendo

1. The locus classicus for a description of all these effects is of course Toynbee 1965, and although the extent of his conclusions has since had to be scaled back somewhat (e.g., by Brunt 1971), the central thesis that the Hannibalic War was a trauma for the SPQR on many levels remains unassailable. For historical surveys of the war, see Briscoe 1989 and Lazenby 2004 (cf. Lazenby 1978); and on Livy's account, see Ridley 2000.

2. Cf. Juv. 10.147–67 ff.

3. Brunt 1971, 62–69, 269–77, and 416–22, emphasizes mainly the loss of life (estimated at nearly 20 percent of adult male citizens) but also points to food shortages and outbreaks of deadly disease.

4. The Hannibalic War marks the obvious low point on the bar graph of triumphs and *ovationes* presented by Rich 1993, 49, but how few celebrations really took place? The Fasti are missing from the triumph of M. Claudius Marcellus (with *spolia opima*) in 222 to that of Q. Minucius Rufus in 197. Degrassi 1947, 550–51, reconstructs six slots in between, based on an estimate of space available for the inscriptions. Marcellus from Syracuse in 211 would presumably take up two places, assuming that the *ovatio* and the triumph *in monte Albano* received separate notices. Next supposedly comes a triumph for Q. Fabius Maximus's capture of Tarentum in 209, which Livy, however, does not attest, and which therefore must remain somewhat dubious (see appendix B below). Another two slots belong to Nero and Salinator from the Metaurus in 207, and Scipio Africanus after Zama obviously held pride of place at the end of the war. As far as we know, there was no one else. Thus Develin 1978, 432, remarks, "During the Hannibalic

series of legendary disasters: Ticinus and Trebia (21.39–47), Trasimene (22.3–7), Cannae (22.38–50).[5] The course of the war—through crisis after crisis to the brink of catastrophe, until a rallying cry and a gathering of forces, and a resounding final success—mirrors on a grand, epic scale the clichéd battle description where Roman valor overcomes all odds.[6] This time, however, the pattern was real. Survival did lie at stake. Hence the collective identity of the SPQR, and the Roman national character as expressed in civic ideology, emerged from the crucible of this conflict with values deeply rooted in the knowledge of having all faced up to the most dreadful fears imaginable and beaten them back together, through sheer determination and discipline, and with the blessing of Rome's tutelary gods.

Against this background, Livy's account of two major triumph debates from the midst of the struggle with Hannibal, and the crowning celebration from the end of the war, will illustrate a number of themes with far-reaching consequences, above all the role of performative rhetoric in negotiating the public status of prominent aristocrats, and the powerful emotional impact of bringing the story of victory home.

M. CLAUDIUS MARCELLUS IN 211: THE RIGHT MAN AT THE WRONG TIME

M. Claudius Marcellus stands out as an individual, a brilliant and illustrious but also a highly controversial figure. He certainly revealed a talent for self-promotion already early on. In 222 he not only triumphed over the Gauls, but for having killed the enemy chief in single combat also won for himself the greater and far more unusual honor of dedicating the *spolia opima,* which resulted in the single longest extant notice from the Fasti Triumphales.[7] In the aftermath of the disaster at Cannae, the people turned to him to help lead the war effort, solely on the strength of a good name earned through previous success. Then in 211, after the fall of Syracuse in a complex and protracted siege operation, as we have seen, Marcellus's political rivals managed through deft deployment of the *deportatio* provision (which seems to have arisen here for the first time) to deprive him of a second triumph. The technicalities of that debate have already been discussed at length in chapter 4 above. What deserves to be brought out here, rather, is the extent to which performative elements abound in this affair from start to finish.

War success was scarce and the time to celebrate a triumph would be hard to find with magistrates in the field for long periods." The former consideration probably weighed more heavily than the latter.

5. Other sources listed by Broughton 1951, 238, 242, 247.

6. Cf. Brunt 1971, 695, and the comments of H. Nissen as cited by Walsh 1961, 158–59.

7. Degrassi 1947, 78–79, 550.

When he first arrived to make his triumph request, Marcellus apparently took it as a personal affront that the *patres* had not allowed him to bring the *victor exercitus* home. Did they not value his achievements enough to do him that courtesy? Of course, given the terrible manpower shortages at that time, the *patres* had good reason to keep Marcellus's veterans in the field in Sicily, especially with more conflict brewing on the island. Yet that does not do much to mitigate the imagined insult, since the conduct of Roman politics was always intensely personal, regardless of any extenuating circumstances. Livy says, though, that Marcellus complained only "gently" ("leniter") and no less on behalf of his veterans left behind in the province than for the sake of his own *dignitas,* as if the would-be *triumphator* were deliberately showing restraint in deference to the occasion of his triumphal *ut liceret* (26.21.2). Though he could not afford to antagonize the body of his peers, he still made his grievance known, willing to toe the line, in other words, but only just. The debate over Marcellus's triumph came down to a choice between two less than ideal outcomes for the *patres:* either snub a commander to his face when they had commended him in his absence, and ignore the *supplicatio* as a token of value, with concomitant risks for the *pax deum,* or pretend that the war in Syracuse was completely finished, which was false, and celebrate a triumph without the army to march in the procession. Livy says that the arguments went on for a long time, emphasizing that the two sides found themselves evenly matched, with neither willing to give much ground, until they all managed to salvage a measure of decorum and consensus within their ranks by granting Marcellus an *ovatio* as a compromise. As noted already in chapter 1, he also celebrated a triumph *in monte Albano,* significantly on the day *before* he entered the city (26.21.3–6).

Practically speaking, with the completion of the official entry rite (and the *ovatio* counts as such) the *imperium* specially granted to him by the assembly for the purpose would have lapsed.[8] He could perform the ritual *in monte Albano* without official sanction, but only by right of his command.[9] In addition, by holding his private ceremony first, Marcellus would be sending a clear signal to his political enemies that he did not appreciate what they had done to him, banishing his triumph outside the *pomerium* when it should be taking place right in the heart of Rome itself. He would also simultaneously register a degree of detachment, as if to let them know that

8. Note that the tribunes act as intermediaries between the senate and the assembly where the question of *imperium* is concerned: "tribuni plebis ex auctoritate senatus ad populum tulerunt ut M. Marcello quo die urbem ovans iniret imperium esset" ("the tribunes of the people by authority of the senate put a motion before the people that M. Marcellus would have *imperium* on the day he entered the city in *ovatio,*" 26.21.5). Cf. 45.35.4, the only other passage where Livy spells out the whole procedure in detail.

9. Note again the precise wording at 33.23.3 ("iure imperii consularis," "by right of consular *imperium*") and 42.21.7 ("sine publica auctoritate," "without the authority of the people").

he would not allow their slighting judgments (*existimatio*) to hold his public image hostage. He knew who he was, and what he had accomplished, and so did his friends and supporters and anyone else who made the trip out to the Alban Mount to view the spectacle. The *ovatio* would appear almost as an afterthought. Then he could afford to be gracious and follow orders, performing his final magisterial duties, including the deposit of money into the treasury, with dignity and aplomb, because he had already told his side of the story on his own terms.

En route through the city to make his thanksgiving sacrifice and deposit in the treasury, Marcellus put on an exotic display, redolent with a mixture of Roman *virtus* and Hellenized *luxuria.* While parading his valor in the old-fashioned martial spirit, this *triumphator* also consciously introduced refinements.[10] A scale model of captured Syracuse, siege engines and all, showed sophisticated military engineering in action. There were also silver and bronze vessels, furniture, textiles, statues, elephants, and more (26.21.6–10).[11] Having specifically named foreign *luxuria* and the greed it inspired as leading causes of Rome's disastrous moral decline (*Praef.* 11–12), Livy has a stake in telling the story of how such influences came to bear.[12] The splendid and unmistakably Greek city of Syracuse lay much closer to home than the Hellenistic kingdoms of the East, yet although the territory of Alexander's conquests had not yet fallen under the purview of Roman *imperatores,* that was about to change. Thus Livy comments that the plunder from Syracuse first brought Greek artworks to prominent attention in Rome (25.40.2), and later has Cato the Elder mention the city in particular when decrying such objects as "infesta" ("hostile") to stern, old-fashioned Roman *mores* (34.4.4).[13]

Even as the spoils of Syracuse came to rest in their new home, Marcellus's *inimici* were seeking new ways to undermine his public image. The fact that he had just been elected consul again for the following year (26.22.12–13) must have stirred up further *invidia* in those who already resented his

10. Holliday 1997, 141, writes that Marcellus "presented himself as a man of culture and discernment, and professed to stimulate Romans to an appreciation and admiration of Hellenic activity." See further Gruen 1992, 241–42; Jaeger 1997, 124–31; Rawson 1989, 432–33. On the interplay of Greek and Roman modes of thought in Livy's account of the fall of Syracuse, including the famous scene of Marcellus weeping over the fate of the city with its glorious past (25.24.11–15), see also Jaeger 2003; Rossi 2000.

11. See Östenberg 2003, 41–43, 206–9.

12. On the theme of *luxuria* in Livy's Preface, see Chaplin 2000, 73–105, especially 97–105, firmly following in the footsteps of Luce 1977, 250–75; also cf. Feldherr 1997a on the damage done by excessive greed to the preservation of historical memory.

13. McDonnell 2006 argues much the same point. At 34.4.4 the reference to *signa* from Syracuse very nicely points both to plundered artworks and to "signs" read by Cato as tokens of impending doom. Cf. Polyb. 9.10 on the dangers of excessive pillaging; and note Gruen 1984a, 348–50.

preeminence. Sheer accumulation of honors—the *spolia opima* not least among them—set him very far apart from everyone else. So the opposition set out both to eliminate the possibility of Marcellus's producing any more *res gestae* worthy of note and to minimize the symbolic value of what he had already accomplished. In a targeted move, they quite literally staged their political offensive by bringing a group of Syracusan envoys to Rome with obviously well-rehearsed laments of ill treatment at Marcellus's hands. They paraded these victims before the *patres,* and even through the streets of the city, in what Livy describes as mock or inverted triumph designed to bring opprobrium rather than *laus* and *gloria* to the commander who had reduced them to their pitiful state (note especially 26.27.16). Marcellus meanwhile adopted a telling counterstrategy, remaining outwardly calm and continuing to show the same moderation and restraint (26.26.9) that had characterized his dealings with the senate all along (cf. 26.21.2).

At first, Livy says, the Syracusans lingered outside the city (apparently in villas owned by Marcellus's *inimici*), and rumors began to circulate that Marcellus was trying to keep their presence a secret, reluctant for people to know about them, much less hear their complaints. Arriving in Rome after the elections ahead of his colleague, he seized both the spotlight and the higher moral ground by making a bold pronouncement that he would gladly take over the role of stage manager for the upcoming encounter. He would bring the Syracusans before the *patres* himself at the first opportunity and answer their charges publicly, with the clear implication that he did not mind running a show, even this one expressly designed to discredit him, since he knew that *existimatio* would finally tell in his favor (26.26.6–7). His willingness to submit questions about his conduct to the body of his peers in the senate completely disarmed any allegation that he had something to hide and pointedly contrasted his own openness and integrity with the evident subterfuge and falsehood of his rivals.[14] His

14. See 26.26.6–7: "scire se frequentes Siculos prope urbem in villis obtrectatorum suorum esse; quibus tantum abesse ut per se non liceat palam Romae crimina edita [ficta] ab inimicis volgare, ut ni simularent aliquem sibi timorem absente collega dicendi de consule esse, ipse eis extemplo daturus senatum fuerit. ubi quidem collega venisset non passurum quicquam prius agi quam ut Siculi in senatum introducantur" ("he knew that there was a crowd of Sicilians near the city in the villas of his detractors; it was so far from the case that they would not be allowed to publicize openly in Rome the false crimes put about by his enemies, that he himself would give them a meeting of the senate immediately, so that they would not pretend he harbored some fear of speaking openly concerning the consul in the absence of his colleague. And when his colleague arrived he would not allow any other business to be discussed before the question of the Sicilians being brought into the senate"). Throughout this passage, Livy pointedly contrasts Marcellus's openness and willingness to discuss things publicly ("palam . . . volgare . . . extemplo . . . non passurum quicquam prius agi") with the furtive, underhanded behavior of his opponents ("crimina edita [ficta] . . . simularent . . . timorem . . . dicendi").

words, actions, and overall demeanor deliberately mirrored the *ut liceret* part of a triumph request in submission to the will of the *patres*.[15]

More histrionics ensued. Sicily was declared a consular province again, effectively ratifying the argument used to deny Marcellus's triumph request, namely that a state of war persisted on the island (26.28.3). Livy says that the Syracusans were standing nearby while the consuls drew lots for their provinces, and when Sicily fell to Marcellus, they made a tearful public scene (26.29.1–2). Soon thereafter they began visiting the homes of prominent senators dressed in mourning garb, with hyperbolic declarations that they would abandon not only their homes, but Sicily altogether, before submitting to Marcellus as their governor again: "It would be better for that island to be engulfed by the flames of Aetna or to sink in the sea than to be surrendered, as it were, to an enemy for punishment" (26.29.4).[16] Their canvassing finally aroused enough talk, through a mixture of pity toward them and *invidia* against Marcellus, that the senate finally held a hearing on the question of provincial assignments (26.29.5). Marcellus relinquished his claim without a fuss, and then he and his colleague quietly arranged to switch places without putting the matter to what might have been an unseemly vote (26.29.6–9).[17] His enemies had won this round, then, inasmuch as he would not be going back to Sicily. Yet it appears that Marcellus was biding his time for the upcoming (and more important) battle over the ratification of his *acta*.

He seems to have felt that he had nothing to lose, and everything to gain, from an open debate in the senate. When that moment arrived, it certainly did not bring any sudden revelations. Everyone in Rome, at least those in élite circles, must have heard about the Syracusans and their complaints by this time. They had done their best to make themselves the talk of the town. And Marcellus had already gone through the process of first crafting and then presenting his *res gestae* narrative to the body of his peers in the triumph debate. There was very little suspense over what he might say at this point. The three crucial factors in the final showdown, therefore, were, first, not so much the content as the quality of the newest performances by the central figures on either side; second, the opportunity for every senator with an opinion to make a statement if he wished, and third, the act of *existimatio* embodied

15. Note the trenchant observations of Barton 2001, 212: "Calling on spectators—or judges, for they were inseparable notions in the Roman mind—of an oath or an action was a Roman's way of saying, 'Go ahead: put me in the spotlight. My words and my actions will stand the test of your scrutiny.' The presence of witnesses made every act into an ordeal."

16. 26.29.4: "obrui Aetnae ignibus aut mergi freto satius illi insulae esse quam velut dedi noxae inimico."

17. Marcellus displays again here the peculiar delicacy of his touch with the niceties of interaction between the senate and magistrates in office, leaving no doubt as to his own interests yet painstakingly deferential at the same time toward both his colleague and his peers.

in the vote to ratify or disavow Marcellus's *acta*. Both the piteous provincials and the dutiful governor were striving to portray themselves in a highly stylized light that would appeal to certain traditional notions and values in their audience. To that end they invoked familiar, exemplary concepts, hoping to become exempla in their own right.[18] The Syracusans themselves would later admit as much to Marcellus in front of a crowd (26.32.8).

The emotional climax of the Syracusans' lament, as Livy describes it, certainly echoes a well-worn topos a city stripped completely bare by the rapacity of its plunderers, down to the empty walls of houses and temples despoiled of their sacred images (26.30.9–10).[19] The stock image deserves special notice here, because not only will it gain further significance for Marcellus in time but it will also find echoes farther afield, in a debate yet to come.[20] The Syracusans' plea to the *patres* to restore if not all their stolen goods then "at least those things that were visible and could be identified" (26.30.10) hints at the intersection between the traffic in symbolic commodities (*laus, gloria, dignitas,* etc.) and material considerations (i.e., money and property).[21] Faced with such accusations, a conqueror would naturally fall back on the *ius belli* to justify his conduct and that of his soldiers. He would also express rightful pride in his accomplishments. Marcellus's speech, as Livy presents it, tempers these predictable elements with allusions to the importance of open debate and avowals of both his loyalty to the *res publica* and his respect for the *auctoritas patrum*.[22] In keeping with the emphasis on exemplary behavior (good and bad) throughout, he displays a keen awareness of the senate's ability to establish precedents (26.31.11).[23]

18. Eckstein 1987, 174, has written, "If the speech of the Syracusan envoys in our sources seems the archetypal complaint of a foreign community oppressed by the arbitrary actions of a Roman commander in the field, then Marcellus's response represents the classic defense of the commander's right—in fact his need (cf. 26.31.10) to take independent action according to his own judgment."

19. References to *templa* or *delubra* (or both) always mark the most sensitive point of contact between conqueror and conquered. Cf. 1.38.2, 3.17.11, 5.41.5, 6.20.16, 7.31.4, 9.9.5, 26.11.9, 26.13.13, 28.36.3, 28.42.11, 29.8.9, 29.18.15, 31.30.10, 37.21.7, 38.43.5, 42.28.12, 43.7.10, 44.7.2.

20. See the charges raised against M. Fulvius Nobilior in 187 (38.43.5).

21. 26.30.10: "orare se patres conscriptos ut, si nequeant omnia, saltem quae compareant cognoscique possint restitui dominis iubeant."

22. Some hint of the tone Marcellus's rhetoric would have adopted, patriotic and self-congratulatory in more or less equal measure, can be found in Livy's notice at 25.40.1. On the *ius belli* in his self-defense, see 26.31.2, and cf. 31.9. On open debate, see 30.12. On Marcellus as proud but loyal servant of Rome, 30.12; also 31.9–10. On his respect for the senate as a body, note the deprecatory use of the title *patres conscripti* at regular intervals throughout and three times in rapid succession at the end (30.12, 31.1, 31.6, 31.9, 31.10, 31.11).

23. Cf. Eckstein 1987, 174: "He argues that it is in the interests of the Roman state for the senate not to make other commanders less energetic in the field in the future by annulling his actions and decisions now."

Then came the senators' turn to speak their minds. After explaining that the debate went on for a long time with many opinions expressed, Livy names T. Manlius Torquatus as a spokesman for the anti-Marcellus group, who offered a poignant memorial to the city of Syracuse and its loyalty to Rome under the dead king Hiero, only to be laid waste by Marcellus's crushing siege works and its spoils carried off as prizes of war (26.32.1–3). In a striking rhetorical and performative flourish (reminiscent of *Hamlet*) Torquatus actually conjures up the hypothetical specter of the king himself (26.32.4):[24]

> If King Hiero, that most faithful friend of the *imperium Romanum,* could rise from the dead, how would it be possible to face either Syracuse or Rome being shown to him, since when he had seen his homeland half ruined and despoiled, entering Rome he would see the spoils of his homeland in the vestibule of the city, almost in the gate?

After allowing the ghost of Hiero to linger for a moment in the minds of his readers, Livy does not describe the rest of the debate in any detail, except to round out the entire episode with a ring composition, ascribing the senate's reaction here again to a mixture of "*invidia* against the consul and pity for the Syracusans" (26.32.5).[25] Beyond that we learn only that Torquatus and his supporters began in the majority but Marcellus's *acta* were ratified nevertheless, with a promise that the senate would look after the Syracusans and instruct consul M. Valerius Laevinus to see to their property, "inasmuch as could be done without damage to the Republic" (26.32.6).[26] The juxtaposition of *res Syracusana* and *res publica* in this passage is highly suggestive, because with it the senate's decree could be referring to the community, the government, and the property of either Syracuse or Rome or both.

There is more going on in this debate than first meets the eye. Livy has carefully framed the invocation of the dead King Hiero to ensure that it would occupy a central place in the whole episode. He clearly wanted his readers to pause here and ask themselves the same hypothetical question that Torquatus posed: *What would Hiero say?* Livy's own earlier narrative of Syracuse's being plundered had contained elements of both pro- and anti-Marcellan versions. In a significant foreshadowing of the commander's own self-defense, he had said that statues and other artworks were plundered

24. 26.32.4: "si ab inferis exsistat rex Hiero fidissimus imperii Romani cultor, quo ore aut Syracusas aut Romam ei ostendi posse, cum, ubi semirutam ac spoliatam patriam respexerit, ingrediens Romam in vestibulo urbis, prope in porta, spolia patriae suae visurus sit?"

25. 26.32.5: "ad invidiam consulis miserationemque Siculorum." Cf. 26.29.5.

26. 26.32.6: "curae senatui fore rem Syracusanam, mandaturosque consuli Laevino ut quod sine iactura rei publicae fieri posset fortunis eius civitatis consuleret." On the phrase "iactura rei publicae" and others like it, see above, p. 111 n. 20.

in accordance with the *ius belli.* But the historian had also singled out the taking of objects from temples as a mark of *licentia* and mentioned that these controversial spoils could still be seen on prominent display during his own lifetime, in the same place near the Porta Capena where Torquatus now pictures Hiero viewing them on a visit to Rome (25.40.1–3). Because of the debate at the time, in other words, the conquest of Syracuse left a mixed legacy behind it, and Livy arranges for Torquatus to give voice here to an act of imagination in which an avid student of history in the historian's own Augustan age might easily indulge when viewing the Syracusan objects in situ in Rome and trying to make sense of complex events and changing loyalties from long ago. The *res gestae* narratives in Livy's history have a political origin in triumph debates. Through them, especially in passages like this, he teaches his readers how to reconstruct their collective past from the monuments surrounding them throughout the city.[27]

With the ratification of Marcellus's *acta* by a consensus of his peers came a powerful vindication, despite all the previous controversy, of what he had accomplished as governor of Sicily. The final concession to the Syracusans about the restoration of their property reads more as a gesture of respect from the senate toward Roman provincials than a personal condemnation of the governor.[28] Yet Marcellus's victory, however gratifying, came at a price that his rivals had exacted at every step of the way: no *deportatio exercitus,* no triumph, no return to the province as consul. Through a series of memorable performative challenges, through scene after scene in and around the senate house, they forced Marcellus to endure heavy, sustained, public questioning of his character, his stature, and his *res gestae.* His entire career seems to have been marked by mixed feelings. Yet he appears to have borne the strain remarkably well, by maintaining decorum and always deferring to the senate.

The dénouement to this episode highlights the theatricality of the entire political process. For the Syracusan envoys, who had at one point apparently told anyone who would listen that they would rather die and have Sicily crumble into the sea than ever have to deal with Marcellus again, now suddenly turned around, *in conspectu omnium* on the front steps of the *curia,* and offered him an apology no less melodramatic than their earlier performances had been. Falling at his feet and begging him to forgive whatever they may have said "for the sake of lamenting their calam-

27. Cf. Feldherr 1998, 38–39, on the creation of monuments as "visible signs" within the urban landscape, both empowering and challenging Rome's citizens to build a coherent understanding of their history. And cf. Chaplin 2000, 201–2: "For a generation undergoing severe dislocation . . . *exempla* provide Livy with the thread to stitch together the past, attach it to his own age, and then present Roman history as one continuous whole."

28. See above, p. 90 n. 23.

ity and lightening it"—that is, in donning all the trappings of suppliants and unquestionably varnishing the truth to make their story conform with conventional patterns (exempla)—they then ceremoniously placed both themselves and their city under his personal protection as their patron (26.32.8).[29] In reciprocity for the respect that the senate had shown to them in their status as provincials, once having gotten what they wanted, the Syracusans reaffirmed their traditionally close ties to Rome. By identifying Marcellus now as the liberator of their city, they championed him, despite what his critics had said, as the true defender of those loyal to Hiero's legacy.[30] Marcellus must have possessed enormous charisma, given the effect of his personality not only on his peers but also on those he had conquered. No Roman aristocrat had ever acquired a *clientela* in a foreign community before.[31]

Marcellus's career illustrates the checks and balances and the occasionally wild volte-face that characterize the *dignitatis contentio* among Roman aristocrats. It must also be placed in context. His return from Sicily and the debate leading up to his *ovatio* appear in Book 26 of Livy, just two short chapters after the appointment of young P. Scipio as a *privatus cum imperio* to Spain in the midst of a terrible crisis. Rome had more armies in the field at that moment, and a greater portion of its resources dedicated to the war effort, than at any other time in the struggle against Carthage.[32] Marcellus's military brilliance under trying conditions would make him stand out in any generation of Romans.[33] He had *imperium, auspicium, ductus,* and *felicitas* to his name—all four (cf. 26.29.10). And as demonstrated by his earlier triumph and the *spolia opima,* plus his reelections to the consulship in 210 and again in 208, he was clearly a master craftsman in the art of self-fashioning throughout his career.[34]

Yet for all that, when he left his province in 211, Roman forces in Sicily and throughout the rest of the *imperium Romanum* were still at war with a deadly enemy against whom the future held no guarantees of a final vic-

29. 26.32.8: "legati benigne appellati ac dimissi ad genua se Marcelli consulis proiecerunt obsecrantes ut quae deplorandae ac levandae calamitatis causa dixissent veniam eis daret, et in fidem clientelamque se urbemque Syracusas acciperet."

30. Cf. the reaction of the envoys from Capua, another rebellious city reduced under siege at about the same time, after the senate had heard their complaints and reinforced the decisions of the commander in charge (26.34.13).

31. So Badian 1958, 157. It is also worth noting the comment of Eckstein 1987, 176 n. 84, that the impetus for the relationship "comes from the Greeks, not the Roman."

32. See Brunt 1971, 66–67.

33. Eckstein 1987, 170, labels the siege of Syracuse as "one of the greatest feats of arms in antiquity."

34. For a detailed study of Marcellus's consummate skill in this direction, see Flower 2000.

tory. His political rivals did not need to invent the *deportatio* provision out of whole cloth. It accurately characterized an unprecedented situation. Marcellus lost out on his *triumphi spes* in 211, that is, not only through the standard, garden-variety workings of *invidia* and aristocratic competition, but also because the Republic in the grips of the Hannibalic War was fundamentally not yet ready to celebrate. Instead, as Livy remarks in a foreshadowing of Marcellus's epitaph, he was destined to end his life in a world where even his greatest achievements simply could not rise above it all (26.29.9–10):[35]

> The exchange of provinces took place between the consuls themselves, with fate carrying off Marcellus toward Hannibal, so that having been the first to seize the distinction of a successful battle over Hannibal, after many crushing defeats, he would become the last of the Roman generals to fall to Hannibal's praise at a time when the war was going most favorably.

This passage would be unintelligible outside the realm of triumphs and triumph debates. The *imperator,* his predecessors, and Hannibal, the great foe, all factor into the symbolic equation, which the historian painstakingly balances. Having captured a measure of *gloria* for the Roman side when they badly needed it, Marcellus only brought more *laus* to Hannibal with his death in what should have been his finest hour. He was the right man on the scene, but at the wrong time.

M. LIVIUS SALINATOR AND C. CLAUDIUS NERO IN 207: TURNING POINT

The joint ceremony that marked the joint victory of M. Livius Salinator and C. Claudius Nero over Hasdrubal at the Metaurus in 207 has already been discussed, including some of its performative features. If indeed, as Livy says, the consuls came up with the idea for their unique hybrid victory procession on their own, then they deserve credit for creating a memorable icon of their singularly memorable campaign. Both men reaped tremendous profits from it in the symbolic coinage of *laus* and *gloria,* and especially Nero, who was seen to have ceded primacy of place to his colleague when he himself deserved the greater honor (28.9.9–11). Paradoxically, that carefully orchestrated self-deprecating gesture only made people admire him all the more, and called all the more heightened attention to

35. 26.29.9–10: "inter ipsos consules permutatio provinciarum rapiente fato Marcellum ad Hannibalem facta est, ut ex quo primus post <adversissimas haud> adversae pugnae gloriam ceperat, in eius laudem postremus Romanorum imperatorum prosperis tum maxime bellicis rebus caderet." Because the compact syntax of interlocking relative and co-relative clauses in this passage is impossible to render into smooth English, I have chosen to repeat Hannibal's name several times. It certainly bears the emphasis.

his *res gestae* as opposed to the outward show of regalia, soldiers in procession, and so on, that this commander did not possess and, in the eyes of his admirers, did not need (28.9.15):[36]

> Let the other consul travel way up high on his chariot pulled by multiple horses if he wanted: the real triumph was riding through the city on a single horse, and Nero would be memorable whether for the *gloria* he acquired in war or for what he had refused in this triumph, even if he entered the city on foot.

Nero's name echoes through this passage in tones of awe: we can almost hear it being transformed into an exemplum for the whole Roman community as the procession travels along. Because we have moved here from the closed aristocratic circle within the senate out onto the larger civic stage of the triumphal ritual itself, Nero's accolades circulate not only or even primarily among his peer group, but rather between him as the focal point of the communal gaze and all the ranks of citizens watching the ceremony, whose comments, jokes, and songs accompanied the *triumphator* to the Capitol (28.9.16).

Livy focuses attention in this scene, as he so often does, on the psychology of the embedded audience.[37] Nero's performance in the public eye—slowly wending his way, with dignity and decorum, through the streets of the city on the back of his emblematic single horse—gradually lends stature and substance to his image as one of Rome's civic heroes, someone who has accomplished almost unimaginable things at a moment of supreme danger to the Republic. As a buzz of interest and approval ripples through the crowd, the incantational power of the dreaded names Hasdrubal and even Hannibal finally begins to weaken in the face of their defeat (28.9.12–14). The historian has very carefully set the stage for this reaction from the beginning of the episode. When the consuls first set off to fight the brothers Barca close to home in Italy, two noteworthy things happened. First, public necessity pressured the consuls, notorious *inimici,* to resolve their differences, at least temporarily, for the sake of the *res publica.* The same unanimity that would later form such a striking feature of their homecoming and victory celebration gave expression here to the depth of the civic

36. 28.9.15: "iret alter consul sublimis curru multiiugis si vellet equis: uno equo per urbem verum triumphum vehi, Neronemque etiamsi pedes incedat vel parta eo bello vel spreta eo triumpho gloria memorabilem fore."

37. Note the highly significant comments of Feldherr 1998, 17: "In presenting a scene . . . as a spectacle, where the responses of the contemporary spectators described in the narrative provide a model for the reader's experience of the event . . . Livy not only draws a parallel between his text and the public spectacles of the state but makes his own narrative the medium through which these spectacles reach a new audience . . . Livy situates his work at the active center of Roman civic life."

crisis (27.35.5–9, 38.9). Second, people anxiously followed their departure, still nursing wounds from the traumas of Trasimene and Cannae and the death of the Scipios in Spain, and not finding grounds for much faith in the rare, tentative successes from the war so far. Livy describes the burden of command in this perilous situation as an oppressive weight (*moles, onus*): everything seemed to hang in the balance (27.40.1–7).

In that tense atmosphere, news of Hasdrubal's unexpectedly speedy crossing of the Alps, and of Nero's even more precipitous and risky march north to meet him and prevent the two Carthaginian armies from joining forces, caused a paroxysm of fear and anxiety among all the inhabitants of Rome. After everything they had already been through, how could they possibly cope with *two* Hannibals at the gates? (27.44.5). Livy writes in broad strokes, emboldened by hindsight, of the way Nero himself drew confidence and encouraged his men on the march. While acknowledging that they were taking a risk by leaving their own camp undefended, he affirmed that the final victory now lay within their grasp. Their impetus would tip the balance (again the image of weights in a scale), and tremendous glory would follow, as evidenced by the crowds coming out to cheer them on (27.45.1–6). In the first of many foreshadowings of triumphal imagery throughout the narrative of the campaign, we learn that Nero's army was met by a flood of people everywhere they went. These spectators invested them as "guardians of the *res publica,* avengers of the city of Rome and her empire," with all their deepest fears, prayers, and hopes about how the upcoming battle would turn out, ready to pay any vow if a *felix pugna* would follow and transform their present anxiety into rejoicing (27.45.7–9).[38] Well-wishers even pressed the soldiers with repeated offers of food and drink, which they politely declined, taking only what they needed (27.45.10–11).

The historian could just as easily have explained to his readers in his own voice how much lay at stake in the Metaurus campaign, but he paints a much more vivid and compelling picture by projecting words and feelings onto a contemporary audience.[39] Moreover, through the repetitive rhythms of the

38. 27.45.7–9: "illos praesidia rei publicae, vindices urbis Romanae imperiique appellabant: in illorum armis dextrisque suam liberorumque suorum salutem ac libertatem repositam esse. deos omnes deasque precabantur ut illis faustum iter, felix pugna, matura ex hostibus victoria esset . . . ut, quemadmodum nunc solliciti prosequerentur eos, ita paucos post dies laeti ovantibus victoria obviam irent" ("They kept calling them the guardians of the *res publica,* avengers of the city of Rome and her empire: in the weapons and right hands of those men rested their safety and freedom and that of their children. They were praying to all the gods and goddesses to grant them a propitious journey, a successful fight, and a speedy victory over the enemy . . . so that just as now they followed them forth with anxiety, so a few days later they might joyously meet them on the way, celebrating in victory").

39. Cf. the *profectio* of P. Licinius Crassus in 171 and the adept analysis by Feldherr 1998, 9–12. Note also Lambert 1967.

annual magisterial cycle, the emotions expressed here become associated not only with this singular moment in Republican history but in fact with any *imperator* setting off anywhere against any enemy at any time. *Profectio* as such was a regular occurrence, of which this merely represents an extreme example, allowing the author to spell out here more fully and memorably than usual (by means of abundant detail and ideologically loaded keywords) what the underlying situation in fact always signifies. There is also a deliberate symmetry between the reciprocal actions of going out to war and coming home again victorious.[40] By studying this episode, then, and calling it to mind whenever the situation recurs elsewhere in Livy's history, albeit sometimes in a highly compressed form, the savvy reader will learn how to interpret the narrative properly and apply its lessons to real life.[41]

Victory at the Metaurus came about just as Nero (and the historian through him) had presaged beforehand: Hasdrubal, his army, and his elephants were cut to pieces. Rather than putting the handful of Carthaginian survivors to death, the consul spared their lives and sent them back to their comrades to begin spreading the fame of their disgrace at the mercy of Roman *virtus* (27.48–49). As the news slowly spreads from the battlefield out on the periphery back to the center of power and meaning in Rome, the symbolic movements and emotional transactions initiated at the moment when the *imperatores* first set out are reversed. If anything, Livy traces this reverse process in even greater detail so as to bring the victory home in all its abiding significance (27.50.2–51.10). Though unheralded, Nero's return journey to the safety of his own camp brings villagers from across the countryside to salute him again. The first inklings of a triumphal procession have begun. Meanwhile a palpable hush has descended on Rome. While waiting for news, with the entire future of the Republic seemingly poised at a pivot point, all the iconic strata of the political and social order have gravitated to their appointed places in the civic geography and remain there night and day, not knowing what else to do: senators and magistrates in the *curia*, ordinary citizens in the Forum, prayerful women wandering from shrine to shrine (27.50.3–5).[42]

40. Cf. Feldherr 1998, 10: "The *profectio* prompts its audience to remember the entire series of past consuls who have marched off to war with the same ceremony, and to anticipate yet a further ceremony when the consul they now watch descending the Capitol will reascend it in his triumph."

41. Thus Feldherr 1998, 11: "Livy's contemporary audience has a place in the same continuum of events recalled by the *profectio,* their own future and past can be mapped by the same series of victories and defeats—the very events that provide the Annalistic structure of Livy's narrative."

42. There are clearly conventional elements at work in this passage: everyone is right where one would expect him or her to be based on societal norms. Livy often points out such

But unlike the inhabitants of the city, Livy and his readers know the outcome of the battle by now, so that the narrative from here on will incrementally close the gap between the privileged viewpoint of history and hindsight on the one hand and the limited understanding possessed by the chorus in the drama on the other. It begins with a tentative whisper at the edges, from the army camp in Umbria, where the first horsemen have come, and then rumors start to grow in the city itself that the Carthaginians have been destroyed (27.50.6). People are incredulous of the good news at first, not daring to hope without more confirmation. A mere two days after the battle, word seems to have traveled too fast for belief (27.50.7). Letters arrive, not yet from the consuls themselves as usual but from the camp in Umbria, where all the rumors started. Even at several removes from the commanders' own *res gestae* narrative, however, this first tangible evidence of events *militiae* nearly sparks a riot *domi,* with everyone clamoring at once and competing to hear. Tensions run high along familiar fault lines in the social and political order of the SPQR, and the *patres* must assert their privileges in order to ensure that the letter will be read in the *curia* first, and only then in the Forum. At this point some people finally make the leap of faith to accept the victory, while others hold out for the arrival of real laureate letters from Nero and Salinator. Then at last comes the flamboyant stage entrance of the consular *legati* L. Veturius Philo, P. Licinius Varus, and Q. Caecilius Metellus to make the official announcement (27.51.1–3).

Livy knows the names of these three men because they took part in a pivotal moment in Rome's history and were remembered: the symbolic equivalent, on the positive side of the ledger, of what certain piously recorded casualties meant on the negative side when singled out by name in the tallies of less-than-bloodless victories. Mobs of people crowd these *legati* from the moment they arrive, as if they themselves were the *imperatores* returning home to celebrate a triumph, rather than just messengers with news of victory. They have to fight their way through to the *curia,* and again the *patres* must intervene to prevent the rabble outside the senate chamber from hearing them first. Their words finally draw a convincing outline of the Metaurus victory and its tremendous scale: *magnitudo rerum gestarum.* At the subsequent *contio* the crowd can barely contain its excitement (27.51.5–6). People rush home to tell their families, and the senate's *supplicatio* decree ushers forth such overwhelming joy, relief, and thanksgiving in all quarters, among men, women, and children alike, that it looks "as if the war were

divisions within a crowd by way of lending colorful detail and verisimilitude to the scene. Walsh 1961, 185–86, cites Quintilian's remarks about the narrative technique known as *eversio* (8.3.63–70).

about to be over" (27.51.9).[43] The balance has indeed tipped, so that people can imagine life finally returning to normal. The resolution of a crisis in the symbolic economy even allows the material economy to function again after the long and crippling paralysis of fear (27.51.10).

Of course the whole process culminates in the arrival of the consuls themselves. When those once heralded as "guardians of the *res publica,* avengers of the city of Rome and her empire" (27.45.7) return at last, having vouchsafed the blessings of *felicitas* through their resounding victory on behalf of the Republic, all the prayers, promises, hopes, and dreams that had accompanied them in anxiety as they first left the city poured forth again to welcome them back.[44] More crowds gather, not only to congratulate their champions but also to touch them, partly for healing (a kind of sympathetic magic) and partly to reassure themselves that the saving heroes of the community are real and not a mere figment. Livy says that the consuls orchestrated their arrival to take place in tandem, just as they had first set off side by side to meet Rome's deadliest enemies, and as they would triumph not long thereafter (28.9.4–6). The telling images of *imperium* in action are deliberately brought full circle. Not long before, the *patres* deftly negotiated a difference in status between the two men by making separate arrangements for their armies (28.9.2–4),[45] and now they tactfully respond in kind by designing their joint victory ceremony as a unique hybrid form of the triumph and *ovatio.* Both men bask in *gloria,* right where this whole discussion began (28.9.8–18).

From start to finish, Livy has painstakingly structured his account of the Metaurus campaign to highlight a dawning awareness on the part of Romans that victory might—just might—be possible over Hannibal and his forces of darkness. The historian clearly views this as the turning point in the war, the one that Marcellus for all his brilliance had never lived to see. The senate's exuberant vote of twin triumphs for Nero and Salinator, with no one standing aside to demur (28.9.9), signals a shift in the balance

43. 27.51.9: "omnia templa per totum triduum aequalem turbam habuere, cum matronae amplissima veste cum liberis perinde ac si debellatum foret omni solutae metu deis immortalibus grates agerent" ("All the temples held an equal crowd throughout the entire period of three days as matrons in loosened garments gave thanks to the immortal gods with their children, released from all their fear, almost as if the war were about to be over").

44. Cf. Feldherr 1998, 10–11: at the *profectio* "the possibilities of victory and disaster are equally present," but by the time the commander returns the outcome is known. To borrow an image from quantum physics, the waveform collapses to reveal the particle's trajectory.

45. At 28.9.3 Livy explicitly calls attention to the separate treatment that the armies received: "id modo in decreto interfuit quod M. Livi exercitum reduci, Neronis legiones Hannibali oppositas manere in provincia iusserunt" ("this was the only difference in the decree, that they ordered the army of M. Livius to be brought back but Nero's legions, who were in place against Hannibal, to remain in the province"). Also see above, p. 69.

of success and failure for the conflict as a whole. So that his readers will appreciate the pivotal moment when it finally arrives, Livy forces them first to relive the anxious interval when everything still hung in midair and no one knew when or how the struggle would end. That is why he spends so long narrating the effect of the news on the people of Rome in such painstaking detail: because it allows him to dramatize just how momentous it all was, with events careening right up to the brink of disaster and then everyone slowly letting their guard down again.[46] In a chilling but unforgettable closing touch, we learn that even Hannibal himself recognized the beginning of the end when he saw his brother's severed head, which Nero had carefully preserved to be thrown in front of the enemy's camp (27.51.11–12). Hannibal's reaction calls to mind the Lady of Shalott: *The curse is come upon me . . .*

P. CORNELIUS SCIPIO IN 201: AFRICANUS AND AFTER

As Hannibal is about to leave Italy and return to Africa in 203, Livy famously shows him lingering on the threshold for a moment, in the knowledge that he has lost his chance and that his powers are already waning. The historian ironically compares his emotions to those of an exile driven from his homeland (30.20.7–9). Two years earlier, as we have seen, complex political maneuvering between senate, tribunes, magistrate, and popular assembly secured authorization for the newly elected consul P. Scipio to take the war onto the enemy's turf (28.40–45). Momentum had started swinging in the Republic's favor since the Metaurus campaign, allowing Romans to get used to the idea that Hannibal might not be invincible. It should hardly diminish Scipio's accomplishment to observe then that the same desperate emotions did not mark his *profectio* as had once followed Nero and Salinator into battle. The *supplicatio* in honor of Scipio's momentous sea crossing, "so that this action might be beneficial for the Roman people and for the leader himself and for his army" (30.1.11), bespeaks a guarded confidence.[47] This champion could set out to slay the mighty dragon with the full blessing of the *res publica* behind him, at least in part because the

46. Lazenby 2004, 234, carefully balances a judicious awareness of Livy's tendency to dramatize against the very real dangers of the historical situation, thus: "Though Livy may exaggerate the alarm felt at Rome when Hannibal's brother, Hasdrubal, reached Italy from Spain in 207, the fact that his conquerors were granted the first triumph awarded in the war is indicative of the relief felt at Rome, and who knows what might have happened had he been able to join Hannibal?"

47. 30.1.11: "decretumque ut supplicatio foret, quod is in Africam provinciam traiecisset, ut ea res saltuaris populo Romano ipsique duci atque exercitui esset." Also see above, p. 101.

dragon's brother, Hasdrubal, already lay dead by a Roman hand. His race was mere flesh and blood after all.

The victory at Zama finally put a decisive end to the nightmare that had kept Italian children awake in their beds through so many summers.[48] Then Scipio, "having brought peace on land and at sea," we are told, and making his way "through an Italy no less overjoyed by peace than by victory, not only with people pouring out of the cities to celebrate his civic honors but also with a crowd of country folk laying siege to the roads, came to Rome and was carried into the city in the most splendid triumph of all" (30.45.1–2).[49] Livy does not record any arguments in the senate. Could there really have been any? If a triumph debate could ever be reduced to the status of a mere formality, this was the occasion. No one among the *patres* would dare to assault Africanus or his *res gestae* now. Indeed he would dominate the Roman political scene for two decades or more, and *invidia* could patiently bide its time (e.g., 35.10.5–7).[50] For Scipio had raised the standard of individual achievement in service to the *res publica* by becoming the first *imperator* to take the name of his *provincia* as an agnomen (30.45.6–7).

Triumphs, and triumph debates, would never be the same again. A new economy of scale took over in the second century, after Hannibal's defeat, as Rome stepped out onto a much larger stage than ever before in the Mediterranean world. The entire legacy of Alexander the Great now came to bear on the city by the Tiber, and vice versa.[51] The lure of the East held unprecedented opportunities for personal enrichment both symbolic and material, tremendous wealth as well as seemingly unlimited pools of *laus* and *gloria,* which intensified the already fierce competition among the élite. Africanus and Salinator were probably the only living *triumphatores* by the year 200, so the field was wide open and the need could not have been greater for new successes, *res triumpho dignae,* to put on display. Such

48. On the Zama campaign see 30.29–38; cf. Polyb. 15.5–19; App. *Pun.* 39–50. Note the assessment by Scullard 1970, 241: "Scipio stands in the centre of the history of Republican Rome. . . . A noble of the nobles, born into one of Rome's greatest families, he shone forth like a star of hope in his country's darkest hour. For nearly ten years the dread Hannibal had swept all before him, but in ten more years Scipio was to bring him to his knees."

49. 30.45.1–2: "pace terra marique parta . . . ipse per laetam pace non minus quam victoria Italiam effusis non urbibus modo ad habendos honores sed agrestium etiam turba obsidente vias Romam pervenit triumphoque omnium clarissimo urbem est invectus."

50. Cf. the remarks of Toynbee 1965, 351, on the "aura of providentiality" surrounding Africanus's career: "Scipio's fellow nobles could not forgive Rome's savior for having been hailed as such by the Roman People at large. Their disapproval eventually condemned him to end his career under a cloud, though he had refrained scrupulously from exploiting his popularity for making anything like a bid for unconstitutional power."

51. Polyb. 1.3.6. See also 1.1.5, with the comments of Walbank 1957, *ad loc.*, as well as the thoughtful discussion by Harris 1985, 107–17.

heightened tensions posed unprecedented challenges in turn to the inner workings of the Roman political system, which is to say the long-established checks and balances between the senate, magistrates, and people of Rome, and between individual identity and the common good, not to mention the precarious perceived commonality of interest within the ruling class.

By all calculations, what followed the long, dark night of the Hannibalic War was a simultaneous increase both in triumph requests and in the struggle to regulate competition through compromise (*ovationes,* etc.).[52] So triumph debates, and angry ones at that, emerge as a prominent feature of the Roman political landscape during the years after Zama, as reflected in Books 31–45 of Livy. Yet the period saw continuity as well as change. The commanders who came after Marcellus, Nero and Salinator, and Scipio Africanus looked to them as exempla in part because these men had all tested the limits of possibility and achievement during a period of national crisis. In addition, they had demonstrated a broad repertoire of performative techniques that any would-be *triumphator* could seek to imitate. The *dignitatis contentio* of the early second century, therefore, with the Hannibalic War firmly in the background, provides the ideal arena for an investigation into the complex individual and group dynamics and powerful ideological symbolism at work in all triumph debates under the Republic, and the place of these episodes within the annalistic scheme of Livy's history.

52. Again note the dramatic upswing in celebrations (triumphs and *ovationes* combined) during the early second century B.C., as charted by Rich 1993, 50.

CHAPTER 8

L. Furius Purpureo in 200

The Centrality of Narrative

The showdown between consul C. Aurelius Cotta and praetor L. Furius Purpureo in 200 began with a sudden emergency. Furius, at Ariminum, had just dismissed the army of his predecessor by order of the senate when he learned that Gauls had attacked two important colonies, sacking Placentia and laying siege to Cremona. He sent out a desperate plea for reinforcements (31.10.2–7). The *patres* gave Cotta, currently preparing to take his post in Etruria, two choices: either go to the rescue of the colonists himself, if his duties would allow, or stay put for now and send his troops to Ariminum in exchange for a small temporary garrison for Etruria, so that the praetor could handle the Cremona situation in his absence (31.11.2–3). They did not instruct Furius to engage the enemy only after the consul's arrival, but no one expected matters to come to a head right away. When Cotta chose the second option, he probably never imagined that the praetor might lead the army into a full-scale pitched battle against the Gauls on his own. The *patres* meanwhile built a contingency into their decree for the sake of any public business that the consul might need to transact in Rome before setting out for his province: "si per commodum rei publicae posset" ("if it were possible to the advantage of the Republic," 31.11.2).[1]

Crises often call for immediate action, even in a system where ad-hoc decisions tend to take the place of careful planning.[2] By authorizing two

1. Cf. 31.22.3 (on Cotta's business in Rome), and note the striking parallels at 26.32.3 (where the senate instructs the consul M. Valerius Laevinus to redress the grievances of the Syracusans) and 35.6.2 (where the consul Q. Minucius Thermus begs off coming home to supervise elections). This is highly formulaic language: the public interest, variously conceived, emerges again and again as an overriding concern.

2. Note Eckstein 1987, xvii.

competing scenarios in advance and leaving events to choose between them, the senators laid fertile ground for later controversy. So once the siege of Cremona had run its course, consul and praetor each sought to exploit the earlier ambiguity for his own designs. A complex, theatrical series of moves and countermoves developed, in which both actors played off each other for the sake of an audience in Rome.

TWO SIDES TO EVERY STORY

The consul, Cotta, tried to have it both ways. At first he agreed to the exchange of troops and lingered over his business in the city, as if preferring to leave the Gallic campaign well alone (31.21.1–2).[3] He must have thought the praetor would be able to handle things for the time being. Then out of the blue came news that Furius had led the consular army to a spectacular victory almost overnight (31.21.2–22.2).[4] Little remained to be done any more, but Cotta suddenly marched off to take command at Cremona after all, and when he got there railed bitterly at Furius for having gone into battle without him (31.22.3). The senators who championed Furius's triumph claim would later note that Cotta had drastically changed his tune (31.48.9). The switch is indeed illuminating: he needed something to show for himself, because the praetor had stolen the march on him in more than just the literal sense. The logic of narrative and representation began quickly to transform *res gestae,* things done on the battlefield, into tokens of symbolic value in the civic political arena. Having engineered the rout of the Gauls on his own, the praetor now had every right, while the consul had none, to boast to the senate of a Roman victory under his command, and to take credit at home for ending a dangerous threat.[5] So he did: the *patres* voted a three-day *supplicatio* throughout the city on receipt of a letter from Furius detailing the scope of his achievement (31.22.1).[6]

Furius's letter is embedded in Livy's own summary of the outcome at

3. Cf. Briscoe 1973, *ad loc.*

4. The praetor certainly lost no time in setting off as soon as the army had come to him, and even after a long forced march did not give the soldiers more than one night to rest before leading them out to face the Gauls in battle (31.21.1–5).

5. Livy uses "prope debellatum erat" ("the war was almost fought to the finish," 31.22.3) and "confectum bellum" (a "completed war," 31.47.4) to describe conditions in the province when the consul arrived. Cf. Furius's own later claims (31.48.11), as well as those of Scipio Africanus (28.40.1), L. Cornelius Merula (35.8.3), and Scipio Nasica (36.39.7), plus the related charge against L. Scipio (37.58.7).

6. 31.22.1: "magna victoria laetaque Romae fuit: litteris allatis supplicatio in triduum decreta est" ("It was a big victory and joyfully received in Rome: on delivery of the [consul's] letter a three-day *supplicatio* was decreed").

Cremona. After remarking that heavy fighting inflicted a major death toll on the Gauls, Livy describes word reaching Rome and the *patres* voting the *supplicatio,* and then gives a second set of casualty figures, balancing the first, but on the Roman side. These men died in the heaviest area of fighting—a neat ring composition (31.21.16–22.2).[7] Despite the reference to Roman losses, the familiar mark of opposition or negative judgment, "nec incruenta victoria fuit" ("nor was it a bloodless victory"), fails to appear.[8] Livy has thus glossed the contents of the dispatch from Furius's point of view and placed the contemporary reaction (i.e., the *supplicatio* vote) in the middle of his account, thereby prompting his readers to join in the act of *existimatio* as part of the living heritage of the Republic. Decisive military action led to civic honors for the commanding officer, but only when presented to the right people in the right way. Even at this early stage, in other words, Furius gained recognition from his peers because he had a particular kind of story to tell. The grandeur of the victory and the intensity of the public reaction reinforced one another: people rejoiced when they saw what great things Furius had done, and his accomplishments gained stature commensurate with the outpouring of civic approval.[9]

The fait accompli left Cotta in the lurch, so he decided to fall back on the provisional authority that the senate had once conferred (nor had he ever explicitly or entirely given it up), to command the troops in Gaul himself. He made a spectacle of his anger, letting it be known loudly, if too late, that the glory of Furius's accomplishments should by right have belonged to him (31.47.4). Although this bit of stage business took place far from the city, he could count on word getting back to the senate in Rome, as it clearly did, since his complaint eventually resurfaced during the triumph debate (31.48.2). Perhaps he even wrote a letter to the *patres* himself to make trouble for Furius's triumph.[10] His grievance against the praetor, "quod absente se rem gessisset" ("that he had done the thing without him," 31.47.4), had at least as much to do with the symbolic capital made available to Furius by his victory as with the victory per se. The praetor had not only waged a battle to write home about but actually written home about it, and to great effect. Cotta could neither take that signal achievement away from him any more nor count on another one of his own to match,

7. Briscoe 1973, *ad loc.*, remarks: "The Gallic losses are very large and probably exaggerated." But for our purposes the actual numbers matter far less than the structure of the narrative and the implication of citing casualty figures at all.

8. On the expression *nec incruenta victoria fuit,* see above, pp. 110–11 and nn. 18, 19.

9. At 31.22.1 (quoted above in n. 6) "-que" ("and") binds together "magna victoria" ("big victory") and "laeta Romae" ("joyfully received in Rome"), balancing the event itself against the public reaction as two sides of the same coin.

10. Livy mentions no such thing here, but he does describe a subversive letter, sent by a *legatus,* which scuttled the triumph hopes of L. Cornelius Merula in 193 (35.6.8).

let alone surpass it—but in lieu of genuine combat he could make a show of force. He shipped Furius very pointedly off to the garrison in Etruria, banishing him forthwith from the scene of the action, and then launched raids on the enemy grain fields with himself in charge (31.47.5).[11] During the triumph debate, as we shall see, he made his presence felt precisely by his absence.

Summarily ousted from his post, the praetor did not take long to realize that any hope for further *res gestae* had come to a dead end for him in Etruria, whereas Rome held the promise of a triumph for the victory he had already won (31.47.6).[12] Livy implies that both these magnets drew Furius in the same direction—one pushing, the other pulling—which means that the lack of military opportunity where he was might have reflected badly on him, just as a triumph would bring him the recognition and status craved by every Roman aristocrat. To extend the prevailing economic metaphor, he found himself cut off then from any additional income, with a major victory in the bank, and so decided to cash in on his dividends sooner rather than later; whereas Cotta put his stock in command of the army to give him control over the means of production of *res gestae,* whether he ever fought a real battle or not. Moreover, since Cotta's efforts to save face required that he stay in Gaul with his troops, the indignant consul had ironically given his rival plenty of room to press his triumph claim undisturbed. Furius dropped everything and rushed home at once to appear before the senate.

The notice in Livy for his formal triumph request beautifully illustrates the typical two-part pattern: first he told the story of his *res gestae* to the assembled *patres,* and then he asked for their permission to enter the city in triumph (31.47.7). Indeed the link between narrative and *triumphi spes* shows up more clearly than usual here, because under the circumstances Furius came home with nothing to offer the Republic by way of booty or captives, only the proud tale of his victory. He and his *res gestae* would stand or fall together, depending on how his peers judged his performance. When all was said and done, what he had would prove enough to win a tri-

11. Because Livy does not mention any provision in the original senate decree for the consul to send the praetor away to Etruria if he chose to lead an expedition against the Gauls himself, Cotta's behavior seems calculated and self-serving. Yet as Briscoe 1973 comments *ad loc.*, "the consul's *imperium* was greater than that of the praetor, and Cotta could thus issue orders to Furius."

12. 31.47.6: "simul quod in Etruria nihil erat rei quod gereret, simul Gallico triumpho imminens quem absente consule irato atque invidente facilius impetrari posse ratus" ("at once because there was no campaign for him to pursue in Etruria, and being intent upon the Gallic triumph, which he thought could be more easily obtained in the absence of the angry and resentful consul"). The balanced construction ("simul . . . simul") neatly couples the lack of activity in Etruria with the tantalizing prospect of a triumph in Rome.

umph—but not for some time yet. Meanwhile Livy says that right from the start the scale of Furius's achievement (*magnitudo rerum gestarum*), coupled with his popularity (*gratia*), did impress a majority of the senators. By voicing their approval a second time, to his face, they began to reaffirm and strengthen the *supplicatio* vote, enriching his store of symbolic capital and enhancing the intrinsic merit of his claim (31.48.1).[13] He drew severe criticism as well, amid the praise, because an outspoken group of elder senators ("maiores natu") picked up on the complaints already raised by the consul in Gaul. Not only had the praetor led troops into battle that belonged to another commander and were hence never rightfully his to command, they said, but he had compounded the offense by arriving in Rome soon thereafter with a selfish and opportunistic triumph bid (31.48.2).[14]

These charges echo the two reasons why Furius had supposedly hurried back to Rome—that is, the *res gestae* that he had to his name and his desire to capitalize on them in the symbolic economy—and turn both against him. By linking the facets of their argument with an *et* . . . *et* ("both . . . and") construction, Livy has made an important point about Roman aristocratic ideology. The two elements clearly refer to different concepts when counterbalanced as things done versus things said, reality versus representation, or warfare versus politics; but taken together from the perspective of the elders in this passage, they led to but a single conclusion. Whether in the field or on the political stage, impetuous zeal for distinction and glory had caused Furius to place blind ambition before his duty as a magistrate of the Republic, spurring him first to engage the Gauls when he should have held back and then to run off in pursuit of a triumph rather than stay in his province for as long as need be. The elders could not bring themselves to condone this unprecedented behavior (31.48.3: "nullo exemplo"), much less reward it. Even while the would-be *triumphator* tried to sculpt himself into a model commander, his critics announced that they could not make the image fit and thereby put themselves forward as defenders of lofty ideals.

Nor can it be accidental that what they claimed Furius should have done so perfectly matched what Cotta was in fact doing at that very moment. The consul's display of righteous indignation had not gone unnoticed. Therefore the plain, unadorned geographical facts—praetor in Rome, consul in

13. 31.48.1: "apud magnam partem senatus et magnitudine rerum gestarum valebat et gratia" ("With a large part of the senate both the scale of his accomplishments and his personal standing weighed in his favor").

14. 31.48.2: "maiores natu negabant triumphum et quod alieno exercitu rem gessisset, et quod provinciam reliquisset cupiditate rapiendi per occasionem triumphi" ("The elders wanted to deny him a triumph, both because he had accomplished the thing with someone else's army, and because he had left his province in a desire to seize an opportunistic triumph").

Gaul—could conveniently be made to cut both ways and serve competing agendas. Furius would get his triumph by working quickly to curry favor while Cotta was away, but Cotta too, by not rushing back, had managed to reach a sympathetic audience among the *patres*. He was engaged, no less than his rival, in a self-fashioning aimed at showing certain people that he had properly lived up to what the Republic expected of its magistrates. We should recall that the senate had shown concern before that Cotta might have pressing business threatening to detain him in Rome (31.11.2). So long as he remained in the field, no one could accuse *him* of shirking responsibilities. He would wait to put in an appearance until the elections brought him home in due course, at the end of the year (31.49.8–11). Those who paid him heed not only forced Furius to face a challenge in the political arena before he could enjoy public honors but also endorsed the consul's decision to stay with the army. Through complementary strategies the two commanders, present and absent alike, sought *domi militiaeque* to increase their political profit margins in Rome.

The opposing routes by which they chose to pursue their goals meant that they would never be seen together. But how could the *patres* properly evaluate what had happened at Cremona if they heard only one side of the story at any given moment? According to Livy, this obstacle was overcome by means of some highly elaborate and subtle stagecraft, in which members of the senate, apart from the consul and praetor, played an unusually prominent role. Any triumph debate put all its participants on display before their peers, because in *existimatio* everyone was always watching everyone else while performing at the same time. What made this a special case was that Cotta could not oppose Furius's triumph request without losing the moral high ground that he had seized, except by proxy. His performance demanded that someone else put on his persona and argue for him, so that he could stay in Gaul. Livy says that a group of *consulares* stepped forward—if this designation is historically accurate, it could signal a concern about Furius's praetorian rank—and urged their colleagues to do now in their deliberations what Furius should have done in the field, namely wait for the consul before taking decisive action (31.48.3–4).[15] The analogy between the military and political domains is explicit: if the praetor should not have acted alone, then when judging his actions the senate should not listen to him alone either.

At the climax of their speech, the *consulares* offer stage directions for an

15. 31.48.4: "quod praetor non fecisset, senatui faciendum esse ut consulem exspectaret" ("what the praetor had not done, the senate should do now: wait for the consul"). In the same sentence they assert that Furius "could have dragged things out ["potuisse . . . rem extrahere"]" in the province until Cotta got there, neatly delineating a better alternative to the undesirable fact of what he had actually done (i.e., *rem gessit;* cf. 31.47.4).

imaginary drama, a play within the play: "ubi coram disceptantes consulem et praetorem audissent, verius de causa existimaturos esse" ("once they had heard consul and praetor debating face to face, they would make a truer judgment in the case," 31.48.5).[16] This is a model for conducting a negotiation or dispute ("causa"), in which two chosen magistrates of the Republic ("consulem et praetorem") would square off for a duel of words ("disceptantes") in a public setting ("coram") before an audience of judges taken from among their peers ("senatus," in the previous sentence) and commissioned to hear them out ("audissent") and seek the truth ("verius")—all designated as part of the ongoing process of assigning symbolic value to their self-fashioning performances on the basis of Roman aristocratic ideals ("existimaturos esse"). Emphasis falls on the comparative adverb, "verius": the hypothetical scene would yield a "truer" result.[17] Compared to what? Livy does not say, but the context points to the senate deliberations as they were currently being conducted: that is, with a face-off between praetor and *consulares* acting on Cotta's behalf instead of directly between praetor and consul.

Taken both on its own and in contrast with reality, the hypothetical scenario operates on several different levels. First, when the *consulares* conjure up ideas about what Cotta might do, were he there to speak for himself, they are warning against letting Furius's account of the battle go unquestioned. Every monologue has its natural limitations as an index of truth, and no real head-to-head confrontation need ever take place for such a reminder to help counterbalance the prevailing bias toward what the praetor had just said. If the *patres* include the absent consul in their *existimatio,* the results will hold more true than if they do not. Second, the self-conscious role of the *consulares* as mouthpieces for someone else underlines the fact that unlike Furius, who abandoned his post, Cotta could still be found with his army, where he belonged. The praetor was seeking to fashion himself into an exemplum in the usual way, by means of a live performance; but under the circumstances the consul could actually become one by failing to appear. Third—and this is crucial—the *consulares* were also performing on the political stage in their own right. By attacking Furius and defending Cotta at the same time, they could take double credit for publicly upholding high standards, fittingly commensurate with their rank.

16. For a close parallel, cf. 35.8.7.

17. Note that the adverb "verius" at 31.48.5 works equally well with both meanings of *existimare:* either taken literally within the monetary realm to denote authentic vs. counterfeit coinage, or understood in the context of aristocratic ideology, in the metaphorical sense of well-founded judgment. Also cf. Barton 2001, 67–68: "As a result of living in a contest culture . . . the 'truth' of what one said was intimately linked with the ability of the speaker to endure a test or trial of some sort."

The image of consul and praetor face to face hangs in the air for a moment, superimposed on the actual scene, just long enough to catch notice and register its effect. Then it fades, leaving the more immediate spectacle with the stage to itself once again. This marks the turning point in the debate. The minority working to make room for Cotta in the picture could not hold out forever amid a growing conviction that the senate's evaluative gaze should finally come to rest on the lone figure of the would-be *triumphator,* who was already right there before them. After all, Furius had exercised his lawful *imperium* to the glory of Rome, decisively rescuing the colonists from deadly peril (31.48.6; cf. 48.10). Elements from the commander's *res gestae* narrative came to the fore again now, as conventional and easily recognizable tokens of symbolic value.[18] Furius's supporters may be appealing to certain basic, long-standing aristocratic ideals about how an *imperator* should behave, but under pressure from the opposition they must still persuade their colleagues to acknowledge *their* benchmark for what entitled someone to a triumph.[19]

Here at last comes Furius's turn to capitalize on the indecisiveness of the original senate decree. Several times along the way different people might have stopped him from ever waging war on the Gauls. When none of them did, "what on earth was the praetor supposed to do?" (31.48.7: "quid tandem praetori faciendum fuisse?"). The *patres* could not maintain that they gave him command over an army but never authorized him to fight. That would send mixed messages, to say the least, to other *imperatores* in the field. They might have forestalled the issue later, when the crisis came, simply by putting Cotta in sole charge of the Cremona expedition instead of leaving him free to make his own dispositions. Even with their decrees as is, if Cotta had so badly wanted to keep Furius out of the action, as he later protested, then he ought to have made a point of marching to the colony at the head of his troops rather than dawdling in Rome and sending them on ahead without him (31.48.8–9). So in order to hold it against Furius that he had rushed into the breach at Cremona, the consul and his supporters could not avoid indicting themselves as well, because they had

18. 31.48.11: "fusos caesosque hostes, castra capta ac direpta, coloniam liberatam obsidione, alterius coloniae captivos reciperatos restitutosque suis, debellatum uno proelio esse" ("the enemy had been put to flight and killed, their camp taken and pillaged, the siege of a colony lifted, the prisoners from a second colony recovered and restored to their families, the war fought to the finish in a single battle"). Notice how the rhetoric of the triumph debate actually outdoes Livy's own remark from the early stages, with only "prope debellatum" at 31.22.3 but "debellatum" (i.e., end of story) here.

19. Hence the references to what the majority "censebat spectare senatum debere" ("agreed that the senate should look to") at 31.48.6 and "spectari debere" ("should be looked to") at 48.11. Both these passages have already been cited as evidence of the extent to which triumphal criteria were open to debate: see above, p. 75 and n. 25.

failed to issue any restraint. The rhetoric suggests an attempt to revoke a closely guarded privilege (i.e., rights to the production and ownership of *res gestae*), on which they placed enormous value and wanted stringent limits.[20] But by now it was too late to undo their earlier decisions.

Critics tried to argue that Furius had no excuse for what he had done, but he had really had no choice (31.48.10).[21] Events had unfolded in a certain verifiable order, against which Cotta's volte-face stood out in bold relief. The consul may have managed to score some face-saving points early on, but now it was time to set the record straight. Furius's supporters also reminded the *patres* of the *supplicatio* decreed in Furius's name. His *res gestae* bore an indelible stamp of civic approval in the sight of the gods, hardly to be gainsaid after the fact (31.48.12).[22] The honor of the whole senatorial order lay at stake in this affair: they would all share the blame if they continued to insist that something had gone wrong, but they could just as easily emerge unscathed together, and even bask collectively in the success of one of their own, by acknowledging what Furius had accomplished. In the end, Livy says, the *maiestas* ("grandeur") that clung to the consul in his absence could not prevail against the *gratia* ("favor") won for Furius through speeches and active self-fashioning on the senate floor. A full session voted for the triumph (31.49.1).[23]

20. 31.48.8–9: "nam si sine consule geri nihil oportuerit, aut senatum peccasse qui exercitum praetori dederit—potuisse enim, sicut non praetoris sed consulis exercitu rem geri voluerit, ita finire senatus consulto ne per praetorem sed per consulem gereretur—aut consulem qui non, cum exercitum ex Etruria transire in Galliam iussisset, ipse Arimini occurrerit ut bello interesset quod sine eo geri fas non esset" ("For had it been the case that nothing must be done without the consul, then either the senate made a mistake when it gave an army to the praetor—indeed just as they wanted the deed to be done not by the praetor's army but by the consul's, so they could have finished with a decree that it should be done not by the praetor but by the consul—or the consul [*sc.* made a mistake], who, when he had ordered his army to cross out of Etruria into Gaul, did not himself go to Ariminum so that he might take part in the war that it would not be right to have waged without him"). This passage is heavily laced with normative language, gradually building in intensity from the relatively mild "geri nihil oportuerit" to the somewhat stronger "peccasse," all the way to "fas non esset," which is tantamount to *nefas* (extreme condemnation). Note the syntactical parallel with the argument of the *consulares* at 31.48.4, which likewise contains a clause introduced by "potuisse enim" (as in "he should have done X, and indeed he could have").

21. 31.48.10: "non exspectare belli tempora moras et dilationes imperatorum, et pugnandum esse interdum non quia velis sed quia hostis cogat" ("The times of war do not wait for the delays and postponements of commanders, and sometimes battle must be joined not because you wish it but because the enemy forces your hand"). Cf. Eckstein 1987, passim, especially 320–21.

22. A strikingly similar argument won a triumph for Scipio Nasica in 191 (36.40.8–10).

23. 31.49.1: "victa est praesentis gratia praetoris absentis consulis maiestas triumphumque frequentes L. Furio decreverunt" ("the favor of the praetor in front of them defeated the grandeur of the absent consul, and a full session decreed a triumph for L. Furius").

Yet the historian pays tribute to both commanders as gifted performers on the political stage, inasmuch as Cotta made his stature felt and known, even from afar. The simple act of airing concerns could help to redress grievances and allowed the *patres* to maintain equilibrium within their ranks. In the course of a debate, *existimatio* brought about a continual circulation and redistribution of symbolic capital among all those who enjoyed their moment in the spotlight, regardless of the final outcome. Nor did the verdict put an end to the issue. Furius's praetorship had helped to legitimize his *res gestae,* so he hastened to celebrate his triumph before his term of office expired (31.49.2). But no prisoners of war led the procession; no booty was put on display; no soldiers followed the *triumphator* up to the Capitolium. According to Livy all these things, everything indeed "except the victory," seemed to belong to the consul (31.49.3).[24] Once again Cotta and the army remained conspicuous by their absence, noticeably depriving the praetor of the manpower he needed. Roman viewers gauged the status of a *triumphator* by the sheer scale and magnificence of his triumph, and the absence of trappings could not help but tarnish his glory.[25]

By the same token, Cotta had also stood back willingly while Furius staged his performance before the *patres,* and that performance had proven that a tale of victory could earn a triumph all by itself. The unadorned *res gestae* narrative was all Furius had—and as it turned out, all he needed—to convince the senate that he was worthy of recognition and honor. Less could be more. Similarly, the lack of adornment in the triumph procession would draw the full force of the public gaze to the lone figure of the *triumphator.* When spectators asked, as they surely would, what had become of the soldiers to swell the ranks of the procession, then the answer would point straight at the invidious Cotta, who had stubbornly kept them to himself because he felt cheated of the victory at Cremona. Everyone could see that the senate had given the prize to Furius, not to Cotta; but the consul had done his best to undermine and usurp the outward marks of that success. Thus the triumph itself bore an imprint of the simultaneous self-fashioning of the *imperator* and his critics during the long course of the debate.

HAVING THE LAST WORD

Now only one further performance remained, because Cotta had yet to appear in person. When elections at the end of the year brought him back to Rome at last, he certainly did not hesitate to act out against Furius.

24. 31.49.3: "omnia praeter victoriam penes consulem esse apparebat."

25. As Chaplin 2000, 144, remarks, "A triumph without a parade of soldiers would have been visually ridiculous." Cf. Itgenshorst 2005, 203–6. Also note Cotta's own comments at 31.49.8–10.

His speech apparently caught the *patres* off guard, but oddly enough not because he made his move so late in the game. Even with the vote long past, and the triumph already over and done with—symbolic capital securely in the bank for the praetor—it came as no surprise that Cotta might still want to go on the record for the opposition. In fact, his hearers took the ongoing theatrical production entirely for granted: they fully expected him to complain, in line with earlier arguments, that they should have postponed their verdict until he could square off with the praetor face to face.[26] Why speak out now, though, when he had obviously forfeited the chance back when he might have actually swayed the decision? The whole scene makes no sense without an understanding that performance and *existimatio* among Roman aristocrats operated continually, beyond the confines of any particular action or decision. In a broader political context, Cotta's gesture, far from empty, emerges as a brilliant parting shot. Cogent reasons had kept him from taking part in Furius's triumph debate, but he had also played a major role in events at Cremona. It is only natural, then, that he would endeavor to sculpt his own public image, and discredit the praetor if he could, when he returned to the city in due time.

Livy's version of his speech blurs boundaries quite explicitly, and tellingly, between the triumph debate and the actual procession. Echoing the *consulares,* Cotta chides the senate for not trying to corroborate Furius's version of events (31.49.10),[27] and at the close of his remarks the *patres* appear in their familiar guise as judges looking for truth in the commander's account (31.49.11).[28] But in between comes a reference to the *populus Romanus* watching a whole cast of characters in the triumph itself. Ancestral tradition called for "*legati,* military tribunes, centurions, and soldiers even, to be on hand for the triumph, so that the Roman people might see witnesses to the *res gestae* of the man to whom such a great honor was being paid" (31.49.10).[29] Irony lies in the suggestion, unproven but

26. 31.49.8–9: "non id quod animis praeceperant questus est, non expectatum se ab senatu neque disceptandi cum praetore consuli potestatem factam" ("he did not make the complaint that they had anticipated in their minds, that he had not been awaited by the senate, nor had the consul been offered any opportunity for debate with the praetor").

27. 31.49.9: "ita triumphum decresse senatum ut nullius, nisi eius qui triumphaturus esset, eorum qui bello interfuissent verba audiret" ("the senate had decreed the triumph in such a way that they did not hear the words of anyone who had been involved in the war except the would-be *triumphator*").

28. 31.49.11: "ecquem . . . fuisse quem percunctari posset senatus quid veri praetor vanive adferret?" ("Who had there been whom the senate could ask what of truth and of falsehood the praetor had reported?").

29. 31.49.10: "maiores ideo instituisse ut legati tribuni centuriones milites denique triumpho adessent, ut testes rerum gestarum eius cui tantus honos haberetur populus Romanus videret." On the role of the army as witnesses to their commander's triumph, also see above, p. 87 and n. 14; and below, pp. 251 and n. 13, 288 and n. 54.

utterly irrefutable, that instead of enhancing the praetor's finest hour by confirming his glorious tale, such witnesses would only have swelled the chorus of his critics. Of course the very people lamented as missing would indeed have taken part, but for the fact that Cotta himself had detained them in Gaul with him all along—yet another reminder of the credibility that came with command of the army.[30] Nevertheless, although he may have tarnished the afterglow of the triumph somewhat, Cotta could no longer hope to change the fact that the senate had officially enshrined Furius's *res gestae* among the annals of great Roman conquests. That kind of history belonged to the victor.

EPILOGUE: RAMIFICATIONS

So we end, as we began, with the *res gestae* narrative, which is what makes this particular episode such a beautiful paradigm. Among the closing arguments from the triumph debate, Livy records that Furius's supporters playfully accused his critics of seeking to put words into the collective mouth of the senate. If the consul and elders had their way, they said, the traditional formula from the *supplicatio* decree, "quod bene ac feliciter res publica a L. Furio praetore gesta esset" ("because public business had been conducted by the praetor L. Furius with success and good fortune"), would have been reworded to say that he acted "male ac temere" ("with failure and rashness," 31.48.12) instead.[31] This bon mot brings the pro-Furius case to a close with a cheerful flourish. Note how neatly the two pairs of adverbs, "bene ac feliciter" and "male ac temere," sum up the arguments on both sides. The witty tone, however, disguises another, more serious verbal twist, one with wide-ranging implications for Roman aristocratic ideology. With so much attention being paid to the idiom *rem gerere* or *res gestae,* the variation here practically leaps off the page: "res publica gesta."[32] The meanings overlap, so that one might almost substitute "res a L. Furio gestae" ("things accomplished by L. Furius) for "res publica a L. Furio gesta" ("L. Furius's handling of public business" [or even simply "the Republic"]), and vice versa.

30. From the point of view of Cotta's self-fashioning we should note that any such invocation of the *mos maiorum* signals a speaker showing off before the all-seeing eyes of *existimatio.* See Habinek 1998, 45–68.

31. 31.48.12: "per triduum supplicationes habitas quod bene ac feliciter, non quod male ac temere, res publica a L. Furio praetore gesta esset" ("Three days' worth of *supplicationes* had been held because the business of the Republic had been conducted by L. Furius with success and good fortune, not failure and rashness").

32. References in Livy to the *res publica* as such are of course far too numerous to list them all here, but two special idioms can be singled out as illustrations of the clear and abiding link between the achievements (*res gestae*) of individuals and the common interest of the whole

Based on this passage and others like it in Livy's history, the conclusion is unavoidable: behind any significant action taken by an *imperator* in the field stood the collective interest of the whole Roman state. Moreover, that same authority would likewise hold him accountable when he came home to tell his story in the hope of gaining public recognition. Productive service to the commonwealth, *res publica bene ac feliciter gesta,* clearly ranks as the single most cherished ideal of Roman aristocrats both at home and abroad, whether they were leading armies into battle as magistrates of the Republic or taking part in the political life of the Forum and *curia.* The activities of commanders out in their provinces counted as *rem publicam gerere* in the profoundest sense, because they were indeed conducting vital public business, striving to bring about glorious achievements that would make them into models of the ideal citizen, and therefore belong not only to them personally but to the entire community. No distinction existed, then, between waging successful war and serving the common good, and the two came together precisely through the narrative and performative elements of the triumph debate. First with the *supplicatio* vote and again by awarding a triumph, the approval of the senate as a body forged a symbiotic link between the commander's personal stature and the civic identity of the SPQR in whose name he had been commissioned to act. Conversely, self-interest and opportunism, as charged against Furius and others, threatened to disrupt that same fragile bond. Roman aristocrats forever carried the weight of the Republic on their shoulders.

Roman state: (1) variations on "rem publicam gerere" or "res publica gesta," as at 31.48.12 and 2.64.5, 8.31.2, 28.9.4, 37.58.5, 39.4.2, 40.36.12, 44.22.11, 45.39.12, 45.39.18; and (2) variations on "rem publicam administrare" or "res publica administrata," found at 1.49.7, 3.42.1, 6.37.8, 7.41.1, 23.49.3, 30.41.9, 34.55.2, 38.48.15, 40.35.14, 45.32.3, 45.41.1.

CHAPTER 9

L. Cornelius Merula in 193

What Could Possibly Go Wrong?

L. Cornelius Merula, consul in 193, learned the hard way about the value placed on a commander's list of achievements. His triumph hopes slipped right through his fingers when his story came unstuck. After defeating the Boii near Mutina, the commander wrote the standard letter to the *patres* proclaiming that his army had won the day (35.6.1), but there was no *supplicatio.* Merula's *res gestae* narrative brought controversy among his peers, not consensus. For meanwhile word had also come to a number of senators, privately, from the *legatus* M. Claudius Marcellus, who had fought in the thick of things at Mutina, and he painted an inauspicious picture of the same events. Livy does not say exactly what prompted Marcellus to turn against his commanding officer, but there were heavy casualties on the Roman side (35.6.8–10; cf. 35.5.14).[1] Marcellus never appears before the *patres* in person and indeed remains a shadowy figure throughout the episode. Yet stories from the field by themselves became such powerful tokens of symbolic value on the political stage in Rome that Marcellus's furtive letter from behind the scenes had fully as dramatic and public an impact on the triumph debate as the official consular dispatch to the senate at large.

We should not allow Marcellus's status as a *legatus* on this campaign to mask his identity as a prominent aristocrat: son of the victor at Syracuse, a paragon of Roman *virtus,* he had already risen to the consulship in 196 (33.24.1) and even triumphed over the Gauls (33.37.10).[2] So he understood how the system worked, shrewdly recognizing that he could get his message

1. At 35.5.1, Livy singles Marcellus out by name as one of two leaders on the left flank of the Roman army, which was hit hard early in the battle (35.5.4–5).

2. On Marcellus's triumph, cf. Degrassi 1947, 78–79, 552.

across about events at Mutina—and no doubt increase his own *auctoritas* in the circles of power as a knowledgeable spokesman on military matters—by winning an unofficial audience among the *patres* who would then serve as his mouthpiece toward the rest. According to Livy, his letter warned that they should ascribe the recent victory to good fortune and the valor of the Roman soldiers rather than give credit to their commander. Indeed poor judgment and bad timing on Merula's part had brought about an indecisive outcome at a terrible cost. Many of the allied troops under Marcellus's command had died needlessly, and Boii had lived through the battle who should have been killed (35.6.9).[3] As discussed previously, casualty figures served as an index of character. If the number slain on the Roman side grew too high, or fell too low among the enemy, it signaled a crisis of leadership, a failure to live up to the best expectations of how an *imperator* should behave.[4] Merula's letter surely had not announced the bare fact of victory and left it at that. It would also have portrayed him as a model soldier of the Republic. The *legatus* knew full well what sort of self-congratulatory tale the consul would tell in his effort to impress the *patres,* and so he carefully targeted his own letter in turn as a deliberate act of sabotage against that account.

Firsthand information from the battlefield allowed Marcellus to set himself up from the beginning as precisely the kind of hostile witness that Cotta had spitefully invoked against Furius after the fact (cf. 31.49.10)—with disastrous consequences for Merula's *triumphi spes.*[5] The discrepancies raised made it impossible for the *patres* to give the consul an automatic stamp of their approval, and they voted to table any question of a *supplicatio* for the time being (35.7.1). Thus although his peers did not openly denounce him

3. 35.6.9: "fortunae populi Romani et militum virtuti gratiam habendam quod res bene gesta esset: consulis opera et militum aliquantum amissum et hostium exercitum, cuius delendi oblata fortuna fuerit, elapsum" ("Thanks for the battle having gone well should be given to the good fortune of the Roman people and the courage of the soldiers: by the efforts of the consul not only were a number of soldiers lost, but the army of the enemy escaped, despite an opportunity to destroy it having been offered"). Note the syntactical gap between the all-important formula "quod res bene gesta esset" and the phrase "consulis opera," clearly set up to demolish the idea (which must have formed the basis of the consul's own letter) that the Republic should reward Merula for his accomplishments as a magistrate. By this subversive account, any *gratia* due should go instead to the *fortuna populi* and the *virtus militum,* both obviously well outside the control of the commander. For *fortuna populi Romani* as a catchphrase, cf. 1.52.3, 2.40.13, 6.21.15, 6.30.6, 7.34.6, 26.41.17, 28.44.7, 38.46.4, 45.3.6 (as listed by Briscoe 1981, *ad loc.*). On *virtus militum* in connection with the failings of *imperatores,* see Rosenstein 1990a, 92–113.

4. Marcellus apparently blamed the high allied casualties on the fact that reinforcements of citizen troops were slow to arrive, and the escape of the enemy on a delayed signal and then a failure to pursue the Boii in flight (35.6.10).

5. The parallel between the two episodes shows that even though Cotta's rhetoric was entirely hypothetical and came too late to change the outcome of the triumph debate any more, it still carried significant weight because it veiled no mean threat, as witnessed by the damage Marcellus inflicted against Merula's triumph bid.

as a failure on the battlefield, they did not commend him for his victory either. Other, more pressing business soon upstaged him (at 35.7.2–5 Livy mentions a fiscal crisis), snatching away his audience at the crucial moment. Marcellus struck just as the consul was reaching out to offer the firstfruits of his victory to the senate, before he had managed to secure their confidence in him or in his *res gestae.* One blow made an illusion of the public image that he was trying so hard to create and severed the delicate symbiotic link, inherent in the *supplicatio,* between the acknowledged success of the commander and the glory of the state he served.

Nor did the situation of mistrust improve with the passage of time, because the consul now faced a decidedly uphill battle to convince his peers that he deserved any recognition at all. *Supplicatio* delayed would also mean triumph denied. When Merula came home, he rather pointedly left Marcellus with the army in the province (35.8.1). His opponents would quickly pick up on this bit of stagecraft as an obvious political ploy to keep the *legatus* out of the debate (35.8.5–7), and if the consul had an answer to this charge, Livy does not record it. He probably wanted the spotlight on himself and himself alone, in hopes of monopolizing the discourse as best he could, even though his audience had largely turned against him. The performance began, naturally, with a showy first-person account of his *res gestae,* reminding the senators of what they already knew, or at least should have known, from his field dispatch (35.8.2). If they had hailed that first report by freely offering thanks to the gods for victory, he might have spoken the *ut liceret* part of the formula now as an equally free gesture of submission, firm in the knowledge that they recognized the value of what he had done. But the vote that should have set the stage in advance for his dramatic monologue had gone awry, leaving Merula no choice as he came before his peers in person, if he still wanted to pursue his triumph bid, but to question their judgment over the *supplicatio.*

Any attempt, however, to vaunt himself as a superior judge of his own worth would only alienate them further. For of course the whole unspoken pact between the *patres* and magistrates of the Republic rested on the willingness of those who sought public honors to bow to the collective authority of those who had it in their power to confer them. Hence the *ut liceret.* Merula took refuge in the tiny window of opportunity left open when they failed to refuse him outright the first time, voicing a pious complaint that the gods should be left unthanked when a Roman army had scored such a decisive success. He asked the senate to remedy the situation at once by decreeing a *supplicatio* and a triumph together, indignation on his own behalf thinly veiled behind an appeal to the common interest (35.8.3).[6]

6. 35.8.3: "questus est cum patribus conscriptis quod tanto bello una secunda pugna tam feliciter perfecto non esset habitus dis immortalibus honos; postulavit deinde supplicationem

In reply, the eminent Q. Caecilius Metellus stated that differing accounts of events at Mutina had surfaced (35.8.4: "litteras . . . inter se pugnantes"). Through the dual-*certamina* trope, Livy often portrays a triumph debate as the political counterpart in Rome to the clash of armies on the battlefield (cf. 39.5.12). Here he takes the further step of setting not the *imperator* and his critics but their narratives, personified, at figurative war with one another on the senate floor. We hear the expression "conflicting reports" so often in our own language that the graphic force of the image in Latin is easily lost, but the *patres* expected a tangible corollary to it in the conduct of the triumph debate. The postponement of the *supplicatio* vote, that is, was supposed to prompt Merula and Marcellus to bring their dispute before the senate in person (35.8.5). Again, as in the episode involving Furius and Cotta, both sides could make much of the interplay between presence and absence on the scene. Merula had little choice but to come back by himself, but it must have looked very suspicious indeed for him to have left Marcellus, of all people, behind in charge of the army. Only someone with something to hide would have reason to fear an open exchange: "It seemed now as though the one had been kept away on purpose who, were he to speak in person what he had written, would be able to argue face to face, and if he reported anything false, to be argued against, until the truth had been found out to the point of certainty" (35.8.7).[7]

Such avowals of faith in the power of a discerning public audience to sort out truth from falsehood are a hallmark of performative rhetoric in Livy (cf. 31.48.5). The judgments of *existimatio* created their own reality. A Roman aristocrat could claim no more worth for himself, after all, than his peers as a body saw in him. While questioning whether Merula's *res gestae* would hold up to that kind of scrutiny, Metellus could also take credit himself for standing there face to face with the consul before the *patres* in Marcellus's place. His performance vicariously enjoyed the political impact of the hypothetical scenario. Even secondhand, the threat of what might happen, were the absent *legatus* to appear, proved strong enough to offset the consul's attempts at self-fashioning in person—an inversion of the outcome in 200 (cf. 31.49.1). Two tribunes promised to veto any decree, and the matter dropped, although for his part Merula never withdrew his request for both *supplicatio* and triumph (35.8.9). Far from giving in to

---

simul triumphumque decernerent" ("He complained before the senators that when so great a war had been brought to a close by a single favorable battle with so much good fortune, no thanks had been offered to the immortal gods; he asked them next to decree both a *supplicatio* and a triumph together").

7. 35.8.7: "nunc videri esse amotum de industria qui, <si> ea quae scripsisset praesens diceret, arguere coram, et si quid vani adferret, argui posset, donec ad liquidum veritas explorata esset."

the attacks against him, he maintained his *dignitas,* and the public record would show that he continued to vouch for his accomplishments to the end. Yet ultimately the senate failed to achieve any consensus about what had happened at Mutina. Consul and tribunes reached a deadlock, and when the curtain closed both sides had scored a certain number of points, but neither had backed down.

This raises an important question: Given the stalemate, what then became of the historical narrative? Whose version of the story does Livy follow? Does he stress the decisiveness of Merula's victory, or its cost? As often happens, Livy's seemingly straightforward battle description looks quite different in retrospect through the lens of the triumph debate. His account appears, in fact, to bear traces of both the consul's self-portrait and the less than flattering view from the *legatus,* with the ambiguity still basically unresolved. On the one hand, Livy shows Merula firmly in command from the start, laying out a deliberate battle plan. He ordered the allies and *extraordinarii* to go out first, tellingly with two *legati,* including Marcellus, in charge, and then had the Roman legions wait for his signal so that they and the cavalry could finish the job (35.5.1–3). When a messenger came with news that the troops were flagging under the Gallic advance, the consul duly sent reinforcements, who vigorously joined the fight (35.5.4–7). Later he dispatched horsemen as well (35.5.7–9).[8] Above all the historian credits Merula with bringing about the final turning point in the battle by encouraging his men that victory lay within their grasp. At his order, they pulled together for one last, brutal assault. The Boii soon broke ranks and fled in all directions—the clear formulaic signal for a rout in progress (35.5.11–12).[9] Marcellus would later claim that Merula had forbidden the cavalry to pursue the Boii in flight, but Livy says that he actually commanded them to do so (35.5.12; cf. 6.10).

This much certainly reads like the *res gestae* narrative of a proud and successful *imperator* and follows a conventional pattern highlighting his leadership at a crucial turning point. On the other hand, the casualties were already beginning to mount when the call for extra troops reached the consul, in an ominous foreshadowing of the triumph debate: "Let him send the other of the two legions to help, if he saw fit, before a disgrace was inflicted" (35.5.5).[10] Livy uses an impersonal passive construction, but who else would bear the brunt of any scandal except Merula? Note that the decision is left up to the commander: "if he saw fit." Such a warning alerts

8. The expression "quod ubi animadvertit consul" at 35.5.8 again places Merula in command, both aware of and reacting to the battle as it unfolded.

9. On Roman battle tactics, see Potter 2004, 74–75.

10. 35.5.5: "legionem alteram ex duabus, si videretur, submitteret, priusquam ignominia acciperetur."

Livy's audience that there might be more than one way to read the rest of the battle narrative. The verdict of *existimatio* will come down to whether people think the commander acted quickly enough in the event, or not. That question belongs to his critics and came to public attention during the triumph debate. In his own voice Livy declares only that the reinforcements did their job once sent, without any comment about how long it took to send them (35.5.5–6).[11] Explicit negative judgment comes later—and in indirect discourse—in the momentous letter from the *legatus* to certain senators. Marcellus of course had to wait in the thick of the fight until relief came, and he believed that too much time had elapsed in that anxious interval at the cost of many lives (35.6.10). The keyword, repeated for emphasis, is "tardius" ("too late").

It is no coincidence that this complaint became the vehicle by which disgrace of a sort did befall the consul on his return. For the triumph debate made its mark on what was said to have happened in the field. Merula achieved his victory, but only at length, and at a terrible price. Despite his battle plan, the Boii showed themselves to be both stubborn and resilient in holding off the Roman advances. Even the "storm of charging cavalry caused confusion at first, and at length disrupted and scattered the battle line of the Gauls, but still did not put them to flight" (35.5.9).[12] The longer the battle went on, the more Roman soldiers died. Marcellus made sure that the *patres* would weigh both sides, and at the end of his narrative Livy dutifully tallies up all the casualties: 14,000 Boii killed and 1,092 captured, including 721 cavalry and three of their leaders with military standards and wagons in tow, but then also more than 5,000 Romans and allies dead, and among them 23 centurions, four *praefecti socium,* and three military tribunes from the Second Legion who made the ultimate sacrifice for the Republic, memorialized forever by name, M. Genucius and Q. and M. Marcius (35.5.13–14). Future generations would look on Mutina as a mixed blessing: perhaps not a catastrophe, but by no means a valuable exemplum either. Livy's account thus leads to the same conclusion that the senators reached in their deliberations. "For the Romans," he says, "it was not a bloodless victory" (35.5.14).[13]

11. Although in the narrative "missa est legio" ("the legion was sent") immediately follows after "legionem . . . submitteret" ("let him send a legion"), and "tum redintegrata est pugna" ("then the battle was rejoined") comes in turn right after "missa est legio" (35.5.5–6), nothing marks the actual duration of or interval between these three events.

12. 35.5.9: "haec procella equestris primo confudit et turbavit deinde dissipavit aciem Gallorum, non tamen ut terga darent." They could also fall back on sheer numerical superiority (see 35.5.7).

13. 35.5.14: "nec Romanis incruenta victoria fuit."

CHAPTER 10

P. Cornelius Scipio Nasica in 191

Family Ties and the Art of Persuasion

In 191, after the defeat and surrender of the Boii in a pitched battle, for which the senate had voted a *supplicatio* (36.38.5–7), the consul P. Cornelius Scipio Nasica returned to Rome supremely confident that a triumph awaited him there. No sooner had the Boii handed over hostages as a pledge of good faith than Nasica disbanded his troops, ordering them to meet him in the city on the day of his triumph (36.39.4).[1] The day after his own arrival, in the Temple of Bellona he gave the senators an account of his *res gestae* and duly asked that they authorize the celebration (36.39.5–10). Livy's narrative makes it all look easy up to this point, perhaps too easy, and sure enough a tribune by the name of P. Sempronius Blaesus soon rose to challenge the consul. As it turned out, then, Nasica could hardly expect to waltz into the senate and summarily demand the highest honor the Republic bestowed; despite or more because of the fact that he bore the name Scipio, he would have to earn his triumph on the political stage as well as the battlefield. The ensuing debate nicely illustrates two significant points that have already appeared but deserve further stress: that the pause to argue both sides before awarding a triumph served a valuable function for the *patres* in its own right, and that in order to impress his peers the would-be *triumphator* had to adopt a very particular stance.

As remarked earlier, Blaesus attacked the consul by a circuitous route, which stands out because of what he did not do. Instead of arguing in any

1. 36.39.4: "inde Romam ut ad triumphum haud dubium decedens exercitum dimisit, et adesse Romae ad diem triumphi iussit" ("From there he dismissed his army, returning to Rome as to a triumph that was hardly in doubt, and he ordered them to be present in Rome for the day of his triumph").

way that the senators should deny Nasica a triumph, he urged only that they wait a while before awarding it (36.39.6). In his haste to triumph over the Boii, said Blaesus, Nasica had passed up a chance at the greater glory of conquering the Ligures as well. These tribes had a history of making common cause against the Romans; neither would truly submit until both had been soundly defeated. Rather than heading home quite so quickly to seek recognition for his one, incomplete victory, the consul should have led his troops on to the aid of Q. Minucius Thermus, consul from 193, who had been struggling with the Ligures in the name of the Republic ever since. Together the two armies might have settled the Ligurian issue once and for all, and they could still do it, if the *patres* would consent to send Nasica back into the field to join Thermus now. Nasica would have every right to expect a triumph as proconsul the following year. Once having entered the city in triumph, Nasica would not then go back into the field,[2] so by this argument if the *patres* wanted him to tackle the Ligures, they should hold off on the award. It would seem that Blaesus recognized the final outcome—a triumph for Scipio Nasica, sooner or later—as a foregone conclusion from the start, yet he spoke out nonetheless. What was he trying to accomplish?

That question leads to another. What did Thermus and the Ligures have to do with Nasica anyway? As everyone in Rome surely knew well, and as the consul himself would quickly say, he had been sent specifically to fight the Boii, not the Ligures (36.40.1; cf. 36.1.9), and Thermus would probably seek his own triumph over the Ligures soon enough (36.40.1–2). Assuming that Blaesus was not just spouting irrelevancies and wasting everybody's time, he must have hoped to score political points for himself with a reminder to everyone that even while Nasica stood before the senate claiming victory, another commander nearby still had a war on his hands. By implication, Nasica had exaggerated both the scale and the finality of his achievement; he had left unfinished business behind. Many an *imperator* had fought many a battle in that region during the past few years. Some had even celebrated triumphs,[3] but the war dragged on. None of these lesser men, that is, could measure up to the exemplum of Africanus at Zama, which receives no mention here but seems to hover like a shadow

2. But cf. a counterexample from 293 at 10.46.1–9.

3. Livy and the Fasti attest the following triumphs over tribes from northern Italy or Cisalpine Gaul in the decade or so before Scipio Nasica: in 200 praetor L. Furius Purpureo over the Gauls (31.48–49 and Degrassi 1947, 551), in 197 consul C. Cornelius Cethegus over the Insubres and Cenomani and consul Q. Minucius Rufus over the Boii *in monte Albano* (33.22–23 and Degrassi 1947, 551–52), in 196 consul M. Claudius Marcellus over the Insubres (38.57.10–12 and Degrassi 1947, 78–79, 552). In addition, in 196 fellow consul L. Furius Purpureo took part in Marcellus's victory and *supplicatio* but does not seem to have sought further recognition (33.37.10). And of course L. Cornelius Merula requested a triumph from Gaul (Boii) in 193, but the *patres* flatly refused (35.8.3–9).

just offstage throughout this debate (cf. 38.51.4). The Roman élite in the early second century found themselves at pains to accommodate the feat of one man who could bring about such a stunningly final victory for the Republic in such a desperate crisis. *Invidia* against Africanus would culminate several years after this in the so-called trials of the Scipios. Meanwhile he had set the standards for everyone else, and his family in particular, very, very high indeed.

Nasica had already borne the brunt of his family's preeminence before, in the consular elections for 192, where backing from his famous cousin had proven more of a liability than an asset (35.10.1–10).[4] In a duel of *auctoritas* against T. Quinctius Flamininus, whose brother was also a candidate, the latter had come out ahead, Livy says, in part because he had previously held back from weighing in with his enormous political influence, whereas Africanus had been continually in the public eye for a decade or more by this time. It helped Flamininus too that he was canvassing on behalf of his brother and trusted *legatus,* not just a cousin: the closer the relationship, the more appropriate, and hence the more effective, the resulting *gratia* at the polls (35.10.5–8).

The following year Nasica came up for the consulship again, this time against Africanus's brother Lucius (35.24.4–5). We may conclude that the Scipios clearly did not act in a unified political block to put forward only one candidate at a time. They openly competed with one another; yet viewed from the outside, they were thus collectively hogging even more space on the political stage. This time Africanus would have had to back his brother over his cousin because of the closer relationship (the flip side of the previous election), and so the vote for Nasica in 191 not only gave him the office he had been denied the year before but also forced Africanus's favorite candidate to wait on the sidelines again. L. Scipio and C. Laelius (another protégé of Africanus, who had been defeated the same year as Nasica) each would have his chance in 190, again with "all eyes on Africanus" ("Africanum intuentibus cunctis," 36.45.9). Nasica would come up short again in the censorial elections for 189, even after his triumph, and again a Flamininus would defeat him, this time the *triumphator*

4. This election has become a famous test case (problematic in part because it is almost unique) in the debate over the role of factions in second-century-B.C. politics. Livy treats it in uncharacteristic detail as a watershed moment for the Cornelii: not only did Nasica lose a close race on the patrician side to the brother of T. Quinctius Flamininus, but in the same year Africanus could not weigh in to help his plebeian associate C. Laelius either. Livy says that people had simply reached a "saturation point" with the Scipios ("ipsa satietate," 35.10.6). Whether or not the defeat for Nasica came as any surprise at the time, it certainly demonstrates the political balancing act of *existimatio* at work. For more discussion see (among others) Briscoe 1972, 48–49; 1981, *ad loc.*; and 1982, 1094–95; Develin 1985, 101–2, 164–67; Gruen 1984a, 209, 218; Harris 1985, 33; Scullard 1951, 122–23; Tatum 2001.

T. Quinctius himself (37.57.9–58.2).[5] The intense competition in alternate years between members of two such illustrious families (and even between members of the same family, in the case of the Scipios) reveals just how little room there was at the very top of the political pyramid. Scipio Africanus, as Livy says, enjoyed the highest stature of all, but that also placed him nearer to the brink of *invidia* (35.10.5). Nasica's position—close to Africanus, but not too close—seems to have shaped his entire career, including the triumph debate in 191.

Before awarding him a triumph, the *patres* would have to reassure themselves on each of two paradoxical fronts: that he deserved the honor, *even though* he had not equaled Africanus, and yet that it would not upset the balance overmuch to honor him, *because* he had not equaled Africanus. The first of these corresponds to the outward form of Blaesus's attack, which Nasica would answer by ostentatiously building up the public image of his *res gestae;* the second, to the subtext of the debate, which would demand a gesture of deference to the collective interests of the Republic as a whole and, above all, to the authority of the *patres* as a body. If this reading holds true, then the tribune lighted upon a discreet means of addressing the broader Scipio question indirectly, without shifting the focus of the debate away from the consul himself, where it belonged, and without resorting to unfounded insults either. Because it raised questions only, the oblique argument about Thermus and the Ligures did more than an outright condemnation would have done to set the stage for an extremely delicate negotiation of status. Simply by voicing a doubt, and no more, about whether or not this *imperator* deserved to triumph just yet, Blaesus could force the senators to hesitate over their decision and thereby create a subtle counterpoise to Nasica's ambition. Threatened only with a delay in his *triumphi spes,* and not a refusal, meanwhile, the consul would hardly apologize for his impertinence and return meekly to the field for another year, any more than he had folded up his tent after the first defeat in the consular elections. This situation cried out for a command performance, designed to swing the consensus in his favor right away. Proudly and boldly, Nasica rose to the double challenge of tackling both the open charges against him and the political subtext, where the real danger lay for his *triumphi spes.*

The surface-level argument came easily enough, as remarked earlier. Nasica had only to say that Thermus would surely take care of the Ligures by himself, while he had accomplished his own task as consul that year

5. Cf. Develin 1985, 172–73; Gruen 1984a, 218; Scullard 1951, 137–38. Scullard 1951, 150, further identifies Nasica as the P. Scipio defeated in the censorial elections for 184 (a noted victory for Cato the Elder) as well, which only strengthens the point argued here; see 39.40–41.

by utterly crushing the Boii (36.40.1–7). He had no trouble pointing out the *magnitudo rerum gestarum,* statistics and all: his army had killed more thousands of Gauls in a pitched battle than any in the past had ever fought at once. Shades of insulted amour propre appear in Nasica's speech as Livy presents it: "Therefore could anyone really wonder why, when not a single enemy remained in the province, the victorious army had come to Rome to celebrate the consul's triumph?" (36.40.6).[6] The soldiers were now waiting expectantly outside the city walls. How could the *patres* send him, and them, back out into the field on a whole new mission without first offering them a reward for their job well done? So far, so good, then. Having through a mixture of righteous indignation and common sense demolished the tribune's token argument against him, he arrived at a point just short of the mark, with *imperium, auspicium, ductus,* and *felicitas* now firmly in hand.[7]

One can easily imagine the quietly wary atmosphere in the senate as the consul neared the end of his speech, with everyone watching intently to see how he would clinch his case. A last issue, delicate but vital, remained left to answer—Nasica's status as a Scipio—which had a no less powerful impact on the proceeding for remaining unspoken. Despite perhaps an appearance to the contrary, this is not a mere figment or an argumentum ex silentio, because Livy himself explicitly calls attention in the election notices to Nasica's family ties more than once, and especially his link to Africanus. Election notices and triumph debates in Livy always go hand in hand, and must be read together both forwards and backwards as facets of the same person's public career. Nasica certainly did not rise to the consulship in a political vacuum, and the senators were very well aware of who he was and what family he belonged to. Moreover, the historian has gone out of his way to ensure that his readers know it as well, so that instead of appearing as an isolated incident, the triumph debate will make sense as part of a broader context. Nasica's crowning gesture in the triumph debate, as we shall see, brings all these ideas together, and coupled with the election notices reveals the silent undercurrents, which had been there all along.

Commanders at a similar crux in their performance would often remind the senate of an earlier *supplicatio* decree, nodding both to religious proprieties and to the fact that the *patres* themselves had already stated their

6. 36.40.6: "itaque id quemquam mirari posse, cur victor exercitus, cum hostem in provincia neminem reliquisset, Romam venerit ad celebrandum consulis triumphum?"

7. Indications of all four canonical elements may be found at 36.40.6 (see previous note). Indeed the two simple phrases "victor exercitus" and "consulis triumphum" tell the whole story between them, by reference to the success in the field by an army under the command of a regularly elected magistrate.

approval of the victory in question. In a brilliant stroke, Nasica accomplished the same effect but on a much grander scale. Whereas a *supplicatio* vote enhanced the public image of the *imperator* only indirectly, through his *res gestae,* Nasica's peroration went beyond such talk to dwell instead with a glaring immediacy on his personal value to the community at large: in 205 the senate had named him, a young man without even a quaestorship to his credit, as the *vir optimus* who should welcome the Magna Mater to the city (36.40.8–9; cf. 29.14.6–8). At that sacred and perilous time, when Hannibal had invaded Italy, the priests had found an oracle from the Sibylline Books promising victory if they brought the goddess from Mount Ida to Rome, and an embassy to Delphi sent back word that they must single out the very best man in the state to receive her (29.10.4–6, 11.6). They had chosen Nasica for this role when the collective stakes could not have been any higher (29.14.6–7), and not long thereafter the dreaded Hannibal fell, to the salvation of all. Now, therefore, even if they should refuse the triumph, Nasica said, he already had enough glory to last a lifetime, because his *imago* would bear the title *vir optimus* forever (36.40.9).[8]

Nasica could not have made more explicit reference either to the *dignitas* of his ancestors or to his rightful place among them. The *imagines* of an aristocratic family hung prominently on display in the atrium of the house as exempla made tangible, a permanent repository for the symbolic capital accumulated through generations of *res e re publica bene ac feliciter gestae.*[9] On one level, then, by first calling to mind for his audience what his *imago* would already look like even without a triumph, and by then declaring that he would be content to leave it as is, the consul proudly made known that his public identity in its present form was fixed and secure. He was already unique and unforgettable—literally the best man in Rome—and so did not need the boost in status that the triumph would confer, because he had reached the pinnacle of his ambition long ago. Especially when the status of *triumphator* usually clinched an aristocrat's identity, and made him and his family justifiably proud,[10] this might almost look like a gesture of defiance, even arrogance, in keeping with his earlier boasts about his military

8. 36.40.9: "hoc titulo, etsi nec consulatus nec triumphus addatur, satis honestam honoratamque P. Scipionis Nasicae imaginem fore" ("by this title, even if neither consulship nor triumph should be added, the *imago* of P. Scipio Nasica would be both honorable and honored enough"). Briscoe 1981, *ad loc.,* notes the etymological link—which says a lot about the complexities of time and identity—between the two elements in "honestam honoratamque": "conferring *honos* and having had *honos* conferred on it," like compound interest on the symbolic capital that the SPQR had invested in him. Cf. also 29.14.7.

9. For an examination of all the various functions performed by the *imagines* in the public and private life of Roman aristocratic families, see the masterful study by Flower 1996. Also cf. Walter 2004, 108–12.

10. Note Polybius's remark on the regalia worn in funeral processions (6.52).

exploits. Yet where had the title of *vir optimus* on which he was staking it all originally come from? He owed it, of course, to a vote from the *patres,* and therefore to an act of *existimatio* on the part of his peers. If he could stand before them now as a Scipio worthy of the name, in other words, they and no one else had made it possible. Thus, his flamboyant assertion of independence and selfhood gave testimony *in the same breath* to the supreme authority of the senate as a body over him and all aristocrats.

What more compelling mask could he possibly put on to impress them now than the idealized effigy that they themselves had carved for him with his name on it, and the unique title that they had already conferred? This appeal to an extraordinary judgment from the past had an equally extraordinary effect on the politics of the present: the senators united in an immediate consensus, and having come together as a body intimidated the tribune into dropping his veto, so that they could vote a triumph for Scipio Nasica then and there (36.40.10).[11] In his victory procession, along with captured prisoners and horses, Livy says that Nasica used Gallic wagons to carry arms, bronze vessels, 1,471 gold necklaces, 247 pounds of gold, 2,343 pounds of wrought and unwrought silver, 234,000 *bigati* coins—an impressive display of *praeda,* if not on the same enormous scale as the royal caches recently brought home by Africanus, Flamininus, and a handful of others like them. He distributed 125 *asses* to each soldier, with double to centurions and triple to horsemen, and the following day *in contione* he criticized the tribune for trying to rob him of the rightful fruits of his victory, then dismissed his troops (36.40.12–14).[12] No scene from any of Livy's triumph debates encapsulates so much of the complex, multilayered interaction between the would-be *triumphator* as an individual and the collective consciousness of the *patres* as Nasica's invocation of his *imago.* In its flair for the dramatic, it recalls Africanus's Day of Zama speech (38.51), but with a complicated additional twist.

For why had Nasica, of all people, emerged in 205 among the citizens of Rome as *vir optimus?* Livy's sources apparently did not say what prompted the *patres* to pick him, and in a classic moment of expressive diffidence the historian declines to pass judgment (29.14.6–9). The result certainly looks like another paradox of *existimatio* at work, however. We should recall that 205 was the very year of Africanus's consulship. With so much riding on their decision, and the name Scipio on everybody's lips, and so much ambition and *invidia* buzzing in the air all around them, the senators had managed to find a Scipio with conveniently nothing else except his (relatively loose) family ties to recommend him—that is, a Scipio who could bear

11. For the notice in the Fasti, see Degrassi 1947, 78–79, 553.

12. By way of comparison: Livy says that Africanus deposited 123,000 lbs. of gold and gave 400 bronze *asses* to each soldier (30.45.3).

the illustrious title of *vir optimus* on behalf of the Republic in crisis and yet not short-circuit the whole symbolic economy in the process. It should be noted that this signal honor, which had obviously brought Nasica's name into the limelight early in his career, was cited as a mark in his favor in Livy's tally of the political assets on both sides of the consular election in 192, when he nevertheless came up short because he could not overcome the tremendous *gratia* of Flamininus (35.10.9).

Returning now to the context of the triumph debate in 191, several significant facts begin to coalesce. Nasica won his triumph by drawing an analogy between two acts of *existimatio* on the senate floor. Reminding the *patres* of an earlier decision allowed him to forge a new consensus. His achievements against the Boii during his consulship clearly bore enough of the requisite signatures of *imperium, auspicium, ductus,* and *felicitas* to place him in the same ranks with other *triumphatores.* He had only to cope with the Scipio effect, therefore, which exalted and damned him in about equal measure. So, as Africanus would eventually do on the day of Zama, he effectively drew himself to his full height and told them he would not cooperate. He was Scipio Nasica, *vir optimus;* what did he need with a triumph, anyway? This defiant posture should have unleashed a torrent of *invidia* on his head—except for one thing. They, the *patres,* had made him who he was, and for good reason. Nasica's full height and Africanus's full height were of two vastly different statures. As they hastened to vote him his triumph, therefore, in addition to the usual civic pride and adulation, the senators may also have felt in part a keen sense of relief, that now, as in 205, they would not be elevating one man too far.

EPILOGUE

Only the fuzziest of boundaries separates the event from its representation. Because of the way Livy dramatizes the scene between Nasica and the *patres,* the text itself becomes the *imago* that he says the consul imagined. The historical narrative acclaims him as *vir optimus* by sanction of the senate's vote in 205 and enshrines him as an exemplum for future generations. Nasica the consul could speak of his *imago* only in the future tense, as a hypothetical construct, because the physical artifact would not appear until after his death. Yet although he would never see the object itself, he could and did observe the slow, lifelong process by which it took shape, and he continually strove to mold it as best he could by producing the *res gestae* that would allow him to accumulate *laus* and *gloria* throughout his career. So at the time of his speech in 191 the formative judgment of *existimatio* naming him as *vir optimus* had already taken place, and had helped, he knew, to determine what the artifact would eventually look like. So too the very invocation of what the past would mean in the future constituted a new political gesture in the present moment and would make its own eventual mark on his *imago* as well, once the senate agreed to grant him a triumph. His self-fashioning became real as long as his peers approved of his performance on the civic stage and voted him the titles and honors that he sought.

Thus every act of *existimatio* inscribed itself figuratively onto his public identity while he lived and literally onto his *imago* when he died, and Livy's text brings the whole ongoing process to life. For Livy the mise-en-scène of such great performances becomes a performance in its own right, passing on the tradition and helping to ensure that the *res gestae* of famous Romans from the past would continue to mean something to the enduring identity of the *civitas Romana.* For of course the historian's contemporary audience found themselves in the opposite predicament from the *imperator* himself in the second century: they could see the *imago* of Scipio Nasica and the monuments around the city that bore his name but could only envision how those signs of status and identity got there in the first place. So by telling Nasica's story—including the story of how Nasica told his story—Livy helps to bridge the gap.

CHAPTER 11

M. Fulvius Nobilior in 187

Staging Hostilities

Livy's account of the *inimicitiae* ("enmity," "political rivalry") between M. Fulvius Nobilior and M. Aemilius Lepidus reads almost like a script for an extended drama played out on the public stage in Rome, scene after scene the joint work of two actor-producers simultaneously crafting self-interested roles, with painstaking care, before an audience of critical judges, both of them striving for effect at every turn. But the mere fact that a notorious rivalry such as that between Lepidus and Nobilior made for such exciting political theater should not imply that it was any less real as a result. Indeed far to the contrary, these two men would never have qualified as *inimici* at all if they had not put on such a memorable spectacle under the watchful gaze of *existimatio.* Romans did not conceive of *inimicitiae* as a matter of personal feelings apart from the visible acts that shaped and manifested relations within the community.[1] Thus the whole course of the rivalry from beginning to end emerges from Livy's narrative as a performative construct, an artifact of the symbolic economy.

Much of the memorable stage business came about when Lepidus worked against Nobilior in his quest for a triumph from Aetolia in 187, beginning with the introduction of envoys from Ambracia into the senate with complaints, carefully coached and rehearsed beforehand, of severe mistreatment

1. So Hellegouarc'h 1963, 186 (my translation): "*Inimicitia* in its most general meaning applies only to exterior manifestations of hostility." As he goes on to observe, this explains the curious fact that the noun *inimicitia* rarely occurs in Latin except in the plural, *inimicitiae,* denoting a series of actions rather than a single abiding state of mind. But Epstein 1987, 11, sounds an important cautionary note: "The importance of the formal signposts of *inimicitiae,* declarations of hostility and reconciliations, must not be exaggerated. Romans themselves often disagreed about whether *inimicitiae* existed in particular instances, because the hostile acts in which *inimicitiae* most frequently originated were so capable of ambiguous construction."

at Nobilior's hands. Yet we cannot regard the triumph debate as the sum of the rivalry, because Livy explicitly marks it as merely a part, albeit a crucial one, of a much longer story within the domain of *existimatio* writ large. The historian portrays Lepidus's decision to bring in the Ambraciot envoys as an outgrowth of something already under way, an expression of deep resentments that stemmed from earlier events in the narrative. Lepidus sought to arouse *invidia* against Nobilior in 187, he says, because he held him responsible for the fact that he himself had reached the consulship only on the third try (38.43.1–2).[2] There has been no real word of the store of resentment building up on Lepidus's part until his open reprisal against Nobilior, but Livy signals his readers to look back now at the consular elections for 189 and again for 188 to see how it all began. This triumph debate, therefore, joins its actors *in mediis rebus:* their drama has been going on, though perhaps unnoticed, for some time already.[3] Suddenly it matters a great deal that these two aristocrats have appeared on the political stage together before.

In the elections for 189, long remembered as a hotly contested race (37.47.6), Nobilior stood as the single plebeian candidate for the consulship on a slate with three patricians: Lepidus, Cn. Manlius Vulso, and M. Valerius Messala. Nobilior was the only one who managed to win a majority of the votes on the first go-round, while the others split the centuries between them, leading to a runoff on the following day. Despite problems with the text of Livy at this point and confusion over the exact procedure followed, it seems reasonably certain that Nobilior presided in some way over the second day of voting, or at least announced the results, and that when all was said and done Messala had dropped out, Lepidus's candidacy was thwarted, and the *comitia* voted in Cn. Manlius Vulso as the second consul (37.47.7).[4] The historian singles out Lepidus among the three patricians to say that he ran for office that year under a cloud. In order to campaign he had left his

2. 38.43.1–2: "inimicitiae inter M. Fulvium et M. Aemilium consulem erant, et super cetera Aemilius serius biennio se consulem factum M. Fulvii opera ducebat. itaque ad invidiam ei faciendam legatos Ambracienses in senatum subornatos criminibus introduxit" ("A rivalry existed between M. Fulvius and M. Aemilius the consul, and above all Aemilius held that he had been made consul two years late by the efforts of M. Fulvius. Therefore in order to stir up resentment against him he brought Ambraciot envoys into the senate, secretly provided with accusations").

3. Although the expression "inimicitiae . . . erant" (see previous note) uses the imperfect tense, it bears connotations best rendered by the pluperfect in English: not just "hostilities existed" but "political actions had taken place that had given rise to hostilities." What looks like a simple comment on Lepidus's state of mind at the start of the triumph debate, in other words, actually characterizes earlier events. Cf. Hellegouarc'h 1963, 187.

4. 37.47.7: "Fulvius consul unus creatur, cum ceteri centurias non explessent, isque postero die Cn. Manlium, Lepido deiecto—nam Messalla iacuit—collegam dixit" ("Fulvius was elected consul by himself, when the others had not filled out the requisite number of centuries, and on the following day, Lepidus having been thrown out, for Messala lay to one side, he

post in Sicily without asking the senate for permission first (37.47.6).[5] His unexpected appearance in the city to canvass for votes constituted a political faux pas, then, because it signaled that he put ambition before duty, his desire for the consulship before his responsibilities in the province.

The voice of *existimatio* said that Lepidus had crossed the very fine but zealously guarded line, perceived less in the observance than in the breach of protocol, that divided merely seeking one's due within the civic order from pursuing harmful self-aggrandizement at the expense of the *res publica*.[6] He had conspicuously failed to pay proper homage to the senate as collective arbiters of *Romanitas*. In this light, his position starts to look very much like that of a would-be *triumphator*. And well it might, for Livy speaks of the requisite gesture here in the identical terms: *ut liceret*. Triumph debates likewise not infrequently raised the question of when and under what circumstances a commander with *imperium* had the right to return to Rome. In chapter 8 we saw how the "maiores natu" accused L. Furius Purpureo of rushing home precipitously to seek a triumph in 200 (31.48.2). Elections and triumph debates took place within the same political and cultural framework. The pursuit of public honors led in a single continuum marked by the common patterns of self-fashioning and *existimatio* throughout. Candidate and critic, victorious general and detractor alike were all taking part in one civic drama.

---

named Cn. Manlius as his colleague"). The procedural interpretation of this passage centers on three phrases: "Lepido deiecto," "Messalla iacuit," and especially "collegam dixit." Just how much say did Nobilior have in the choice of his colleague? See Briscoe 1981, *ad loc.*; Broughton 1991, 5–6 and nn.; Mommsen 1887, 3.217 n. 4; Rilinger 1976, 18 n. 42; Scullard 1951, 135 n. 4. Also note Warrior 1990 (on the alternative reading "collegam duxit"). Technicalities aside, it seems clear that (1) the runoff took place after Nobilior had already secured his slot as consul, (2) Lepidus definitely lost out, and most important for the origin of the *inimicitiae*, (3) he blamed Nobilior for it later (cf. 38.43.1).

5. 37.47.6: "M. Aemilius Lepidus petebat adversa omnium fama, quod provinciam Siciliam petendi causa non consulto senatu ut sibi id facere liceret reliquisset" ("M. Aemlius Lepidus ran for office with everyone whispering against him, because he had left his province of Sicily in order to run for office without the senate having decreed that he would be allowed to do this"). Lepidus had gone to Sicily as praetor for 191 (32.2.6), taking command of the army from his predecessor L. Valerius Tappo, but keeping Tappo in the province as propraetor and dividing the territory between them (36.2.10–12). Early in 190 the senate authorized a new praetor, C. Atinius Labeo, to take command from Lepidus in turn and to write back for reinforcements on his arrival, with no mention this time of prorogation for Lepidus or any new or continued division of the province (37.2.8). Yet either Labeo arrived late, leaving Lepidus in charge for the time being, or Lepidus took over for Tappo in 190 after relinquishing his own previous command to Labeo. In any event when the elections for 189 took place he still evidently held *imperium* in the province, which meant that everyone in Rome, and the *patres* especially, expected him to stay with his army through to the end of the season.

6. We rarely learn about the existence of the established rules until or unless someone is said to have broken them. Cf. Brennan 2004, 41.

Did Nobilior join in the invidious talk around town that so effectively scuttled Lepidus's candidacy in 189? Livy does not say: the rumormongers remain anonymous. It is at least conceivable that Nobilior was not among them, that he antagonized Lepidus in some other way. Issues from the campaign aside, Lepidus may have felt wronged primarily because he would have to wait his turn, whereas Nobilior had won the consulship without a struggle and even secured an illustrious command for himself against the Aetolian League in northwestern Greece. Sadly too, when Lepidus finally did serve as consul, in 187, the *patres* saw fit to send both him and his colleague to unglamorous Liguria instead of the East (38.42.8–13). But then again, in 189 Lepidus could not have foreseen all that. Besides, if pure envy sparked his resentment, then by rights he should have seen the threat in fellow patrician Cn. Manlius Vulso, the man who had actually beaten him out. As the lone plebeian candidate, Nobilior had not taken the consulship away from Lepidus simply by being elected.[7] Nor did any longstanding rivalry develop between Lepidus and Vulso. So there must have been more to the story with Nobilior, some direct provocation that would count in Lepidus's eyes as a tangible first sign of *inimicitiae* in the making.[8]

It stands to reason, then, that Nobilior did play a prominent role in the allegations that marked Lepidus with *invidia* in 189. Perhaps candidate Nobilior even led the outcry *in contione* over Lepidus's unsanctioned return to Rome. Alternatively, he may have bowed to the wishes of those speaking out against Lepidus and agreed to officiate somehow over the formal procedure blocking his candidacy. Though the inference comes easily enough, however, in actual fact Livy's readers must draw their own conclusions. We can only speculate about where Nobilior fits into the picture, even on the broadest possible view of his bias against Lepidus and the degree of his leverage over the choice of a colleague, because of the syntactical gap inevitably left between the subject of a main clause and the unstated agent in a perfect-passive ablative absolute (37.47.7–8: "Lepido deiecto . . . collegam dixit"). On its own, such an admittedly tiny detail all but vanishes in passing, but it suddenly stands out in sharp relief when placed side by side with Livy's notice on the next set of elections, for 188, when Nobilior appears as the unmistakable subject of the same verb in the perfect indicative, actively blocking Lepidus on his second try at the consulship.[9]

7. Note Develin 1985, 310.

8. The expression "M. Fulvii opera" ("by the efforts of M. Fulvius") later on at 38.43.2 also suggests deliberate intervention on Nobilior's part.

9. 38.35.1: "creavit consules M. Valerium Messalam et C. Livium Salinatorem, cum M. Aemilium Lepidum inimicum eo quoque anno petentem deiecisset" ("He named as consuls M. Valerius Messala and C. Livius Salinator, after he had thrown out the candidacy of his rival M. Aemilius Lepidus, who was running again this year"). Here Nobilior, as the presiding consul, is explicitly the grammatical subject of both "creavit" and "deiecisset."

Of course the two constructions are roughly equivalent, but not exactly, almost perfectly parallel, but not quite. A *cum* clause does spell out certain things that the compressed form of an ablative absolute leaves unsaid. This contrast suits the progression of Livy's narrative in several ways. In the elections for 188, not only was Lepidus conspicuously running for the second time in a row, but now as consul Nobilior was acting in an established, official capacity, with a clear mandate from the *patres* to oversee the elections (37.50.6–7), a far cry from the odd circumstances of the previous year. It would also appear that since those earlier events had taken place, Nobilior was already known by this point as the *inimicus* of Lepidus, because Livy does not hesitate now to designate him as such (38.35.10). Together in this order—the ambiguous case first, followed by the more highly elaborated, clear-cut one—the two election notices form a distinct pattern within the bounds of normal *variatio,* conveniently allowing Livy to dramatize the steady growth of the rivalry by stages, visible primarily, if not exclusively, in retrospect.

On the third try Lepidus's persistence finally paid off. He reached the consulship at long last for 187, in what appears to have been an uneventful election, presumably because Nobilior did not make it back to Rome to campaign against him one more time (38.42.4). Both Nobilior in Aetolia and his colleague Cn. Manlius in Asia had had their *imperium* prorogued, leaving the new consuls for 188, M. Valerius Messala and C. Livius Salinator, with far less coveted assignments to Liguria and Cisalpine Gaul (38.35.8–9). When the question of provinces arose again in the following year for Lepidus and his colleague, the senate voted to send them to Liguria as well (38.42.8; cf. 39.1.2). Lepidus had not sought a consular command for three years running in order to be "fobbed off with Liguria once again, while Fulvius and Manlius still nominally held charge of all the East."[10] In a defiant bit of stagecraft he stood up and challenged the senate to give him his due, at least by summoning Nobilior and Vulso back to Rome if not also choosing himself and his colleague to take their place.

The senators recalled the two standing *imperatores* at once but stopped short of rewarding Lepidus's self-seeking bid for an Eastern command of his own. He would remain Liguria bound (38.42.12–13). *Existimatio* operated through a system of checks and balances: one must weigh the identity of each individual against the collective interests of the Republic as a whole. Both Vulso and Nobilior had enjoyed quite a long tenure already, and to extend it any further might upset the distribution of status within

10. Gruen 1984a, 218. The perpetual need for Roman troops on patrol in Liguria made it both well suited as a training ground between major conflicts and a convenient place to send magistrates not judged worthy by their peers, for whatever reason, to hold one of the coveted eastern commands.

the ranks of the *nobiles.* There Lepidus had certainly struck a chord.[11] But meanwhile, by doing nothing to change the provincial assignments as they stood, the *patres* sent out a signal that war in the East was concluding itself and held no place for Lepidus. He must not push his ambition too far, consistent with the earlier verdict that he had shown himself overly eager for self-advancement already in the elections two years before. Again *existimatio* put him in his place. Yet by Livy's account Lepidus had actually seen this coming and even suggested the compromise himself. This implies that the senators must have given him what he wanted most when they brought Nobilior's stint in Aetolia to an end.

Thanks to Nobilior, *invidia* had placed the opportunity for the *res gestae* that Lepidus had hoped to achieve on the battlefield beyond his political reach. Now instead he would seek to maximize his stature in Rome at his rival's expense, by mounting a spectacular challenge to his triumph bid. He set out to win back some of the prestige that he had lost in the course of his three frustrating trips to the *comitia,* by ensuring that if Nobilior eventually won a triumph, it too would come only after a heated political struggle, prolonged as far as possible for all to see. Accordingly, Lepidus did his best to anticipate the steps that Nobilior would take on his return, so that he could throw obstacles into the path of the would-be *triumphator.* Since his preemptive strategy was designed to subvert the conventional postures of Roman triumphal discourse, it points them up rather nicely in the process. Lepidus knew that Nobilior would try to mold the narrative of his *res gestae* into an exemplum for future generations and that the tale would probably culminate with the sack of Ambracia, Pyrrhus's former royal capital now allied with the Aetolian League (38.3.9).[12] The town had in fact surrendered willingly, under terms negotiated by the Athymanian king, Amynander, but only after a prolonged siege (38.9–10).[13] The fall of Ambracia had meant sumptuous spoils for Nobilior and his troops because

11. Thus Gruen 1984a, 218: "Annual commands, Lepidus argued with some justice (and self-interest), had been the rule and should continue to be so. The *patres* recognized the force of that claim."

12. During the siege of Ambracia, the defenders ingeniously used bellows on a barrel pierced many times and crammed full of smoldering feathers to produce acrid smoke, which poured into the Roman tunnel under the city wall and drove back the invaders—a striking example of ancient chemical warfare. Livy is cryptic about the technology (38.7.13), but thankfully Polybius's original and far more lucid description of the apparatus is extant (22.11). Citing this example, among others, Walsh 1961, 4, memorably remarks that Livy "is so ignorant of the practical aspects of soldiering that he can never have thrown a *pilum* in anger. It seems clear that he stayed home and read." For a more balanced and sympathetic treatment of Livy's siege narratives, see now Roth 2006. Also cf. Hammond 1967, 143–48; Walbank 1971, 61–62.

13. For the final negotiations and terms of surrender, cf. Polyb. 21.29.1–30.10.

of all the splendid artwork, both statues and paintings, that adorned the old royal palace (38.9.13).

Just as Marcellus's enemies had done with the Syracusans in 211, Lepidus arranged to put the victims of Nobilior's rapacity on display before the *patres:* not as silent captives led in triumph, which the commander himself might do, or as unseen, hypothetical witnesses invoked for a speech he himself might make bewailing their plight, but in the starkest possible light, appearing as actors on the political stage in their own right. He brought the victims from Ambracia into the *curia.* Though they appeared unwilling at first to speak the worst, Livy says, the consul led them to divulge a litany of their woes: "war waged against them with all the trimmings, murders, fires, ruin, plunder of the city" (38.43.5).[14] Their lament reached a suitably heartbreaking climax with a description of how the Roman soldiers under Nobilior's command, in their hunger for booty, had carried off the cult statues from all the temples of the city, taken away the very gods themselves, and left the poor Ambraciots with only empty walls and barren doorposts to hear their prayers. This piteous spectacle, so clearly contrived for dramatic effect, cannot be anything other than deliberate political stagecraft aimed against Nobilior and his *triumphi spes* (38.43.6).[15] The other consul, C. Flaminius, apparently saw right through it. Ambracia had not suffered worse than any besieged and conquered city might have done (38.43.10).[16] Nobilior would proudly carry the spoils in his triumph and hang them up at his house as badges of honor (38.43.10–11; cf. 23.23.6).[17]

Once again the debate hinges on a byplay of presence and absence. Lepidus made a deliberate show of the dark side of Nobilior's *res gestae*

14. 38.43.5: "omnia exempla belli edita in se caedibus incendiis ruinis direptione urbis." Asyndeton enhances the cumulative effect for heightened pathos. Note also the striking use of exempla here: battle narratives fell into conventional patterns, easily recognized as such. On what was considered normal behavior for Roman generals with regard to captured cities, see Ziolkowski 1993; and on Livy's accounts of siege works, see Roth 2006.

15. 38.43.7: "interrogando criminose ex composito consul ad plura velut non sua sponte dicenda eliciebat" ("By questioning them reproachfully by prior arrangement the consul lured them to say more, as if against their will"). Cf. 38.43.2: "subornatos criminibus" ("secretly provided with accusations"). The rapacious Roman army must have left more behind them in Ambracia than just bare walls. Cf. Pliny *NH* 35.66; Varro *Sat. Men.* fr. 52 Astbury. See also Gruen 1992, 107–10.

16. 38.43.10: "facta quae captis urbibus soleant" ("actions that typically befall captured cities"). Cf. 38.43.8: "veterem viam et obsoletam ingressos Ambracienses dixit" ("he said that the Ambraciots were treading an old road, and an obsolete one"). These two passages amount to the same thing as "omnia exempla belli" ("war with all the trimmings") at 38.43.4, except that the narrative has been polarized in the opposite direction.

17. At 38.43.11 Flaminius singles out "Ambraciam captam" ("captured Ambracia": i.e., an image or model of the town) among the spoils likely to be displayed in Nobilior's triumph, yet Livy's description of the triumph itself (39.4.13–17) contains no reference to such a thing. Also see Östenberg 2003, 210–11.

narrative without him there to tell his own story ("absente M. Fulvio," 38.43.14; cf. "praesente Flaminio" in the next sentence, 44.2)—the reverse of the triumph request, where the general would speak for himself and his victims would most likely never appear—and more important, he got there first, for maximum impact. Flaminius meanwhile refused to deal with the subject of Ambracia at all until Nobilior arrived. Matters stood at an impasse between the feuding consuls for two whole days (38.43.13–44.2, in which words such as *inimicus* and *inimicitiae* occur three times). Only when Flaminius called in sick did the *patres* give way at last to pass a decree making amends to the Ambraciots: they declared the town free and self-governing, and ordered all property carried off in the siege to be restored to its rightful owners (38.44.3–5). This represents "a direct and deliberate slap at Fulvius" in his absence, and a victory for Lepidus.[18] Yet on the single most sensitive issue, regarding the stolen cult statues, the senators took no direct action, voting merely to refer the whole question to the college of *pontifices,* and even that only on Nobilior's return. So although they could not ignore such serious allegations, once raised, against one of their commanders, they did not rush to judgment without hearing from him in person first. One also notes that in addition to a triumph, Nobilior apparently also requested a *supplicatio* on his return, implying that the senate had not decreed one previously (39.4.2).

Livy takes pains as well to show what a close and bitter struggle Lepidus had to face before getting his way in the end. His vendetta went only so far as he could push it by sheer determination and political pressure, more *certamen* than *consensus.* The first decree must not have done enough to satisfy his grudge, because he surreptitiously put through another *senatus consultum* at a poorly attended session, to the effect that Ambracia did not appear to have been taken by force (38.44.6).[19] Once again Livy quietly shows up Lepidus's maneuvering: if more senators had voted on it, the narrative implies, this second decree would never have passed.[20] Lepidus could not expect to hold out against Nobilior's supporters forever, but he based his strategy on the confidence that a single sign (i.e., a captured town) might be manipulated to point in two different directions, at least briefly, within the ever changing dynamics of the *dignitatis contentio* (38.4.4

18. Gruen 1984a, 310–11.

19. 38.44.6: "neque his contentus consul fuit, sed postea per infrequentiam adiecit senatus consultum, Ambraciam vi captam esse non videri" ("Nor was the consul content with these things, but afterwards at a poorly attended session he added a decree of the senate to the effect that Ambracia did not seem to have been taken by force").

20. The procedural detail "per infrequentiam" at 38.44.6 (quoted in the previous note) may reflect a pro-Nobilior slant in the historical tradition, inasmuch as it suggests a certain sneakiness on Lepidus's part. On the technicalities of *infrequentia* under the Republic, see Bonnefond-Coudry 1989, 357–435; Feig Vishnia 1996, 190–91; Ryan 1998, 13–51.

vs. 43.7). There was no such thing as an empty political gesture: even if Nobilior went on to triumph in the end, it would count for something, on balance, that he would now arrive home to be greeted by a decree from his peers that flew in the face of his triumph claims.

Nobilior arrived in Rome at the end of the year.[21] At a meeting of the senate in the Temple of Apollo he gave a full formal account of his *res gestae,* just as Flaminius had anticipated, and he solemnly asked the *patres* if they saw fit, because he had served the Republic so well, both to thank the civic gods and to grant him a triumph (39.4.2).[22] The consuls had not yet made it back from Liguria, but before leaving, knowing that his *inimicus* would probably appear while he was gone, Lepidus had charged the tribune M. Aburius to hold off any vote on the triumph pending his return (39.4.3–4). He conveniently found someone to go on the record for him, so that he could display again his power to steer the debate, even in absentia. The tribune spoke for Lepidus, saying that the consul wished to speak for himself. Livy has Aburius make quite a striking admission about the nature and limits of political showmanship: "Fulvius was suffering a loss of time only. Even with the consul present, the senate would decree what it wanted" (39.4.4).[23] Despite the terrific lengths to which Lepidus had gone in order to stir up *invidia* against his rival, that is, he understood that he probably could not block the triumph altogether. He would ultimately have to bow to the *consensus patrum* like everybody else. This should not come as too much of a surprise, however, because it marks a perfect quid pro quo with the earlier provocation: Nobilior had not deprived him of the consulship in the end either, but only forced him to wait.[24]

Nobilior would now strive both to defend his honor against Lepidus in the eyes of his peers and to win a triumph over the Aetolians—not two acts of self-fashioning but one and the same. Lepidus had worked hard to make the combined task as formidable as possible, but Nobilior could turn that

21. Livy seems to stress the hiatus by placing not one but two major senatorial controversies—the debate over another triumph, for Nobilior's colleague Cn. Manlius Vulso, and the so-called trials of the Scipios—in the interim between the *senatus consulta* dealing with Ambracia at 38.43.3–6 and Nobilior's return at 39.4.1.

22. 39.4.2: "isque ad aedem Apollinis in senatu cum de rebus in Aetolia Cephallaniaque ab se gestis disseruisset, petit a patribus ut <si> aequum censerent, ob rem publicam bene ac feliciter gestam et dis immortalibus honorem haberi iuberent et sibi triumphum decernerent" ("And at a meeting of the senate in the Temple of Apollo, when he had given an account of his accomplishments in Aetolia and Cephallania, he asked the *patres,* if they saw fit on account of public business conducted with success and good fortune, both to order that honor be paid to the immortal gods and to grant him a triumph").

23. 39.4.4: "Fulvium temporis iacturam facere: senatum etiam praesente consule quod vellet decreturum." On the phrase "temporis iacturam" here, see above, p. 111 n. 20.

24. Politically the two-year delay had left Lepidus not crippled, but only embarrassed. Broughton 1991, 6, notes that went on to become "famous for his brilliant career as consul for

very challenge to his own advantage. For the display of deference to the collective judgment of the senate and avowals of service to the interests of the Republic as a whole, which the codes of *existimatio* demanded from the would-be *triumphator,* also enabled Nobilior to seize the moral high ground against his rival. The rhetoric of this speech, as Livy presents it, strongly contrasted Lepidus's vindictive and unseemly behavior all along with Nobilior's own, strictly in accordance with the *mos maiorum* (39.4.5–13). He asked the *patres* to deem him worthy, at once because and in spite of the fact that his *inimicus* was acting out of such unmistakably personal bitterness. To see the fruits of his *imperium,* they need look no further than the conquering army ("victor exercitus": cf. 36.40.6) outside the gates, laden with booty and captives. Aburius held out the promise of an outcome in his favor somewhere down the line, but Nobilior understood as well as his opponents did that every moment of further delay was playing straight into their hands by further attenuating his *laus* and *gloria* (39.4.6–7).

On their own merits his *res gestae* would answer the charge, openly, that the second, furtive *senatus consultum* had made official by such questionable means (39.4.8; cf. 38.44.6). A straightforward account of siege works and tunnels, fifteen days of struggle to enter the city, followed by a long day of fighting after the Roman soldiers had crossed the walls, and more than three thousand enemy casualties demonstrated that Ambracia had fallen by deadly force under his legitimate command as a magistrate of the SPQR (39.4.9–10). This is a beautiful example of how casualty statistics and the like functioned within the Roman political game. With that kind of narrative to vouch for him, Nobilior could gain both symbolic capital and material wealth together, justifying the plunder of Ambracia's art treasures by appeal to the unwritten laws of war, as Flaminius had said he would do (39.4.12; cf. 38.43.9). He would be made a laughingstock if all these tangible, traditional claims, now that he stood before the senate in person, could not outweigh the machinations of the absent consul trying to influence the debate from afar (39.4.13). But no commander, however successful, could do more than submit himself to *existimatio* and wait for his peers

---

a second time, censor, pontifex maximus, and princeps senatus." Cf. Brennan 2004, 33–34, citing Münzer 1920, 158, who accords Lepidus "truly princely status." Also cf. Gruen 1984a, 242 (as cited below, p. 210). Develin 1979a charts the intervals between magistracies for this period, and Lepidus certainly does not fall behind the curve. And cf. 39.32.6 on repeat candidates in another election: "veteres candidatos, et ab repulsis eo magis debitum, quia primo negatus erat, honorem repentes" ("old candidates, and seeking again an honor that was owed to them from refusals because it had first been denied"). Note also what Develin 1985, 165, says about ambitious young *nobiles* who "actually stood [for the consulship] in advance of their expected date of success *in order to have their names before the public*" (my italics). What looks like frustration, in other words, could actually prove beneficial in the long run. Cf. Broughton 1991; Konrad 1996.

to decide. Mayhem broke loose as everyone jumped in to beg Aburius or take him to task (39.5.1–7). The competing interests of Lepidus on one side and Nobilior on the other could not be resolved, even by an emerging *consensus patrum* in Nobilior's favor, until the one remaining spokesman for the losers agreed to back down.

At length only an appeal to the welfare of the Republic at large—the base currency of all *existimatio*—brought arguments to a close. Ti. Sempronius Gracchus, better known as the father of the Gracchi, reminded Aburius that magistrates in general and especially tribunes bore a civic trust that came with a heavy responsibility to put collective needs ahead of all personal quarrels. Aburius could not possibly stand up by himself to this sort of political pressure, especially since he was not even making trouble on his own behalf, and the senate would not stand by and wait for Lepidus to appear in person any longer. Gracchus had finally touched on the limits to what the consul could hope to achieve in absentia against Nobilior's *triumphi spes,* and Aburius knew when he was beaten. Nobilior would have his due: they voted him a triumph. Livy records his thanks to the *patres.* By now he must have felt not only grateful but relieved as well. But even at that he had not yet heard the last from his rival. News that only a sudden illness had held up Lepidus on his way back to Rome yet again prompted Nobilior to hold his triumph two weeks earlier than he had originally planned—"lest," as Livy wryly remarks in the bon mot with which this whole investigation began, "he face more of a struggle in his triumph than he had in the war" (39.5.12).[25]

Lepidus probably aimed only to obstruct the triumph, not to bar it outright ("ad impediendum triumphum," 39.5.12). But he did not need to prevent the ceremony from ever taking place in order to make his point. In fact, he did not even need to make it all the way back to Rome. The *triumphator*'s sudden change in schedule at the mere threat of his appearance would have had Lepidus's name all over it. Under the strain of these circumstances, when Nobilior did celebrate his triumph certain elements of the display were pointedly directed at his opponents. He asked that a quantity of gold be set aside to fund games that he had vowed to Jupiter Optimus Maximus "on the day when he captured Ambracia" (39.5.7).[26] The contro-

25. 39.5.12: "ne plus in triumpho certaminum quam in bello haberet." This is, oddly enough, the second fortuitous illness in Livy's account of these machinations. (Cf. 38.44.3.) One almost wonders whether the historian is not using the motif as a way to dramatize the intensity of disagreements in the senate that would perhaps not have been settled otherwise.

26. 39.5.7–8: "adiecit ludos magnos se Iovi optimo maximo eo die quo Ambraciam cepisset vovisse; in eam rem sibi centum pondo auri a civitatibus conlatum; petere ut ex ea pecunia quam in triumpho latam in aerario positurus esset id aurum secerni iuberent" ("he added that he had vowed great games to Jupiter Optimus Maximus on the day when he captured Ambracia; to that end he had brought with him a hundred pounds of gold from the cities; he asked that

versial artworks had a prominent place in the triumphal procession, as did a huge sum of money conspicuously bound for the public treasury, and a vast collection of captured weapons and artillery. This was primarily a military show, designed to counter the charges that he had not won Ambracia by force (39.5.15–16).[27] In addition, Nobilior held a *contio* in the Circus Flaminius on the day of the triumph, where he showed broad largesse to his army as partners in his success and distributed prizes (*dona militaria*) to those who had distinguished themselves in battle under his command (39.5.17). Cato the Elder sharply criticized this bit of extravagance: "Who has seen anyone granted a crown when a town had not been captured or an enemy camp burned?"[28] He clearly had Lepidus's *senatus consultum* in mind here, but so it would seem did Nobilior. Aulus Gellius says that in making his awards Nobilior especially singled out conspicuous siege works, no doubt at Ambracia. The *imperator* must have aimed to silence grumblers on the day of his triumph, Cato among them, by highlighting the valor of his troops.[29] Nobilior would stress over and over, for anyone who cared to listen, that Pyrrhus's capital had indeed been taken by force and in accordance with the triumphal formula: *imperio auspicio ductu felicitate.*

HISTORIOGRAPHICAL EPILOGUE: LIVY TAKING SIDES

So much, then, for the story of the sack of Ambracia as a token of symbolic value on the second-century political stage. What of the story of the sack of Ambracia as a historical event earlier in Livy's narrative? For much as

---

they order that gold to be separated from the money that he would place in the treasury after carrying it in his triumph"). Note the remark of Walsh 1994, *ad loc.*, that Fulvius here perpetuates "the fiction of the capture of the town." This is consistent with Walsh's slant on the whole episode, effectively championing Lepidus's arguments against Nobilior's as an implicit indictment of Livy's integrity as a historian. Walsh is plainly biased, but both rival claims have left perceptible traces in the narrative.

27. Cf. L. Richardson 1977, 355: "The celebration seems to have been a sober one, marked by its emphasis on the military accomplishment and on Fulvius' decoration and reward of his troops." For the display of siege engines in particular, see Östenberg 2003, 43. Oddly enough, Livy singles out Nobilior's colleague, Cn. Manlius Vulso, not Nobilior himself, for the topos denouncing Eastern decadence and luxury (39.6.7–9). Also see Gruen 1992, 106–7.

28. Cato *ORF* fr. 148 *apud* Gell. 5.6.24: "quis vidit corona donari quemquam, cum oppidum captum non esset aut castra hostium non incensa essent?" Cato may well have joined in the earlier flap over Ambracia, but this particular remark should be seen as a later offshoot of that debate. Nobilior distributed prizes to his army on the day of the triumph, so Cato must have used the earlier *senatus consultum* as ammunition to decry excessive and overly conspicuous spending, which was one of his favorite rhetorical hobbyhorses.

29. Immediately after quoting Cato (as seen in the previous note) Gellius adds (*NA* 5.6.24): "Fulvius autem, in quem hoc a Catone dictum est, coronis donaverat milites, quia vallum curaverant, aut qui puteum strenue foderant" ("but Fulvius, against whom this was said by Cato, had given the soldiers crowns because they had looked after a rampart or dug a well quickly").

Lepidus stole the march on Nobilior with the Ambraciot envoys in 187, so Livy has ensured that his readers would hear his own authorized account long before the consul Lepidus would ever stage that production for the benefit of the *patres*—as an integral part of the campaigning season in 189. Of course Livy maintains a distinction throughout his work between battlefield and *curia:* even on a syntactical level, by switching from the unadorned perfect indicatives of his own battle narratives to accusative-plus-infinitive or other constructions of implied or explicit indirect discourse in the triumph debates. First he tells us in his own voice what Roman commanders did, and then how they talked about what they had done, weaving together an idealized autobiography for public consumption. Yet unavoidably the boundaries between these two narrative categories tend to blur, especially when controversy grew up around a particular military campaign. Which version made its way into the tradition to become official Roman history? Or does Livy's narrative reflect the confusion? In this case, the historian appears to be explicitly taking sides in the triumph debate: "The statues of bronze and of marble and painted pictures with which Ambracia was more richly adorned than the other cities of that region were, since the palace of Pyrrhus had been there, were all taken up and carried away; nothing besides was touched or violated" (38.9.13–14).[30]

Thankfully the relevant passage of Polybius has survived for comparison as well: "After taking Ambracia, Marcus let the Aetolians go under treaty terms and carried off the statues of gods and of men and the paintings from the city, which were even more numerous because Ambracia had been the royal capital of Pyrrhus."[31] Although Livy follows the Greek model fairly closely, one point of translation deserves special note. Polybius lists ἀγάλματα, literally "ornaments" and usually the technical term for cult statues, among the art treasures that Nobilior carried off from Ambracia. The word could possibly refer more loosely to any decorative art, but Polybius signals the technical meaning in this passage by placing it in a parallel construction with ἀνδριάντας, implying a strong contrast between statues of deities and those of human beings. Livy substitutes for ἀγάλματα and ἀνδριάντας a contrast not of representation (gods vs. men) but of material

30. 38.9.13–14: "signa aenea marmoreaque et tabulae pictae, quibus ornatior Ambracia, quia regia ibi Pyrrhi fuerat, quam ceterae regionis eius urbes erant, sublata omnia avectaque; nihil praeterea tactum violatumve."

31. Polyb. 21.30.9: ὁ δὲ Μάρκος παραλαβὼν τὴν Ἀμβρακίαν τοὺς μὲν Αἰτωλοὺς ἀφῆκεν ὑποσπόνδους, τὰ δ' ἀγάλματα καὶ τοὺς ἀνδριάντας καὶ τὰς γραφὰς ἀπήγαγεν ἐκ τῆς πόλεως, ὄντα καὶ πλείω διὰ τὸ γεγονέναι βασίλειον Πύρρου τὴν Ἀμβρακίαν. Note that the Greek verb παραλαμβάνω can mean either "take possession of, take in pledge" or "take by force, seize forcibly" (LSJ, s.v.), so that this passage cannot be used to settle the argument about how Nobilior captured the town.

(bronze vs. marble).[32] In addition, he adds one last qualifying clause, which does not appear anywhere in the Greek text: "nothing besides was touched or violated." With each of these changes to what he found in Polybius, and especially with the two of them together, Livy quite insistently champions the commander's own version of events at Ambracia over what Lepidus would have had the *patres* believe.[33]

We have in fact already witnessed the same tendency throughout Livy's treatment of the triumph debate. He calls attention several times to the artifice and stagecraft behind Lepidus's crusade against Nobilior—just as Nobilior did in the speech that eventually won him the triumph (39.4.5–13). The *inimicitiae* between these two aristocrats obviously had a dramatic effect on what their contemporaries came to believe had happened at Ambracia, or at least on how their contemporaries viewed the way they had sought to portray those events. Both of them expended a great deal of effort to appear in the best possible light at all times before the judgments of *existimatio*. They sought to maximize their symbolic capital, which was always in flux, the insubstantial, ephemeral product of audience responses to each performance in turn. Yet something endured. All along each of them was sculpting a public identity that he hoped would live on as an exemplum, a model of how Roman aristocrats ought to behave. Every time one succeeded in making a mark on the official public record, that particular act of self-fashioning would become part of a historical tradition that belonged to the whole Republic, *res publica bene gesta*. When Livy came to write his history, he found two conflicting legacies—the *senatus consulta* against Nobilior and the triumph awarded to him; the complaints of the Ambraciots and the tale of the siege—side by side, both sanctioned by the same collective body.

Polybius's account makes it clear that Roman siege engines had been used against Ambracia, regardless of anything Lepidus may have argued later. But Livy also had to take notice of the Roman aristocratic tradition, where he found the whole story of the triumph debate, and the *inimicitiae* to which that debate belonged. What emerges, then, is a narrative where Nobilior's version of the military campaign won out, as it had done the moment the *patres* voted for his triumph, and yet Lepidus still scored many political points along the way through the workings of the symbolic economy. The *senatus consultum* said that "it *looked as if* Ambracia had not been taken by force" ("Ambraciam vi captam esse non videri," 38.44.6). That judgment, though eventually superseded, still remained suspended in time, reflecting one point of view and one man's efforts to decide which

32. Cf. Walsh 1993, *ad loc.*

33. The discrepancies between Livy's account and Polybius's were noted and attributed to his composition of oversimplified literary "set-pieces" by Walbank 1971, 61–62.

story would be told. With political sleight of hand Lepidus had made the siege of Ambracia disappear—if only for a moment. He could not rewrite history altogether, any more than he could actually block the triumph, but he emerges as the consummate actor on the political stage. His artifice dazzles the eye, even though his rival still went on to gain recognition for his accomplishments. In other words, neither one of them lost out completely, because a memory of the *certamen* outlasted them both.

POLITICAL EPILOGUE: THE LIMITS OF *INIMICITIAE*

And yet, although the collective memory in Rome proved long enough to preserve a legacy of the spectacular strife between these men, the backlash from the triumph debate still came to a definite end. After an unsuccessful bid in 184 (39.40.3), Nobilior was elected censor for 179, and in a stroke of bitter irony the *comitia* chose as his colleague none other than his old *inimicus* (40.45.6–7). Of course everyone knew of the infamous public acrimony between them. This meant trouble, because although no one would doubt their qualifications—Nobilior had triumphed over the Aetolians, after all, while Lepidus ranks as "probably the most distinguished man of his day"[34]—any antagonism between the censors could jeopardize the symbolic unity of the Republic, which that most solemn of civic offices tended to represent.[35] So Livy records a scene in which a group of eminent senators approached the *inimici* right after their election to secure a reconciliation (40.45.8–46.13). Q. Caecilius Metellus, acting as spokesman, begged the new censors to live up to the ancient formulaic prayer of their office: "that what you will pronounce publicly in almost all the prayers, 'May this endeavor turn out with success and good fortune for myself and my colleague,' you wish will happen truly and from the heart, and make it so that we might believe that even as human beings, you want what you will have prayed for to the gods" (40.46.9).[36]

Not, of course, without a last rehearsal of their well-known grievances

34. Gruen 1984a, 242.

35. The Romans valued *concordia* between the censors not only because it helped them fulfill their duties if they worked together, but also because they were supposed to set an example for others, and *inimicitiae* could mar decorum. Cf. the "magna inter se concordia" (32.7.3) between Scipio Africanus and P. Aelius Paetus, censors in 199. As a counterexample, although Nero and Salinator (another famous pair of *inimici*), managed to lay aside their personal differences for the sake of the Metaurus campaign, yet the hostilities between them resurfaced during their censorship in 204, as if needing an outlet (29.37). It was always a matter of balancing one's own personal interests against the public good.

36. 40.46.9: "quod in omnibus fere precationibus nuncupabitis verbis 'ut ea res mihi collegaeque meo bene ac feliciter eveniat,' id ita ut vere, ut ex animo velitis evenire, efficiatisque ut quod deos precati eritis, id vos velle etiam homines credamus." Varro *LL* 6.86 gives a more complete version of the ritual formula.

with one another, the two agreed finally to submit to the interests of the community at large and to lay aside their long-standing quarrel in the sight of all. The praise heaped by the senate on this striking public scene (40.46.14–15) demonstrates once again the extent to which the *patres* saw *concordia* between the censors as vital to the common interest. Livy's version of Metellus's speech places particular emphasis on the need for genuine reconciliation, not just the end of open hostility (note the visual verbs at 40.46.3–4); and quite remarkably, as the year went on the two of them fulfilled their duties "with faithful unanimity" ("fideli concordia," 40.51.1). It was no accident that the same public context in which these men had played out their *inimicitiae* for so many years should then demand that they reconcile for the sake of civic business, but simply another twist in the plot of the political drama. Lepidus and Nobilior were no more than two small actors in the huge pageant of Roman history, fully as old as the Republic and as long as Livy's tale. The historian would have been hard pressed to invent a more elegant ring composition, bringing an end to the rivalry that had grown out of consular elections a decade before.

CULTURAL EPILOGUE: NOBILIOR AND ROMAN HELLENISM

We must not let M. Fulvius Nobilior go without pausing to acknowledge his prominent place in the history of Roman Hellenism. Like Marcellus before him and Paullus after him, among others, in the process of first attaining and then memorializing his stature as a military figure, this *imperator* engaged in a variety of cultural activities that fused, or at least conjoined, both newly imported Greek and traditional Roman elements. We have seen that the plunder from Ambracia that Nobilior brought back to Rome for his triumphal parade included artworks, sculptures and paintings, from Pyrrhus's Hellenistic royal palace (38.9.13–14, 43.10–11). As a further spectacle, he engaged the services of Greek artisans to help him celebrate *ludi* that he had vowed during his campaign in Aetolia, combining a wild-beast hunt with competitions performed by Greek athletes, the first such seen in Rome (39.22.1–2).[37] In addition to these ephemeral displays, he also created a more permanent and intriguing memorial: the Aedes Herculis Musarum in the Circus Flaminius, where he dedicated a statue group of nine Muses taken from Ambracia alongside a figure of Hercules playing a lyre.[38] He then transferred an *aedicula* to the Camenae,

37. On Nobilior's victory games, see Klar 2006, 165–68, 170–71, 176–80. She argues with some compulsion that the display of plundered artworks in temporary structures built for victory games may have had a formative effect on the architectural development of the elaborate *scaenae frons* as a permanent fixture in Roman theaters.

38. An inscribed base, apparently from the Ambracian Muses, has survived (*CIL* 6.1307): "M. Fulvius M. f. | Ser. n. Nobilior | cos. Ambracia cepit" ("M. Fulvius Nobilior, son of Marcus

attributed to Numa, from the Temple of Honos and Virtus to his new shrine.[39] We also know that the poet Ennius, famous as the one who first explicitly identified the Greek Muses with the Roman Camenae in his hexameters,[40] had accompanied Nobilior to Aetolia and wrote poems celebrating his victories there.[41]

The Aedes Herculis Musarum thus brought together three diverse but deeply significant elements: Hercules, perhaps the earliest Greek deity to arrive in Rome from southern Italy, and notably the subject of a number of other dedications along the triumphal route, which passed near his primeval Ara Maxima; plus the Greek goddesses of artistic inspiration, the Muses, whose images had been captured by Nobilior *militiae* and brought to the city as *spolia* under his name, and their newly designated Roman counterparts, the Camenae, enshrined in Latin literature as such by the very poet to whom Nobilior acted as patron. Taken as a composite whole, and viewed in the context of Nobilior's *res gestae* and subsequent self-promotion, the juxtaposition of Hercules, Muses, and Camenae in a single monument emerges as a deliberate and delicately crafted synthesis, with a marked message about Roman cultural identity in contact with the Hellenistic world, and Nobilior's role in helping to shape it.[42] Before he died, the *triumphator* himself deposited an annotated copy of the Fasti in the Aedes Herculis Musarum, which later went on to become the meeting place for the Collegium Poetarum in Rome.[43] Nobilior's legacy endured.

---

and grandson of Servius, captured this as consul from Ambracia"). So has a set of coins with what might be images of the statue group: see Crawford 1974, no. 410. The temple appears on the Severan Marble Plan: Castagnoli 1961; Nash 1968, 471. For further ancient testimonia, cf. Ov. *Fasti* 6.799–812; Pliny *NH* 35.66; Plut. *Quaest. Rom.* 59; Macrob. *Sat.* 1.13.21. The monument has generated a sizable bibliography. See among others Boyancé 1972; Cancik 1969; Gruen 1992, 107–10; Holliday 1997, 141–42; Martina 1981; Moevs 1981; Orlin 1997, 6, 65–66, 132–33, 137–39, 155, 177; L. Richardson 1977; Welch 2006a, 502 and nn.; Wiseman 1975.

39. Serv. *ad Aen.* 1.8.

40. Ennius *Ann.* 487: "Musas quas memorant nosc nos esse Camenas" ("Learn that we, whom they call Muses, are the Camenae").

41. On Nobilior's connection with Ennius, see Cic. *Arch.* 27, *Tusc.* 1.3, plus a reference in Eum. *Panegyrici Latini* 9.7.3 (veiled in the words "summi poetae amicitia," "the friendship of the greatest poet"; cf. Nixon and Saylor Rodgers 1994, *ad loc.*), and a notice in *De Vir. Ill.* 52. Cicero even claims (*Brut.* 79) that Nobilior's son, who had learned from his father to appreciate literature, as triumvir actually gave Ennius citizenship, although Badian 1968, 185, is clearly right in condemning this story on the basis of its impossible chronology, given that the son in question would have been only 12 years old at the time. Also cf. Bettini 1979; Martina 1979; and recently Fantham 2004; Klar 2006, 168–70; Welch 2006c, 9.

42. Holliday 1997, 142, argues that Nobilior "sought to identify personal with national accomplishment through a complex interweaving of artistic, literary, religious, and political elements."

43. On Nobilior's Fasti, see Macrob. *Sat.* 1.12.16. On the Collegium Poetarum, see Val. Max. 3.7.11; Pliny *NH* 34.19; Juv. 7.38; also cf. Crowther 1973.

CHAPTER 12

Cn. Manlius Vulso in 187

Beyond Allowable Limits?

Cn. Manlius Vulso and M. Fulvius Nobilior must have made quite a pair. When they reached the consulship together in 189 (37.47.7), both men took on coveted provincial assignments in the East—Asia and Aetolia, respectively (37.50.1–8)—and both had their *imperium* prorogued for the following year (38.35.3), by no means an automatic privilege in the early second century.[1] Ordered back to Rome by the senate in 187 (38.42.12–13), they both went on to celebrate triumphs (39.5.14–16, Nobilior; 39.6.3–7.2, Vulso), but not without first igniting two of the most volatile and dramatic triumph debates on record in Livy. Unlike his colleague, however, Vulso did not owe the *certamen* over his triumph to a long-standing rivalry with any one person. Rather, two men joined forces at the head of the opposition, L. Furius Purpureo and L. Aemilius Paullus—notably a former *triumphator* and a future one—and not merely on their own behalf, but as spokesmen for the *decem legati* sent to help iron out terms for a peace with Antiochus (37.55.4–7). They accused the commander of behaving in the province like a law unto himself, with no regard for the communal interests of the Roman state, which he supposedly served (38.45.4–7). As Livy presents it, this controversy explicitly tested the limits of individual ambition within the magisterial system and the degree of freedom with which a Roman commander could afford at home to exercise his *imperium* in the field. Stagecraft mirrored ideology to a rare degree even for a triumph debate: the one versus the many.

Vulso claimed a triumph because as consul in Asia in 189 he had crushed the Galatians, driving them into the mountains and forcing their complete surrender (38.12–27).[2] The *legati* questioned not so much what

1. On the noninevitability of *prorogatio* during this period, see Gruen 1984a, 214–19.

2. Cf. Polyb. 21.33–39, Diod. 29.12–13.

he had accomplished as by what right he had acted in the first place. He should never have launched a Galatian campaign, they said, when the SPQR had not declared war against the Galatians through the solemn fetial rituals sanctioned by centuries of Roman tradition (38.46.12). He had gone ahead on his own initiative, far overstepping the bounds of his command (38.45.4–5). The ancient sources indeed do not record any formal declaration of war, and Vulso apparently admitted as much himself, quite openly (38.48.7–9). Livy's account also skips from rather vague foreboding in Rome of a possible Galatian threat before Vulso set out, to the scene of him in the province actually mounting his offensive (37.51.10, 60.2; cf. 38.12). So the *legati* did not trump up a charge out of thin air, and yet there were very definitely two sides to the story. The *patres* therefore found themselves confronted with a dilemma. Did the end justify the means? How could they reward Vulso for his behavior and achievements, as he asked, without jeopardizing their own authority over the magistrates of the Republic? These questions pointed to certain deep-seated ambiguities and tensions that the senate did not, indeed could not, fully resolve. In their typical ad-hoc way they eventually arrived at a settlement, but only a temporary and uneasy one, characteristic of the period.

The *legati* stressed that Vulso's military success had come at an awful price. Specifically, the casualty list from his stint in Asia bore the name of Q. Minucius Thermus from within their own ranks (38.41.3; cf. 46.7). The death of Thermus must have shaken his nine remaining colleagues deeply on a personal level, but in the performative context of the triumph debate it became a very public token of symbolic value. Furius and Paullus put it on display before the *patres* as an exemplum, from their own firsthand knowledge, of the dangers inherent in giving a general too much free rein. After paying tribute to their fallen colleague, they asked, "A triumph is sought for *these* accomplishments?" (38.46.9: "pro his triumphus petitur?"). Thermus died late in 188 at Thracian hands, when the Roman army—already victorious over the Galatians and laden with booty—fell into an ambush on its westward trek to winter quarters in Epirus (38.41.3). Nevertheless the effectiveness of the appeal suffered little from the fact that the Thracian skirmish did not technically belong to the campaign for which Vulso was seeking a triumph (38.48.16). For like the commander's own *res gestae* narrative, the story of the slain Thermus gave the audience an index of character on which to base their judgments. It allowed the *legati* to call to remembrance a brave man who had died serving the Republic and to cast a dark shadow thereby on the reckless one they held responsible for such a grievous loss.[3]

3. 38.46.7: "Q. Minucius Thermus, in quo haud paulo plus damni factum est, quam si Cn. Manlius, cuius temeritate ea clades inciderat, perisset, cum multis viris fortibus cecidit" ("Q. Minucius Thermus fell with many brave men, in which far more damage was done than if

The triumphal criteria implicit in this attack put surprisingly little weight on the facts or the intrinsic merit of the Galatian victory, resting instead on a strenuous effort to shape the public identity of the commander to whom that victory belonged. What sort of Roman was Cn. Manlius Vulso? As with Scipio Nasica, what should his *imago* look like? Only once, by Livy's account, did the *legati* denigrate the value of the battles themselves that Vulso had fought against the Galatians, saying that he had nothing to brag about in conquering a decadent people, more like animals than human beings, who hardly qualified as a worthy foe (38.45.11). Again emphasis falls on Vulso's flaws as a leader: the Galatians must be feeble, for inasmuch as the *imperator* set a standard for his troops in this case (a core assertion of any would-be *triumphator* hoping to take credit for his army's success), none of them would have escaped alive to bring home news of their defeat had they gone up against the more robust European Gauls (38.46.2). Yet Furius and Paullus also admit that those same Galatians might easily have overwhelmed the Roman army because of their sheer numbers and superior tactical position. Vulso later called attention to the contradiction, but it did not matter to his critics, who were trying to make a point by discrediting him either way. Even a conventional trope like overcoming unlikely odds could reflect badly on him: the enemy fled in terror, but only because the fame of past victories by other Roman generals did all the fighting (38.46.3–5).

By far the most serious charge against Vulso had to do with neglect of proper fetial procedure.[4] An *imperator*—that is, a citizen imbued with *imperium,* the quasi-magical power to act on behalf of the community—answered finally to the solemn authority of the SPQR. That authority rested in the collective will of the Roman people, who had gathered to name him as a magistrate and to declare war, and of his peers in the senate, who would assess the fruits of his labor when he returned. He could expect to triumph if he faithfully completed the task that they assigned to him as his province: *imperio, auspicio, ductu, felicitate* (38.46.9).[5] Everything he did in the field would redound to his own greater glory on the political stage, but only so long as the audience believed he had acted for the glory of Rome. If he

---

Cn. Manlius had perished, by whose shamelessness this slaughter had begun"). Note the emphasis on Vulso's *temeritas.* The Thracian ambush receives the label of *ignominia* at 38.46.9.

4. On the role of the *fetiales* in officially declaring war, see Beard 1990, 26–27; Harris 1985 166–75; North 2006, 268 and nn.; Rich 1976; Rüpke 1990, 97–117.

5. 38.46.9: "de quibus hostibus triumphum peteres? de iis, ut opinor, quos tibi hostes senatus aut populus Romanus dedisset" ("Over which enemy would you seek a triumph? Over the one, as I see it, that the senate or Roman people gave to you as the enemy"). Note also 38.50.3: "devictis perduellibus, confecta provincia" ("with the enemy conquered and the province completed"), with the comment of Walsh 1993, *ad loc.,* that "the archaic word for *hostibus* is apt in this formulaic context."

should disobey or disregard his obligations to the senate and people, and take matters too far into his own hands, at that moment his *res gestae* would lose their value as tokens in the symbolic economy, because they ceased to belong to the state as a whole. The Roman aristocratic ethos drew a fine line indeed between righteous self-interest properly allied with patriotism and the destructive brand of blind arrogance bordering on hubris.[6]

Once having crossed that line, a commander categorically forfeited any attempt to justify his actions. Now no longer his country's general but a brigand, instead of a lawful and honorable war in the name of the Roman people such a man could wage only an illicit campaign of pillage and piracy for personal gain: "publicum populi Romani bellum" versus "privatum latrocinium" (38.45.7).[7] The first corresponds to the commander's own idealized self-portrait; the second, to the antithesis of Roman aristocratic ideals. The same deeds could thus potentially register as either cause for national celebration or something tantamount to high treason, depending solely on the judgment of the *patres*. By Livy's account Furius and Paullus framed the question in black and white: "How are we supposed to say, Gnaeus Manlius, that what you did counts as X and not Y?" Yet to understand the debate in its performative aspect, it is vitally important to mark a distinction between the *legati* raising the issue as part of their performance and the senate pronouncing a final verdict on the triumph. For although the rhetoric of exempla (good and bad) tended toward stark alternatives, in actual practice the mechanisms of *existimatio* had many checks and balances built in. The *patres* would get the last word over whether Vulso had genuinely transgressed or not, and they did not rush to endorse radical doubts about one of their own.

Nor did the debate take place in a political vacuum: indeed, far from it. When Vulso was allotted the province of Asia, he expected to take over the ongoing operations against Antiochus. Then came news that L. Scipio's stunning victory at Magnesia had brought that campaign to an abrupt end,

6. 38.45.4–5: "circumegisse exercitum ad Gallograecos; cui nationi non ex senatus auctoritate non populi iussu bellum inlatum. quod quem unquam de sua sententia facere ausum?" ("He had then led his army around against the Gallogreeks, a nation on which war was not launched by authority of the senate or by order of the people. Who had ever dared to do such a thing of his own accord?"). Note the emphatic contrast between actions sanctioned by the senate and Roman people and those arising from the commander's own initiative ("de sua sententia"). Cf. 38.45.11: "pro temeritate imperatoris, nullo gentium iure bellum inferentis" ("according to the rashness of a commander bringing war by no law of the nations"). The death of Q. Minucius Thermus is likewise credited to Vulso's *temeritas* (38.46.7).

7. 38.45.7: "quid eorum, Cn. Manli, factum est, ut istud publicum populi Romani bellum et non tuum privatum latrocinium ducamus?" ("Which of these things, Gnaeus Manlius, was done in such a way that we should consider it a public war of the Roman people and not your own private banditry?")

just as the new consuls were preparing to head out into the field. The senate decreed that Vulso should still go to the province as planned, but now mainly to supervise negotiations for peace and to handle possible mop-up operations rather than to wage a full-scale war. They left his army intact, however, citing some fear of the Gauls, who had fought among Antiochus's allies.[8] Livy's narrative then marks a steady progression from the initial indication of concern in the senate about a possible threat (37.51.10), to a statement that grounds existed for war against the Galatians (37.60.2), and finally to Vulso in the province actually waging a war (38.12.1).

One explanation for the decision to send Vulso to Asia with a limited mandate lies in a familiar quarter: the senators shrank from allowing L. Scipio to stay in the province, where he would then take credit for a lasting settlement on top of his already unexpected victory.[9] T. Quinctius Flamininus had enjoyed such a privilege in 196, but only because two tribunes stepped in to secure it for him when the annual provincial assignments came up for debate, a sure sign of *existimatio* at work painstakingly parceling out honors among the élite (33.25.4–11). The fact that Africanus had gone to Asia with his brother in the role of *legatus* no doubt added to the senate's already chronic anxiety over what heaping too many accolades on the Scipios might do to the fragile balance within their ranks. They did grant L. Scipio a triumph over Antiochus on his return (37.59.2–6),[10] but the notorious litigation that followed soon thereafter bespeaks the unmistakable *invidia* against him and his family.[11] We shall see that Vulso would not emerge unscarred from that controversy either.

Meanwhile, on his arrival in Asia, he found himself not only overseeing the developing peace talks but commanding an army as well, the same troops whom the senate had originally assigned to him for the major assault he would now never mount against Antiochus (37.51.10). A recent study has linked Vulso's rather curious meandering progress through Asia Minor to a careful strategy that allowed him, first, to keep all his troops fed and to pay them, both at Seleucid expense; second, to forestall any possibility of a renewed offensive on the part of Antiochus's forces, which if ignored might still pose a considerable threat, while, third, still strictly

8. On the complex patchwork of alliances on both sides in the Asian war, see Grainger 1995, 30–31.

9. See Gruen 1995, 69.

10. On Asiaticus's triumph, cf. Polyb. 21.24.16–17; Cic. *Prov. Cons.* 18; Val. Max. 4.1.8, 5.3.2, 5.5.2; Pliny *NH* 33.148, 35.22; Plut. *Cat. Mai.* 18.1; Gell. 6.19.3.

11. As already remarked, the garbled historical record cannot yield many firm conclusions about the obscure events now known as the trials of the Scipios. But whatever happened, bitter *invidia* certainly played a crucial role. The word occurs no fewer than four times in Livy's account of the episode: 38.51.4, 38.54.10, 38.59.7, and 38.60.10. Cf. Gruen 1995, 78 n. 75.

abiding by the terms of the truce so that the ongoing peace negotiations could proceed unmolested.[12] With these genuine policy concerns in the province, plus soldiers under his command, a typical drive toward glory in battle, and a ready target to hand, he had lacked neither means, nor motive, nor opportunity (f. 37.60.2).

Indeed, the senate may even have meant the broad hints about the Galatians as more than a consolation prize to Vulso, as it might appear at first glance, in compensation for the larger campaign where Scipio had stolen his march. Moreover, Vulso may have used the Galatian campaign as a deliberate cover to mask the hidden anti-Seleucid agenda behind his movements, long enough so that by the time his real adversaries figured it out, it would be too late, because he would already have achieved his objectives and vastly depleted their war chests to feed his army. Whether by senatorial directive, or through Vulso's own broadly sanctioned initiative within the boundaries of his *provincia,* this was in fact exactly how things turned out. He could legitimately claim that the original declaration of war against Antiochus had at least implied, even if it did not outright announce, an umbrella authorization to hunt down any Seleucid allies remaining hostile in the province after the king's defeat. Since Galatians had fought alongside Antiochus against the army of L. Scipio, he had merely set out to finish what his predecessor had begun (38.48.7–9).

In their mutual efforts to impress the *patres,* Vulso and the *legati* managed to turn the ideology of Roman *nobiles* against itself. The charge of *latrocinium* spoke to the vested interest that the senate had in demanding deference from commanders in the field.[13] But Vulso likewise invoked a concept dear to aristocratic thinking: *felicitas* (38.48.15). His military success meant ipso facto, he argued, that the gods had bestowed on him their sanction and blessing to fight as Rome's champion against the enemies of the Republic (38.48.14–16). If the higher powers had not approved of the Galatian campaign, it would have ended in defeat. Nathan Rosenstein has shown that this kind of reasoning often helped to shield Roman generals who had lost battles from humiliation on their return home: no one could blame them for failure if success was never meant to be.[14] So Vulso could lament the death of Q. Minucius Thermus in Thrace as a sad misfortune,

12. See Grainger 1995. It is particularly gratifying to see the alternating positive and negative strands in Livy's narrative of the campaign traced back to the politics of the triumph debate, where Vulso's critics circulated one story and the general himself and his supporters another. Also cf. Grainger 2002, 337–50; Pagnon 1982.

13. Furius's and Paullus's speech contrasts with Vulso's rash, presumptuous conduct in ignoring the fetial rites with the exempla of recent *triumphatores,* including M'. Acilius Glabrio, T. Quinctius Flamininus, and Scipio Africanus (38.46.10–12). Cf. 36.3.7.

14. Cf. Rosenstein 1990a, passim, especially 114–52.

but it was not his fault (38.49.8–9). And more important, in a twist on the familiar paradox, he could proudly take credit for his accomplishments against the Galatians by acknowledging that victory did not belong to him alone. He and his army merely wanted to share in the glory that the state owed to the civic gods. He sought to cast himself in a favorable light as an individual by appeal to the general character of the Roman polity (38.48.14).

Just as the alleged breach of fetial procedure threatened to banish him from legitimate service to the Republic into the realm of *latrocinium,* so too an emphasis on the triumph as an act of civic religious duty, alongside the *supplicatio,* allowed Vulso to tie his public identity back to the community again. Here the symmetry of the triumph celebration works to his advantage. For by carrying the firstfruits from his victory up to the Capitolium, the very spot at the center and heart (literally the "head") of the city from which he had initially set out, Vulso *triumphator* would be giving the state its due and fulfilling the task assigned to him on behalf of the Republic in the best possible way (38.48.16).[15] This argument did not so much resolve the question of mandate as gloss over it, by diverting attention from the ambiguous rights and policies behind his *res gestae* toward their indisputable yield. With the defeat of the Galatians, the entire province now lay at peace (38.47.6, 10–16).[16] To deny honors for such an achievement would constitute blind *invidia* (38.49.5).[17] The senate could not afford to endorse any commander who shamelessly flaunted disobedience and disrespect for the common interest, because that cut dead against the grain of the magisterial system (38.48.15). But if, notwithstanding the charges against him, Vulso could both fashion a convincing image of his *res gestae* as valuable public property and offer his peers a visible and noteworthy gesture of submission to their collective authority, then he might at length win their commendation.

Only at very great length indeed did the verdict arrive. Arguments on

15. 38.48.15–16: "postularem ut dis immortalibus honos haberetur et ipse triumphans in Capitolium escenderem, unde votis rite nuncupatis profectus sum" ("I would ask that honor be paid to the immortal gods and that I myself should climb to the Capitolium in triumph, whence I set out having announced my vows according to ritual").

16. Note the striking collocation "prospero eventu pravo consilio rem gesserunt" ("they accomplished the thing with a successful outcome, but a flawed plan") used at 38.48.13 to describe commanders executed by the Carthaginians, unlike Roman practice. By implication, the *patres* might well condemn Vulso's strategy, but even so the result would speak for itself (38.48.15): "tantam nationem sine ulla militum iactura devicimus" ("we conquered so great a nation without any loss of our soldiers"). On the phrase "militum iactura" and others like it, see above, p. 111 n. 20.

17. 38.49.5: "caeca invidia est, patres conscripti, nec quicquam aliud scit quam detractare virtutes" ("*Invidia* is blind, senators, nor does it know anything else except how to disparage virtues").

both sides took so long that the *patres* could not vote until the following day.[18] In the process, Vulso came perilously close to losing out on his triumph before winning in the end. How did that happen? And what do we make of the unusual timing? Livy's account hinges on the following passage (38.50.1–3):[19]

> On that day the accusations would have outweighed the defense had they not prolonged the exchange until late. The senate adjourned in such a frame of mind that it seemed as if they would deny the triumph. The next day the relatives and friends of Cn. Manlius pressed on with their best helping efforts, and the *auctoritas* of the elder senators also prevailed, saying that no exemplum had been committed to memory whereby a commander who had brought his army home, with the enemy conquered and his province completed, should enter the city without a chariot and laurel wreath, as a private citizen and unhonored. The shame induced by this appeal overcame ill will, and a full session voted the triumph.

Superficially speaking, if nothing mattered about a triumph debate except the outcome, the contrary-to-fact condition in the first sentence here would suggest that the *legati* set out to thwart Vulso's *triumphi spes* and failed because they could not convince the *patres* fast enough. They had almost reached their goal but lost their momentum when everyone went home at nightfall. So from their perspective the extravagant display of speechmaking before the senate, on both sides, simply went on too long.

Overnight the judging audience had time to reflect and reconsider, and things looked very different in the morning. So Vulso got his triumph, leaving Furius and Paullus with apparently nothing to show for themselves but unfulfilled potential and a lost cause. If only the speakers on the first day had managed to show restraint, to be a little less longwinded, then maybe a quicker verdict would have gone the other way. Or would it? Such a narrow view may be missing the point. Even though it obviously made a big difference to all concerned whether the senate would award the triumph or not, these debates still yielded more than a

18. Few other would-be *triumphatores* in Livy met with such vehement and long-winded opposition. In 197, two commanders who had joined forces tried to make a joint request but were forced to apply separately, so that one triumphed although the other did not (33.22.10). And in 167, a group of soldiers trying to block their own commander's triumph prolonged the arguments until nightfall on purpose and, ultimately, in vain (45.36.1–2). Cf. above, p. 76 and n. 39.

19. 38.50.1–3: "plus crimina eo die quam defensio valuisset, ni altercationem in serum perduxissent. dimittitur senatus in ea opinione ut negaturus triumphum fuisse videretur. postero die et cognati amicique Cn. Manli summis opibus adnisi sunt, et auctoritas seniorum valuit, negantium exemplum proditum memoriae esse ut imperator, qui devictis perduellibus, confecta provincia exercitum reportasset, sine curru et laurea privatus inhonoratusque urbem iniret. hic pudor malignitatem vicit, triumphumque frequentes decreverunt."

zero-sum, yes-or-no answer before they were finished. We must never allow the end result of the political process to obscure the value of the process itself—the ongoing, precarious balancing act of the Roman aristocratic élite, forever struggling to negotiate and maintain a livable distribution of status within their ranks. Rather than dwelling on how much the delay may have cost the *legati,* therefore, we should focus instead on what they gained through that long day of arguments, remembering that regardless of what they might say, Vulso had the raw material for the conversion of *res gestae* into elements of public identity firmly in his possession all along: *imperio, auspicio, ductu, felicitate.*

There were certainly two sides to the debate, with two plausible ideological constructs vying for the attention and approval of the *patres.* Livy labels it an *altercatio* (38.50.1) and carefully dramatizes the face-off with a matched pair of elaborate speeches.[20] Yet in one important respect the theatrical staging worked in Vulso's favor right from the start. Tradition ensured that any would-be *triumphator* would tell his story first, before the senate heard arguments from the opposition. The same procedure held even when the commander had only the shakiest hope of impressing his peers, and this one could boast with confidence that he had wiped out a very real threat to security throughout his province. So by the time Furius and Paullus got up to speak, Vulso had already sculpted a brilliant effigy of himself as loyal and diligent in his service to the Republic (38.44.10–11). When all was said and done, precisely that image prevailed. In the end the senators had to admit that they owed honor to Vulso on three major counts. These were not criteria per se, but compelling tokens of symbolic value derived from the *res gestae* narrative in the course of the debate: he had thoroughly crushed the enemy, completed the assignment given to him as his province, and brought his army home (38.50.3). The distribution of air time on the senate floor guaranteed that he would have a political *aristeia* to match his success on the battlefield, so people would have been able to gauge the strength of his chances early on.

Far from spelling disaster for the *legati,* then, the fact that the debate ran over into a second day may even have held the key to their strategy, a measure not of their failure in the political arena but of their success.

20. At 38.47.1 Livy admits to having taken a degree of license in his presentation of the speeches from this debate: "talis oratio Furi et Aemili fuit. Manlium in hunc maxime modum respondisse accepi" ("Such was the speech of Furius and Aemilius. I take it that Manlius replied essentially like this"). Walsh 1993, 9, remarks: "This content is clearly at least in part fictitious reconstruction rather than a record of what was actually said . . . the significance of the issue for readers recalling Marius' foundation of a personal army, which through Sulla and Pompey led to Julius Caesar and monarchy, is set out unambiguously." Yet if Livy is sermonizing for his contemporary audience here, the message lies as much in how the conflict was eventually resolved without bloodshed as in the precise wording of arguments on either side.

When they went home in the evening, Furius and Paullus could feel gratified that they had kept up their fight for so long, regardless of how the senate might vote the next day. In the passage cited above (38.50.1–3), Livy uses the same verb, albeit in different moods, to describe the political weight carried by the arguments on both sides. So when their viewpoint prevailed ("valuit," perfect indicative, 38.50.3), Vulso's supporters achieved in reality what his detractors had seen only as a potential hope that never materialized ("valuisset," pluperfect subjunctive, 38.50.1). But the senators adjourned at nightfall pointedly *in a state of mind* engineered by Vulso's critics (38.50.1). *Existimatio* would take its own course from here on, and Vulso had many friends and family members, not to mention the "auctoritas seniorum" (38.50.3), to back him up. Other voices besides theirs could still be heard, but nonetheless the *legati* had made a dramatic impact on their peers that day. So once having seized the floor they pressed their advantage as strenuously as they could, seeking to score points for themselves for as long as that all-important senatorial audience cared to listen. They were fashioning their own public identity out there in the limelight, even while speaking out against Vulso, and they put on a very convincing show. Surely those efforts did not go entirely to waste.

Then came the pause overnight, stillness marking the end of a rousing performance, like the intermission between one act of a play and the next. The *legati* had capitalized on their time at center stage, and when deliberations resumed it was Vulso's turn again. Political performance under the Roman Republic typically followed this rhythm: a commander who met with opposition to his triumph request would persevere and win civic honors in the end more often than not, by forging a consensus after his critics had their say (see appendix B). The formal and deliberate (if heated) exchange of speeches in the senate tended gradually to dispel tension and thus to restore the precious equilibrium of status among the élite, which a hasty or ill-considered verdict might endanger. This case stands out because the issues raised proved divisive in the extreme. Vulso had brought home *res gestae* that deserved recognition, but first the senate had to wrestle past the formidable charges raised by the *legati.* Such closely matched negotiations put a terrible strain on the symbolic economy. Both sides pushed harder than usual, and to compensate, the pendulum of audience response had to swing out very far in one direction before coming back to settle in the other. As a result, the whole process went into slow motion, as when a composer, to borrow another metaphor, writes *molto ritardando* into his score to make room for a crucial harmonic shift.

Instead of giving up at the start of day two, Vulso's relatives and friends rallied behind him, renewing the debate (38.50.2). Livy singles out the elder senators for bringing their recalcitrant colleagues to a consensus at last, in favor of the triumph, by stirring a very specific emotion in them. At the prospect of leaving such an impressive catalogue of achievements unrewarded, he says, the *patres* finally felt ashamed: "pudor malignitatem vicit" (38.50.3: "shame overcame ill will"). Nowhere else does Livy directly credit the award of a triumph to the workings of *pudor,*[21] and the passage stands out all the more because those workings had wide social and cultural ramifications. The capacity for shame lurks at the permeable boundary between an individual's own internalized view of himself and his status in the eyes of a valued external audience. *Pudor* typically strikes when a person realizes that something he has done, or (less often) might do, will result in making him look bad to someone who matters. Because it grows out of lifelong exposure to and sensitivity toward the judgments of *existimatio,* it appears in its most highly developed form among those with the greatest investment in the elaborate patterns of self-fashioning: aristocratic men in public life.[22]

Since the *patres* wielded the power to grant or withhold the most sought-after prizes of honor in Rome, their collective sense of shame had a huge impact on the symbolic economy as they struggled to keep aristocratic competition in line. The *auctoritas* of the elders in particular made them heard as the repository for Rome's collective memory and the voice of the civic conscience. When these men announced that they found no exemplum for a given course of action—whether strict factual history backed them up or not—the person caught pursuing that course felt a double dishonor: first for the supposed lack of precedent and again for meeting with the elders' public reproof.[23] Worse, if that person happened to come from among their own ranks, then his conduct would reflect poorly on the entire senatorial order. In the present passage, Livy says that *pudor* assailed the *patres* as a group, almost as if they formed a single consciousness held in the sway of the Vulso's critics until the *seniores* set them straight. Shame jerked them out of complacent assent to the belittling of one of their own, which would have branded them all as *maligni.* Only rarely does *pudor* actually stop

21. Forms of *pudor* or *pudere* appear 75 times in extant Livy, but only three times in the context of a triumph debate: at 38.50.3 (the present passage) and again at 45.39.2, 18. Both of the later examples come from the speech by M. Servilius (consul 202) on behalf of L. Aemilius Paullus's triumph after Pydna in 167. The first belongs to a hypothetical (contrary-to-fact) scenario imagined by the speaker, and the second, in the negative, refers to feelings from which the speaker himself is happily immune. See below, pp. 265–66, for a detailed discussion.

22. Cf. Kaster 1997, 13: insofar "as it acted as a brake upon mere self-regard and self-assertion, [*pudor*] would tend to regulate the vigorous competition for prestige and honor among the élite." See also Barton 2001, 199–288.

23. At 38.50.3 Livy does not say merely "pudor malignitatem vicit" (referring to shame in general), but "hic pudor," i.e., "*this* shame," namely the one arising from an unprecedented action duly reprimanded by the elders in a public way.

someone from doing something that he might later regret, as opposed to thinking back with a new critical self-awareness on deeds in the past.[24] Livy also suggests that the senators' shame overcame more than a mere threat of *malignitas,* so perhaps we should look for a hidden retrospective element here as well. But what mean thing had they already done?

Happily, an explanation lies near at hand in the realm of performance. For if the song and dance on the senate stage had an intangible substance on which Roman aristocrats placed a high social value, then just taking part in a public debate where a well-earned triumph came under fire would already count by itself as *malignitas,* even short of a vote against the would-be *triumphator,* especially when such participation drew open reprimand from the *seniores.* It was the judgment of an authoritative audience in Rome, linked to success on the battlefield but also distinct from it, that made the merit of a triumph claim truly real and no longer negotiable. Strictly speaking, the *patres* could have found precedent to deny Vulso's triumph if they had wanted to. The three facts mentioned earlier that emerged at the start and eventually won the day for the commander—that he had soundly defeated the enemy, finished his task in the province, and brought his army home—did not become genuine tokens of symbolic value until the right people vouched for them publicly (38.50.3).[25] As soon as the elders had spoken, however, any lingering doubt about the potential worthiness of Vulso's *res gestae* narrative would have ceased. Now his peers saw their reluctance to hail Vulso so far as meanness and coalesced behind him, thereby not only staving off deeper trouble ahead, should the triumph not take place, but also averting an immediate crisis for equilibrium among themselves.

The conclusion of this debate therefore boils down to the one versus the many again, on a number of levels. Individual senators, each reminded of his duty toward the community at large, acted together as one on behalf of the Republic to extol a commander who had just given a spectacle of allegiance to that same communal interest, and of deference toward them in turn as the lawful arbiters of civic identity in Rome. The charges raised by Vulso's critics had very nearly threatened to banish him from the circle of those who served the state honorably, but his carefully crafted and overwhelmingly civic-minded performance reaffirmed his identity as a loyal soldier who was now bringing home the firstfruits of his victory to the SPQR. His request that the *patres* grant him a triumph, ceremonially offered at the start of the proceedings and later reiterated and glossed as an act of civic piety, served to place his fate in their hands and to acknowledge

24. For the short list of examples of "prospective *pudor,*" see Kaster 1997, 12 n. 28.

25. As Gruen 1995, 65, remarks, the elders' claim that no precedent existed was "inaccurate—but true enough to carry the day." It might not have been "true enough" coming from a less highly esteemed source.

them as the keepers of the flame in regard to both the *pax deum* and the distribution of honors. Vulso had friends in high places, too, for he won his triumph in the end when his supporters among the senior ranks of senators exerted their tremendous *auctoritas* on his behalf to shame the others into following their lead. With the final vote, his *res gestae* at last bore their official stamp.

The paired gestures of the commander's request and the senate's approval are evenly matched and perfectly correspond—first *ut liceret,* then *licet*—each reinforcing and legitimizing the other within the same ideological framework. Vulso owed his triumph to an act of persuasion and a line of thought that often helped to save defeated generals from disgrace. When push came to shove, Roman aristocrats shared a stake in ensuring that praiseworthy deeds received due public recognition. All of them stood to profit from the transaction and to lose otherwise.[26] Tellingly, at the moment of the final appeal from the *seniores,* the commander's name disappears. The exemplifying discourse of *existimatio* has transformed Vulso, the individual with a unique story to tell, into an anonymous *imperator qui,* a normative cultural type (i.e., exemplum) to whom as such the senators were then called upon to feel certain obligations (38.50.3). The irony is, of course, that when he put his *res gestae* on display, a would-be *triumphator* aimed his self-fashioning at precisely this depersonalizing effect, since only thus, inscribed in the Fasti for all time, would his name gain stature by association with universalized Roman ideals (cf. 8.30.8–9).

AFTERMATH AND BACKLASH

Whereas the honor conferred by a triumph endured, however, the political settlement brought about by the triumph debate simply could not, because *existimatio* kept symbolic capital in constant circulation among the élite. The charges raised by the *legati* had been very serious ones, with broad implications beyond the triumph itself, and a favorable outcome in the senate did not keep Vulso out of trouble for long. Livy's narrative breaks off with the award of the triumph instead of moving on straightaway, as it usually would, to the celebration itself.[27] In between, he recounts another

26. Reflecting on the pattern observed by Rosenstein 1990a, 114–52, that Roman aristocrats, despite the intense competition among them, would ultimately unite to protect their own from embarrassment or disgrace, Kaster 1997, 15, remarks: "The dynamics originate not so much in the thought 'there but for the grace of God go I' as in the self-protective recognition that recriminations, once begun, could leave oneself scarred, and, more important, undermine the public perception of excellence that was the premise of the aristocracy's life." Note the echo in 38.50.3 of the passage from Vulso's speech at 38.49.5, cited above, p. 219 n. 17.

27. Livy's account of the debate ends at 38.50.3, ten chapters before the end of Book 38, but he does not get to the triumph itself until 39.6.3.

episode so momentous and volatile that he says it eclipsed the triumph debate altogether: the trials of the Scipios (38.50.4). Details of these events remain hopelessly obscure and need not concern us here, save that terrible suspicion arose, further fueled by lingering *invidia,* as pointed out earlier, over L. Scipio's handling of money and booty taken from Antiochus and those under him, which had never found its way into the public coffers (38.54.3).[28] In a brilliantly theatrical outburst, as noted in chapter 6, Africanus defiantly tore the account books to shreds (38.55.10–13).[29] That display of *dignitas*—or "arrogant gesture," as others have called it[30]—did not stop L. Scipio from being fined and imprisoned, but then one of the ten tribunes intervened to secure his release, so that in the end a measure of *invidia* landed also on the heads of those who had brought the complaints in the first place (38.58–60).[31] Vulso meanwhile found himself implicated in the controversy surrounding his predecessor. A charge was leveled against the Scipios of "regnum in senatu" ("reigning in the senate like kings"), and L. Furius Purpureo, again on behalf of the *decem legati,* demanded an account of all money gathered in Asia under the recent peace (38.54.6–7).

Fearing the prosecution to which he would be liable as soon as he entered the city and became *privatus,* Vulso remained outside the *pomerium,* postponing his triumph until the very end of the year, when the praetor in charge of the tribunal no longer had enough time left in office to try his case. After that the matter was dropped (39.6.3–4). It would seem that he had indeed inherited financial responsibilities in Asia: L. Scipio had collected only five hundred talents from Antiochus, out of a total indemnity of three thousand, and Vulso gathered the rest as part of the Apamea settlement.[32] The fact that both men came under fire, and Vulso from the same quarters as in his triumph debate, reveals that more lay at stake here than just the often cited fear of giving Africanus and his family free rein. In the early second century, Rome's deepening involvement in the affairs of the Mediterranean world tended to arouse ambitions. Choice new provincial assignments held seemingly limitless promise of personal advancement in service to the Republic, not to mention the untold wealth pouring into the city year after year with each new spectacular conquest. Laws against electoral bribery (*ambitus*), sumptuary legislation, and con-

28. Cf. 38.55.5–8 for more monetary details, and Gell. 4.18.7–8, which says that the senators demanded an account of *pecunia* (money) and *praeda* (booty) both.

29. Cf. Polyb. 23.14.8–11, Gell. 4.18.7–12, Val. Max. 3.7.1, Diod. 29.21.

30. So Walsh 1993, 4.

31. On *invidia* in particular, note especially 38.60.10.

32. Gruen 1995, 74 nn. 58–60, cites the evidence from Polybius: 21.17.5 (total indemnity of 3,000 talents), 23.14.9 (500 talents given to Scipio), 21.41 (remaining 2,500 talents part of Apamea settlement). Also see Grainger 1995, 39–42.

cern over the disposition of wealth from the East are all emerging features during this period, and represent efforts to rein in individual aristocrats who were seen to have overstepped the traditional bounds of what was good for the *res publica*.[33] These trends also expose the structural links, or what Bourdieu would call the homology between the two economies, symbolic and material.[34]

Generally speaking, the money and other booty brought home by Roman armies was earmarked for the civic treasury. Commanders had custody over their personal share of the takings (*manubiae*), however, and could direct the flow of this special category of public property toward temple dedications or displays of largesse to their troops.[35] Relative freedom from scrutiny encouraged *imperatores* to seek profit from both rapacity abroad and generosity at home, but the staggering sums involved gave growing cause for alarm over apparent abuses. The historical record preserves catalogues "in loving detail" of the fabulous objects carried in triumph during the years after the Hannibalic War.[36] Certainly no exception, Vulso put on a lavish display notable for the tonnage of precious metals involved: "golden crowns weighing 212 pounds, 220,000 pounds of silver, 2,103 pounds of gold, 127,000 Attic four-drachma pieces, 250,000 cistophori, 16,320 gold Philip coins, and arms and many Gallic spoils loaded on carts, and 52 leaders of the enemy led before his chariot" (39.7.1–3). In addition to a bonus for each of his soldiers, with extra for the centurions and even more for the cavalry, Vulso gave them all double pay. Moreover, the money he deposited in the *aerarium* enabled the *patres* to wipe out a sizable public debt (39.7.3–5).[37]

It might help to compare what Livy says about L. Scipio's Asian triumph in 189. He carried "224 military standards, 134 models of towns, 1,231 ivory tusks, 234 golden crowns, 137,420 pounds of silver, 214,000 Attic four-drachma pieces, 321,070 cistophori, 140,000 gold Philip coins, 1,423 pounds of silver vases—all were embossed—and 1,023 pounds of gold. And 32 royal generals, prefects, and nobles were led before his car." He also handed out double pay and other rewards to his troops, including a special

33. See Lintott 1972, 631–32.

34. So Bourdieu 1977, *passim*.

35. Booty was public property, after all, and should therefore be used in cooperation between magistrates, senate, and people to serve the general good. See especially Churchill 1999 and Orlin 1997, both cogently arguing against the former *communis opinio* (best articulated by Shatzman 1972) that the senate and people exerted little or no formal control over individual commanders in the disposition of money and *praeda*.

36. The quotation is from Gruen 1995, 71. Livy's triumph descriptions include precise amounts of coins and other precious metal objects wherever possible from 293 onwards. See Östenberg 2003, 57–76, 97–107; cf. the statistics compiled by Grainger 1995, 42.

37. See Gruen 1984a, 293–94.

distribution after the battle on the spot (37.59.3–6). In both cases, Livy intimates that sheer extravagance made the *triumphator* suspect. For while L. Scipio may have far surpassed his brother Africanus in the parade of captured wealth, he could not equal him in civic stature. Likewise, though no doubt justifiably grateful for the generous rewards they had received, Vulso's troops sang his praises so loudly and openly that he almost looked as if he had bought their favor for the sake of his own ambition, taking the triumph away from the Roman people, to whom it properly belonged (39.7.3).[38]

Against this background, the accusations over misappropriated Seleucid funds marked a tentative step toward establishing the need for some kind of restraint: Vulso's experience formed part of a much larger trend. Similarly, and not long before, M'. Acilius Glabrio had been forced to withdraw from the censorial elections of 189 amid allegations that he had not carried certain items captured from Antiochus in his triumph after Thermopylae, nor deposited them into the treasury. Cato the Elder, himself a candidate for censor that year, testified boldly that he had seen vessels of gold and silver among the original booty that did not appear in the triumph. Tribunes proposed a fine and pressed charges for two of the three statutory days, only to drop them on the third, as soon as Glabrio had pulled out of the election (37.57.12–58.1).[39] Thus three commanders celebrated triumphs from the province of Asia in the course of about two and half years—Glabrio, L. Scipio, and Vulso—only to be accused one by one of misusing the spoils of conquest. The truly striking thing, however, is that none of them paid the proposed penalty. Each time the public proceedings as such seem to have done the trick politically, merely by airing a discussion and allowing both sides to tell their stories. Then the collective self-preservation instinct of the Roman aristocracy stepped in to save face for everyone before recriminations went too far.

Such performative posturing and display was anything but void of substance. It served a vital purpose as the Republic wrestled with the challenges posed by its heady new role on the Hellenistic stage.[40] Only one further element remains in order to understand how the Vulso controversy fits into its proper context both in the turbulent times of the early second century and in Livy's narrative scheme. Livy singles out this commander as the target for a moralizing diatribe in his own voice about the evil influence of Eastern opulence on traditional Roman values: *luxuria* came from

38. Cf. the soldiers' songs from Caesar's triumph over the Gauls: Suet. *Iul.* 49.4, 51.1.

39. For Cato's conspicuous testimony, see especially 37.57.13–14, with the remarks of Walsh 1992, *ad loc.*

40. Cf. Gruen 1995, 89–90.

outside the city, he says, and was literally "carried within" in Asian triumphs (39.6.7).[41] Of course the historian programmatically blames the decline in Roman morals that led to the Civil Wars on the deleterious effects wrought by imported foreign wealth on the austerity of the *mos maiorum* (*Praef.* 11–12). Armies returning from the East introduced a weakness for amenities such as bronze couches, elegant and exotic textiles, one-footed tables and sideboards, musicians, and elaborate banquets, which led to the elevation of cookery from the lowest form of servitude to the status of an art. Such novelties, Livy says, were barely the beginning, and indeed spelled the beginning of the end (39.6.7–9).[42] Other authors share a preoccupation with imported *luxuria* as a cause of moral decline, particularly when looking back on the fall of the Republic.[43]

Livy dramatizes history in order to train his audience in the ethical discourse of the Republic, so that they can learn how to sort out the good exempla from the bad (*Praef.* 10). Situated right in the middle of an ongoing series of *certamina,* each of which tried the limits of the Republican system in a different way, the Vulso controversy becomes a perfect test case for the method by which Roman aristocratic ideology was supposed to work out its problems. He therefore uses the triumph debate as a showcase for divergent voices speaking from within the value system at a moment when it already showed the signs of strain but still maintained structural integrity. The pendulum swing of the *consensus patrum* over Vulso's triumph, first one way and then the other, not only illustrates the performative dynamic at work, giving both sides their due in turn, but also demonstrates at the same time how precarious and fragile the balance really was. The system had both strengths and weaknesses. Above all, equilibrium came at a price: citizens could not put their own self-advancement ahead of whatever the *res publica* might demand.

Behind the portrait of an *imperator* who oversteps the bounds of his authority, defies the senate, and behaves in his province like a law unto himself, while claiming continually that he is acting as a loyal servant in the best interests of the Republic, looms the specter of Julius Caesar, who swore that nothing other than old-fashioned aristocratic *dignitas* had

41. 39.6.7: "luxuriae enim peregrinae origo ab exercitu Asiatico invecta in urbem est" ("For the origin of foreign luxury was carried into the city by the army from Asia"). Note that the expression "invecta in urbem est" closely echoes the triumphal formula: Livy is almost making a pun.

42. Cf. Östenberg 2003, *passim;* and Flower 2004b, 339.

43. For the *luxuria* trope outside Livy, see, e.g., Polyb. 9.10, 39.2; Sall. *Cat.* 10–11, *Jug.* 41; Flor. 1.47.7; Pliny *NH* 34.14. Other primary sources listed by Lintott 1972. Cf. also Earl 1961 and more recently Barton 2001, *passim,* especially 92–93, 268; Gruen 1984a, 260–66.

driven him to cross the Rubicon on that fateful day, in the firm conviction that he deserved recognition for his accomplishments.[44] We must never forget that Livy and his readers possessed the terrible knowledge, which history spared to the *nobiles* of the second century, that through an excess of aristocratic self-fashioning Roman society eventually came apart at the seams in the cataclysm of civil war.[45]

44. Caes. *BC* 1.7.7, and again at 1.9.2. Cf. Cic. *Att.* 7.11.1: "atque haec ait omnia facere se dignitatis causa" ("And he said that he did all of these things for the sake of his *dignitas*").

45. As Gruen 1974, 497, remarks: "The fierce struggle for personal *dignitas* was not incompatible with the *res publica*. Indeed it was as old as the *res publica* itself."

CHAPTER 13

M. Popillius Laenas in 173

Inverting the Paradigm

The Fasti Triumphales contain no record of any triumph for M. Popillius Laenas, consul in Liguria in 173. Nor does Livy state anywhere that Laenas made a triumph request on his return from the province. Not even once, in fact, does the historian ever use the word "triumph" in his whole account of Laenas's consulship, which he characterizes as a thoroughgoing breach of protocol and the antithesis of Roman ideals. In particular, Laenas refused to play by the established rules and bow to the authority of the *patres* (cf. 42.9.1). Yet the series of confrontations between him and the senate belong squarely in the context of all the other dramas played out when generals came home from the battlefield in hope of glory. Livy's treatment of the episode has a distinctive shape, marked by the steady annalistic rhythm of dealings between the *patres* and magistrates of the Republic. Even without any mention of a triumph, that is, the familiar concepts, performative elements, formulaic expressions, and basic expectations from a triumph debate still underlie the historian's narrative, but subtly hidden, because they have all been systematically overturned or transgressed by the negative exemplum. In short, what we have here is a triumph debate turned on its head, which will demonstrate just how pervasive an influence the triumphal discourse of the *res publica* had on the foundations of Livy's history.

FIRST PHASE: *PESSIMUM EXEMPLUM*

Livy's account of the pitched battle where Laenas defeated the Ligurian Statellates follows a predictable pattern. A thunderous charge by the Roman cavalry, carefully timed, turned an otherwise even fight into a rout. Panicked Ligurians fled in all directions, making ready prey for Roman swords (42.7.5–10). As usual Livy crowns the narrative with casualty figures: some ten thousand of the enemy were killed and more than seven hundred captured, along with eighty-two military standards. Then he adds that Laenas's hard-won success came at a considerable cost to Rome, with the loss of more than three thousand men. Here as elsewhere the grim litotes "incruenta victoria fuit" ("nor was it a bloodless victory," 42.7.10) sounds an ominous note with its hint of opposition to what Laenas had done. Of course news of death tolls from the field served to memorialize and enshrine the noble deeds of those soldiers, centurions, military tribunes, and *legati* who made the ultimate sacrifice for the Republic, but these statistics also bore a significant political weight for the *imperator* himself, inasmuch as he had a personal stake in everything that took place under his command and sought to maximize the symbolic capital from his *res gestae.*

The Statellates gave Laenas their unconditional surrender, hoping, Livy says, that at least he would not behave any worse than earlier Roman commanders had done, a telling hint at precedents and paradigms (42.8.2).[1] In response Laenas summarily confiscated their weapons, laid waste to their town, sold their belongings, and condemned them all to slavery. One should note that these actions, though harsh, were certainly well within the bounds of a commander's rights in response to a surrender.[2] Laenas then wrote a letter to the senate proclaiming his accomplishments (42.8.3). By now we have certainly seen enough different examples of such letters to recognize quickly the performative aspect of this self-fashioning gesture, so often the prelude to a *supplicatio* vote. The consul wanted everyone at home to know that he had done his duty in the province, so that he could claim the reputation and other rewards that would come with acknowledged success on the battlefield (cf. 42.9.5). But Livy shines an unusual light here on an otherwise unremarkable performative exchange, by dramatizing the surrender of the Statellates very much from their point of view and thereby setting up a striking contrast between the treatment they expected, based on the Roman character as they had known it before, and what they received now from Laenas. As much as Laenas bragged to his peers about his *res gestae,* he had broken the rules, at least as his victims saw them, and Livy's narrative voice begs sympathy for their plight.[3]

1. 42.8.2: "dediderunt sese, nihil quidem illi pacti; speraverant tamen <non> atrocius quam superiores imperatores consulem in se saeviturum" ("They surrendered, making no further stipulations with him; nevertheless they hoped that the consul would not rage against them more violently than earlier commanders").

2. Note the lesson on stern Roman practice that M'. Acilius Glabrio gave to the Aetolians who had surrendered to him in 191, by throwing them all into chains: 36.28.5–6, and cf. Polyb. 20.10. See Walsh 1990, *ad loc.,* on differences between Livy's version and Polybius's.

3. The syntax at 42.8.2–3 carefully balances the Statellates' cautious hopes against Laenas's outrageous behavior, with first several highly pejorative terms negated in indirect discourse (future tense: see above, n. 1), and then a string of perfect indicatives for what the consul

This built-in tension between two stories of the same battle—one told by Livy and the other by the *imperator* himself—will set the stage for the entire Laenas episode from here on. The historian has cast his own implicitly negative vote in the *supplicatio* debate before even allowing the consul's letter to reach the senate floor. Then, during the marked pause while praetor A. Atilius reads the letter aloud in the *curia,* Livy cues his audience to cast their votes as well, and to test their reaction, in some sense, against the authoritative reading of Laenas's *res gestae* narrative by the body of his peers and critics in the senate. Had he acted "atrocius quam superiores imperatores" ("more violently than earlier commanders," 42.8.2), or not? Through the byplay of storytelling and judgment, Livy teaches his readers step by step how to understand Roman history by sharing in the *existimatio* of the second-century aristocrats.[4] Laenas for his part had clearly expected his self-congratulatory letter to win him a rousing endorsement from the *patres* and make his deeds an exemplum for future generations of Romans. And indeed the senators did come to a united verdict based on an understanding of traditional Roman values, but emphatically not as the consul would have hoped. For the *consensus patrum* lined up solidly against Laenas rather than behind him, joining the Statellates (and, significantly, also the narrator) in a tough condemnation of the consul's behavior, with unmistakable verbal links to the earlier passage (42.8.5; cf. 42.8.2).[5]

The political theater of the *curia* once again shows its power to transform deeds from the provinces into tokens of symbolic value at home. But this time, instead of celebrating the victory, the senators brand Laenas's *res gestae* as the opposite of Roman ideals and the worst possible role model for future commanders: *res numquam gerendae,* as it were (42.8.5–6).[6] The

actually did: "ademit" ("he took away"), "diruit" ("he demolished"), "vendidit" ("he sold"). The effect is not unlike a double negative. The net effect of this rhetorical sequence—that is, "We hoped that he would not commit worse atrocities than his predecessors, but then he did all these (plainly terrible) things"—is not unlike a double negative, highlighting the painful disappointment experienced by Laenas's victims.

4. Thus the ethical language throughout the episode does not represent a superficial bias on Livy's part, beneath which the unembellished historical truth lies hidden, *pace* Harris 1985, 270–71: "Over this [i.e., the enslavement of the Statellates] a political conflict arose which Livy embroiders with moralizing sentiments. . . . Some may well have been voiced, but disapproval was far from unanimous." In fact, because the mechanisms of *existimatio* serve as the foundation for the kind of *res gestae* history that Livy has set out to write, the "political conflict" is not easily disentangled from the "moralizing sentiments," because both arise from the same ongoing drama of aristocratic self-fashioning in Rome.

5. In an obvious echo of "saeviturum" at 42.8.2, Livy pointedly ends the decree with "saeviendo in adflictos" ("by raging against the afflicted," 42.8.8).

6. 42.8.5–6: "atrox res visa senatui, Statellates . . . deditos in fidem populi Romani omni ultimae crudelitatis exemplo laceratos ac deletos esse . . . ne quis umquam se postea dedere auderet, pessumo exemplo venisse" ("it seemed a terrible thing to the senate that the Statellates, . . . having surrendered to the good faith of the Roman people, were cut to ribbons

patres may have had ample incentive, with another major war brewing in Macedonia, to keep Liguria quiet just now and avoid unnecessarily provocative actions there. It did not matter much whether the consul's deeds actually fell within the bounds of the *ius belli* or outside them. At a different moment another *imperator* who had dealt with the Statellates no less harshly might well have met with praise rather than censure.[7] The mechanism at work here is the flip side of the broad and flexible definition of triumphal criteria, which likewise left the senate leeway to award triumphs ad hoc and make their judgments stick, except that when Laenas wrote home about his deeds, he earned a stiff rebuke instead of civic honors. Bad enough that the people he had conquered expected better things from a Roman, but this assessment by his peers in *existimatio* scored a direct hit at his public identity. He had failed to live up to Rome's highest standards in the eyes of the people whom he sought most to impress, and they had real authority to make or break his quest for *laus* and *gloria*.

The *dignitatis contentio* created its own brand of truth, and in the process a commander's narrated *res gestae* could easily gain value or lose it. So once the *patres* had passed a decree condemning Laenas as a negative exemplum, it became a political and ethical fact in Rome that this consul had mistreated the Statellates.[8] The highly theatrical process of telling the story of his campaigns to the crucial senatorial audience could allow a commander to reap tremendous political profits. Likewise, by alienating that same audience, Laenas had now suffered a net loss of symbolic capital, and at this point he could hope to recoup those losses only by undoing his *res gestae*. For the senators did not halt at simply denying him the honor of a public thanksgiving for his victory. They issued what amounts to an anti-*supplicatio* decree, actively disowning, indeed rescinding the consul's actions. They demanded that he buy back the slaves and restore them their

---

and destroyed in every typical pattern of extreme cruelty. It set the worst sort of precedent . . . so that no one after them would dare to surrender"). This rhetoric culminates in the final outrage of having sold the suppliants into slavery (42.8.6). Cf. the complaints from the citizens of Ambracia against M. Fulvius Nobilior in 187: "omnia exempla belli" ("war with all the trimmings" 38.43.5).

7. This demonstrable fluidity in the terms of senatorial debate prompts Harris 1985, 271, to remark that "M. Popillius' offense, in so far as he was genuinely believed to have committed one, was to have achieved traditional ends by an untraditional, even if technically permissible, response to the Statellates' act of *deditio*."

8. We should therefore be wary of the game, popular among modern scholars, of trying to second-guess the *patres* by exposing their judgments as capricious and false, or, perhaps worse, by doubting the historical record if the reported results of their *existimatio* do not seem to harmonize with our own evaluations of people and their actions. The fact that the consul escaped prosecution in the end does not mitigate the charges against him so much as demonstrate how the symbolic economy allowed Roman aristocrats to save face by negotiating political compromises.

freedom as well as their belongings, weapons included, and then they forbade him to return to Rome until he had finished the job—this last an ironic twist on the *deportatio* provision (42.8.7–8).[9]

The outcome rests on a fundamental duality at work throughout Livy's account of the episode: the *imperator* sought to paint one self-portrait whereas the solemn vote of his aristocratic peers inscribed something quite different into the historical record. Instead of reaping all the intangible benefits of a *clara victoria* recognized in his name, the consul came up against the opposite label. Each of two alternative *res gestae* narratives—Laenas's own and the hostile official version (which also pointed out what he should have done to earn a real reward)—corresponds to an exemplum good or bad, each exemplum to a *consensus patrum* for or against, and each *consensus patrum* to a sanctioned public spectacle or the absence of one (42.8.8).[10] Again, as so often, the *supplicatio* debate could stand by itself as a one-act drama in the performance of *existimatio.* The preliminary transaction sketched the outlines of what would follow in due course when the commander appeared in person to demand recognition for his deeds.

Laenas's next confrontation with the *patres* no more qualifies as a successful triumph bid, or even a proper triumph debate, than the senatorial fiat in response to his letter created any symbiosis between one man's personal glory and the civic pride of the whole SPQR. One inverted paradigm leads to another. After the débâcle over the *supplicatio,* Laenas might have decided to save face by following the senate's instructions and coming home quietly, letting the matter go by. Instead he descended on Rome with a vengeance: "That same savagery of mind he had employed among the Ligures he [now] brought to bear on disobeying the senate" (42.9.1).[11] It would be hard to exaggerate the gulf separating this attitude on Laenas's

9. The passage referred to here (42.8.7–8) begins "quas ob res placere senatui" ("On account of these things it pleased the senate"), but coming as it does immediately after the alternative senatorial version of Laenas's battle narrative (42.7.4–6), it might have read *quas ob res gestas* ("On account of these accomplishments"), to reflect the link between what the *patres* felt Laenas had accomplished in the province, most of it bad, and their decision here about how to "reward" (i.e., punish or chastise) him.

10. 42.8.8: "claram victoriam vincendo oppugnantes, non saeviendo in adflictos fieri" ("A victory becomes illustrious by defeating an assault, not by raging against the afflicted"). Note the implied contrafactual condition: if Laenas had wanted his victory to become genuinely *clara,* then he should have brought home the right sort of battle narrative ("vincendo oppugnantes"). As it was, he had only set a bad example, with the echo in "saeviendo" of the Statellates' fears, "in se saeviturum" (42.8.2, cited above in n. 3). Perhaps we may put a bit of extra weight on "fieri" here as well, to suggest that the *res gestae* of a *triumphator* do not just happen on the battlefield but are actually fashioned by the political process in Rome.

11. 42.9.1: "consul qua ferocia animi usus erat in Liguribus, eandem ad non parendum senatui habuit."

part from that of an ideal would-be *triumphator*. Every successful triumph bid in Livy's account hinges on a credible stance of submission by the general to the collective *auctoritas* of the senate as the body empowered to assess the worthiness of people and their actions in service to the Roman state. A Laenas dead set on disobeying the *patres* flew right in the face of those expectations.[12] In a spectacular blurring of the well-worn boundaries between warfare and battle narrative, combat and politics, military campaign and triumph debate, Livy says that Laenas now brought home onto the senate floor not only a tale of war but war itself. What is more, since the *patres* had already decreed Laenas's treatment of the Statellates as cruel and unusual punishment, he was misdirecting a brand of hostility that did not belong even on the battlefield, let alone in Rome.[13]

At this moment, just when Laenas needed most to bow to the judgment of his peers so that they might evaluate what he had done for the Republic, he ignored their explicit command to remain in his province with the army until he had set the enslaved Statellates free, sent his troops immediately to their winter quarters at Pisa, and hurried back to the city (42.9.2). Note the illuminating contrast with the praetor L. Furius Purpureo in 200, who also came home sooner than expected. The *supplicatio* vote in Furius's favor made all the difference for how people in Rome would react to his return. Even so, the consul Cotta and his supporters accused the praetor of rushing home precipitously in search of honors, but Furius managed to capitalize on his *res gestae* and did win a triumph, whereas Laenas was defying a senate that had already united against him, so that he arrived not just perhaps a bit too quickly, but against their express wishes. He was working from two steps back, in other words. And if Furius displayed eagerness and self-confidence, Laenas let loose anger and righteous indignation against his peers who gathered in the Temple of Bellona, site of so many triumph debates, to hear what he had to say for himself.

12. In the passage just cited Livy does not refer to Laenas by name but solely by his title of office. One wonders whether perhaps this undeniably typical bit of Livian *variatio* might nevertheless be tinged with a gentle reminder that a consul was expected to play a particular role in the life of the Republic. A certain weight naturally falls on "consul" as the first word in the sentence and as its grammatical subject. Closely after it follows "ferocia animi," the hostility appropriate toward enemies abroad, now radically and perilously displaced onto the senate at home. Since the danger stems precisely from Laenas's failure to act like a proper consul, at the very least the use of his title appears as a happy coincidence, if not a deliberate choice by the author.

13. There are no direct verbal echoes, but the sense of "qua ferocia animi usus erat in Liguribus" at 42.9.1, marked here as historical or at least narrative fact by the pluperfect indicative, clearly hearkens back to the complex of ideas discussed earlier in the byplay of the words *atrox* and *saevire* during the *supplicatio* debate (42.8). The senate did not approve of the way Laenas had behaved on the battlefield, and now he brought that same transgressive spirit into the political arena, where it became doubly dangerous.

In a long speech he laid out his *res gestae* narrative, as any would-be *triumphator* would have done—but with one important difference. This self-congratulatory monologue took the form of an attack on the praetor Atilius, who had brought the motion against Laenas instead of pushing for a *supplicatio* to thank the civic gods that the Roman army had won the day in Liguria. Laenas tried to reconfigure his victory over the Statellates as a job well done ("ob rem bello bene gestam," "on account of a success in war"), with all that that entails (42.9.3).[14] Without the stamp of approval from the *patres,* he would not be able to say that he had accomplished anything of value: a victory not welcomed on the political stage in Rome was no real victory at all. Atilius had effectively sided with the enemies of Rome to strip the consul of his laurels and hand them over to the beaten Statellates. Laenas moved to place a fine against the praetor for slandering him and began issuing his own demands: first that the *patres* repeal the decree against him, negating their negation, as it were, so as to give him back his *res gestae,* and next that they make amends by finally accepting his offering of firstfruits from those *res gestae* and granting here and now and to his face the *supplicatio* that they should have authorized in his absence before (42.9.4–6).

Once again we see the familiar rhetoric of a triumph debate turned inside out: instead of using a *supplicatio* to clinch the higher honor, Laenas had to try to make up for the absence of a *supplicatio.* Yet despite this attempt at saving face, against a firm *consensus patrum* he could not and did not prevail. The senators would not back down so easily having once passed a definitive judgment against someone. Various of them rose up with fiery speeches, just as they had done when his letter first arrived. Denouncing his conduct in a wholesale reaffirmation of what had gone on record before, they summarily turned down both his requests.

Having been met with a second inflexible ruling, the consul duly returned to Liguria, but not entirely in disgrace. Subtly perhaps, but still perceptibly, his appearance in the *curia* and the open debate about his *res gestae,* with performative speeches on both sides—*existimatio* at work—had begun to dispel the tension between the two conflicting accounts of his deeds as consul. On one level, it is true, Laenas made a set of politically impossible, outrageously selfish demands, which the senate flatly refused.

14. 42.9.2–3: "senatuque extemplo ad aedem Bellonae vocato, multis verbis invectus in praetorem, qui cum ob rem bello bene gestam uti dis immortalibus honos haberetur referre ad senatum debuisset, adversus se pro hostibus senatus consultum fecisset, quo victoriam suam ad Ligures transferret, dedique iis prope consulem praetor iuberet" ("Having summoned the senate right away to the Temple of Bellona, in a long speech he denounced the praetor, who, when he should have brought a motion to the senate that honor be paid to the immortal gods on account of success in war, had instead come up with a decree against himself in favor of the enemy, so that the praetor could transfer his victory to the Ligures, and practically order the consul to surrender to them").

Nor could he reasonably have hoped for a different outcome, given the force of the opposition. The senators would hardly overturn their earlier verdict or grant a *supplicatio* at this late date. So if he never had any real chance of accomplishing what he outwardly claimed he sought to do by coming before the senate, why did he bother with that hasty, futile trip all the way back from Liguria to Rome? Once again the answer must surely lie in the efficacy of public performance per se, apart from decrees and the last word, as a vehicle for negotiating status and identity.

Laenas returned to his province having made his point, and he did not press the issue further. Meanwhile, an audience of his aristocratic peers had listened to his side of the story, which would thereby enter the historical record in some guise even though they still would not officially endorse his behavior toward the Statellates. It would be wrong therefore to categorize the outcome as a fruitless impasse just because the good results lay within the symbolic arena and did not take any immediately tangible form. As we have seen in one episode after another, air time counted for much in the day-to-day workings of the *dignitatis contentio,* where everyone who took part always had something to gain just by participating and being seen to participate in the processes of public life.

The debate had obviously branded Laenas as a negative exemplum, however, and he would never celebrate a triumph. Nor, since the struggle with the senate continued for a considerable time after this, should we see the final resolution here. That would be not only premature but naive as well, and would make nonsense out of the ensuing acts in the drama. Nevertheless, Laenas's return to Liguria after the failed triumph bid, if we may name it such, marks a watershed and should serve to place the *supplicatio* debate and its rhetoric into the proper broad context. The simple passage of time itself played a role in diffusing potentially volatile situations, especially given the periodic cast changes that came about as a natural result of the annual electoral cycle. As it happened, the following year (172) found Laenas's younger brother, C. Popillius Laenas, elected to the consulship (42.9.7–8). The *supplicatio* débâcle had obviously not left an indelible stigma on the whole family.[15]

15. Harris 1985, 271, reads these election results in 172 as evidence that "disapproval [of M. Laenas] was far from unanimous," especially since Marcus did not himself preside over the polls. Obviously without a hint from the sources we have no way to measure the true unanimity of any reported *consensus patrum,* but the majority of the senators had voted once for the stern decree against M. Laenas, and again a second time when he appeared to argue his case in person. Livy bears no record of dissent among them, or of support for Laenas, but only of their opposition as a body to his conduct in Liguria. Family connections counted for a lot in the formation of a Roman's public identity, and magistracies became signposts in a public career—yet, still, given the force of the decree against M. Laenas, the immediate election of his brother to the consulship suggests some degree of separation within the realm of *existimatio,*

SECOND PHASE: RAMIFICATIONS

The elder Laenas may have left the scene, but his ultimate fate and that of the injured Statellates still remained very much in doubt when his brother took office (42.10.9). The stern critics who had pushed for the decree against him now urged for strict enforcement and an end to unfinished business. They persuaded the other new consul, P. Aelius Ligus, to move for a reissuing of the decree, but C. Laenas staunchly defended his brother, threatening a tribunician veto, and strong-armed his colleague into joining his cause. The resulting stalemate set both consuls alike at odds with the *patres* (42.10.9–11).[16] Several other factors contributed: first, before 173 no Popillius had been elected consul since 316;[17] second, the Fasti mark 172 as the first time in the history of the Republic when two plebeians held the consulship together;[18] and third, all this maneuvering on the senate floor took place amid rumors and under the darkening shadow of the soon-to-be Third Macedonian War. At first only a murky connection appears between the domestic political standoff of 173 and the growing tensions in the East between Rome and Perseus of Macedon. Yet that link, on closer scrutiny, provides an important clue to what the senate was up to both at home and abroad.

Livy says that C. Laenas and his colleague, Aelius, had hoped to see Macedonia as one of their consular provinces, but the senate voted to send the two of them off to join M. Laenas in Liguria instead unless they agreed to back down and accede to the motion against him after all (42.10.11–12). Since they had just made it clear that they would do no such thing, the consuls had to accept the proffered posts in unglamorous Liguria, letting the question of Macedonia drop.[19] But how do the various pieces fit? As suggested before, the senate may have gone after M. Laenas in the first

---

either between elections and triumph debates, or between family members, or both. The fact that Roman aristocrats as a body tended to protect their own (cf. Rosenstein 1990a, 114–52) may thus have shielded C. Laenas at the *comitia* to some extent.

16. Note especially 42.10.11: "patres eo magis, utrique pariter consuli infensi, in incepto perstabant" ("The senators, equally hostile to both consuls, persisted all the more in what they had begun").

17. Before M. Laenas in 173, the last consul from the gens Popillia had been M. Popillius M. f. M. n. Laenas, consul in 316: see 9.21, the entry in the Fasti Capitolini, and Diod. 9.55.

18. This has been challenged by Palmer 1970, 294–95. If he is right, then the unquestionably obscure status of the gens Popillia will still go a long way toward explaining the hostile prevailing attitude among the *patres.*

19. Livy says nothing explicit, but the particle "deinde" in the next frustrated request of the consuls (42.10.12) implies that the *patres* had forced them to back down on the issue of provinces, which certainly does not come up again. A further hint comes shortly thereafter in the consuls' announcement that they would soon depart "in provinciam" ("to their province," singular), and therefore of course to the same one together, i.e., Liguria not Macedonia (42.10.15).

place the year before to "quiet the Ligurian theater in preparation for the imminent war in Macedonia."[20] One can readily understand the desire to avoid a messy entanglement in Liguria on the eve of a major assault in the East, but it is hard to see why they would then opt to send both consuls in 172, obviously sympathetic to the offending commander and themselves eager for a fight, into the very province they wished to pacify. The presence of three *imperatores* together in Liguria might just as easily force the restless tribes there to take up arms against the massing Roman invaders as cow them into tranquil submission. Neither for that matter had the decree against him restrained M. Laenas: in his brief tenure as proconsul he had already managed to spark a new rebellion (42.21.2–3).

It would seem that the *patres* had to balance the risks in Liguria against their deeper concern to avoid any overtly inflammatory step just yet on the Macedonian front.[21] If the senators were not quite ready to spark a wholesale Mediterranean conflict, they would have recognized that naming Macedonia a consular province would look like an act of aggression, something tantamount to a declaration of war against Perseus. They could use the threat of a decree against M. Laenas to force the new consuls' hands and conveniently quell the Macedonia issue for a while, buying more time for themselves to gather information and test alliances.[22] Further, despite the allure of a prestigious, not to say lucrative, Eastern command, they could tell that C. Laenas would not abandon his brother's cause for the sake of his own advancement, ensuring then that both consuls would acquiesce and go to Liguria, safely distant from Hellenistic affairs. The *patres* probably hoped that Aelius and the two Popillii would help to keep each other out of trouble.

Moreover, though the star of the Popillii was certainly in the ascendant with two consuls in as many years, the symbolic economy would ensure that it did not rise either too high or too fast. Time had not completely obliterated the ancient battle lines between patrician and plebeian either. That the first election of two plebeian consuls did not escape public notice we know from the comment in the Fasti. The old guard must have sensed that this unprecedented circumstance had potential to stir up trouble within senatorial ranks. Better then to keep this pair of consuls in line than risk endowing them with the extra prestige of a high-profile command in the East. The *patres* would declare war against Perseus in their own time—as it

20. Harris 1985, 271.

21. On the selection of consular provinces for 172, in the context of the buildup to the Third Macedonian War, Gruen 1984a, 409, writes: "The *patres* eschewed provocative action."

22. Hence the fact-finding mission of C. Valerius and others sent out to Macedonia in 173 (42.6.4). They returned in 172 (42.17), apparently after the appearance of Eumenes with his long list of grievances against Perseus (42.11–13). See again Gruen 1984a, 407–10.

happened, the following year—and in their own way, by putting a motion before the centuriate assembly and acting as a governing body for the Republic as a whole rather than pandering to the ambitions of any individuals, patrician or plebeian, magistrates or no (42.30.8–11).

The threat of war in Macedonia certainly made itself felt. When the consuls, now Liguria bound, requested new armies, or at least new recruits to strengthen the old ones, the senate once again said no, most likely seeking to conserve resources for what lay on the horizon (42.19.12–13). Doubly frustrated, therefore, in their hopes to lead fresh troops to glory in an Eastern campaign, the consuls announced angrily that they would be setting off for Liguria as soon as possible, "and that they would not take on any public business save what pertained to the government of the provinces" (42.10.15).[23] Macedonia was now a dead issue. This declaration brought the decree against M. Laenas back to center stage. Not only did it allow C. Laenas to follow through on the considerable political investment that he had already made in defending his brother's name against lingering charges, but a refusal to cooperate with the senate gave both consuls an outlet for their new grievances as well. Meanwhile the senators dug in their heels too, insisting that they would not take up any other motion without first securing that decree. Now for a time everything hung in abeyance (42.21.1), though, tellingly, Livy does not say so at first.

Instead, immediately after the consuls' pronouncement, without any mention of a countermove from the *patres,* the narrative leaves Laenas and Aelius aside, presumably to go off to their province, and launches into several long chapters dealing with various embassies and reports to the senate, including a personal appearance from Eumenes of Pergamum, all bearing news of Perseus's activities about the Mediterranean (42.11–20).[24] The shift of focus does not call attention to itself. In the annalistic books of his history Livy generally breaks down the account of each year by theaters of operation, following a geographical and thematic sequence rather than a strictly chronological one. That pattern, bred of the aristocratic, senatorial history Livy has set out to compose, leads readers to presume that the consuls of 172 did what they said they would do and left for Liguria straightaway, while back in Rome the senate listened to envoys from the East. It comes as a shock, then, to find them still in the city many chapters later, with the old, long-standing deadlock as yet unresolved (42.21.1).

23. 42.10.15: "consules ob ea irati senatui . . . in provinciam abituros esse denuntiarunt, nec quicquam rei publicae acturos praeterquam quod ad provinciarum administrationem attineret."

24. Livy highlights the psychological effects of an imminent war by describing a series of portents around the city and the measures taken by the haruspices to deal with them (42.20.1–2), all part of the steady buildup to the formal declaration of war.

The jolt dramatizes an important point: the lingering controversy between the senate and the brothers Laenas, by disrupting the changing of the magisterial guard, has now actually come to threaten the very coherence and stability of Livy's narrative. The annual cycle organizes his conception of Republican life on such a fundamental level, and thus so deeply conditions the responses and expectations of his readers, that the political crisis in the historical past sparks a crisis in the text as well. As the chain of events wanders further astray from the usual paradigm, the narrative structure endures a greater and greater strain, until Livy cannot properly tell his story any more. The succession of magistrates brings order and intelligibility to Roman history—history as *res gestae,* first won on the battlefield and then brought home to the *curia*—and shows us the Republic at its best. But C. Laenas and P. Aelius will never have any *res gestae* to speak of unless they consent at last to go out into their province and get to work. The impasse demands that they find a way to overcome their differences with the *patres,* and soon, not only so that M. Laenas can finish saving face, but more pressingly so that another set of consuls and praetors can finally take office in due course, allowing Livy to get on with his tale.

Just then, with matters at a complete standstill, the defiant M. Laenas took the stage again with—of all things—yet another *res gestae* narrative. A letter arrived saying that he had fought the Statellates a second time and killed six thousand of them, provoking the other tribes of the region to take up arms in turn against the Romans (42.21.2). So the proconsul was embroiled in another fight with Ligurian tribes who had already surrendered once, when he should have been busy repairing the damage he had caused the last time he defeated them. A decree against him had been rendered toothless and left unenforced because of political wrangling in Rome. And the current consuls were both literally and figuratively refusing to budge. This situation did not please the *patres* at all. Speeches flew, full of righteous indignation on all sides, until finally enough was enough (42.21.3–5). At length two tribunes, M. Marcius Sermo and Q. Marcius Scylla, introduced a new motion dealing with the entire Laenas problem all at once. They proposed a fine against the consuls if they did not go to their provinces immediately and a law to be set before the Roman people to prosecute the man responsible (i.e., M. Laenas) if any of the ill-used Statellates should remain enslaved after a certain date. When with the blessing of the *patres* the tribunes put the law to a vote in the assembly, the people approved the *rogatio Marcia* with a resounding consensus, and the senate named praetor C. Licinius to head the investigation (42.22.5, 8).

The plebiscite disabled any further objection from the consuls, because they could not overrule the people. So they went to Liguria at last, and on arrival even took over command of the army from M. Laenas as a prelude to his return home (42.22.1). Livy mirrors the relief in the *curia* once they had finally set off by a palpable easing of the structural tension in his narrative. We have no way of knowing how long all the political posturing took in real time, days or weeks, but in the narrative space that Livy has created the psychological effect on the reader—what might be termed the dramatic as opposed to the actual time—drags out considerably, and clearly on purpose. The historian makes sure that this episode will stand out from its background through repeated hints that the chain of events should fall into a certain pattern, which it stubbornly refuses to fit.[25] On the brink of the long-awaited resolution, with the *rogatio Marcia* about to come to a vote in the assembly, Livy interrupts the narrative one more time to insert the extraneous notice of the triumph *in monte Albano* by C. Cicereius, who had been praetor in 173. It is as if he wants to postpone an end to the stalemate for as long as possible, so that his readers will see the paradigm reflected in its breach (42.22.6–8).

EPILOGUE

Even at that, one final chapter remains to the whole affair, namely the homecoming of M. Laenas himself. We have alluded more than once to the possibility that despite all the controversy and the public actions taken against him, checks and balances within the symbolic economy might eventually allow Laenas to save face in some measure, to escape without suffering total disgrace in the end. He never stopped seeking to maximize his symbolic capital at every turn. He had defied the original *senatus consultum,* ordering him to stay in Liguria until he set the Statellates free, by returning to Rome to make a proud stand before the *patres.* Now, in the opposite way, when the assembly had summoned him home to stand trial under the *rogatio Marcia,* he chose to linger in the province for a while, avoiding prosecution, after handing over command of his army to his brother and P. Aelius. He knew that the odds were stacked against him and that the city was not waiting with open arms to welcome him back, the conquering hero. Indeed C. Licinius, the very praetor who had officially set the *rogatio* in motion, now presided over the case and stood ready to judge

25. Livy's subtle signals produce a striking cumulative effect when viewed all together: at the beginning of the year the senate had unfinished business from the year before because of M. Laenas (42.10.9); then they turned down one request after another from the uncooperative consuls (42.10.12), who finally announced themselves about to depart (42.10.15); then comes the long break for embassies and speeches on the growing threat from Perseus of Macedon, the conclusion of which finds the two of them still in Rome (42.21.1); then the senate's irritation at their failure to leave (42.21.3), the suggestive wording of the tribunes' decree (42.21.4), and the intrusion of the triumph for C. Cicereius before the consuls' departure (42.21.6); finally the plebiscite is voted (42.21.8), and "tum demum consules in provinciam profecti sunt" ("then at last the consuls set out for their province," 42.22.1).

Laenas's *res gestae* once and for all (42.22.2). Laenas could do no more than only postpone the inevitable, perhaps, but he still had this one gesture of self-justification left. Of course presence in the *curia* and absence from the scene could both produce a memorable performative effect under the gaze of *existimatio.*

Then the tribunes raised the stakes yet again, threatening, should the proconsul fail to appear in Rome in person before a certain deadline, to authorize Licinius to pass judgment in his absence, a more ignominious fate than allowing him to speak for himself (42.22.3). This brought down the final curtain on his performance in Liguria, and as Livy says, "when he had returned, dragged by this fetter, he came into the senate amid enormous resentment" (42.22.4).[26] Many a senator took advantage of the opportunity to be seen joining in the consensus against him that day, affirming that the *patres* as a body had the power to judge people and their actions in service to the Republic. The new decree, broader than the first, restored freedom and allotted land in the region across the Po not only to the Statellates enslaved by M. Laenas in 173 but to all Ligures who had not been enemies of Rome for the past seven years, since 179. Fittingly, in order to bring home the message that even renegades must bow at length to the collective will of the senate, they charged the consul C. Laenas with the task of distributing that land (42.22.5–6).

By issuing a blanket declaration, the senators reached back in time to set a more or less arbitrary terminus ante quem for the land distribution that would guarantee full restitution to all injured parties among the Ligures and leave no doubt that the senate meant business now in defending its interests and curbing men like Laenas. This decree, we must remember, came at the end of a prolonged and bitter struggle between the senate and several magistrates of the Republic, a far cry from the ceremonial *ut liceret* of the formal triumph request. The *patres* needed to take a firm, decisive stand and then ensure that their instructions would be duly carried out. Case closed: "Many thousands of people were given back their freedom by this *senatus consultum,* and land was assigned to them across the Po" (42.22.6–7). With the ill-used Statellates thus taken care of, the workings of the *rogatio Marcia* were left to deal with the commander himself. He faced a curtain call with the threat of punishment on one side and a last chance to save his good name on the other.

By law the trial went on for three days. Laenas stood before C. Licinius for two of the three. Then at the very last possible moment the praetor gave in, according to Livy, to "the reputation of the absent consul" (i.e., Marcus's brother C. Laenas, serving in Liguria) "and the entreaties of the Popillii

26. 42.22.4: "hoc tractus vinculo cum redisset, ingenti cum invidia in senatum venit."

as a family," who no doubt thronged around him in a visible show of support. Licinius simply could not bring himself to pass the final, irrevocable judgment, and instead he found an ingenious way out of the dilemma. He scheduled the third day of hearings for the Ides of March, when the new set of magistrates would take office, making him a *privatus* and hence no longer authorized to preside over a trial (42.22.7–8). M. Laenas had been elected consul and had tried to serve the Republic in good faith, and he did come from one of the oldest noble families in Rome. In practical terms there had been enough scandal and upset for one year already, without having to declare a sentence against the brother of a magistrate in office.

Not only that: M. Laenas had already paid a huge political price for his misdeeds, having borne the brunt of first one *senatus consultum,* and then a plebiscite, and then a second *senatus consultum* against him, not to mention the cost in air time alone with the countless speeches and two days of hearings full of public outcry against him. So whether or not we choose to join with Livy in labeling the eleventh-hour stay of political execution a "deceptive ruse" (42.22.8: "arte fallaci"), the dénouement of the Laenas affair should stand as a powerful emblem for the very real way in which the symbolic economy in Rome allowed the circle of aristocrats to protect their own. He did not endure any lasting disgrace. For all its rhetoric of black and white, good exempla and bad, *existimatio* was simply and most emphatically not a zero-sum game. Everyone who took part had everything to gain by it, and in practical terms surprisingly little to lose.

CHAPTER 14

L. Aemilius Paullus in 167

Rogatio ad Populum and the Soldiers' Revenge

The debate over the triumph of L. Aemilius Paullus in 167, coincidentally also the closing episode in extant Livy, brings the *populus Romanus* firmly back into the picture. Despite the letter *P* in SPQR, we have not heard from the democratic element in a triumph debate for quite a while, ever since the handful of celebrations *sine auctoritate patrum populi iussu* discussed above in chapter 1. For of course the senate took customary care of awarding civic honors from the mid-third century onwards, and in Livy's Books 21–45, the people of Rome generally play only two major roles in triumphal politics: as voters in the *comitia* at the start of the cycle and as spectators or receptors at several key points thereafter, most notably the *profectio imperatoris,* the news of victory or defeat in public mourning or *supplicatio,* and finally, if all goes well, the culminating procession and sacrifice. The *patres* as a body had a vital stake in continuing to interpose themselves between magistrates and citizens when it came to granting or denying triumphs, for two reasons: first, because this allowed them to maintain their say over the distribution of status within their own ranks (which seems to have been the reason behind many of their decisions in individual cases, as we have seen), and second, because it helped them to secure their collective position as the élite within the overarching social and political hierarchy.

The whole elaborate transaction between a would-be *triumphator* and his peers in the senate would be utterly meaningless without the prize itself, the opportunity to put on a show for the assembled masses both in one's own name and with the stamp of official approval from the senate acting on behalf of the SPQR. Because of the unusual way in which the challenge to Paullus's triumph came about, it placed not only his personal status but the *patrum auctoritas* itself at risk. By watching the aristocratic response to that challenge, therefore, we may learn much of the precarious balancing act between various interest groups that was triumphal politics, and indeed politics in general, under the Roman Republic.

THE NEWS OF VICTORY

If the *patres* could have ensured that Paullus would celebrate a triumph just by voting him one, then he never would have had any problem. As soon as he arrived in the city, together with his fleet commander, Cn. Octavius, and ex-praetor L. Anicius Gallus, who had taken charge of the campaign against the Illyrian king Gentius (one of Perseus's allies), the senate met and awarded triumphs to all three, apparently without hesitation or controversy (45.35.4). The stunning victory at Pydna ranks among the great decisive achievements of the time (44.32.5–42.9),[1] and Livy calls attention to it as such in a number of ways, not least by describing Paullus's homecoming in terms reminiscent of Scipio Africanus in 201 (30.45.1–2) and T. Quinctius Flamininus in 194 (34.52.23), both obvious examples of undisputed triumphs.[2] Moreover, the historian was sowing seeds of Paullus's eventual *gloria* from the beginning, in a manner that should by now be very familiar. Before setting out for his province in 168, the new consul declared *in contione* that he had been judged worthy of bringing an end to the long-ongoing Macedonian war (44.22.3), and a crowd much larger than usual gathered to see him off, wishing him success and looking forward to an exceptional triumph (44.22.17). A sizable chunk of Livy's account of the battle itself is lost in a lacuna,[3] but from the extant text we can see at least that he pauses at the end to relish the statistics: all his sources agreed that more Macedonians were killed at Pydna than in any other single engagement; very few Romans and allies perished, and only nightfall prevented an even more complete rout (44.42.7–9).

From there the historian marks the solemnity of the occasion—and with it the *magnitudo rerum gestarum*—just as he had done with the Metaurus campaign forty years earlier, by narrating the arrival of the news from Pydna as a crescendo through incremental stages.[4] Right away the consul sent three messengers to Rome with his letter announcing the victory, and we

1. Cf. Polyb. 29.14–18, with the comments of Walbank 1957, *ad loc.* For a full-scale modern account, see Hammond 1988, 512–63. Also note the effort by Gruen 2004, 254–57, to downplay the long-term administrative impact of Paullus's victory.

2. Note also the explicit comparison drawn between Paullus's achievement in bringing the Macedonian war to an end and what C. Lutatius Catulus did in the First Punic War and Scipio Africanus in the Second (45.38.4).

3. Two whole quartos are missing from the single surviving manuscript for Books 41–45 of Livy at the end of 44.40, right in the midst of the battle description from Pydna.

4. Walsh 1961, 184–85, draws an explicit parallel between the two episodes as examples of Livy's vivid evocation of the "atmosphere of stunned joy" in a crowd.

learn their names, a sure indication that this moment warranted memory, even down to such details (44.45.3). At their arrival several chapters later, having made the journey as fast as they possibly could, we discover that the news had somehow preceded them. For they had barely set out when a sudden murmur went up in the Circus, significant as a public place where citizens gathered for spectacles, to the effect that a battle had been fought in Macedonia and the king beaten (45.1.1–4). No one had been able to discern who started the buzz, but the story gained strength "as if [it had come] from a reliable source" and was seen as an omen.

Some days after that, as the consul was about to start the chariot race for the Ludi Romani, a man ran up to him with a laureate letter, allegedly from Macedonia, and as soon as the race was completed the people rushed to the Forum to hear the consul officially proclaim, in greater specificity now, that "his colleague L. Aemilius had fought a pitched battle with King Perseus; the Macedonian army had been cut down and routed; the king had fled with a few men, and all the cities of Macedonia had come under the jurisdiction of the Roman people" (45.1.8–9).[5] The men then went home to tell their wives and children, bringing a wider spectrum of society into the picture, and the senate voted a *supplicatio* the following day, making the word official on the assumption that the anonymous messenger had come on behalf of Paullus's *legati*—a claim that they themselves later never confirm or deny (45.2.1–2).

The real *legati* finally make their dramatic entrance into the city at a precise date and time that Livy painstakingly records. Some source must have included this information too, like the men's names, showing just how vividly the moment was enshrined in the civic consciousness (45.2.3). And when they fight their way through the crowds to tell the senate, as cited previously, "how great in number the forces of the king had been, foot soldiers and cavalry, how many thousands of these had been killed, how many captured, with the loss of how few [Roman] soldiers so great a slaughter of the enemy had been accomplished, with how few followers the king had fled" (45.2.4–5),[6] they are bringing not the first, or even the second, but the third public announcement of Paullus's victory—never mind the fact that the historian has already narrated all these events in his own voice as well.

5. 45.1.8–9: "denuntiavit populo L. Aemilium collegam signis conlatis cum rege Perseo pugnasse; Macedonum exercitum caesum fusumque; regem cum paucis fugisse; civitates omnes Macedoniae in dicionem populi Romani venisse."

6. 45.2.4–5: "tantum temporis retenti dum exponerent quantae regiae <copiae> peditum equitumque fuissent, quot milia ex iis caesa quot capta forent, quam paucorum militum iactura tanta hostium strages facta, †quam pauci† rex fugisset." Also cited above, p. 106 and n. 6. As noted there, I have done my best in the translation to cope with the impossible crux in the manuscript text.

Oddly enough, Livy does not pause to offer any explanation, miraculous or otherwise, for this strange superabundance of news from Pydna. He is not interested in the possible causes, only the dramatic effect: both the inhabitants of Rome at the time, and the readers of his text, whoever, wherever, and whenever they might be, have heard Paullus's achievement heralded over and over again, each time a little bit louder, in front of a larger crowd, and in more detail, so that by the end the initial rumor has been amplified into a resounding certainty and an acknowledged fact. The repetition takes nothing away from Paullus's prestige, indeed only enhances it, as brought out by the heightening of emotion, along with what looks like either a second *supplicatio* decree or perhaps an extension of the earlier one (45.2.6–8, 12).

Nor even at this point was the story in Rome complete; even more momentous events were still unfolding in the field. Shortly after news of the victory at Pydna came word from another pair of non-anonymous *legati* that ex-praetor L. Anicius Gallus had destroyed the Illyrian army and taken King Gentius prisoner. The senate decreed another *supplicatio* (45.3.1–2). Meanwhile, at the end of their announcement Paullus's *legati* had told of unfinished business, soon to be concluded: Perseus had fled from the battlefield, but the consul had dispatched the fleet to his expected point of refuge in Samothrace so that he could not hope to escape by land or sea (45.2.6). Livy uses the verb "existimari" (45.2.5) to denote Paullus's authoritative personal judgment. Thus Paullus himself, in his camp at Amphipolis, had to learn of Perseus's capture at a distance; and by describing his reaction—for he obviously heard about it sooner than anyone else—Livy keeps his readers one step ahead of the senate and people in Rome, still waiting for news. Having read the dispatch from Cn. Octavius saying that the king was in custody and on his way to him under guard, Paullus offered a grateful sacrifice, "because he thought of it as a second victory, which indeed it was" (45.7.1).[7] Note the authorial comment in affirmation of the commander's perceptions, ensuring that readers will understand the full import of what has just occurred.

A sentence or two later, Livy claims that the largest crowd *in history* pressed around the camp to catch a glimpse of Perseus being led to the Praetorium in chains, as if the shining figure of Alexander the Great himself had now fallen prisoner to the Roman army (45.7.2–4). People sensed that they were watching the end of an era, and once again, as with the realization that the Metaurus campaign marked the turning point in the Hannibalic War, this assessment emerges from implied indirect discourse, an actual element of the scene the historian describes rather than just his opinion. Livy gives

7. 45.6.12–7.1: "Octavius regem in castra ad consulem misit, praemissis litteris ut in potestate eum esse et adduci sciret. secundam eam Paullus, sicut erat, victoriam ratus, victimas cecidit eo nuntio."

his own summation of the rise and fall of Macedon, and his *hommage* to the stature of Alexander at the end of his empire's ascendancy, several chapters later (45.9.2–7), by which point his views have already received indirect confirmation from the reactions of the embedded audience here. When at last another letter brings the news of Perseus's capture to Rome, then, it effectively fills in the only missing piece for the perfect outcome of the entire mission, the answer to everyone's most cherished hopes from the *profectio* of Paullus, Anicius, and Octavius (45.13.9). Civic joy redoubles, and with yet another round of *supplicationes* in honor of the two foreign kings and their territories now "in potestate populi Romani" (45.16.7–8), plus a string of foreign dignitaries offering their congratulations,[8] Livy makes sure that the senate's untroubled decision to vote triumphs for all three commanders has already attained the status of a fait accompli by the time they reach Rome in person one by one (45.35.1–4).

COURAGE UNDER FIRE: PAULLUS *IMPERATOR*

After approving the triumphs, the *patres* next authorized the urban praetor to ask the tribunes to put a motion before the assembly that the *triumphatores* should have *imperium* on the day they entered Rome, one of two places in the extant portions of his history where Livy describes this significant triumphal procedure in full (45.35.4).[9] With tribunes presiding, the people voted by tribes: *comitia tributa.*[10] On this occasion, they appear to have met on the Capitol, emphatically mentioned three separate times (45.36.1, 36.6, 36.7). The *imperium* in question, specifically designated for the ritual entrance into the city, across the *pomerium,* was thus functionally limited both in space and in time. With so little evidence, however, and especially because Marcellus in 211, the only other example, also represents something of a special case, we do not know exactly how the stipulation about *imperium* for the day of the triumph related to the enigmatic *lex*

8. Envoys arrive from Eumenes and Attalus of Pergamum (45.13.12) and Massinissa in Africa (45.13.12–14.7), as does an embassy from Egypt to thank the senate for the intervention of *legatus* C. Popillius Laenas, whose circle in the sand at Eleusis (45.12.1–8; cf. Polyb. 29.2.1–4, 27) had just forestalled an invasion by Antiochus IV.

9. 45.35.4: "mandatumque Q. Cassio praetori cum tribunis plebis ageret ex auctoritate patrum rogationem ad plebem ferrent, ut iis, quo die urbem triumphantes inveherentur, imperium esset" ("A charge was given to Q. Cassius the praetor to work with the tribunes of the plebs so that they would bring a motion before the people on the authority of the senate to the effect that these men might have *imperium* on the day when they entered the city in triumph"). Cf. 26.21.5 (the *ovatio* of Marcellus in 211).

10. Livy mentions the tribunes several times as the officials in charge of this assembly (45.35.4, 36.1, 36.10, 39.20), whose job it was to call the tribes to order and ask their votes, yes or no (hence the term *rogatio,* as at 35.4 and again at 36.1). On procedure, further note 36.7 and also 39.20.

curiata de imperio customarily passed at the outset of a magistrate's term, nor whether the rule applied to promagistrates only or to all *triumphatores,* although the latter view seems to have gained some acceptance.[11]

At any rate, in Paullus's case the *rogatio ad populum,* which was supposed to be a rubber stamp, unexpectedly set the stage for controversy when the army decided to turn against their commander over the distribution of booty and to use the assembly vote as a platform to voice their grievances in public. Simply put, the soldiers felt that they deserved a greater portion of the spoils. According to Livy, some of them had suggested a boycott of the assembly to register their complaints, for people would certainly notice their absence, but Ser. Sulpicius Galba, a tribune from the Second Macedonian Legion later destined to become a famous orator (although at this point having held no elective office), spurred on his comrades instead to "come out in force to the polls, so that they might take revenge on their domineering and mean-spirited general by voting against the bill that was being proposed concerning his *imperium*" (45.35.8–9).[12]

What we see here is a breakdown at a crucial node in the network of exchanges: by Galba's reasoning, because Paullus failed to give his soldiers an adequate share in the rich royal *praeda* that they had helped him to win, they in turn should now exercise their power to ensure that he would not receive his reward either. In order to ensure the maximum symbolic benefit for himself in the *gloria* of a triumph, in other words, a commander must first earn respect and gratitude through the conspicuous display of generosity in the material economy. Galba's complaints not only shed a whole new light on the stagy ceremonies by which *triumphatores* rewarded their armies with *dona militaria* and sums of money carefully calibrated to their respective ranks, as we have seen more than once already, but also reveal what critics of commanders whose troops could not be present for the triumph debate meant when referring to the soldiers as witnesses of a job well done or the opposite.[13] They could make their opinions powerfully felt, especially when aggrieved.

11. On this special vote of *imperium* for the day of the triumph, see Mommsen 1887, 1.132 and nn., arguing that the stipulation applied only to promagistrates. As noted above (p. 36 n. 12), Versnel 1970, 192, broadens the argument to include all *triumphatores,* and more recently Brennan 1996, 316, follows Versnel's lead.

12. 45.35.8–9: "sed eos Ser. Sulpicius Galba, qui tribunus militum secundae legionis in Macedonia fuerat, privatim imperatori inimicus, prensando ipse et per suae legionis milites sollicitando, stimulaverat ut frequentes ad suffragium adessent. imperiosum ducem et malignum antiquando rogationem quae de triumpho eius ferretur ulciscerentur." On Galba's family connections and army rank see Linderski 1990, especially 69–71; on his later oratorical fame, see Cic. *Brut.* 82, 86.

13. On *dona militaria,* see above, p. 140 n. 44. On soldiers as witnesses to a triumph and to the *res gestae* of their commander, see 26.21.4 (Marcellus) and 31.49.10 (L. Furius Purpureo). Also see above, pp. 87 and n. 14, 178 and n. 29; and below, p. 288 and n. 54.

Once Galba had the floor, Livy says, he deliberately kept talking until nightfall, so that the arguments thus prolonged ran over into a second day (45.36.1–2), as they had previously in only two other triumph debates: C. Cornelius Cethegus and Q. Minucius Rufus in 197 (33.22.10) and Cn. Manlius Vulso ten years later (38.50.1-3).[14] Declaring in hyperbole that the conquered Macedonians were better off than Paullus's own troops, deprived of honor even in victory and crushed by harsh treatment as well as the normal dangers of war (45.36.3–5, a passage laden with the economic imagery of cost-benefit analysis), Galba urged his fellows to give notice by appearing in force on the following day. "If they were on hand the next day to vote down the law," he argued, "the men in power would understand that not everything lay in the leader's hand, but there was something also in the hand of the soldiers" (45.36.5).[15] The one triumph debate in Livy 21–45 taking place before the people as opposed to the senate therefore emerges as an outgrowth of a clash between the soldiers of the rank and file and the commander who belonged to the Roman élite. Paullus's disgruntled and vengeful troops attempted to redress their grievances from what happened *militiae* by driving a wedge into the midst of the harmonious workings of the political machine *domi,* effectively pitting the *populus Romanus* against the *patres* for their own ends (45.35.9).

From the beginning, however, Livy unmistakably sides with Paullus. He says that almost no one bothered to argue for the motion before the people "as if in a cause that was barely in doubt" ("ut in re mimime dubia," 45.36.1). Defenders of a proposal customarily spoke first to lay out their case, and Paullus's supporters did not expect him to come under attack. As far as they were concerned, and the historian obviously concurs, the *existimatio* of his senatorial peers should have had the last word about the commander, his *res gestae,* and his service to the community. Especially when they were talking about the man who had defeated an enemy tantamount to Alexander the Great, no one should have dared to interfere with the triumph any more once the *patres* as a body had spoken (cf. 45.37.3).[16] Livy further contends that Galba was hardly acting on principle but rather was pursuing a personal rivalry (45.35.8). Most revealing of all, in the very first sentence introducing the debate, he labels the would-be *triumphator* as a fine upholder of traditional military discipline and the backlash against him as an outgrowth of the malicious envy ("invidia") and verbal attacks

14. Also see above, p. 76 and n. 39.

15. 45.36.5: "si frequentes postero die ad legem antiquandam adessent, intellecturos potentes viros non omnia in ducis, aliquid et in militum manu esse."

16. There was of course always recourse to the law courts too, as amply illustrated by the post-triumph experiences of M'. Acilius Glabrio (37.57.9–58.1) and Scipio Asiaticus (38.50.4–60.10).

("obtrectatio") that predictably take aim at those in high places. After all, how would it look if underlings like Anicius and Octavius triumphed and their high commander did not? This same hypothetical image, fraught with embarassment and shame, will resurface at a key moment later in the debate (45.35.5; cf. 39.2).[17] Meanwhile, says Galba, if Paullus had indulged the rapacious greed of his soldiers, there would have been nothing left from all the royal wealth of Macedon to place in the public coffers (45.35.6).

Not only does this statement pick up on a prominent theme from Livy's Preface, with its references to the perils of greed and other desires piqued by Eastern conquest and the promise of *luxuria* (*Praef.* 11–12). It also calls to mind Polybius's unapologetically admiring portrait of the financial dealings by the *imperator* whose family had served as his patrons in Rome.[18] Throughout this study, based on the consistent parallels between the arguments raised in triumph debates and the apparent biases expressed in the narrative portions of Livy's history, I have urged that the historiographical tradition that Livy is following owes much, albeit often at several distant removes, to the *res gestae* and other aspects of the public image propagated by Roman aristocrats themselves during their lifetimes and by their families after their deaths. Here, if nowhere else, we have evidence of a direct and concrete link, because of Polybius's close personal ties with the commander and his sons.[19] For of course we know that Livy relied on Polybius. In following Livy's account of the triumph debate, therefore, we may rest assured that when the emerging image of L. Aemilius Paullus as a champion of austere Roman values, an impeccable exemplum, a darling of the senatorial establishment, and in many ways the last of his breed varnishes the truth, as it must to a degree, then it does so in precisely the idiom that he himself and those nearest to him would have deployed to shape his memory.[20]

The obvious authorial bias in Livy's account of the triumph debate gains further confirmation from the way he has already described Paullus's han-

17. 45.35.5: "intacta invidia media sunt: ad summa ferme tendit. nec de Anici nec de Octavi triumpho dubitatum est; Paullum, cui ipsi quoque se comparare erubuissent, obtrectatio carpsit" ("The middle heights are untouched by *invidia:* it generally reaches for the top. There was no hesitation over the triumph of either Anicius or Octavius; the urge to disparage singled out Paullus, to whom these very men would have blushed to compare themselves.").

18. Polyb. 18.35 (especially 4–5), 31.22 (with the remarks of Walbank 1957 on both passages, *ad locc.*), and note Plut. *Aem.* 28.10. On the subject of fiscal probity as a particular mark of moral character in Polybius, see Eckstein 1995, especially 230–33; and more recently M. F. Williams 2000.

19. On Paullus and his sons as Polybius's likely sources, see Reiter 1988, 62 n.73, with references to previous scholarship.

20. For a modern attempt to strip away the varnish and expose the realpolitik behind the mask, see Reiter 1988, 109–62.

dling of booty during the campaign. Immediately after the battle at Pydna, the *imperator* conceded a measure of plunder to his troops, provided that they did not take too much time about it to the neglect of their duties (44.45.4). Somewhat later we learn that the senate had designated the booty to be confiscated from the cities of Epirus, which had defected to Perseus and thereby betrayed the Roman cause, for the army and no one else, and that Paullus, following orders, took scrupulous care over its proper collection and subsequent distribution. According to the one extant Livian manuscript, riddled with errors,[21] on proceeds from the sale of property plundered from Epirus, the cavalry received four hundred denarii apiece, and the infantry two hundred (45.34.1–6). Plutarch, meanwhile, either accurately reflecting what he read in Livy (from a text presumably less corrupt than ours), or perhaps emending it so as to account the better for the soldiers' complaints, says that they each received only eleven drachmas, a much more modest sum.[22] One is tempted in light of the triumph debate to speculate about which ancient author had stronger motives to distort the real numbers in one direction or the other, Livy upwards or Plutarch downwards; but the discrepancy may reflect scribal errors and nothing else, and especially without the evidence from Polybius there is no way to cross-check.

Livy does tell us, however, that Paullus distributed still more money to his troops on the day of his triumph: a hundred denarii to each soldier, plus the usual double to centurions and triple to cavalry, with a comment that these amounts would have been twice as large if the soldiers had not opposed their commander's triumph request (45.40.5). Cn. Octavius and L. Anicius also rewarded their men handsomely, particularly the former, who was also drawing from the Macedonian pot.[23] Even if Paullus was holding back on his troops out of pique over the triumph debate, the figure of a hundred denarii represents two to four times the customary amount, judging from what Livy says about other commanders in the early second century who followed the practice of distributing money to their troops.[24]

21. In his editorial preface Briscoe 1986, vi, remarks: "errores codicis . . . tanti et tam varii sunt ut causa corruptionis haud semper inveniri possit" ("The errors of the codex . . . are so great and so varied that the cause of corruption can hardly ever be located"). Elsewhere he comments that the same manuscript "is extremely corrupt—indeed one sometimes wonders whether the scribe understood Latin at all" (Briscoe 1993, 40).

22. Plut. *Aem.* 29.5. Historical, not to say cross-cultural, monetary equivalents are notoriously difficult to calculate, but Plutarch may have used δράχμα as a rough gloss for *denarius*. Each at any rate represented approximately a workman's daily wage. On equivalences and terminology, with some indication of Plutarch's vocabulary, see Thomsen 1957, 36–47.

23. Octavius distributed 75 denarii to each of his sailors, with double to ship pilots and quadruple to captains (45.42.3), whereas Anicius gave each infantryman 45 denarii, with the usual double to centurions and triple to cavalry (45.43.7).

24. According to Livy, C. Cornelius Cethegus from Cisalpine Gaul in 197 gave 70 *asses* (= 7 denarii) to each regular soldier (33.23.7); T. Quinctius Flamininus from Macedonia in

Perhaps the most bitter indignation really stemmed from Paullus's apparent failure to include double pay in the package, as notably L. Cornelius Scipio Asiaticus and Cn. Manlius Vulso before him had done.

As to the contents of the Macedonian royal treasury, the sources are all in agreement that Paullus directed as much of it as possible to the public coffers in Rome. Plutarch does not specify the amount, but according to Polybius the total added up to more than six thousand talents.[25] Livy says that Perseus absconded with most of the gold and silver when he fled (44.45.12), so that when the Roman army first came to Pella, surrounded by its impenetrable swamps (44.46.5), they found there only three hundred talents of silver that Perseus had earlier designated for the ransom of prisoners from the Illyrian king Gentius and then withheld (44.46.8).[26] As Perseus made his way to his point of refuge, some fifty talents went to appease the inhabitants of Crete, so that he arrived in Samothrace with approximately two thousand talents (44.45.13–15). Cn. Octavius recovered as much as he could (45.6.11; cf. 45.40.1–3), and in the end between those funds and the plunder of luxury goods from the palace and elsewhere, such as gold and silver vessels, ivory carvings, statues, and other artworks, Paullus deposited a truly dazzling sum in the *aerarium,* enough indeed to cancel the direct taxation of Roman citizens for a time.[27] Octavius's naval triumph too was unadorned with prisoners or spoils, so that Paullus had the honor of making the full deposit (45.42.2).

The other major source of resentment among the soldiers in addition to the question of finances, namely Paullus's insistence on a severe version of the traditional Roman *disciplina militaris,* has also been on Livy's mind all along, as if the historian were anticipating the arguments from the triumph debate and attempting to forestall any criticism of the would-be *triumphator* in advance. Early in his tenure as consul Paullus raged against armchair *imperatores* among the aristocracy in Rome, who sat around "in all the social

---

194, 250 *asses* = 25 denarii (34.52.11); P. Cornelius Scipio Nasica from Cisalpine Gaul in 191, 125 *asses* = 12.5 denarii (36.40.13); L. Cornelius Scipio Asiaticus from Asia in 189, 25 denarii and double pay (37.59.6); M. Fulvius Nobilior from Aetolia in 187, 25 denarii (39.5.17); Cn. Manlius Vulso from Asia in 187, 42 denarii and double pay (39.7.2–3); Q. Fulvius Flaccus from Nearer Spain in 180, 50 denarii (40.43.7); Ti. Sempronius Gracchus from Nearer Spain in 178, 25 denarii (41.7.3); L. Postumius Albinus from Farther Spain in 178, 15 denarii (41.7.3). All these passages say that centurions received double the stated amount, and cavalry triple.

25. Polyb. 18.35.4. Cf. Plut. *Aem.* 28.10.

26. For the prior history of this particular money, see 44.23, 27.8–12.

27. Cic. *Off.* 2.76; cf. Pliny *NH* 3.56; Plut. *Aem.* 38.1; Val. Max. 4.3.8. There was some precedent for this: in 187 the friends of Cn. Manlius Vulso arranged with the senate for taxes paid by the people into the treasury to be reimbursed with money from the triumph (39.7.4–5). For a general discussion of the *tributum* and other forms of public taxation in Rome, see Nicolet 1980, 149–206.

circles and even, may it please the gods, at dinner parties," second-guessing what commanders in the field ought to be doing (44.22.8–9):[28]

> There are those who would lead the army into Macedonia, who know where camp should be pitched, which spots should be occupied by guards, when and by what pass Macedonia should be invaded, where granaries should be placed, by what routes on land and sea supplies should be transported, when battle should be joined with the enemy and when it is better to remain quiet. Not only do they determine what should be done, but whatever has been done otherwise than they themselves had advised, they also hold against the consul as accusations, as if bringing him to trial.

This passage suggests that senators avidly discussed political and military affairs during off-hours, a compelling image. The heavy concentration of passive-periphrastic constructions outlines the areas of an effective general's competence and allows Paullus to claim them all for himself. In his insistence that the *imperator* himself is the only one who should be reading the landscape and making judgments as to timing and appropriate tactics (as must have been the case in any event, given the difficulties of communication across long distances, etc.),[29] the consul emerges as an *imperator* who definitely knows what he is doing and has no qualms about taking command.

During the buildup to the battle at Pydna, Livy tells of Paullus's careful reforms to the daily routine of the army along these same lines (44.33.1–11). First he earned respect and admiration by helping to secure a fresh water supply. Next he gave orders to the troops to ready their weapons, presumably to keep them busy, and went out himself with a few chosen leaders to reconnoiter. Finally he devised his new rules: an established chain of command from *imperator* to military tribunes to centurions to soldiers, ensuring that orders would be accurately passed along down the ranks and duly performed; a prohibition against sentries' carrying shields, which allowed them to drowse on duty; and a system of staggered shifts to keep troops fresh rather than wearing them out with constant patrols. He announced all this *in contione,* with the twin provisions that there would be only one *imperator* in this army, and that the ordinary soldier for his part should look after just three things, his physical condition, his weaponry, and his rations, leaving everything else to his superior officers and to the

28. 44.22.8–9: "in omnibus circulis atque etiam, si dis placet, in conviviis sunt qui exercitus in Macedoniam ducant, ubi castra locanda sint sciant, quae loca praesidiis occupanda, quando aut quo saltu intranda Macedonia, ubi horrea ponenda, qua terra mari subvehendi commeatus, quando cum hoste manus conserendae, quando quiesse sit melius. nec quid faciendum sit modo statuunt, sed quidquid aliter quam ipsi censuere factum est, consulem veluti dicta die accusant."

29. Thus Eckstein 1987, passim, especially 320–21.

gods: "They should not ask what was going to happen; when the signal was given, then they should do their duty as soldiers" (44.34.5).[30] Apart from any contribution to the immediate war story, all this vivid detail serves naturally enough to portray Paullus *imperator* as a disciplinarian in accordance with stern Roman tradition, so that Livy's readers will be forearmed against the triumph debate when it comes (45.35.6).[31]

Similarly, when the two armies were encamped opposite each other at Pydna but neither seemed ready to make the first move, Scipio Nasica, one of the military tribunes, took it upon himself during a council to question why the consul had not yet engaged the enemy but appeared to be holding back. In so doing, Nasica claimed, he ran the risk of losing a golden opportunity (44.36.9–12).[32] Paullus's magnanimous response in dramatic *oratio recta* showcases his superior knowledge and *auctoritas*, urging caution and restraint until the right moment comes: "'I also,' he said, '[once] had that mind, Nasica, that you now have, and the one that I have now, you will. From many chances of war I have learned when to fight and when to refrain from fighting. . . . Ask for my reasons at another time; now you will be content with the *auctoritas* of a veteran commander'" (44.36.12–13).[33] This utterance had the immediate effect of silencing the young man (44.36.14), and it is not much of a leap to imagine Livy hoping to silence any like-minded critics among his readers, especially when he gives Paullus a speech repeating the same arguments to the whole army *in contione* on the following day and enlarging on the theme: "I am so far from regretting the inactivity yesterday that I believe the army was saved by me with this plan" (44.38.4).[34] Since the battle of Pydna was later famous for starting almost by accident, after hesitancy and delays on both sides, when a packhorse suddenly shied into a nearby stream (44.40),[35] Livy goes

30. 44.34.5: "illos nihil quid futurum sit quaerere; ubi datum signum sit, tum militarem navare <operam>."

31. 45.35.6: "antiqua disciplina milites habuerat" ("He had held his soldiers with old-fashioned discipline").

32. This P. Cornelius Scipio Nasica Corculum (consul 162) was the son of the Nasica who triumphed in 191 and therefore a cousin of Africanus. Since the son of Africanus adopted one of Paullus's two elder sons (P. Cornelius Scipio Aemilianus), a family tie of sorts existed between Nasica and the *imperator*. On Nasica's rank in 167, see Linderski 1990, 69.

33. 44.36.12–13: "'et ego' inquit 'animum istum habui, Nasica, quem tu nunc habes, et quem ego nunc habeo, tu habebis. multis belli casibus didici quando pugnandum, quando abstinendum pugna sit . . . rationes alias reposcito; nunc auctoritate veteris imperatoris contentus eris."

34. 44.38.4: "tantum abest ut me hesternae quietis paeniteat ut servatum a me exercitum eo consilio credam."

35. Note especially 44.40.3: "neutro imperatorum volente, fortuna, quae plus consiliis humanis pollet, contraxit certamen" ("At the will of neither commander, the element of chance, which is mightier than human plans, brought about the fighting"). Plut. *Aem.* 18.1–2 includes

out of his way to establish Paullus as an exemplary leader beforehand, in anticipation of political attacks eventually leveled against him.

The historian had another reason to give Paullus as broad a stage as possible for his performances *militiae* as well: because *domi* he would have to entrust his cause to others who believed in him and were willing to argue on his behalf. For of course one conspicuous result of the triumph debate conducted *ad populum* instead of before the senators—whose resounding vote in his favor arrived so swiftly and surely that Livy did not even allow him to step down from the resplendent royal barge in which he had made his dramatic entrance, much less narrate his accomplishments or pose the traditional question, before we learned that his triumph had been granted (45.35.3–4)—is that that the would-be *triumphator* himself could not appear. He had to remain outside the *pomerium.* So the debate in this case, unlike any of the others that we have seen, reflects the self-fashioning of the commander at one remove. He has already done his part of the job in securing the approval of the *patres,* who must now speak for him to the populace of Rome, justifying their decision and therefore placing their collective *existimatio* on display and asking the people to affirm their *auctoritas* by voting to ratify it. If Paullus's peers, and more to the point, Livy's readers, are to follow the proceedings with a proper appreciation, then, the historian must allow the great man to speak for himself early and often.

SERVILIUS TO THE RESCUE: HOW TO BRING OFF A MAJOR TRIUMPH

The Roman people did not have the benefit of this testimony, however, when listening to Galba's vituperations against his superior officer, because Paullus's supporters, naively imagining that the triumph was a shoo-in, had not bothered to make much of a case for the *rogatio* (45.36.1). They were in for a nasty surprise. For the legionaries did what Galba had urged and turned up on the Capitol the next morning in such great numbers that they left no room for anyone else. It was only when the first several tribes voted no that the leading senators realized what was happening and rushed to the scene (uphill from the *curia*?), "shouting out that it was a disgraceful deed for L. Paullus, victor in so great a war, to be stripped ["despoliari"] of his triumph" (45.36.6–7).[36] Livy describes the resulting uproar as an aristocratic attempt to squelch the spirit of insubordination

---

an alternative account that releasing the pack animal was actually part of Paullus's plan, thus taking Livy's defense of the *imperator* one step further.

36. 45.36.6–7: "his vocibus incitati, postero die milites tanta frequentia Capitolium conpleverunt, ut aditus nulli praeterea ad suffragium ferendum esset. intro vocatae primae tribus cum antiquarent, concursus in Capitolium principum civitatis factus est, indignum facinus esse clamitantium L. Paullum, tanti belli victorem, despoliari triumpho."

and mutiny among the lower classes: "What would happen if soldiers were made the masters of their commanders?" (45.36.8).[37] A venerable senator emerged as their leading spokesman, M. Servilius Pulex Geminus, former consul (30.27.5) and *magister equitum* (30.24.4) from the latter stages of the Hannibalic War. He persuaded the somewhat bewildered tribunes to let him address the crowd and afterwards to start the now hopelessly disrupted voting process over again (45.36.9–10).

Servilius's speech, though long, nevertheless deserves an attentive close reading, because it is a genuine tour de force. Through it Livy offers his most sophisticated exposition anywhere of what the triumph signified in Roman civic life, and, equally crucial for the present investigation, graphically illustrates how the specifically performative aspects of the triumph debate served to articulate the status both of individual aristocrats and of the aristocracy as such within the social and political order of the *res publica*. We should recall the setting: this debate took place on the Capitolium, in the very center of the city, familiar site of both the *profectio imperatoris* and the culminating triumphal sacrifice to Jupiter Optimus Maximus. It is a place where exempla become real, where every *triumphator* in all of Roman history has stood before, where Paullus's command began and where it should ideally end.[38] And Servilius is addressing the people on behalf of the *patres* as a body, who have already voted in the commander's favor, so that his performance iconically represents a collective effort by the Roman élite to defend their right of arbitration over the distribution of civic honors to one of their own. Galba has effectively challenged that right, and Servilius must reassert it in order for Paullus's hard-earned and well-deserved triumph (cf. 39.4.6) to go forward.

The opening words signal the central act of *existimatio* at the heart of the entire process with an indirect question about Paullus's achievement, which Servilius simultaneously hurls back at Galba in a scathing indictment before his fellow Romans (45.37.1–2):[39]

> If it could not be judged, citizens, from anything else how great an *imperator* Lucius Aemilius has been, this would have been enough, that although he had in his camp soldiers so mutinous and unsteady, and an enemy so high-ranking, so brash, and so well spoken in spurring on a crowd, yet he had no mutiny in his army. The same severity that they now hate restrained them then.

37. 45.36.8: "quid si domini milites imperatoribus imponantur?"

38. On the potent symbolism of the Capitolium as "head" of Rome, see the provocative essay by Jaeger 1993.

39. 45.37.1–2: "quantus imperator L. Aemilius fuerit, Quirites, si ex alia re nulla aestimari posset, vel hoc satis erat, quod cum tam seditiosos et leves milites, tam nobilem tam temerarium tam eloquentem ad instigandam multitudinem inimicum in castris haberet, nullam in exercitu seditionem habuit. eadem severitas imperii quam nunc oderunt tum eos continuit."

The simple address to the assembled citizens as "Quirites" signals a call to duty and reminds the audience of their shared responsibility, while also marking the speaker as a properly civic-conscious individual who has all their collective interests at heart. At the same time, Galba is singled out for seeking to undermine the communal values entrenched in Paullus's "antiqua disciplina" ("old-fashioned discipline"), not incidentally a perfect echo of Livy's own earlier phrase (45.37.2; cf. 36.5).

By standing up to defend Paullus before the Roman people, then, and excoriating Galba, Servilius allies himself, the *imperator,* and all upstanding aristocrats with the good of Rome as a whole. Any reader of Cicero should be long familiar with this basic rhetorical strategy, followed throughout the speech.[40] Now speaking on behalf of the *patres* as a body, whose authoritative assessment of Paullus is being inappropriately called into question, Servilius urges that Galba should not attempt to interfere with the triumph that the senate has already voted to Paullus as owing to him in exchange for his tremendous victory (the economic imagery is Livy's), but rather should wait and bring him to trial as a *privatus,* so that in addition to receiving his due, he might pay the penalty for any actions unworthy of his *gloria* old and new (45.37.3–5). In order to avoid disrupting the proper order of things, in other words, Galba should keep the redress of his grievances separate from the award of a triumph, which is supposed to be a transaction between the senate, magistrates, and people of Rome.

Next, as if to illustrate the intrusion of an agenda foreign to the matter at hand, Servilius imagines two separate assemblies of the groups currently commingled in the crowd before him: the accusing army, and the *universus populus Romanus,* dressed in white togas to signify their purity of judgment, who participate in civic life *domi* and whom the army *militiae* is supposed to protect and defend. In an inversion of roles, having just mentioned Galba possibly taking Paullus to court at some later date, he calls on him to appear here and now as a defendant rather than the accuser, and to make his case before his fellow citizens rather than his comrades at arms. Complaints about stern discipline in the military, commanders who take their job seriously, and money bound for the public treasury in Rome sound very different to that audience, who expect nothing less (45.37.8–11). A complex rhetorical geometry is at work in this passage, because although Servilius has conceptually divided soldiers from citizens, he is still talking to both groups at once, so that each may hear and reflect on what he says to the other. By repeating Galba's arguments and defining the alternate reactions to them among the two groups (soldiers driven to mutiny vs. *Quirites* made patriotically proud), he not only demonstrates to the citizen body

40. For an important reading of authoritative speech in Roman literature generally, see Laird 1999.

from his opponent's own words that Paullus has acted in accordance with traditional Roman values *domi militiaeque* (his primary ostensible purpose) but also displays himself as a qualified speaker on behalf of those values and shows up the greed, laziness, and disloyalty to Rome of *milites* who would dare to say such things with the opposite meaning.

With a reference in passing to the famous clash during the Hannibalic War between Q. Fabius Maximus *dictator* and his *magister equitum* Q. Minucius Rufus, illustrating the need for stern discipline (*severitas*) as a counter to excessive ambition (45.37.12),[41] Servilius quickly dispenses with his address to the people, assured that he has already won their support through the delicate series of maneuvers, detailed above, by which he has so closely allied himself with their interests. All that remains now, therefore, in the greater part of his speech, is to deal with the mutinous soldiers. Ideally he would like to set their priorities straight for them and then manage to reintegrate them and their newly realigned values into the *res publica* as a literally triumphant and harmonious whole. But in order to reach that goal he has had to isolate them from everyone else first. As he turns to address them, he exerts the full force of his gaze *in conspectu omnium* in order to induce shame: "Let us cross over to the other *contio;* nor do I think I will address you as citizens, but rather as soldiers, if this name at least might be able to bring a blush to your cheeks and induce a certain scruple about committing an outrage against your commander" (45.37.14).[42]

The word *pudor* does not appear in the passage just cited, but it will soon, and meanwhile "ruborem" ("blush") and "verecundiam" ("scruple") between them come close enough to make this moment unmistakably similar to the turning point in the debate over the triumph of Cn. Manlius Vulso, as discussed in chapter 12, except that an additional social stratum has been introduced into the scenario here, which thus takes on a new complexity. Rather than merely older senators shaming younger ones within the closed circle of their peers for the good of the aristocracy (albeit understood as what is good for Rome), we have a single older senator instead, acting openly in front of the whole citizenry as a figurehead and spokesman, on behalf of the aristocracy, to shame a group who represent a cross-section of the body politic and who should know better, including a single younger member of the élite who has been serving as their ringleader and needs especially to be brought back into line, and performing for the

41. *Magister equitum* Q. Minucius Rufus had openly opposed the adoption of Fabian tactics in 217. Driving ambition led him to be elevated to the status of co-*dictator* with his rival, only to get himself and his army into terrible trouble with Hannibal, from which Fabius then had to rescue him (22.24–30).

42. 45.37.14: "transeatur ad alteram contionem; nec Quirites vos sed milites videor appellaturus, si nomen hoc saltem ruborem incutere et verecundiam aliquam imperatoris violandi adferre possit."

sake of the *res publica* to which all of them belong—soldiers, citizens, and senators alike. Everything else that Servilius says from here on must be interpreted in this marked social and political context.

He acknowledges first that he can tell the difference between speaking to the two hypothetical audiences, the citizens *domi,* here within the city of Rome, and the soldiers who operate as such only *militiae* (45.38.1). Within the civic sphere, all Romans share in the identity of the *universus populus Romanus,* and the primary dynamic is either individual versus collective or subgroup versus subgroup, whereas out on the battlefield the champions of that mutual interest come into conflict with foreign aggressors, Romans versus non-Romans or "us" versus "them." The triumph, then, especially one with the enemy king led in chains as Paullus's promises to be, is supposed to bring the conquered enemy into the city center so that the inhabitants may draw the full benefit, both material and symbolic, from the fact of victory. Now Servilius pointedly invokes the name of that conquered enemy to spark the fury of the *milites* and direct it elsewhere (45.38.1–2):[43]

> What do you say, soldiers? Is there anyone in Rome, except Perseus, who does not want a triumph celebrated over the Macedonians, and would you not tear him to pieces with the same hands with which you defeated the Macedonians? The one who is preventing you from entering the city in triumph would have prevented you from winning if he could have done.

Anyone in Rome who would deny the triumph for a victory once achieved on behalf of the Republic thereby marks himself off as a *hostis* as opposed to a *civis,*[44] and because of the soldiers' fierce defense of their earlier hard-won success, such a person becomes subject to the same graphic violence, the same patriotic *sparagmos,* as a foreign foe on the battlefield. So Nobilior's twin *certamina* meet again, in a chilling reminder of what Roman legionaries were expected to be capable of always at a moment's notice.[45]

Servilius has just instantaneously united the soldiers against a common

43. 45.38.1–2: "quid †etiam† dicitis, milites? aliquis est Romae, praeter Persea, qui triumphari de Macedonibus nolit, et eum non isdem manibus discerpitis quibus Macedonas vicistis? vincere vos prohibuisset, si potuisset, qui triumphantis urbem inire prohibet."

44. On *civis* vs. *hostis* as conceptual categories, see Roller 1996, 322.

45. Livy does not often describe people ripping each other to pieces with their bare hands. Aside from this moment in Servilius's speech, in fact, the phrase *manibus discerpere* appears in only two other places: first in one of the veiled rumors about the mysterious death of Romulus, suggesting that the group of senators who were nearby when he disappeared had taken their gruesome revenge (1.16.4: "discerptum regem patrum manibus," "the king was torn apart by the hands of the senators"), and again in connection with the Bacchanalian conspiracy of 184, voicing the fears of an informant as to what might befall him (39.13.6: "qui se indicem manibus suis discerpturi essent," " who would tear him apart with their own hands as a finger-pointer"). The graphic idiom clearly bespeaks a righteous fury seeking to obliterate its victim in defense of something held very dear indeed.

threat, reaffirming their sense of solidarity and purpose; only now instead of resentment at their commander's *disciplina* as before, the threat has to do with their being deprived of their due should anyone—like Galba—try to take Paullus's triumph away from him. The process of first reconfiguring their loyalties and then weaving them back into the social and political order has now begun in earnest, and the ritual of the triumph provides the conceptual framework within which Servilius will accomplish his task. He explains that by seeking to sabotage the triumph they were choosing the wrong weapon against Paullus, because it actually belongs as much to them and to the whole Roman people as to the commander personally, so that in their desire for vengeance against one individual they would end up damaging not only themselves but everyone around them (45.38.3).[46] Paullus's title, *imperator,* does not appear here by accident. *Imperium* as such, along with *auspicium, ductus,* and *felicitas,* creates a unique relationship between its bearer and the community at large, and because the triumphal ceremony was designed to articulate that relationship, the various elements within it cannot be treated as isolated entities apart from the whole.

According to Servilius, Paullus does not need the triumph to secure his preeminent status as conqueror of the Macedonian phalanx, nor will the ritual help to make him a great *imperator.* For his *res gestae* (and the senate's endorsement, although he does not mention that) have already ensured that no one will ever be able to deprive him of the badge of honor for having brought the war to a close. During a triumph, all eyes are fixed on Rome, watching among other things how the community treats its most illustrious citizens: Athenian-style ostracism should not be an option (45.38.4–6). We thus come around to the touchy subject of *invidia* from the perspective of the city's overall reputation, which Servilius claims has been damaged by exempla from the past like Camillus and Africanus, both of whom ended stellar careers in exile and disgrace, to the abiding shame of all. Since Paullus already ranks alongside these men, all loyal Romans must work together now, like good soldiers of the Republic, to prevent him from suffering a similar fate at their hands (45.38.7–8). Yet Servilius carefully does not push this negative argument too far when instead he can stress the communal benefit of triumphs and their power to enhance the *gloria* of the whole Roman people. "With so many triumphs celebrated over the years from perennial battlegrounds like Gaul and Spain and Carthage," he asks (loosely translated), as if suddenly looking back over the course of Livy's history up to this point, "can we really say that they belonged only

46. 45.38.3: "erratis, milites, si triumphum imperatoris tantum, et non militum quoque et universi populi Romani esse decus censetis" ("You are mistaken, soldiers, if you believe that the triumph is a badge of honor for the commander only and not also for the soldiers and the whole Roman people").

to the commanders as individuals?" In a clever manipulation of formulaic language, he reminds his audience that the ritual names not only single kings and famous leaders but entire tribes and peoples brought under subjection; conversely, therefore, whenever an *imperator* triumphs, all Romans triumph with him (45.38.11).[47]

Having briefly sketched out the schematic link between *triumphator* and *universus populus Romanus* in this way, Servilius now addresses the specific concerns of the soldiers again, first as significant participants in the triumphal ritual and then on that basis as people with a genuine stake in seeing to it that the ritual takes place. The troops who march in a triumph all wear laurel crowns of their own, and those who can boast of special acts of valor have medals and other prizes (*dona militaria*) to put their *virtus* on display.[48] In addition, they contribute to the sounds of the triumph as well as the sights, by shouting *Io, triumpe!* and singing hymns of praise throughout the city for themselves and their commander (45.38.12). We should notice that Servilius is speaking in the third person here about any soldiers in any triumph. Hearing this, his audience of Paullus's particular troops should identify with the description and start to imagine themselves performing the same actions when their turn comes to fulfill the generic role. Emotions follow suit: in a sudden reflection on the meaning of the *deportatio exercitus,* Servilius explains that armies left behind in the province when their commanders come home to triumph deeply resent not being able to take part in person, and yet also share in the ritual in spirit, even across long distances, because they know that they had a major hand in making victory a reality (45.38.13).

That reference to the very hands that brought about victory, the second in the speech, builds a rhetorical bridge from soldiers in general (third person) to Servilius's audience (second person), and recapitulates the earlier call to unite. The speaker can now pose a devastating hypothetical question with only one logical answer, which will force them to confront their own behavior and motivations, and expose the contradictions inherent in continuing to follow Galba's lead (45.38.14):[49]

47. 45.38.11: "tot de Gallis triumphi, tot de Hispanis, tot de Poenis, ipsorum tantum imperatorum an populi Romani dicuntur? quemadmodum non de Pyrrho modo nec de Hannibale, sed de Epirotis Carthaginiensibusque triumphi acti sunt, sic non M'. Curius tantum nec P. Cornelius, sed Romani triumpharunt" (Here is a more literal translation than the one offered in the text: "Are so many triumphs over the Gauls, so many over the Spanish, so many over the Carthaginians said to belong to the commanders only or to the Roman people? Just as triumphs were celebrated neither over Pyrrhus only nor over Hannibal, but over the Epirots and the Carthaginians, so neither M'. Curius only nor P. Cornelius but the Romans triumphed").

48. On *dona militaria,* see above, p. 141 n. 44. Also see above, n. 13.

49. 45.38.14: "si quis vos interroget, milites, ad quam rem in Italiam deportati, et non statim confecta provincia dimissi sitis, quid Romam frequentes sub signis veneritis, quid

> If someone were to ask you, soldiers, why you were brought home to Italy and not dismissed at once the moment your mission was done, why you have come to Rome en masse under your military standards, why you have been lingering here and not going back in separate directions, each to his own home, what else would you answer, except that you wanted to be seen in triumph? You ought certainly to have wanted to go on display as conquerors.

Servilius proceeds to answer his own question, and not once but twice, using the repetition to instill in his audience a growing certainty that he must indeed be right as they pause to acknowledge that, yes, they do feel the things that he has ascribed to people in their position. Notice the abundant alliteration in the last line, linking the soldiers themselves ("vos"), their success ("victores"), their desires ("velle"), and the act of being seen ("videri"). Everything in Roman civic life, as Polybius says, comes down to earning and enjoying the esteem of one's community in exchange for a job well done,[50] and that in turn inevitably entails spectacle, ceremony, and public display.

Next comes a string of evaluative comparisons among various splendid triumphs recently celebrated or soon to come, occasions for *existimatio,* which serve to point up the absurdity of a triumph denied to Paullus, of all people, who has not only engineered his enemy's defeat but actually taken the king and heir of Alexander prisoner (45.39.1–4; cf. 39.7). Servilius paints a vivid image of Anicius and Octavius, resplendent in triumphal purple, riding past their superior officer clad in the simple white toga of a *privatus* among the spectators, and when challenged by him using their names (another deeply significant hypothetical question with only one valid response) ceding their place of honor and stepping down off the chariot in shame, handing over their insignia, and allowing him to take their place in the triumph (45.39.2).[51] The specific identification of the feeling that inspires this striking secondary spectacle as *pudor* echoes the speaker's earlier admonition to the soldiers that they should be ashamed of themselves for opposing Paullus and asks them now to imagine the kind of scene that makes even *triumphatores* blush. What must their own reaction be now? The

---

moremini, hic et non diversi do<mos> quisque abeatis vestras, quid aliud respondeatis, quam vos triumphantis videri velle? vos certe victores conspici velle debebatis."

50. Polyb. 6.52.11 (cited above, p. 132 n. 17).

51. 45.39.2: "quod si in curru scandentes Capitolium, auratos purpuratosque, ex inferiore loco L. Paullus, in turba togatorum unus privatus interroget 'L. Anici Cn. Octavi, utrum vos digniores triumpho esse an me censetis?', curru ei cessuri et prae pudore videntur insignia ipsi sua tradituri" ("Now if Lucius Paullus, one private citizen in the crowd of men wearing togas, were to ask them from below as they climbed the Capitolium in the chariot, clad in gold and purple, 'Lucius Anicius, Gnaeus Octavius, do you think that you are more worthy of a triumph, or that I am?' they would be seen ready to relinquish the chariot to him and for shame to hand over their insignia to him").

analogous and more personal thought of having to sit by and watch the army from Illyria and the sailors from the fleet enjoy their celebrations, for what were after all only sidelights to the main Macedonian war, helps to bring the issue of fairness into much sharper focus (45.39.3–4).

While all this *existimatio* is being transacted along various axes, and in between the imagined shame of Anicius and Octavius and the rising indignation of the soldiers, comes a direct address to Servilius's other audience, forgotten for a time: "And you, Quirites: Would you rather see Gentius led in triumph than Perseus?" So discreetly that he almost does it in passing, the speaker places citizens and soldiers side by side in his hypothetical scenario as undifferentiated spectators to the triumphs of the lesser commanders and then locates Paullus, the supreme would-be *triumphator* himself, right in their midst, dressed as one of them and therefore distinguished only by everyone's knowledge of exactly who he is and what he has accomplished. As the scene crystallizes, suddenly the two *contiones* that Servilius has been pretending to conduct separately collapse into one again, leaving only an awareness of the *universus populus Romanus* to which both citizens and soldiers belong, and at the same time L. Aemilius Paullus emerges from the crowd as an unmistakable champion and hero. He simply must have his triumph now, so that all of them can resume their rightful places in the Roman social and political order.

Moreover, the reference to *pudor* felt by Anicius and Octavius at the prospect of Paullus being deprived of his triumph also picks up on Livy's introductory remarks at the start of the whole debate about what caused it all! (45.35.5). The speech connects solidly with its frame, therefore, as does Servilius's aristocratic agenda with the historian's own broader patriotic purpose. The speaker has been deftly manipulating a very complex rhetorical situation between several different interest groups, and throughout his speech Livy has been speaking through him to his readers, instructing them in the proper interpretation of Rome's triumphant past as his *Ab Urbe Condita* presents it. For by following the speech to its conclusion, it is possible to learn through the mouthpiece of an exemplary aristocratic figure to recognize the various elements of triumphal ritual and to understand how they are supposed to fit together—and what is more, to do the same thing with the various competing interests within the *res publica,* all of whom have a stake in the triumph debate: senators, magistrates, soldiers, *populus Romanus.*

In his peroration, with Paullus's upcoming triumph starting more and more to look like a sure thing, as it should have been all along, Servilius proceeds to break the spectacle down into its component parts and to dwell for a moment on the significance of each. The legions have already received detailed attention as a target for his persuasion, because he has had to remind them of their proper role in order to secure their allegiance. Having inquired at last whether Paullus's troops are truly prepared to watch the triumphs of others when their own has been annulled (45.39.4), he can rest assured that they will give the correct response to his rhetorical question, and move on to the rest. Next, he asks if all the accumulated royal treasures, money, art objects, luxury goods, weapons, and so on, piled up outside the city gates and waiting to be proudly displayed in the triumphal procession as badges of honor, must instead be sneaked into the treasury under cover of darkness, or perhaps even shipped back to Macedonia (45.39.4–6). These things are destined to become public property, *res publica* in the etymological sense, and as such should be ceremoniously welcomed. Nor do the people often get to see the especially dramatic and stirring spectacle of a great king led in chains through the streets of the city (45.39.6).[52]

The triumph also represents the perfect fulfillment of a crucial cycle. For the commander himself, L. Aemilius Paullus—whose name stands in metonymy for his stature in the community, a proud family heritage augmented by his own accomplishments—was chosen by the electoral process as an officeholder and endowed with *imperium* and *auspicium* to fight as champion on behalf of the SPQR. He set off to his province at the start of his campaign from the Capitol amid hopes and good wishes for the speedy completion of a war that had already dragged on to everyone's shame (again that word *pudor*) for nearly forty years. Having now completed his allotted task to the glory of Rome, he deserves to come home and receive his just reward, to enjoy his moment at the center of the city's highest honor (45.39.8–9).[53] Paradoxically, the same distinctions that set him apart from the community as a prominent individual also mean that his interests are closely allied with the collective needs and corporate identity of the *res publica* as a whole. What Paullus has accomplished is what the whole system was designed to make possible, for everyone's benefit.

Moreover, to deprive Paullus of honor would also mean breaking a

52. 45.39.6: "illud spectaculum maximum, nobilissimus opulentissimus rex captus . . . victori populo ostendetur" ("that greatest of spectacles, a king of highest birth and tremendous riches . . . is put on display before the people in victory"). On the display of enemy captives, most notably kings, in triumphal processions, with particular reference to Perseus and Paullus, see Östenberg 2003, 126–64, especially 132–35.

53. 45.39.8–9: "ipsum L. Paullum, bis consulem, domitorem Graeciae, omnium oculi conspicere urbem curru ingredientem avent; ad hoc fecimus consulem, ut bellum per quadriennium ingenti etiam pudore nostro tractum perficeret. cui sortito provinciam, cui proficiscenti praesagientibus animis victoriam triumphumque destinavimus, ei victori triumphum negaturi <sumus>?" ("The eyes of all are eager to see Lucius Paullus himself, twice consul, the conqueror of Greece, riding into the city in a chariot; to this end we made him consul, so that he might bring an end to the war that had dragged on for four years even to our enormous shame. When his province was allotted, and when he set out, we marked him out for victory and triumph with minds that predicted the future; [*sc.* now that he has returned] as victor will we deny him a triumph?")

promise to the immortal gods, because it would violate ritual symmetry. The ceremonies performed in the same sacred space in connection with both *profectio* and triumph, and indeed the vows and sacrifices highlighting the outset and completion of any significant action within the civic sphere, always serve to bind the activities and concerns of the human world, social, political, and military, to the cosmic order as well. The text of this passage is terribly corrupt, but the legible words reveal that Servilius invokes both the ancestors and the gods, and mentions the Capitol twice, as the point of both origin and return for *imperatores* and their *res gestae.*[54] He appears to stress that a commander's *felicitas* signals the extent to which the gods have been looking out for his success and for the well-being of Rome, in keeping with proper ritual procedure. Once his efforts have been crowned with victory, it would not do to disrupt the *pax deum* by failing to offer appropriate thanks where thanks are due (45.39.9–13). When we recall then that Servilius and his audience are standing on the Capitolium themselves as he calls these images to mind—half in memory, half in prophecy, as it was, is, and shall be to come—their evocative power, the power of exemplum and authority and of Rome's place in the cosmos, emerges in even bolder colors. We can imagine him and his audience lifting their eyes to the Temple of Jupiter in recognition of how much lies at stake.

Hypothetically, at least, the elaborate civic pageantry of Paullus's triumph is now complete, and indeed if the speaker has done his performative job right, those images will soon become a reality. Quickly going back through the list of core elements one more time, and issuing a final call to the soldiers to repudiate Galba as a spreader of lies (45.39.13–15), Servilius ends with a dramatic performative flourish on his own behalf, focusing attention on himself as the right man to have made this particular speech (45.39.16–19):[55]

> "I have fought the enemy twenty-three times . . . I have brought back spoils from all those with whom I have fought hand to hand; I have a body distinguished by the marks of honorable scars, all of them received on the front." Then he is said to have uncovered himself and to have narrated which wounds he had received and in what wars.

He stands before his fellow citizens as the literal embodiment of Roman values and an icon of the aristocratic ethos, not only someone who has

54. Cf. Jaeger 1997, 3–5.

55. 45.39.16–19: "'ego ter et viciens cum hoste †per provocatio† pugnavi; ex omnibus cum quibus manum conserui spolia rettuli; insigne corpus honestis cicatricibus, omnibus adverso corpore exceptis, habeo.' nudasse deinde se dicitur, et quo quaeque bello volnera accepta essent rettulisse." For Servilius's coins with images of *spolia,* see Crawford 1974, 264 (cited by Morstein-Marx 2004, 87 and nn.).

fought bravely *militiae* and proudly shed his own blood on behalf of the Republic, but also a skilled speaker and self-promoter *domi,* who knows how to tell the kind of story that will impress his audience, whether he is speaking to his peers in the senate ("Look what I did for Rome") or to the assembled citizen body ("Look what I did for you"). The scars on his flesh tell their own stories.[56] All in front, they function on his behalf as signifiers, bearers of culturally determined meaning, forming a nonverbal framework or visual aid for the performance of his *res gestae* narrative, and (by extension) Paullus's as well.[57]

And then comes the unforgettable moment when the act of lifting his toga to display his body as text unwittingly exposes his private parts, the "things that should remain hidden." It is no wonder that the nearest onlookers could not suppress a laugh (45.39.17).[58] His swollen groin is the stuff of Plautine (or Aristophanic) comedy, hardly displaying the *dignitas* and decorum incumbent upon a prominent aristocrat at the crowning moment of a speech before the people, especially when he has been relying on the sight of his flesh to produce a very different effect in his audience.[59] Yet Servilius does not so much as flinch and immediately turns the tables on anyone who would misinterpret his performance or second-guess his *auctoritas.* The swelling arose from long tireless days in the saddle, he explains, and therefore betokens the very devotion and service to the Republic that he has been seeking to demonstrate from the start.[60] His battle-scarred body marks him indelibly as the old soldier speaking to a group of new recruits, whose pristine hides would likewise give them away: "Let Galba strip his!" (45.39.19).[61] After this Livy's account of the final vote is missing in a lacuna, but as Servilius's voice rises above the murmur of the crowd to summon the tribunes, and perhaps to remind the soldiers of their duty one last time, is there any doubt at all what the outcome will be?

One final question: How much of this debate is conceivably historical? Livy's sources would have preserved some record of the senate vote and

56. Cf. Sall. *Jug.* 85.29–30, and see the comments of Brilliant 1999, 221–22.

57. On scars as visible symbols of aristocratic *virtus,* see Leigh 1995; Oakley 1985; Rosenstein 2006, 367.

58. 45.39.17: "quae dum ostentat, adapertis forte quae velanda erant, tumor inguinum proximis risum movit" ("While he was showing off his scars, those things that ought to have been hidden were by chance exposed, and the swelling in his groin brought a laugh from those nearest to him").

59. On physical peculiarities (including strange swellings) interpreted rhetorically as signs of deformed character, see Corbeill 1996, 14–56, especially 42–43, 48–49, 55–56.

60. On cavalry service as a hallmark of the Roman aristocracy, see McCall 2002.

61. 45.39.19: "ego hoc ferro saepe vexatum corpus vetus miles adulescentibus militibus ostendi: Galba nitens et integrum denudet" ("I, the old soldier, have shown this body of mine, often marred by the sword, to teenage young soldiers: let Galba strip his, shining and unblemished").

subsequent recourse to the popular assembly at least, along with an indication of the soldiers' complaints at having received less than their fair share of the loot, probably the names of Galba and Servilius as participants in a cause célèbre, and certainly the final outcome in favor of the would-be *triumphator* through the timely intervention of his aristocratic peers to forestall what would have been a deeply embarrassing incident if the *rogatio* had failed. The historian probably did not invent Servilius's final performative flourish either, since even without Paullus's family to preserve the memory by passing it on to Polybius, a juicy story like that would have burned itself indelibly into the civic consciousness and immediately become the stuff of legend. Everything else, and especially the extended discourse on the components of the triumphal ritual and of the sociopolitical order in Rome, to which so much time and attention has just been devoted, Livy obviously must have extrapolated and expanded, tweaked and tailored to suit his own rhetorical purposes. Yet instead of throwing out the entire episode as a product of Livy's hand in giving it its distinctive shape, we should acknowledge the fact that history and historiography are interwoven, in order to arrive at an adequate appreciation of the tremendous value of Servilius's speech as a detailed reader's guide to the triumphs, and the triumph debates, that form such a prominent feature of the civic landscape in the *Ab Urbe Condita*.

SPECTACLES BETWEEN EAST AND WEST

Thanks to the efforts of Servilius and others who intervened to prevent a disastrous vote in the assembly, Paullus received his special grant of *imperium* and went on to celebrate a magnificent triumph (45.40.1–4), which lasted for three days, rivaling the grandiose spectacle staged by T. Quinctius Flamininus, victor over the previous Macedonian king three decades before (34.52.4–12). Much of Livy's description has fallen away in the same lacuna that also swallowed the tail end of Servilius's speech and the final assembly vote, but many details of Paullus's triumph can be reconstructed from Diodorus and Plutarch.[62]

On the first day, trumpeters led the way in front of 1,200 wagons filled with bronze shields, 300 laden with weapons, and 800 panoplies: this was above all a military pageant. On the second day began the parade of wealth and luxury goods: 1,000 talents of coined money, 2,200 talents of coined silver carried in 750 huge vessels, 500 wagons loaded with statues of gods and men, golden shields, dedicatory plaques. On the third day came 120

62. Plut. *Aem.* 32–34, Diod. 31.9–12. For the notice in the Fasti, see Degrassi 1947, 80–81, 556. On the precious-metal items in particular, with some useful calculations, see Jacobsthal 1943, 308–9.

white oxen for sacrifice, 220 wagons of gold talents, a single ten-talent gold libation bowl studded with jewels, 2,000 elephant tusks, an ivory chariot with gold and jewels, a horse in jeweled battle array, and a golden couch. Then finally, crowning the spectacle, King Perseus in chains with his family (45.40.6), followed by 400 garlands from various cities and kings, and at last Paullus himself in the triumphal chariot with his two elder sons close by him,[63] and the infantry marching in ordered ranks behind (45.40.4). Valerius Antias reported that the gold and silver that Paullus deposited into the treasury totaled 120 million sesterces, and although the true sum must remain incalculable, it was clearly an astronomical amount of money, enough to cancel the *tributum* or tax on individuals, which was apparently not reinstated for another hundred years (45.40.1).

Shortly afterwards, Cn. Octavius celebrated his naval triumph, unadorned with prisoners or spoils, having secured both the royal prisoner and the contents of his treasury for inclusion in Paullus's celebration (45.42.2). Anicius followed with another grand procession to mark his victory over Gentius and the Illyrians, including many military standards, royal furniture, 27 pounds of gold and 19 of silver, 13,000 denarii, 120,000 Illyrian silver coins, plus the king and his family led before the chariot (45.43.1–8).[64] According to Valerius Antias again, he deposited 20 million sesterces into the treasury (45.43.8).[65] He also staged a performance, a twist on traditional Roman gladiatorial games, involving Greek dancers, musicians, and pugilists.[66] The Roman world was changing, and exotic elements were gaining increasing prominence.

63. These were Q. Fabius Maximus and P. Scipio Aemilianus. Of Paullus's two younger sons, who should have ridden in the triumphal chariot with him, the youngest (12 years old) died five days before his triumph, and the other (14 years old) three days later. Since he had given his two elder sons away in adoption, this meant the end of his family, and the circumstance prompts a touching *contio* in which he contrasts his own personal losses with the glory and good fortune of Rome (45.40.6–41.12). His speech seems to echo the sentiments expressed by M. Fabius Vibulanus, consul in 480, who turned down a triumph because his brother and his son had perished in the battle (2.47.10–11). By displaying civic pride in the midst of immense family sorrow, L. Aemilius Paullus *triumphator* became a Roman legend and a "documentum humanorum casuum" ("example of human misfortunes") in a manner that linked his fate to that of the captive King Perseus (45.40.6). On Livy's debt to Polybius here, see Eckstein 1995, 230–32. Note also the foreshadowing in Livy's narrative of the battle of Pydna, where Paullus returns to his camp amid anxiety about the fate of his elder son, P. Scipio Aemilianus, who had disappeared from his sight earlier during the fighting (44.44.1–3), only to discover him safe and sound.

64. Cf. Diod. 31.8.10. See also Degrassi 1947, 80–81, 556.

65. Note the remark of Gruen 1984a, 290 n. 9: "also the triumph of L. Anicius, lesser in character because earned against the Illyrians, but Anicius turned it into a memorable event."

66. Polyb. 30.22. On the complex cultural politics of this Hellenized spectacle staged in Rome, see Gruen 1992, 215–19, and more recently Edmondson 1999, 81–84.

Whereas people like Marcellus, M. Fulvius Nobilior, and Anicius incorporated Greek elements into the ancestral customs of their homeland, Paullus's stage as a performer of *Romanitas* extended well beyond Rome, even beyond Italy, to include the famous cities of the fabled East. Between his victory and his homecoming, he went on a grand tour of Greece, visiting all the legendary places: Thessaly, Delphi, Lebadia, Chalcis in Euboea, Aulis, Attica, Athens, Corinth and the Isthmus, Sicyon, Argos, Epidaurus, Sparta, Megalopolis, Olympia, Demetrias (45.27.5–28.6).[67] In a very short compass, Livy presents his readers with a sweeping tableau of *Graecia capta* through the eyes of its captor.[68] Fragments of Polybius reveal that Paullus took note of the fortifications and strategic possibilities of various cities as he passed.[69] He also offered conspicuous sacrifices at a number of important shrines, particularly those to Zeus, whom he identified with Jupiter Optimus Maximus, the Roman triumphal god.[70] At Delphi, oracular site and showcase of Greek self-promotion since time immemorial, he found a square column where a statue of Perseus had been destined to stand and placed his own equestrian image atop it instead, commissioning a figural relief below that depicted scenes from the battle of Pydna in vivid historical detail, including the packhorse whose shying started the fight, and an inscription, still visible to this day outside the Delphi Museum, that proclaimed him as conqueror—in Latin—for all the world to see: L. AIMILIVS L.F. INPERATOR DE REGE PERSE MACEDONIBVSQVE CEPIT ("L. Aemilius the son of Lucius, [*sc.* Roman] commander, seized this from King Perseus and the Macedonians").[71] One imagines Greek visitors to Delphi peering up at the impressive equestrian statue and then squinting to puzzle out the inscription, possibly getting their first glimpse of the Roman alphabet from Paullus's name and the title *inperator.*

At Amphipolis, prior to his departure for home, with *theōroi* from the Greek cities in attendance, he orchestrated a parting spectacle on the same grand scale and along much the same lines as any major Panhellenic

67. Cf. Polyb. 30.10; Plut. *Aem.* 28. As A. F. Stewart 1990, 220, has written, "Having smashed the Macedonian army for ever, this dignified, courteous, and ascetic senator turned tourist after his great victory."

68. Cf. Jaeger 1997, 1–3, 5 n. 13.

69. See Polyb. 30.10.3–4, noting the acropolis at Corinth and the fortifications of Sicyon and Argos.

70. These associations were particularly strong at Olympia, because of the Phidias statue and its famous imperious gaze. See 45.28.5 and Polyb. 30.10.6.

71. *ILLRP* 323. Cf. 45.27.7. For a reconstruction of the monument, including a drawing, and an interpretation of both its Greek and its Roman elements, see A. F. Stewart 1990, 220–21, 231, and plate 786. In addition to reproducing a drawing originally published by Künzl 1988, fig. 65, and similar to Stewart's, Flower 2004b, 328–35, includes some lovely photographs of the surviving sculptural reliefs. See also Kuttner 2004, 298, 306, 312; Gruen 1992, 141–45.

gathering, yet not at one of the Panhellenic shrines. Rather, Amphipolis had been designated to become the Roman administrative center for one of the four *merides* into which the former kingdom of Macedonia was now being divided in plans laid out by Paullus's *decem legati* (45.29.9–10).[72] Having invited local dignitaries to the new seat of power, Paullus treated them to games and sacrifices, with performances by artisans and athletes, men and beasts.[73] He then served them a splendid feast, saying that skill in "both hosting a party and preparing *ludi* belonged to a man who knows how to conquer in battle" (45.32.11).[74] Before setting sail, and to mark the close of his campaign, he ceremoniously burned a huge pile of weapons as a dedication to Mars, Minerva, and Lua, an archaic Roman practice (45.33.1–2),[75] while laying out an opulent display of gold, silver, bronze, ivory—all symbols of Eastern *luxuria* (45.33.5–7). These same objects would eventually appear in his triumph, and here, as there, they manifested his *res gestae* and the power of Rome. Yet although his army would have been on hand for the festivities, and could certainly tell stories to the people at home when they returned, Paullus at Amphipolis was addressing primarily not the conquerors but the conquered, allowing them to gaze on the undeniable splendor of the Macedonian kingdom one last time before loading it all onto his ships and carrying it away forever. The notable "gathering of Europe and Asia" ("in illo conventu Europae Asiaeque," 45.33.3) at his behest heralded a new status quo: Paullus was leaving, but Rome had arrived on the Hellenistic scene and was here to stay. People had best get used to the idea.

The answering festival of Antiochus IV Epiphanes at Daphne shows that the communication worked both ways.[76] We have therefore reached a critical moment in the interaction between East and West. The Greeks, and in particular the Hellenistic kings, had developed an elaborate visual language of monument, statuary, and court ceremonial that marked the centers of power and set Alexander's heirs apart.[77] As Rome emerged victorious over Hannibal and became enmeshed in the affairs of the Hellenistic world, the *imperatores* who conducted campaigns in the East brought home unprecedented amounts of gold, silver, ivory, artworks, and other luxury goods, which enriched and indelibly Hellenized both the material and

72. See Edmondson 1999, 78.

73. On Paullus's victory games, see recently Klar 2006, 168–75.

74. 45.32.11: "et convivium instruere et ludos parare eiusdem esse qui vincere proelio sciret."

75. For the burning of weapons to various deities, see 8.30.8, 10.29.19, 41.12.16; Rüpke 1990, 199–201. On the ancient cult of Lua Mater, see also 8.1.6.

76. See Edmondson 1999, 84–89.

77. On Hellenistic royal display, see (among others) Gruen 1985; Herman 1997; Kuttner 1999; Rice 1983; R. R. R. Smith 1988; A. F. Stewart 1993.

the symbolic economies in Rome, as we have seen. Meanwhile, by their actions abroad and by staging spectacles in the Hellenistic mode, men like Paullus also made known the presence of their city, and the power of her *imperium,* to a much wider audience than would ever have the opportunity to experience a triumph on the Capitolium. In 167 Rome stood at an important historical threshold, poised for deeper and deeper involvement across the whole Mediterranean.[78] Looking both forward and back, L. Aemilius Paullus inherited a tremendous legacy from those who had gone before him—Marcellus, Africanus, Flamininus, Asiaticus, Nobilior, Vulso, Glabrio—and paved the way for the even more formidable figures who eventually followed in his triumphant footsteps: Sulla, Marius, Pompey, Julius Caesar, Augustus, Trajan, Constantine.

78. See Kallet-Marx 1995.

Conclusion

Triumphs and Roman Values

THE PAGEANTRY OF POWER

The earlier discussion of triumphal criteria and the byplay between the senate, magistrates, and *populus Romanus* eventually led to a focus on the performative elements in triumph debates. Similarly, that focus leads in turn to an examination of triumphs as spectacle. As seen from the rhetoric of Servilius's speech on behalf of L. Aemilius Paullus in the previous chapter, triumphs allowed the SPQR and its constituents to feast their eyes on the tangible benefits of conquest and to ponder the intangible ones as well (45.36–39). The whole city gathered to celebrate and fully realize the glory of each new *triumphator* as he added his name to the Fasti and his *res gestae* to the cumulative history and legacy of Rome at arms. No greater performance took place on the civic stage than the triumph, which was one of the foundations of Roman public life (thus 30.15.12).[1] The time has come, therefore, to attempt a decoding of the triumph as religious ritual, political display, and cultural pageant. To the Romans of the Republic, it was a familiar and significant feature of their civic calendar and urban landscape, and in Livy's history it becomes a ruling metaphor and governing symbol of Roman identity, individual and collective. Technicalities will abound from start to finish, making details often hard to pin down, but there is much to be learned from the broad sweep and evocative power of images, ideas, and concepts.

First and foremost, of course, the triumph was a victory celebration, orchestrated to show off the Romans to themselves as the proud and right-

1. Hesberg 1999, 73, remarks: "Public life, of course, can always be understood as a spectacle." Cf. Wiseman 1989, 154: "Public life, or spectacle? The two categories cannot be separated."

ful conquerors of defeated foreign foes.[2] Public events on a grand scale always hold a peculiar fascination because of what Clifford Geertz, in one of his typically elegant turns of phrase, calls the "symbolics of power." His lively description of three comparative case studies in the art of political showmanship—royal progresses from Elizabethan England, fourteenth-century Java, and nineteenth-century Morocco—immediately brings the Roman triumph to mind, and not only because of the latter's supposed origin in the period of kings. Geertz points out the inherent staginess of power:[3]

> At the political center of any complexly organized society . . . there is both a governing élite and a set of symbolic forms expressing the fact that it is truly governing. . . . [The members of that élite] justify their existence and order their actions in terms of a collection of stories, ceremonies, insignia, formalities, and appurtenances . . . that mark the center as center and give what goes on there its aura of being not merely important but in some odd fashion connected with the way the world is built.

So it matters little whether the *triumphator* happened to be an Etruscan warlord in his primitive splendor, a dutiful magistrate of the SPQR at its height, or the *Princeps* who held the whole vast Empire under his personal sway. By their very nature as public spectacles, Roman triumphs from any era embodied, and thus helped to constitute, the ruling ideology of the day. In so doing, they served to locate everyone who came under their purview within four reference frames: time, space, community, and cosmos.

Ceremonies of Eternal Return: Triumphs and Time

Its precise origins may be obscure, but we know that the celebration of triumphs in Rome to mark military victories was an extremely venerable practice, dating back at least as far as the age of Etruscan domination, and perhaps even farther.[4] The Latin word *triumphus,* though ultimately derived from the Greek θρίαμβος, first came into the language via Etruscan.[5] As already noted, both Livy and the Fasti claim Romulus himself as the first

2. Östenberg 2003, passim, summarized neatly by Flower 2004b, 340.

3. Geertz 1983b, 124.

4. For theories on the Etruscan origins and subsequent development of the Roman triumph, see Coarelli 1988, especially 363–437; Künzl 1988; Lemosse 1972; Versnel 1970; Warren 1970 (all with copious reference to earlier works). Recently Rüpke 2006b (cited by Rüpke 2006a, 225 and n. 27) has provocatively argued that both the triumphal ritual and the funeral procession with the *imagines* originated not in the Etruscan period but in fact as late as the fourth century, when the senate began seeking to exert control over civic honors, notably public statues, by limiting them to officeholders. *Contra,* however, see Versnel 2006, in defense of the *communis opinio* that his own earlier work (Versnel 1970) did much to establish.

5. See Forsythe 2005, 118, with reference to Versnel 1970, 11–55; Warren 1970.

triumphator.[6] Whether or not the legendary founder ever really existed, the proud assertion of such a vast, unbroken continuity stands on the Fasti inscription, for all to see, as a signpost of Roman identity, strikingly defined by the existence of the ritual.[7] In the solemn procession through the streets of the city and thanksgiving sacrifice to Jupiter Optimus Maximus on the Capitol, the *triumphator* of later eras still bore the ancient sacral insignia of the Etruscan kings, which Jupiter's cult statue also wore: purple robes, an embroidered tunic, and red-lead face paint, with a crown of laurel on his head and an eagle-topped scepter in his hand.[8] Having made its debut

6. For the earliest entries in the Fasti Triumphales, including both Romulus and the Etruscan kings, see Degrassi 1947, 64–65, 534–35 (also cited above, p. 33 n. 2). A beautiful photograph of the stone with Romulus's name appears in Künzl 1988, 57 fig. 30. Cf. Plut. *Rom.* 16.5–8. Livy does not mention a triumph for Romulus per se but does describe him dedicating the *spolia opima* to Jupiter Feretrius on the Capitolium (1.10.5–7).

7. The prominent mention of Romulus at the head of the Fasti inscription gains added ideological point from the fact that the list was carved not on the Regia as previously believed but on the inner face of the triumphal arch built by Augustus, the self-styled new Romulus, in 19 B.C. (see Degrassi 1947, 17–19 with plates 8–10, as well as the drawing at Künzl 1988, 56). On the complex archaeology of the arch itself, see Scott 2000. Anyone who passed under the arch, symbolically reenacting Augustus's triumph, would learn that the history and identity of the Republic led from the first founder to the new founder in a single, perfect chain. The neat summation of Augustan ideology offered by Barchiesi 1997, 271–72, is immediately relevant: "To write an ending to the annals of triumphs, a supplement to the *carmen arvale,* to close Janus, to reclaim the Golden Age, to gather the *Annales maximi,* to describe an accurate geography of the known world: Augustus defines himself not only as the First, but also as the Last and Definitive Man of Rome." Cf. Wallace-Hadrill 1987; Zanker 1988, 206. Needless to say, the role of triumphs and triumphal imagery in the establishment of the Principate makes a fascinating study unto itself. In addition to Zanker 1988, especially 88–96, 188–96, 198–204, and 213–17, see by way of example Favro 1996, especially 236–44; Hickson 1991; Itgenshorst 2004; and 2005, 1–12, 219–26; Koortbojian 2006. It should be noted that a detailed comparison between exempla from Livy's history and the *elogia* of the *summi viri* in Augustus's Forum brings out contrasts between the historian's catalogue of heroes and that promulgated by the *Princeps* and culminating in himself: see Luce 1990 (also cited by Feldherr 1997b, 137 and n. 5; Kraus 1994, 9 and n. 36).

8. On the triumphal insignia, see the long and detailed discussion by Versnel 1970, 56–93, with a concise list of testimonia for Etruscan elements in the Roman triumph at 83 n.1. By contrast with Versnel's synchronic view, Warren 1970, 58–62, stresses the gap between the original Etruscan forms and later Roman (especially Hellenistic) borrowings, again with copious notes. These two treatments, published in the same year, make a wonderful study in contrasts. At 10.7.10 Livy describes a *triumphator* as "Iovis optimi maximi ornatu decoratus" ("adorned with the accoutrements of Jupiter Optimus Maximus"). The statue of the god wore the same equipment; cf. Juv. 10.38, Serv. *ad Ecl.* 10.27. See Favro 1999, 216 n. 22. This has led to misleading speculation, now and again, that the regalia signified actual deification of the *triumphator,* whereas Ehlers (1939, 495), Versnel (1970, 84–93), Warren (1970, 59–60), and others are clearly right to argue that the Etruscans simply gave their cult statues the attributes of regal power, decking out their gods in man's image rather than the other way around. On significant links between the Roman victor who is king for a day and his vanquished royal foe led in chains, see Östenberg 2003, 131–44, 281–85. Also note G. Stemmler 2003.

appearance in the earliest phase of Rome's history, the spectacle returned frequently: under the Republic multiple celebrations often occurred in a single year, and from 220 to 70 B.C., even taking the relative drought of the Hannibalic War into account, Romans saw triumphs on average once every year and a half.[9] Even when Augustus put an end to triumph debates once and for all by restricting the *ius triumphandi* to himself and members of the imperial family,[10] the celebrations still continued unabated. The institution, functionally if not strictly as old and familiar as the seven hills, lived on under the Empire: Orosius says that 320 triumphs took place between the founding of the city and the reign of Vespasian.[11] Warfare and *triumphi spes* practically formed a hendiadys in the Roman imagination.[12] Then, after lying dormant for centuries, the ritual came to life again with all its powerful symbolism as late as World War II, when Mussolini staged a triumph for himself.

Because of the primordial memories encoded within it, the triumphal ritual always stirred deep resonances from the distant past, and the continuing presence of very old triumphal monuments helped to reinforce that sense of connection across the ages.[13] Not surprisingly, however, as the city of Rome developed and its empire grew over the course of its long history, so both the outward trappings and the political symbolism of the triumph gradually changed as well.[14] Indeed ironically, within the ancestral framework, novelty became a familiar hallmark of triumphs, marking each

9. See Favro 1994, 152. Also appendix B below and the similar calculations by Develin 1978, 436.

10. See Hickson 1991, among others.

11. Oros. 7.9.8.

12. Livy records the following responses from the haruspices during the second century when asked about the omens, should the Republic go to war: against Philip in 200, "et prolationem finium victoriamque et triumphum portendi" ("both the expansion of boundaries with victory and a triumph was foretold," 31.5.7); against Antiochus in 191, "eo bello terminos populi Romani propagari, victoriam ac triumphum ostendi" ("by this war the borders of the Roman people were being extended, victory and a triumph promised," 36.1.3); and again against Perseus in 171, victoriam, triumphum, propagationem < . . . portendi> ("victory, triumph, expansion [*sc.* of boundaries] was foretold," 42.30.9). The formulaic language is suggestive. Harris 1985, 122, cites these passages to support his claims about raw expansionism as a self-conscious Roman aim, but they reveal the close link between conquest and triumph just as well. If anything, in fact, the strength of that latter connection lends credence to Harris's argument, since like the Romans we too take it more or less for granted that victory meant *triumphi spes*.

13. Thus Kuttner 2004, 319, remarks: "Only the most privileged had the right to ancestor masks, but Rome displayed the whole city's ancestral actors, in the form of statues . . . [that] let the modern, living Romans trespass back into time, as far back as the woodland valley of the satyr kings."

14. On the "inherent heterogeneity" of the Roman triumph in its ritual context, see Plattus 1983, passim, but especially 97.

new significant conquest as greater than the last.[15] Because of these various complex strata, modern scholars have repeatedly tried to reconstruct the original form and function of the triumph and the stages of its evolution.[16] The intricacies of their elaborate, often highly speculative arguments lie well outside the bounds of the present discussion.[17] Nor, for that matter, would an accurate account of the early phases effectively solve the problem of what the triumph meant to Romans at a later date.[18] For triumphal pageantry came to encompass many diverse elements, ranging from the ineffably primitive to the glaringly contemporary, from the native and traditional to the imported and exotic—all operative at once somehow, and juxtaposed side by side, challenging the trained eye of the Roman spectator to sort things out and tell the difference. Make no mistake: the triumph played profound, complex, and deliberate tricks with time.[19]

This brings us back to one of the core ideas in Roman aristocratic culture. As we have seen, Polybius describes how family members at élite funerals would don the ancestral *imagines* and sit in an imposing row to hear the *laudatio* of the newly deceased, who would thereby ceremoniously join their ranks.[20] The performative chronicle of *res gestae* through generation after generation of the clan—offices held, enemies defeated, triumphs celebrated—from the earliest ancestors to the present day, was offered by an up-and-coming young man, often at the start of his public career along the same path, thus binding the aspirations of the living to the achievements of the dead. When not in use for the funereal context, the *imagines* would then prominently hang in the atrium of the family's house as tangible reminders of status, values, and expectations for daily life. Aristocrats looked to their forebears and were always symbolically watched over by them in a reciprocally constitutive gaze, which took place more in public than in private and identified members of the family as such to their

15. Cf. Flower 2004b, 339: "The impact of the empire at home was often first felt in the novelties to be seen in the triumphal procession, as each returning general aimed to outdo his predecessors." See also Östenberg 2003, passim.

16. For references, see above, n. 4.

17. Warren 1970, 50, expresses very well the state of radical uncertainty about the primitive triumph: "There is, of course, bound to be a lot of conjecture in such an enquiry, in a period of history where we are almost literally moving in the dark."

18. Marshall 1984, 126, reasons that "significance of any social institution cannot be restricted entirely to its earliest beginnings and must accordingly be traced through time as an evolving function of the historical life of the parent society." Cf. similar comments by Coarelli 1988, 366; Nicolet 1980, 352; Warren 1970, 49.

19. Thus Östenberg 2003, 272, observes that the twofold division between spoils (i.e., inanimate objects) and captives (i.e., living beings) endured for centuries, allowing the Romans to categorize items of conquest and thus "to embrace the new within the frames of the well known."

20. Polyb. 6.53.1–54.2. For references to modern scholarship, see above, p. 132 n. 18.

fellow citizens. In much the same mysterious way, on a full-community scale, each new triumph, both in the iconic person of the *triumphator* and in the reenactment of the familiar ritual procession and sacrifice, brought the city's glorious present into dynamic, living rapport with its glorious and continually revivified past.[21]

Triumphal imagery derived much of its power from its uncanny ability to transcend time while also existing inside it; exemplarity in action, it marked the ephemeral present moment in the most dramatic way possible with an imprint of the eternal.[22] Centuries' worth of triumphal monuments lined the processional route on all sides, so that the *triumphator* not only followed in his predecessors' footsteps but actually performed under their watchful eyes, as well as before the masses of living spectators who saw him in continuity with them, and likewise saw themselves in continuity with the similar crowds who had gathered before and would gather again for triumphs past and future. In the usual course of events, after completing the ritual, this commander would add his own manubial contribution to the fabric of the city, knowing that he would then symbolically participate in future triumphs, just as an aristocrat could count on his *imago* living on after him, alongside his illustrious forebears, as long as his family and its ritual practice endured.[23] Livy and his contemporaries would have had a heightened awareness of the temporal dimension too, because like civic *imagines,* the statues and *elogia* in the Forum Augustum famously linked the achievements of the *Princeps* and his family to the legendary heroes of Rome and thereby served as a communal atrium for the whole *civitas Romana,* with Augustus permanently enshrined as *paterfamilias.* The conceptual framework of this quintessentially programmatic monument obviously has deep organic roots in the self-fashioning of *nobiles* throughout the centuries, even while it also represents a newly concerted effort to rebuild Roman identity in the aftermath of civil war. Livy's history of the Republic presents a different catalogue of heroes from the Augustan Forum but belongs to the same anxiously nostalgic context.[24]

21. On the connection between funerals and triumphs, see App. *Mith.* 17.117 (portraits substituted for people missing from triumphal processions), and cf. Bodel 1999; Flower 1996; Rüpke 2006b; Walter 2004, especially 89–112.

22. The triumph demands a viewpoint somewhat akin to the synchronic mode of perception peculiar to the fictional inhabitants of the planet Tralfamador in Kurt Vonnegut's *Slaughterhouse Five,* who see human beings as embodiments of their whole lifespans all at once: "great millipedes—with babies' legs at one end and old people's legs at the other" (Vonnegut 1968, 87).

23. Cf. Favro 1994, 159; Kuttner 2004, 316 (on aristocratic self-fashioning); Plattus 1983, 97.

24. On Augustus as father of Rome, see Favro 1992, closely followed by Favro 1996, 123–28. On the *elogia* from the Forum Augusti, see Chaplin 2000, 168–96, as well as Luce 1990. Much has been made of the discrepancies that Luce identifies between Augustus's catalogue of heroes and Livy's (e.g., Feldherr 1997b, 137 n. 5; and 1998, 19 n. 52, 36 n. 105; Jaeger 1997, 183 n. 13;

Mapping Imperium: Triumphs and Space

On the day of a triumph, the participants would muster in and around the southeastern Campus Martius, where the ceremonial distribution of booty to the soldiers would usually take place. From there the procession would wend its way through the streets of the city, with the *triumphator* in his four-horse chariot right in the middle, preceded by the display of booty and captives from foreign parts and followed by the loyal Roman army.[25] The path circled the Palatine hill in the primordial amburbial route that it shared with periodic rituals such as the Lupercalia and *lustratio*. By retracing the sacred perimeter carved out with a bronze plow by Romulus himself long ago, it symbolically embraced the whole city, culminating in the steep climb up to the central shrine on top of the Capitolium, where the *triumphator* would make his thanksgiving sacrifice of a white bull to Jupiter Optimus Maximus.[26] Yet although every triumph had to incorporate the same three basic components in the proper order—Campus Martius, Palatine, Capitol—no two followed exactly the same path, allowing each *triumphator* a measure of creative autonomy in directing the procession past monuments and vistas of his own choosing, such as those built by members of his family or by other favorite exemplary predecessors with whom he particularly wanted to identify himself, or rather wanted people to identify him. As a result, "the improvised street formed by the triumphal parade remained always new and vital, redefined periodically with each ceremonial event," even while it also conformed to the recognizable sacred topography of the city.[27]

Triumphs as spectacle sought to compel the civic imagination through the charismatic and transformative use of public space in front of an audience. They bound the Roman community together as such by taking place quite literally in the midst of it.[28] From the most ancient times the city of

Kraus 1994, 9 and n. 36), and yet it is important to bear in mind that the search for historical exempla goes on in both places, equally prompted by the crisis of the Civil Wars. I wholeheartedly agree with Feldherr 1998, 36 n. 105, that "the Forum can provide an analogy for the type of historical representation to which Livy's text aspires."

25. On the significance of this rigid order of placement, see Östenberg 2003, 264–66.

26. On the triumphal route generally, see Favro 1994, passim, especially 153–57. For maps and diagrams, see Favro 1994, 151; Hölkeskamp 2006, 484 (probably the best illustration); Künzl 1988, 15; Plattus 1983, 98. For specific monuments and other points of interest along the route, particularly as it made its way through the uncertain topography of the Forum Boarium, see Coarelli 1988, 363–414. His remarks about the meaning of *amburbium* at 388 are particularly helpful. Cf. Hölkeskamp 2006, 485.

27. Favro 1994, 157. Cf. Hölkeskamp 2001; and 2006, 487; Plattus 1983, 111.

28. Cf. Flower 2004b, 338: "Roman culture took on its full value in its own context, and that context was provided by the topography of the city of Rome itself." Also note Favro 1994, 160: "After the last trumpet had sounded, residents . . . carried home a sense of security tangibly evidenced by the active presence of their impressive army and by the manifest power of the place where they lived."

Rome enjoyed the protection of its sacred boundary, the *pomerium*.[29] A charmed augural circle concretely set everything within it apart from what lay outside, allowing the Romans to articulate in their religious practice between center and periphery, *urbs* and *ager, domi* and *militiae*.[30] The triumph was intimately connected with this threshold. Commanders set out from Rome crossing from *domi* to *militiae* and wielding the twin powers of *auspicium* and *imperium*, which between them constituted a quasi-magical authorization to test the will of the civic gods for the carrying out of public business and to lead the Roman army into battle in the field as the official representative and anointed champion of the whole SPQR.[31] Because of the strict taboo (*nefas*) forbidding the exercise of military command within the bounds of the city proper, as already noted, the senate always met outside the *pomerium* to hear triumph requests from victorious generals, often in the Temple of Bellona or another shrine nearby.[32] Triumphal processions traditionally began by solemnly crossing the *pomerium* into Rome through the Porta Triumphalis, "a real gate into an ideal, or at least ritually idealized city."[33] Consistent synecdoche in formulaic language actually marks this passage into the city—not, as one might expect, the crowning sacrifice

29. The line traced by the *pomerium* at any given time in Roman history bore a close but not necessarily identical relation to the circuit of stone fortification walls. See Coarelli 1988, 386. The many technicalities simply cannot concern us here. For ancient testimonia on the meaning of the word *pomerium* (probably derived from *murus,* as in *postmoerium*), see Varro *LL* 5.43, 1.44.3–5; Gell. 13.14.1–3. The original circuit was extended several times, first by Servius Tullius, and apparently not again until Sulla. On the early phases, see Magdelain 1976, cited helpfully by Coarelli 1988, 385–88. For later developments, see Boatwright 1984 and 1986; L. Richardson 1992, s.v. "Pomerium."

30. Gellius defines the *pomerium* as the "locus . . . qui facit finem urbani auspicii" ("place . . . that marks the boundary of the urban auspices," 13.14.1). On *urbs* vs. *ager* ("city" vs. "country"), see, e.g., Val. Max. 2.9.3; Amm. Marc. 14.6.22. The distinction between *domi* and *militiae* is of course ubiquitous: e.g., Ter. *Ad.* 495; Livy 2.58.4, 5.12.4, 7.19.5, 24.18.1; Vell. Pat. 1.13.3; Quint. 12.11.23; Val. Max. 9.2.2. For explicit statements regarding the *pomerium* as dividing line between *imperium domi* and *imperium militiae,* see Cic. *Rep.* 1.63; *Leg.* 3.6, 3.3.8; *Nat. D.* 2.

31. Develin 1977, 61, writes that "the magistrate was given power equal to that of the state itself, so that in theory he was the *populus Romanus,* the city incarnate outside the city opposing the enemies of the city." This passage refers to the *auspicia populi Romani,* but cf. Develin 1985, 18, characterizing a Roman general in the field as "a surrogate of the people, the conceptual equivalent of the state with full *imperium*." Also see Versnel 1970, 319–55 (on the *lex curiata de imperio*).

32. On meeting places of the Roman senate outside the *pomerium* specifically for triumph debates, see Bonnefond-Coudry 1989, 137–60, and Coarelli 1988, 395–99, both cited above, p. 36 n. 11.

33. So Plattus 1983, 102. A vast literature surrounds the Porta Triumphalis as a monument, if indeed it was a fixed monument and not a temporary gate set up for each new triumph in turn. For recent treatments, see Brennan 2004, 42; Coarelli 1988, 363–414 (a revision of his earlier arguments from Coarelli 1968); Favro 1994, 153; Kleiner 1989, 201–4; Künzl 1988, 30–44; L. Richardson 1992, 301; Versnel 1970, 132–63.

to Jupiter Optimus Maximus—as the defining moment in the ritual: *triumphans urbem inire* or *invehi,* or *triumphans in urbem regredi* or *redire.*[34]

Partly on the basis of these formulas, and also drawing on a vast store of comparative material from Egypt, Babylonia, and Greece, Henk Versnel compellingly argues that the triumph was in essence an entrance ritual, formally ushering the talismanic *dynamis* of the victorious general across the sacred threshold of the *pomerium* into the city and effectively channeling that positive energy to ensure continued safety and prosperity for all Rome.[35] The *pomerium* taboo had after all one notable exception: by vote of the people a *triumphator* could bear *imperium militiae* within the city limits on the day of his triumph (26.21.5, 45.35.4; cf. 8.26.7). Triumphal ritual perfectly mirrored the *profectio imperatoris,* as we have repeatedly seen, because the power of an *imperator* emanated from the center, precisely so that he could take it out across the sacred boundary to the periphery, use it well in his *provincia* on behalf of the whole SPQR, and then return to the point of origin on the day of his triumph to lay down his arms, proudly and patriotically vouchsafing the glorious benefits of his *res gestae,* both material and symbolic, for the community that had sent him out as its champion in the first place.[36] With the help of the gods and in the name of the Republic, he triumphed *imperio auspicio felicitate ductu,* quite literally mapping his success onto the urban landscape at the center and fulcrum of the Roman world.[37]

The concept of *imperium Romanum* gradually carried over from the raw

34. For the variety of expressions, see 1.38.3, 2.7.4, 2.16.6, 2.20.13, 3.24.8, 3.29.4, 4.10.7, 4.20.2, 4.29.4, 5.28.1, 5.49.7, 6.4.1, 7.13.10, 8.37.1, 9.40.20, 9.43.22, 10.1.9, 10.5.13, 26.21.2, 28.9.7, 31.20.3, 31.47.7, 34.52.2, 35.8.9, 36.39.5, 37.46.2, 38.44.10, 38.51.14, 40.43.6, 41.28.9, 45.38.2. Livy also uses *triumphans in Capitolium ascendere* at 38.48.16 and 42.49.6. Versnel 1970, 163, remarks: "If the passage through the Porta Triumphalis were nothing but a lustration-ritual"—that is, a rite of purification from the miasma of war—"it would be difficult to understand why so much stress was laid on the entry into the town." See also Phillips 1974a and 1974b; Plattus 1983.

35. In the closing pages of his book Versnel 1970, 371–97, neatly sums up his own conclusions. On the ritual homecoming (εἰσήλασις) of victorious athletes in the Greek world (one of Versnel's main parallels), see also Kurke 1993, especially 156 n. 7, where she cites Versnel.

36. Plattus 1983, 103, emphasizes a cycle that formed "an organic and apparently intransitive whole: beginning on the Capitol with the assumption of the *imperium militiae,* exercising the command successfully, returning to and entering the city with that power intact, displaying its fruits, and finally relinquishing the *imperium* and dedicating the spoils upon return to the Capitol." Cf. Feldherr 1998, 10–11. Also cf. Develin 1977, 58, on the importance of the *pomerium.*

37. Note Plattus 1983, 99, on the reciprocity of the ritual: "The triumph . . . represented a double responsibility—owed by the city to the victor and by the victor to his urban sponsor. It was . . . a two-edged sword. If the *triumphator* seemed to perpetuate a ritual conquest of the city, he was also in turn *captured* by the city, which re-confirmed, and at the same time enhanced, its own identity and mythic stock of good fortune."

power of legions and their commanders—its original meaning—to denote also the territory they controlled, which we still call the Roman Empire. Under the Republic, limited terms of office and designated *provinciae* set boundaries for *imperium* in both time and space. So the two dimensions are oddly intertwined wherever *imperium* is concerned, and thus the ritual of the triumph proclaimed to participants and spectators alike, *You are here, right where you belong,* within both sets of coordinates. Recurring spectacles led to the construction of many manubial buildings along the triumph route, which meant that the pattern of return to the origin continually reinforced itself. Through repeated cycles of ephemeral ritual and permanent commemoration, Romans came to value triumphs as occasions to celebrate their civic pride and, conversely, to identify their city as the home of conquerors, the privileged locus where triumphs took place. Indeed the fact that triumphs always tied the periphery back to the center in the same familiar, predictable way made the whole process of imperial expansion both real and comprehensible to the city's inhabitants, enabling them to assimilate change and maintain, renew, and reformulate their sense of Roman identity.[38] This understanding led to the development of the triumphal arch as an unmistakably Roman architectural form, utterly meaningless apart from an awareness of the dynamic relationship that triumphs engendered between spectacle and spectator in a civic space.[39]

Other monuments followed suit, as exemplified by Livy's description of the *tabula* that Ti. Sempronius Gracchus set up in 174 inscribed with his *res gestae* in the Temple of Mater Matuta after two triumphs in rapid succession from Spain and again from Sardinia (41.28.8–10).[40] Through proper exercise of the military authority vested in him, Gracchus had led his army to victory and brought a key piece of conquered territory back under Roman control, a perfect embodiment of *imperium Romanum* in both its meanings. By putting this object on permanent display as a dedication

38. So Kuttner 2004, 320: "The intense monumentalization of the republican city over time shows how the community kept its bearings as Roman trade and conquest spread outward, reaching almost unimaginable distances." On reciprocities in the triumph between center and periphery, Roman self and foreign Other, see also Östenberg 2003.

39. Thus Plattus 1983, 110: "As the ever more elaborately 'triumphal' arches proliferated along the processional route, they reflected back to each successive pageant the accumulated tradition of the ritual and the reiterated diagram of the ritually established relationship between the act of entry (as embodied in the form of the arch), the display of spoils (as depicted in the decorative iconography), and the urban apotheosis of the *triumphator,* monumentally mounted in his *quadriga* atop the arch."

40. Part of the inscription from Gracchus's tabula was cited above, p. 25 n. 2, because it uniquely preserves the entire fourfold triumphal formula (40.52.5: "auspicio imperio felicitate ductuque eius"). On the dedication itself, see further Galli 1987–88; Östenberg 2003, 189–95.

to Jupiter, Gracchus could ensure that his triumph would be continually reenacted every time anyone paused to read the words. Moreover, Livy goes on to say that the plaque itself took the shape of the island of Sardinia and bore depictions of battles ("simulacra pugnarum") alongside the narrative within the very frame or outline of the *provincia* where the memorable deeds took place. Visually striking, the *tabula* traced Gracchus's accomplishments to a recognizable, significant Mediterranean location. The composite of word and image, verbal and nonverbal texts, created a complex, multilayered representation of an exemplary performance, demonstrating that Gracchus's *res gestae* and his place in the Roman world, literally and figuratively, were one and the same.

Senate, Magistrates and People: Triumphs and the SPQR

We have repeatedly witnessed the operation of the twin economies, symbolic and material, in the ostentatious spectacle that was the Roman triumph. As one recent author has put it: "Inevitably, conquest was confiscation."[41] During the period covered by Books 21–45 of Livy's history, especially from campaigns in the East came literally tons of gold, silver, art objects, weaponry, and even miniature symbolic images (*simulacra*) of captured towns, all of which were duly marched on display through the streets of the city. With the greater economy of scale in the Late Republic and of course all the more under the Empire, triumphs paraded an astonishing variety of captured foreign stuff before the eyes of the eager spectators: not only material things either, weapons and booty, but also exotic animals and even trees, plus models of cities, nations, and rivers, lively tableaux vivants of battle scenes, and so on.[42] *In contione,* usually before the triumph, commanders would ceremoniously distribute a share of the spoil to their loyal troops, according to rank: so much to the infantry, twice that to the centurions, three times to the cavalry, with special prizes to single out acts of particular valor. The bulk of the money was then deposited into the public treasury, enriching the common-wealth (*res publica*) in the literal, material sense. At the discretion of the *patres* public funds were used to pay *supplicationes* and for triumphal processions, which included a sacrifice and meat feast.[43] Further, if the *imperator* had vowed a temple on the eve of his great victory, then money would be drawn back out of the treasury for that as well, again by a senate decree, allowing him to fulfill his vow—or one of

41. Östenberg 2003, 285.

42. The table of contents in Östenberg 2003, with its exhaustive catalogue of all the various objects and persons put on display in Roman triumphs, reads just like the familiar extended ekphrasis so beloved of ancient authors, including Livy.

43. On the triumphal feast, see D'Arms 1999; Favro 1994, 158–59; Kajava 1998.

his descendants, or perhaps even someone unrelated to him, if the *patres* saw fit. The dedication of manubial temples, like the conduct of military campaigns, called upon individuals to act as agents of the community at large.[44]

Amid all the complex interactions between the magistrates, senate, and people of Rome under the Republic, triumphs served to broadcast, from the top down, a self-image fashioned for the entire commonwealth specifically by the élite.[45] From the third century onward, that meant the patricio-plebeian senatorial aristocracy, made up of officeholders and priests both past and present, a group whose identity was always in flux but who sought to portray themselves as forever firmly in control.[46] Although at any given time a relatively small cluster of names seem to have dominated the political scene, nonetheless the boundaries between those inside the senatorial group and those outside it proved notoriously permeable, allowing a steady trickle of *novi homines* from previously unknown families to enter the ranks here and there. This has frustrated modern prosopographers seeking to establish a strict genealogy of power. A functional tautology marks the only truly reliable way to define the *nobiles* as a social group, despite the exasperating circularity of it all: "Whoever played a political role belonged to the aristocracy, and whoever belonged to the aristocracy played a political role."[47] No simple system of privilege based on birth or primogeniture existed in Rome. Each successive generation of so-called aristocrats needed to earn their right to social and political privilege all over again by seeking election to public office. Who one's father was mattered a great deal—hence the proud patronymics in the Fasti, the Scipionic epitaphs,

44. On manubial temples, see Orlin 1997, followed by Orlin 2000 with a particularly intriguing case study.

45. Östenberg 2003, especially 1–15 (the introduction to methods and theory), seems to equate any emphasis on the political dimension of triumphs with the reductionist view that nothing matters except the *triumphator*. Any talk of politics once dismissed, however, the spectacle is divorced from its civic context, and the author is at pains to elucidate how the complex power structures at work in Rome, especially under the Republic, but also as they evolved under the Empire. As a result, while claiming to address the diversity and complexity of the interaction between triumphs and the Roman audience, not to mention the changes in the ritual over time, the argument continually shies away from the underlying social and political developments. Yet how else can one try to make sense of the complexities involved? The nature of the subject demands a balanced synthesis among all these various elements.

46. On the formula *patres et conscripti*, see Mitchell 1990, especially 25–26 and 108–16; on the composition of the élite at different times, see among others Afzelius 1945; Briscoe 1982; Broughton 1991; Burckhardt 1990; Hölkeskamp 1987, passim; Mouritsen 1990; and of course also Syme 1939.

47. Thus the famous chiastic formula of Meier 1966, 47: "Wer Politik trieb, gehörte zum Adel, und wer zum Adel gehörte, trieb Politik." The same is cited and translated by Millar 1998, 4–5 n. 6: "Whoever participated in politics belonged to the nobility, and whoever belonged to the nobility participated in politics." Also cf. Hölkeskamp 1987, 248.

and elsewhere—but although lineage certainly did count as an asset, especially when properly presented, it still held no guarantees.[48] Therefore, despite the various overlapping hierarchies imposed on the citizenry by the census, by membership in tribes, *curiae,* and centuries, and by rank in the military, the social and political structures of the SPQR remained inherently flexible to a great degree, and as a result the status both of individual aristocrats and of the aristocracy as such was always open to redefinition and to challenge from below.[49]

The Roman Republic constituted not a rigid system but a dynamic and delicate balancing act between various elements that could work together but could also readily realign themselves and were continually tugging and pulling at each other. Members of the élite engaged in a dialogue with the *populus Romanus* at every stage in the political process.[50] Magistrates became magistrates to begin with only by popular vote, and when successful commanders came home in search of triumphs, the tribunes and at times even the assembly could countermand the *consensus patrum,* as we saw in chapter 1. Because only officeholders could triumph and the senate had made itself the acknowledged authority to dispense civic honors, the *nobiles* together held an effective monopoly between them over both the right to triumph and the process of deciding who among themselves had earned that right. It was very much in their interest, individually and collectively, to hang onto that monopoly and to provide a continual display, because it helped them to shore up their position at the top echelon in the social pyramid. Indeed the very word *nobilis* in Latin derives from the idea of being well known or conspicuous.[51]

Triumphs and the elaborate discursive techniques that surrounded them formed only a part, albeit a crucial one, in a broad repertoire of self-promotional strategies adopted by the Roman élite, which were all aimed at the same basic goal. In their campaigns for office, in their political speeches, in their daily appearances in the Forum, surrounded by a retinue of clients and admirers, in the *elogia* at their funerals, and finally in the monuments and *imagines* through which they lived on after their deaths, Roman aristocrats strove to keep their *res gestae* always in the public eye.[52] The fierceness of triumph debates reflects the prevailing competitive

48. Millar 1998 repeatedly stresses this point. See also Hopkins and Burton 1983; and the remarks of Flower 1996, 60–90.

49. Cf. David 2000, 36 (my translation): "They were inscribing into the collective memory the important facts of their lineage, lending belief to the notion that the destiny of the community was linked to that of the descendants of those who had made it so great in the past."

50. Hence North 1990b, 285: "The popular will of the Roman people found expression in the context, and only in the context, of divisions within the oligarchy." Also cf. Flower 2004b, 335.

51. Flower 2004b, 324.

ethos among them and the extent to which they zealously maneuvered to maintain a balance of status within their own ranks. Yet the triumphs that they so piously celebrated and so vociferously argued over among themselves would have meant nothing to them without the involvement of the whole Roman people, to whom in so many ways the élite owed their status.[53] Only rarely does Livy interrupt his lovingly detailed accounts of the objects carried in various triumphs to comment on what the spectators were doing. In his focus on the spectacle itself, he takes the observers themselves almost entirely for granted.[54] Nevertheless, the presence of the Roman people, collectively, always lies just below the surface of the historian's triumphal ekphrasis, giving coherence, substance, and weight to all the pomp and circumstance, which would be meaningless otherwise. For the center of a spectacle, after all, can manifest itself as center only by dint of the circle around it. Public displays demand an audience—and the bigger, the better.

The triumph was "a public display of the first order: the City admiring itself in its victorious army, and the conqueror offering himself to be admired."[55] Or as another study has recently phrased it:[56]

> The triumphal parade was sufficiently extraordinary to constitute a "special event"—transitory, to be sure, but so well defined institutionally that it provided all Romans with the opportunity to affirm their cohesiveness and their superiority over "others" through the agency of the triumphator. Thus, as both a unifying structure and one dominated by a resplendent protagonist, the triumphal procession established an ideologically significant distinction between a single, hegemonic presence and his many spectating subjects.

Throngs of people from every stratum of Roman society and foreign visitors as well came out to see the show, lining the grassy slopes along the parade route where they could, or sitting on balconies with a view, or pack-

52. The comment of David 2000, 36 (as cited above, n. 49) is also pertinent here.

53. Cf. Parker 1999, 176, on the crowd who "had the right of life and death over the gladiators competing with each other in the arena . . . [and] also might help decide the fate of the nobles who were competing with each other in a different arena."

54. Oddly enough, the two most obvious exceptions to Livy's usual reticence about the spectators at victory celebrations in Books 31–45 belong to the same episode: the triumph of L. Furius Purpureo in 200. At 31.49.3, Livy describes how Furius's triumph looked ("apparebat"), yet strikingly does nothing to identify the observers. Shortly thereafter, Furius's main opponent says that soldiers were expected to take part in the triumph of their commander "ut testes rerum gestarum eius cui tantus honos haberetur populus Romanus videret" ("so that the Roman people might see witnesses to the *res gestae* of the man to whom so great an honor was being paid," 31.49.10).

55. Nicolet 1980, 353.

56. Brilliant 1999, 222. Cf. Flower 2004b, 323, with reference to "a coherent system [of spectacles], representing the Roman community and its place in the world through display and performance within the space of the city itself."

ing themselves into the theaters, circuses, and special wooden bleachers (*tribuni*) put up for the purpose in the Forum and elsewhere.[57] As Juvenal says about a different spectacle: "Today the circus captures all of Rome."[58] Clearly the stakes could not be much higher for those concerned with fashioning and propagating their public image. Individual triumphs showcased the *res gestae* of individual aristocrats on behalf of the Republic, and the succession of triumphs year after year served as a continual reminder of the benefits bestowed on Rome and all its citizens by the members of its élite as such. These signals helped to bolster the continuation of the sociopolitical status quo.[59]

To a degree, it is easier to consider how the triumph made its meaning felt as a performative and symbolic act than to reconstruct precisely what it meant, the latter being subject to endless fragmentation and permutation depending on the moment and one's precise point of view.[60] We cannot ever hope to conjure up the full range of individual responses felt by so many throngs of diverse viewers and participants.[61] Yet the triumphal procession exercised a powerful universalizing logic over everyone who came into contact with it—those who took part in the parade as well as those who came out to watch it—because it conspicuously called attention to itself as something that belonged to the city (and by extension, to the Roman Empire) as a whole.[62] "Ritual participation," as one recent author has written, "shaped [a] sense of oneness . . . in the pronounced exhibition of the defeated as other."[63] People stood in mingled shades of awe and wonder as the procession made its loud and colorful yet stately progress through the streets, past shopkeepers, merchants, and farmers, local residents, Italian visitors, and foreigners, *matronae*, children, and slaves.[64] Somewhere in the spectacle, regardless of who they were, both Romans

57. Künzl 1988, 69–72. Rüpke 2004, 184, remarks: "The splendor and the material rewards of watching a triumph must . . . have produced a huge number of spectators." Indeed Ehlers 1939, 502, estimates that a typical audience for triumphs under the Republic was probably on the order of 300,000–400,000 people. Note Plut. *Aem.* 32.2, and Jos. *BJ* 7.131.

58. Juv. 11.197: "Totam hodie Romam circus capit."

59. Thus most notably Hölkeskamp 1987 (especially 114–203) and 1993.

60. On the reactions of people from different social backgrounds to the same urban environment, see Favro 1996, especially 6–11.

61. So Beard 2003, 28, refers to "the noisy, messy, probably rowdy and almost entirely irrecoverable events of the ceremony 'as it really happened.'" This same passage is quoted more than once by Östenberg 2003, 6, 11.

62. Images of carvings and paintings that communicate this idea appear most notably in Brilliant 1999 and Plattus 1983.

63. Östenberg 2003, 266.

64. On the diversity of the crowd, see Favro 1994, 151, 153–54, 162 n.13; Künzl 1988, 71. Also note Brilliant 1999, 222, on the triumph's appeal to multiple senses (especially sight and hearing).

and non-Romans alike saw themselves mirrored in complex relation to the whole *res publica Romana* and its various constituents.[65] Ancient literary and visual representations of triumphs are typically crafted to have the same or a similar effect on readers, viewers, or both.[66]

The *triumphator* himself appeared right at the center of the procession. The experience of gazing down from his chariot at the assembled crowd, while surveying the train of spoils and captives in front of him and the ordered ranks of his army behind, was the pinnacle of honor and glory to which every Roman aristocrat aspired. Because of his "elaborate makeup, costume, and props . . . [the figure of the *triumphator*] has seemed to some to be the god Jupiter, to others a king-for-a-day based on an Etruscan model, and finally to others a gory warrior returning from battle steeped in blood and spoils."[67] In a sense he was all three at once. Not without reason did the slave holding a victory wreath over his head whisper in his ear throughout the procession to remind him of his mortality.[68] His family and clientèle basked in his reflected glory. Senators and other civic leaders also took a proprietary interest. The army cried *Io triumpe!* and sang songs and made jokes expressive of manly solidarity with their commander.[69] We have already heard an eloquent description of their stirring feelings above in chapter 14 from the speech of the ranking senator Servilius on behalf of L. Aemilius Paullus in 167 (45.38.11–13). Roman citizens among the spectators knew that the victory of the army belonged to them too, with all its attendant benefits (*dynamis*). It is easy to imagine them swelling with pride, satisfaction, and gratitude while their applause and shouts mingled with the *carmina* of the army, adding to the general din.[70] The enemy hostages and prisoners of war, meanwhile, endured an almost unimaginable

65. Cf. David 2000, 28 (my translation): "Each citizen had a place to hold and a role to play: some spoke while others listened; enthusiasm followed respectful silence according to forms that manifested a clinging to that point necessary for civic equilibrium, whose absence would have been a sign of crisis and herald of conflict."

66. We have already seen many examples in Livy. On triumphal art and architecture, and its deliberate manipulation of the intended audience, see among others Brilliant 1999; Holliday 1997; Kuttner 1999 and 2004; Plattus 1983.

67. So Plattus 1983, 103.

68. For the whispered words of the slave, see Tert. *Apol.* 33.4: "respice post te, hominem te memento" ("Look behind you; remember that you are a man"); cf. Zonar. 7.21. Note Barton 2001, 241: "The triumph, like all ceremonies that brought one extreme attention, shamed even as it honored." Also see Favro 1994, 154, 161 n.12; Köves-Zulauf 1998.

69. On the *carmina* sung by the soldiers in a triumph, see 3.29.5, 4.20.2 (Camillus equated with Romulus), 7.10.13, 10.26.11, 28.9.18 (Nero and Salinator), 39.7.3, 45.43.8; Varro *LL* 6.68; Suet. *Iul.* 51. Also note the interpretive comments of Corbeill (1996, 68, 87 n. 95, 204–5) linking the Roman impulse toward public insult and mockery to anxieties about too much success.

70. Cf. Brilliant 1999, 225, on mass psychology.

agony of shame and humiliation as they marched toward their execution. Cleopatra was only the most famous to commit suicide rather than face the jeering mob.[71] The power of the spectacle could be overwhelming. Any noncitizens or foreigners in the crowd were forcibly compelled to submit themselves to the power of Rome and to admire it in all its awesome strength.[72]

No matter who you were, in other words, whether or not you could read and write or would ever run for public office, the sights and sounds of the Roman triumph provoked a visceral, emotional reaction.[73] The spectacle was designed to make itself memorable.[74] The social and political ramifications of the reciprocal gaze between center and periphery correspond fully and resonate deeply with the way in which triumphal ritual inscribed itself into the urban landscape: to adapt another of Geertz's emblematic phrases, the triumph was "a story that [the Romans told] themselves about themselves."[75] Indeed, when Livy decides to add elaborative detail of reactions in the city to his account of bringing the story of victory home prior to a triumph, as we saw especially with the Metaurus campaign and the battle of Pydna, he breaks the community down into the same various iconic constituencies who would gather to watch the final spectacle: magistrates, senators, ordinary citizens, women and children. These are the deep structures through which the historian imagines civic and political life under the Republic. The annually recurring rituals of officeholding and triumphs functioned as one unbroken cycle, continually reformulating a concept of Rome's civic and imperial identity and reproducing it over and over again for all to see.[76]

71. On Cleopatra's suicide by snakebite, see Plut. *Ant.* 86. An Egyptian cobra was probably the snake in question: see Herodotus 4.191. On the enormous role played by Cleopatra in Octavian's triumph nonetheless, see Östenberg 2003, 143–44 and nn.; cf. Green 1990, 679–82.

72. Thus Östenberg 2003, passim. Also cf. Brilliant 1999, 222: "triumphators did not conceal the acts of violence that had laid the foundations of victory, but rather sublimated them to the ceremonial display . . . for all to see and remember."

73. Among others Bergmann 1999, 10, stresses the importance of nonverbal communication through spectacle in illiterate and semiliterate societies.

74. Many passages from Latin authors in both poetry and prose testify to the power of the triumph over the Roman imagination. In addition to those already cited, note in particular Mart. 7.6.7–8, Prop. 3.4.11–22, Pliny *Pan.* 22–23, Ov. *Tr.* 4.2, Cic. *Pis.* 60. Also cf. Brilliant 1999, 221, with reference to "the transcendent triumphator, the cynosure of all eyes."

75. Geertz 1973, 448. Also note Kuttner 2004, 312–13: "Triumphal paintings often mirrored the citizen soldiery back to itself . . . Roman historical art is overwhelmingly an art about crowd scenes and participatory rituals, intended to energize participatory looking by the living crowd."

76. Cf. Plattus 1983, 104.

Pax Deum: Triumphs and the Cosmic Order

Secular displays may of course manipulate time, space, and civic identity to the mutual advantage of both ruler and subjects; but the triumph gained an added measure of solemnity and power from the fact that it had always been and would always remain fundamentally a religious ritual, an act of devotion and thanksgiving offered by the community to the gods who protected the city *domi* and manifested their good will *militiae* by giving courage, strength, and victory—in a word *felicitas*—to Roman armies. As we saw above in chapter 14 from the peroration to Servilius's speech on behalf of Paullus (45.39), triumphs used the ritual topography of the city of Rome to articulate the human world, the *res publica,* in all its intricate diversity and then weave it into the fabric of the divine and cosmic order. From *profectio* to triumph, from the Capitol to the battlefield and back to the Capitol again, every Roman had a stake in the *pax deum,*[77] and the aristocrats who served as priests in the civic cult took a special role in mediating between the citizens and the gods. Within the framework of the SPQR, as discussed in chapter 1, this sacral responsibility to authorize, fund, and oversee the exercise of religious functions contributed in no small way to the status of the senate as an élite with the vital interests of the whole community at heart: *patrum auctoritas.*[78]

As a spectacle, then, the triumph paid both personal tribute to the victorious commander with his army, who were put on display, and religious homage to the civic gods and specifically to Jupiter Optimus Maximus, who received the offering and sacrifice. Scholars who have worked on the early history of triumphal practice generally envision a secularizing trend, whereby the religious ritual came first, with the political emphasis arising only later, as an outgrowth or devolution of the original.[79] Yet this type of argument can easily go too far. On the one hand, because it took place by definition at the charismatic center of the community, the lavishly conspicuous act of honoring the gods in a triumph could not help but bring honor among his fellow citizens to the *triumphator* personally, at any stage

77. Cf. David 2000, 28.

78. On the senate's predominant role in overseeing Roman state religion under the Republic, see Beard 1990; Mitchell 1990, especially 11–15, 228–29; Orlin 1997 and 2000; also Sziemler 1972.

79. Versnel 1970, 164, comments that under the Republic the pure form of the primordial triumph "changed its character, gradually developing, or perhaps degenerating rather, into a personal homage to the victorious general." The negative tone is striking. Cf. Hölkeskamp 1993, 29, for a less biased assessment: "The archaic character [of the triumph] was supplemented, if not marginalized and eventually replaced, as it were, by a more 'secular' objective: the demonstrative and increasingly lavish celebration of an individual commander, his *virtus, gloria,* and almost divine charisma of victory." See also Ehlers 1939, 495; Warren 1970, 65.

in Rome's historical development. The prestige factor did not suddenly appear out of nowhere during the Middle Republic.[80] Though perhaps underemphasized earlier, it had always been there, and merely came to the fore, gradually but strikingly, in an increasingly volatile political climate of intense aristocratic competition.[81] On the other hand, politics and personality never effaced the religious element altogether either. If the men who triumphed under the Republic gained tremendous stature as a result, they did so not on their own but by virtue of having been chosen to carry out a solemn ancient rite in the sight and on behalf of the whole Roman people. The very fusion of the two domains, then, or more accurately the dynamic tension between them, gave the Republican triumph its unique character.[82]

Keeping in mind both religious and political aspects, we must now carefully distinguish between the four classes of victory celebration in Rome, all generally grouped together under the broad heading "triumphs" but in fact representing different honors on a descending scale: the full triumph, the naval triumph, the *ovatio,* and the triumph *in monte Albano.* Everything said so far applies without qualification only to the full triumph, by far the most common and most prestigious of the four, the culmination of an aristocratic career and the perfect completion of the ritual cycle. The remaining three vary significantly from the paradigm of the full triumph in one degree or another. Naval triumphs were very rare: only three took place in the whole period between 201 and 167, all awarded by the senate to men who had served as praetors in charge of the fleet while a larger campaign fell under someone else's higher command.[83] Details of the ceremony remain obscure. The Rostra that stood in the Forum for centuries after the regular triumph of consul C. Maenius in 338 (8.14.12) and the *columna rostrata* set up in strategic spots after the first official naval triumph by the consul C. Duillius in 260 suggest that the beaks of captured enemy ships may have played a prominent role as trophies of conquest at sea.[84]

80. So Warren 1970, 65, admits that this feature "had been slowly developing but now becomes very clear."

81. Cf. Develin 1985, 213.

82. Thus Warren 1970, 49, writes: "the triumph was, more than other religious festivals, a part of the political life at Rome."

83. The three were L. Aemilius Regillus against Antiochus in 189 (37.58.3), Q. Fabius Labeo from Crete in 188 (37.60.6), and Cn. Octavius against Perseus in 167 (45.42.2; cf. Diod. 31.8.10).

84. Ehlers 1939, 497, flatly remarks (my translation): "on the manner of its institution nothing is known." Also see Östenberg 2003, 45–55. On C. Duillius, who celebrated the first naval triumph after defeating the Carthaginians at Mylae in 260, see Livy *Per.* 17; Val. Max. 3.6.4; Pliny *NH* 34.20; Sil. 6.664; Tac. *Ann.* 2.49. For the *columna rostrata,* see in addition 22.20.1, Quint. 1.7.12, Serv. *ad G.* 3.29. The honorific inscription to Duillius from the *columna*

Judging from the way Livy describes both the debates and the celebrations themselves, the *triumphus navalis* would appear functionally equivalent to a full triumph, more or less, though perhaps a fraction lower in rank as a subsidiary rite.[85]

Dionysius of Halicarnassus calls the *ovatio* ὁ ἐλάττων θρίαμβος ("the lesser triumph"), and Livy pointedly refers to it as a "medius honos" ("middle-grade honor," 39.29.5).[86] As we saw from the discussion in chapter 3 of the unique celebration devised by Nero and Salinator in 207, in the *ovatio* the *imperator* entered the city not in a four-horse chariot but on horseback or even on foot. In place of the *ornatus triumphalis* he wore the more ordinary *toga praetexta,* his head crowned with myrtle rather than laurel leaves. He carried no regal scepter, and the subdued sound of flutes, not blaring trumpets, saluted his progress.[87] But the procession, however modest by comparison, still began by formally crossing the *pomerium:* Livy's formula is *ovans urbem inire* (or *redire,* or *ingredi*).[88] It also followed the same traditional route through the streets of Rome and likewise culminated with a thanksgiving sacrifice to Jupiter Optimus Maximus on the Capitol. In an *ovatio,* therefore, no less than in a full triumph, the ritual cycle was complete and the commander's *imperium* brought to a happy conclusion, albeit without all the trimmings.

The triumph *in monte Albano,* by contrast, took place entirely outside the

---

has survived in an Imperial copy (*ILS* 1.65, *ILLRP* no. 319). See Hölkeskamp 2006, 485–86; Welch 2006c, 3–4 (with reference to Hölscher 1978); also Flower 1996, 159–84, with other references. Elaborate aquatic spectacles commemorating famous naval victories became a noted feature under the Empire, on which see, e.g., Coleman 1993.

85. On the award of naval triumphs, see 37.58.3 ("magno consensu patrum," "by an overwhelming consensus of the *patres*"), 37.60.6 ("causam . . . triumphi navalis impetrandi ab senatu," "the reason for obtaining a naval triumph from the senate"), and most revealing, 45.35.4, describing the award to Octavius in 167 in the same breath with full regular triumphs for Paullus and Anicius: "tribus iis omnibus decretus est ab senatu triumphus" ("a triumph was awarded to all three of these men by the senate"). Livy also designates the celebrations by verbs that might equally apply to a full triumph: "triumphavit" (of the commander) and "translatae sunt" (of the booty) at 37.58.4, and "navalem triumphum egit" at 45.42.2 (for "triumphum egit," see 7.11.9).

86. Dion. Hal. 8.67.10; cf. 5.47.2. Cf. Pliny *NH* 15.19: "minoribus triumphis ovantes."

87. On the *ovatio,* see Rohde 1942, and cf. Ehlers 1939 (on the triumph). Versnel 1970, 166, admits that there are difficulties in sorting out the truly salient features of the two rituals, and then writes as follows: "suffice it to say that the *ovatio* lacks precisely those elements which make the triumph into the triumph." Warren 1970, 51–52, would like to see the lesser, simpler rite as a relic of the pre-Etruscan "proto-Latin" triumph, but her conjectures cannot be proven.

88. For variations on the idiom *ovans urbem inire* or *redire,* see 3.10.4, 4.43.2, 4.53.11 ("urbem ovans introiret"), 7.11.9, 26.21.5, 26.21.6 (where he also uses "ovans praedam intulit"), 31.20.5, 31.20.6, 32.7.4, 39.29.6, 40.16.11, 41.28.3, 41.28.6. For the related idiom *ovans urbem ingredi,* see 5.31.4, 33.27.1, 34.10.4, 34.10.6, 36.21.11, 36.39.2. On formulas for the *ovatio,* see also Phillips 1974a, 270–71.

city limits, without ever crossing the *pomerium,* and thus did not require the same official sanction. Such celebrations could be held "iure consularis imperii" ("by the right of consular *imperium,*" 33.23.3) and "sine publica auctoritate" ("without the authority of the people," 42.21.7). Any *imperator* could mark his victory in this way under his own authority—and at his own expense—if he so desired. It should be self-evident by now, however, that within the overwhelmingly civic ideology of the Roman triumph a private ceremony of this kind simply did not belong to the whole SPQR, as the others did, and thus did not bestow anywhere near the same degree of fame and privilege in the public eye. The Fasti record *ovationes* and triumphs *in monte Albano* right alongside full triumphs, but savvy Roman audiences could tell the difference (cf. 33.23.8).

TRIUMPHS AND TRIUMPH DEBATES

Rich as they were in significance both civic and religious, it is no wonder that triumphs became such coveted prizes for those who competed on the public stage. Yet a victorious Roman general who had cherished hopes of a triumph on his return might find himself turned away or left with one of the lesser honors instead. What made the crucial difference in any given case? The answer, of course, is *existimatio:* before he could triumph, he and his *res gestae* had to be judged worthy by the SPQR through performance, evaluation, and debate.

What this generally meant was that he had to satisfy his peers among the aristocracy, because although the triumphs *sine auctoritate patrum populi iussu* stand as eternal reminders of the fluidity within the political framework and of the power of the democratic element to seize control on occasion, nonetheless by the mid-third century the senate held a firm though not entirely undisputed grip on the *ius triumphandi.* Every triumph request had to go through them, and their decisions, with the acquiescence of the tribunes, were usually regarded as final. If on some occasion they felt for any reason at all that they must deny a full triumph, they could still reward success on a more modest scale by resorting to the *ovatio* as a political compromise. At the next level down, an *imperator* whom they refused altogether could save face with a triumph *in monte Albano* so as not to emerge completely empty-handed. Both his personal status and prestige as an individual and theirs as a body were hanging on the result.

When a commander came before the senate, he set forth the narrative of his victory as evidence that he had lived up to the highest ideals of service to the state—*res (publica) bene ac feliciter gesta*—and submitted himself to the judgment of the *patres.* If no one objected and they all agreed without hesitation, as happened to Scipio Africanus in 201 or T. Quinctius Flamininus in 194 (to choose the most illustrious examples from Livy's history), then the accolades poured over him unimpeded in a torrent of public acclaim, first from his peers and then from the whole Roman people on the day of his triumph.[89] But of course it did not always happen that way, for many of the men who arrived home victorious faced serious opposition to their triumph claims from within the senate. Political rivalries blazed openly between individuals, such as Lepidus and Nobilior. In addition to personal tensions of that sort, the Roman élite as a peer group with a collective consciousness seems to have suffered deep anxieties about elevating any one of their number too quickly or too far above all the others, either because he was perceived as having distinguished himself to such a degree that the honor of a triumph would set him on an exalted plane too far out of reach or because it might debase the coinage in *laus* and *gloria* for them all if they bestowed the highest reward without a qualm on his not-so-stunning victory. Either way, as a counterpoise to the uplifting effect of winning a triumph, the senators could demand that he earn it first by sweating out a challenge.

Viewed as a confrontation between the one and the many, a single performer before the critical audience of his peers as a body, the commander as an individual versus the *patres* altogether, a triumph debate clearly helped to regulate the status of prominent people within the community by keeping personal ambition in check. *Invidia* lay in wait for all those who refused to submit to the higher authority, *ut liceret.* No one man could be allowed to fashion his public identity without regard for the acknowledged interests of the Republic as a whole, and the senate functioned as the official go-between in the enforcement of that vital rule. And even within the ranks of the élite there was more to the story than a single negotiation, however complex and nuanced, between an *imperator* and the senate. For he was not the only one on display, seeking to impress his peers by performing on the political stage. Whenever anyone took some active role in the debate—standing up to lead the opposition or helping to build a consensus in the commander's favor, encouraging others to join a particular side or admonishing them not to pursue a dangerous course, making his presence felt when it came to the final vote or even, at times, pointedly keeping silent—he did so in order to craft his own public persona, playing to his audience all the while in the hope of scoring points for himself. No one escaped the all-seeing eyes of *existimatio.*

Conceptually, it is useful and revealing to divide the discursive process of a triumph debate into two distinct phases or levels, depending on the performers and the audience involved. The first phase, on the floor of the senate, had to do above all with gradations of honor among aristocrats

89. Cf. Cic. *Phil.* 1.29 (cited above, p. 131 and n. 14).

and fostered an emphasis on rules and restrictions that limited access to civic honors; the second, as we have seen, on the broader public stage, negotiated the balance of power between aristocrats collectively and the rest of the commonwealth, which meant a pressing need to keep *laus* and *gloria* always in circulation (see appendix B). The Roman aristocratic ethos effectively grew out of the creative tension between these two overriding concerns, and the shift from the first phase to the second explains the oscillation often observed between internal discord among the *patres* at the start of a triumph debate, calling a commander's *res gestae* into question, and the resounding consensus at the end, which regularly validated his contribution to the Republic after all and led to an award and celebration. Further, the confrontation in front of the assembly in 167, as Livy describes it, demonstrates the potency of a threat to the Roman élite when one of their own was set to triumph and had won the support of his peers, and then ran into difficulties from an unexpected quarter within the social and political hierarchy: immediately galvanized, the senators rushed to the scene en masse and brought out one of their big guns to make the best and most eloquent case on their behalf.

A political structure based on annual commands and provinces normally assigned randomly, by lot, presupposed that all those privileged enough to gain election to the highest civic offices should in fact be functionally interchangeable one for another.[90] Distinctions did exist among them, of course—lest we inadvertently begin to transform the Roman Republic into some imaginary socialist utopia, which it most manifestly was not, even considering only the narrow ranks of the political class as a state unto themselves, not to mention their privileged position overall. Yet by the same token, despite their seeming obsession with status, the fierce competition among the aristocrats did not degenerate into a Hobbesian free-for-all, *bellum omnium contra omnes*—or at least not yet. By the first century the stakes had grown considerably higher, with fewer and fewer Great Men in Rome demanding ever more and more from the Republic that they served, and eventually the whole system tore itself to pieces. Civil war erupted then, but not before. Generations of Romans could still maintain a firm distinction between battlefield and political arena.

With reference to Nobilior's twin *certamina,* where this whole investigation began, we come at last to the role of triumphs and triumph debates in Livy's history. For although a well-recognized doomsday shadow looms over the whole narrative of the *Ab Urbe Condita* from beginning to end, the story would not be worth telling if it did not contain good exempla as well as bad. For a long time the safety valves designed to diffuse tensions and

90. On the ritual allotment of *provinciae* and its effect on the distribution of opportunities, see Rosenstein 1993 and 1995; R. Stewart 1998.

maintain a balance and solidarity among conflicting interests—individual and collective—within the traditional framework of the SPQR actually still worked, and in Books 21–45 Livy shows us those mechanisms in occasionally volatile yet stable operation. It is thus that he seeks to provide desperately needed means of healing for a society traumatized by civil war. The historian constitutes his text as a triumphal monument and the pageant of *res gestae* narrated within it as an ongoing triumphal spectacle, so that his audience can contemplate the heroic men whose character and achievements *domi militiaeque* first made Rome great. His assumption thereby, or at least his prayerful hope, is that the same traditional values will continue to sustain the *res publica* and perhaps even lead to greater things in the future (*Praef.* 9–10).

APPENDIX A

Fasti Liviani

Requests For Triumphs, 218–167 B.C.

The following catalogue of recorded homecomings by victorious Roman military commanders runs from the Second Punic War to the end of extant Livy and is intended as a supplement to the list of celebrations found in the *Fasti Triumphales*.[1] The idea was to chronicle the broad history of triumph requests, as opposed to triumphs per se. In most of these cases, Livy records the request with varying degrees of detail about the debate. He notes some triumphs granted and others denied, as well as *ovationes* and triumphs *in monte Albano*. He occasionally remarks on the conspicuous lack of any request, and sometimes, although he may describe a victory, a *supplicatio*, or both, he makes no mention of a triumph request at all. I have tried to encompass the entire range of possibilities. Each entry below indicates the year of the commander's return to Rome, with his full name, rank at the close of his term of office or *prorogatio*, defeated enemy or theater of conflict, and the end result of the triumph request, plus a reference to the passage or passages in Livy where the debate or celebration (or both) or the lack thereof may be found. As a prosopographical aid, each commander's name is also accompanied by a rank and year in parentheses, which can not only give a general sense of where the events in question fall within the commander's career (in the case of promagistrates a special effort has been made to indicate the nature of the original appointment) but also help to distinguish between different individuals with the same name.

[1] 211: M. Claudius Marcellus (consul 222); proconsul, Sicily; *supplicatio* (26.21.3); both *ovatio* and triumph *in monte Albano* (26.21.1–13)

1. For the relevant entries in the Fasti, see Degrassi 1947, 78–81, 551–56.

[2] 209: Q. Fabius Maximus Verrucossus (consul 233); consul, Tarentum; triumph attested by *elogia* (14, 80) but no reference to triumph in Livy (see 27.20.9) and Fasti not extant

[3] 207: M. Livius Salinator (consul 219); consul, Carthaginians in Italy; *supplicatio* (28.9.9) and triumph (28.9.5–20)

[4] 207: C. Claudius Nero (praetor 212); consul, Carthaginians; *supplicatio* (27.51.8, 28.9.9) and triumph-*ovatio* blend (28.9.5–20)

[5] 206: P. Cornelius Scipio, later Africanus (consul 205); proconsul (*privatus*), Spain; *supplicatio* (27.7.4) but triumph denied (28.38.2–5)

[6] 201: P. Cornelius Scipio Africanus (consul 205); proconsul, Hannibal; *supplicatio* (30.17.3, 40.4) and triumph (30.45), no recorded debate

[7] 200: L. Cornelius Lentulus (consul 201); proconsul (*privatus*), Spain; *ovatio* (31.20)

[8] 200: L. Furius Purpureo (consul 196); praetor, Gaul; *supplicatio* (31.22.2) and triumph (31.48–49.3)

[9] 199: C. Cornelius Cethegus (consul 197); proconsul (*privatus*), Spain; apparently no request made (see 31.49.7)

[10] 199: L. Manlius Acidinus (praetor 210); proconsul (*privatus*), Spain; even *ovatio* denied (32.7.4)

[11] 197: C. Cornelius Cethegus (consul 197); consul, Cisalpine Gaul; *supplicatio* (32.31.6) and triumph (33.22–23)

[12] 197: Q. Minucius Rufus (praetor 200); consul, Cisalpine Gaul; *supplicatio* (32.31.6) and triumph *in monte Albano* (33.22–23)

[13] 196: Cn. Cornelius Blasio (praetor 194); proconsul (*privatus*), Nearer Spain; *ovatio* (33.27.1), arguments not recorded

[14] 196: L. Stertinius (no other office); proconsul (*privatus*), Farther Spain; lack of request recorded (33.27.3)

[15] 196: M. Claudius Marcellus (praetor 198); consul, Cisalpine Gaul; *supplicatio* (33.37.9) and triumph (33.37.10–12), arguments not recorded

[16] 196: L. Furius Purpureo (praetor 200); consul, Cisalpine Gaul; *supplicatio* (33.37.9) but apparently no request made (see 33.37.10)

[17] 195: M. Helvius (praetor 197); proconsul, Farther Spain; *ovatio* (34.10.3–5)

[18] 195: Q. Minucius Thermus (praetor 196); proconsul, Nearer Spain; triumph (34.10.5–7), arguments not recorded

[19] 194: M. Porcius Cato the Elder (consul 195); proconsul, Spain; *supplicatio* (34.21.8, 42.1) and triumph (34.46.2–3), arguments not recorded

[20] 194: T. Quinctius Flamininus (consul 198); proconsul, Macedonia; *supplicatio* (33.24.5, 34.42.1) and triumph (34.52), no real debate

[21] 193: L. Cornelius Merula (praetor 198); consul, Gaul; both *supplicatio* and triumph denied (35.8.3–9)

[22] 191: M. Fulvius Nobilior (praetor 193); propraetor, Farther Spain; *ovatio* (36.21.10–11), arguments not recorded

[23] 191: P. Cornelius Scipio Nasica (praetor 194); consul, Italy; *supplicatio* (36.38.7) and triumph (36.39.5–40.14)

[24] 190: Q. Minucius Thermus (consul 193); proconsul, Ligures; triumph denied (37.46.1–2)

[25] 190: M'. Acilius Glabrio (consul 191); proconsul, Graecia; *supplicatio* (36.21.4–11) and triumph (37.46.1–6), subsequent trial for misappropriation of booty (37.57.9–58.1)

[26] 189: L. Aemilius Paullus (praetor 191); propraetor, Farther Spain; *supplicatio* (37.58.5) but apparently no request made (see 37.57.5–6)

[27] 189: L. Aemilius Regillus (praetor 190); praetor, fleet against Antiochus; *supplicatio* (37.47.4) and naval triumph (37.58.3)

[28] 189: L. Cornelius Scipio Asiaticus (consul 190); consul, Graecia; *supplicatio* (37.52.2) and triumph (37.58.6–59.6), subsequent trial for misuse of funds (38.50.4–60.10)

[29] 188: Q. Fabius Labeo (consul 183); praetor, fleet off Crete; naval triumph (37.60.6), arguments recalled later (38.47.5)

[30] 187: Cn. Manlius Vulso (consul 189); proconsul, Asia; triumph (39.6.3–7.5) with debate at 38.44.9–50.3

[31] 187: M. Fulvius Nobilior (consul 189); proconsul, Aetolia; triumph (39.4.2–5.17)

[32] 185: L. Manlius Acidinus Fulvianus (praetor 188); propraetor, Nearer Spain; *ovatio* (39.29.4–7)

[33] 184: C. Calpurnius Piso (consul 180); proconsul, Farther Spain; *supplicatio* (39.38.6) and triumph (39.42.2–3)

[34] 184: L. Quinctius Crispinus (praetor 186); propraetor, Nearer Spain; *supplicatio* (39.38.6) and triumph (39.42.2–4)

[35] 182: A. Terentius Varro (praetor 184); propraetor, Nearer Spain; *ovatio* (40.16.11)

[36] 182: Cn. Baebius Tamphilus (praetor 199); consul, Ligures; *supplicatio* (40.16.5) but apparently no request made (see 40.17.6–8)

[37] 181: L. Aemilius Paullus (consul 182); proconsul, Ligures; *supplicatio* (40.28.9) and triumph (40.34.7–11), arguments not recorded

[38] 180: P. Cornelius Cethegus (consul 181); proconsul, Ligures; triumph (40.38.8–9, "nullo bello gesto"), arguments not recorded

[39] 180: M. Baebius Tamphilus (consul 181); proconsul, Ligures; triumph (40.38.8–9, "nullo bello gesto"), arguments not recorded

[40] 180: Q. Fulvius Flaccus (praetor 182); proconsul, Nearer Spain; *supplicatio* (40.36.12) and triumph (40.43.4–7), arguments not recorded

[41] 179: Q. Fulvius Flaccus (praetor 182); consul, Ligures; *supplicatio* (40.53.3) and triumph (40.59.1), arguments not recorded

[42] 178: Ti. Sempronius Gracchus (praetor 179); propraetor, Nearer Spain; probable *supplicatio* (41.6.4)[2] and triumph (41.7.1–3)

[43] 178: L. Postumius Albinus (praetor 179); propraetor, Farther Spain; probable *supplicatio* (41.6.4)[3] and triumph (41.7.1–3)

[44] 177: C. Claudius Pulcher (praetor *suffectus* 180); consul, Istria and Ligures; *supplicatio* (41.12.4) and triumph (41.13.6–7)

[45] 175: Ti. Sempronius Gracchus (consul 177); proconsul, Sardinia; *supplicatio* (41.17.4) and triumph (lost in lacuna from Livy 41 but recovered from the Fasti; also cf. 41.28.8–10)

[46] 175: M. Titinius Curvus (praetor 178);propraetor, Nearer Spain; triumph (lost in lacuna in Livy 41 but recovered from the Fasti), subsequent trial for improper taking of prisoners (43.26)

[47] 175: M. Aemilius Lepidus (consul 187); consul, Ligures; *supplicatio* (41.19.2) and triumph (lost in lacuna from Livy 41 but recovered from the Fasti)

[48] 175: P. Mucius Scaevola (praetor 179); consul, Ligures; *supplicatio* (41.19.2) and triumph (lost in lacuna from Livy 41 but recovered from the Fasti)

[49] 174: Ap. Claudius Centho (praetor 175);propraetor, Nearer Spain; *supplicatio* (41.28.1) and *ovatio* (41.28.3, 28.6)

[50] 173: M. Popillius Laenas (praetor 176); consul, Ligures; *supplicatio* denied (42.9, 21–22)

[51] 172: C. Cicereius (praetor 173);propraetor, Sardinia and Corsica; triumph *in monte Albano* (42.21.6–7)

[52] 172: C. Popillius Laenas (praetor 175); consul, Ligures; triumph(?) apparently denied (42.28.2–3)

[53] 168: M. Claudius Marcellus (praetor 169);propraetor, Spain; apparently no request made (see 45.4.1)

[54] 167: L. Aemilius Paullus (consul 168); proconsul, Macedonia; *supplicatio* (45.2.8, 2.12, 16.7–8) and triumph (45.35–39) with much of the celebration lost in a lacuna (but see 45.40.1–4)

[55] 167: Cn. Octavius (praetor 168); proconsul, fleet (Macedonia); *supplicatio* (45.16.7–8) and naval triumph (45.35.4–5, 42.2–3)

[56] 167: L. Anicius Gallus (praetor 168);propraetor, Illyrians; *supplicatio* (45.3.2) and triumph (45.35.4–5, 43.1–8)

2. Livy seems to have neglected to report a *supplicatio* celebrated on this occasion, but it seems highly improbable that the senate would have failed to decree one when a commander came home to request both a triumph and a *supplicatio* at the same time (41.6.4) and the triumph did take place (41.7.2–3).

3. See previous note.

APPENDIX B

Success Rates of Triumph Requests

218-167 B.C.

Because the Fasti Triumphales by definition record only celebrations and not refusals, any attempt to measure success rates for triumph requests in the Middle Republic must hinge, with all due caution, on Livy and his sources. *Triumphi spes* may have been canvassed on occasion in varying degrees of seriousness without leaving so much as a trace in the historical record, but such cases should probably remain marginal to the discussion of triumph debates, having probably never even made it to the floor of the senate. Be that as it may, between the state of the evidence—more than likely incomplete and impossible to verify, not to mention the small sample size as well—no self-respecting statistician would ever give these data a second glance. But since the question of numbers has already entered into the discussion among ancient historians,[1] the relevant calculations deserve closer scrutiny, if only to show how little they do, in fact, actually prove in and of themselves.

As a starting point, in the period covered by Livy Books 21–45, from the outbreak of the Hannibalic War in 218 down to 167, the question of a triumph for a returning commander seems to have come up at least 56 times.[2] This figure comprises the total number of triumphs and *ovationes* actually granted, plus triumphs *in monte Albano,* triumph bids rejected outright, and a handful of additional requests that were apparently never made but could have been. Now let us look more closely at the numerical breakdown.

Six *imperatores* during the period produced deeds worthy of notice but

1. Witness the exchange between J. S. Richardson 1975 and Develin 1978, cited above, p. 115 n. 3 and p. 116 n. 4.

2. See appendix A above for names, dates, and other details.

as far as we know never asked for a triumph: C. Cornelius Cethegus in 199, L. Stertinius in 196, L. Furius Purpureo also in 196, L. Aemilius Paullus in 189, Cn. Baebius Tamphilus in 182, and M. Claudius Marcellus in 168. Only with Stertinius does Livy explicitly state that he made no request, although he does not say why (33.27.3). We are told that Purpureo's colleague deliberately left room for his *triumphi spes* (33.37.10), but then he apparently never did anything about it. Amid Livy's silence we have to presume that the other four did not make requests either. All six may well have taken themselves out of the running for fear of rejection, although in the absence of evidence the real explanation is anyone's guess.

In the case of Q. Fabius Maximus, who recaptured Tarentum in 209, Livy follows a distinctly hostile version of the *res gestae* and does not even record a pursuit of civic honors (27.15.9–17.17).[3] An alternative tradition, however, best represented by the *elogia,* attests that Fabius celebrated a triumph on this occasion, and Attilio Degrassi reconstructed a notice for this triumph in a lacuna in the Fasti.

If his reconstruction were to prove correct, it would be the only case in the period covered by Livy 21–45 where the Fasti contain a reference to a celebration that Livy does not include. There were clearly both pro- and anti-Fabian stories in circulation during the Augustan era. Taking that into account, plus the well-known rivalry between Fabius and Africanus (as illustrated, e.g., by the debate over Scipio's crossing to Africa at 28.40–45) and the paucity of triumphs from the rest of the Hannibalic War, two more or less equally probable explanations suggest themselves: either someone at some point along the line tried to enhance the prestige of Scipio Africanus, the final victor over Hannibal, by suppressing the notice of Fabius's earlier triumph (in which case the guilty party would have to be Livy or one of his sources or his sources' sources, etc.), or else someone in the pro-Fabian camp tried to make him out as the great unsung hero of the war by concocting one of the false honors for which the *elogia* are

3. Livy raises explicit doubts about the manner in which the city was betrayed to the Romans (27.15.9–19, 20.9–10, including the strange intrusion of a love-story element, and the appearance of a shady local character whose involvement with Fabius makes the whole thing look like a dirty trick) as well as possible qualms over the indiscriminate slaughter and plundering depicted in the latter stage of the battle (27.16.1–7). These traces smack of triumphal spin-doctoring on the part of Fabius's critics, who would have tried to make his victory look as insignificant or underhanded (or both) and as costly as possible. And note the later summary (27.20.9) making an explicit comparison to his archrival Scipio Africanus: "Romae fama Scipionis in dies crescere, Fabio Tarentum captum astu magis quam virtute gloriae tamen esse" ("in Rome the fame of Scipio was growing daily; nevertheless for Fabius the capture of the city of Tarentum brought glory for more than mere valor").

4. See Degrassi 1937, 14, 80; and 1947, 551. For the pro-Fabian story, cf. Plut. *Fab.* 23.2, Str. 6.3.1, *De Vir. Ill.* 43.6, although none of these is a particularly reliable or independent witness.

5. Cf. 8.40.4–5, and see also Wiseman 1986 and more recently Chaplin 2000, 168–96.

so notorious.[5] Certainty is impossible. Just to keep things on a even keel, I will simply leave Fabius out altogether for the calculations that follow. One triumph or triumph request more or less will not swing the results very far in either direction.

That leaves 49 requests documented by Livy, only a few of which appear to have resulted in no public victory celebration of any kind: L. Cornelius Scipio (later Africanus) in 206, L. Manlius Acidinus in 199, L. Cornelius Merula in 193, and Q. Minucius Thermus in 190. The renegade brothers M. and C. Popillius Laenas in 173 and 172 actually fall into a special indeterminate category of quasi requests and were soundly rebuffed. Q. Minucius Rufus in 197 and C. Cicereius in 172 met with opposition in the senate and chose to forgo the stamp of official approval, triumphing under their own authority *in monte Albano.* So did M. Claudius Marcellus in 211, except that the *patres* had already awarded him an *ovatio* for the same victory.[6] Whatever we make of that peculiar (indeed, unique) scenario, Marcellus clearly does not belong among the outright rejections, which then (between the six who came up empty-handed and the two *in monte Albano*) would account for eight out of 49, or roughly one in seven (16%) of the total request pool.

Setting all the failed attempts aside, then, the 33 attested triumphs (30 regular and three naval) and eight *ovationes* together translate into 41 out of 49, or a success rate of 84-percent in securing a public victory celebration among those we know to have asked for one. This hardly amounts to a dazzling display of senatorial control over the *ius triumphandi* or a crackdown on illegitimate triumph requests. It should also be noted that no fewer than 33 of those 41 commanders triumphed by full consensus of the *patres,* so that the eight *ovationes* make up only 19.5 percent, just less than one in five, of the publicly authorized victory celebrations. The remaining 80 percent are all full triumphs (73% regular, 7% naval). So far I have counted the twin débâcles of M. and C. Popillius Laenas in 173 and 172 as rejections, when in fact the chances are that neither of them ever really placed a formal triumph request. Removing them from the calculation would leave only six rejections in 47 requests, or an 87-percent success rate—nearly nine out of ten. And if we follow a lead from the Fasti and count triumphs *in monte Albano* among legitimate victory celebrations, that number may climb as high as 91 percent.

6. Degrassi 1947, 551, argues that either or both of the Cornelii who served as *privati cum imperio* in Spain, namely P. Scipio (the future Africanus) in 206 and L. Lentulus in 200, could very well have triumphed *in monte Albano* despite Livy's silence. Two pages later Degrassi finds fault with another scholar for postulating a similar situation with L. Aemilius Paullus in 189, because such triumphs would have appeared in the Fasti. He cannot have it both ways: if Marcellus, Minucius, and Cicereius were not the only ones to celebrate triumphs *in monte Albano* during this period, the others are all unattested and therefore matters of guesswork.

Conversely, however, if we keep the Popillii and the triumphs *in monte Albano* as rejections and add the six nonrequests (mentioned above) to the list of failed triumph bids, then we can pare the results down to 41 celebrations granted out of 55 that might once have been considered, or only 74.5 percent. It is also possible to justify interpreting the *ovatio* as a mark of senatorial control and therefore not entirely a success. If we take only full and naval triumphs into account, then, subtracting the eight *ovationes* from the tally above, we have 33 triumphs granted out of 49 that were requested and 55 that might have been, thus either 67 or 60 percent. Not surprisingly, the odds now start to look much less promising for the would-be *triumphator*. If we treat naval triumphs as second-class celebrations, moreover, those figures shrink once again, to 30 full triumphs out of either 49 requests or 55 possible requests, 61 or 54.5 percent. At last, by eliminating as tainted by scandal the eight triumphs that were awarded only after a fierce debate about whether or not the commander deserved them, we can claim that only 25 (or even 22, depending on the status of naval celebrations) out of the 49 commanders who asked for triumphs or the 55 who might have done—something on the order of 40–50 percent—actually came home to an ideal (i.e., thoroughly unobstructed) triumph.

It obviously makes an enormous difference whether we are finally talking about nine out of ten triumph bids succeeding or something less than half, and such starkly contrasting results do not come about by accident. Everything depends on how the various subcategories are either grouped together or treated separately: that is, imagined as equivalent or differentiated and ranked according to a hierarchy of value. And the problem of categorization leads right back in turn to a familiar string of tricky questions—the very questions, in fact, that the numbers themselves were originally supposed to answer. Should the success rate take account of requests that were never even made, or not? To what extent do such cases provide evidence of informal prescreening of senatorial opinion? Do *ovationes* count as successes or failures? What about naval triumphs and triumphs *in monte Albano*? How much should a fierce or protracted triumph debate (or one that was both) be seen to vitiate the final result? How seriously did senators take their role as gatekeepers of the triumph? And amid constant pressure to innovate, how much constraining force did the unwritten *mos maiorum* really exert?

Throughout this book I have sought to demonstrate, based largely on the disputes from the second century that Livy recounts in some detail, that the *patres* used triumph debates to maintain both the balance of *dignitas* within their own ranks and their lofty position as self-proclaimed collective arbiters of Roman identity. When a lengthy discussion led to a positive result in the end, this came about in two stages: first, through the political theater of the debate, the senators allowed some limited free play to competition and judgment (both positive and negative) among themselves; and then, after those potentially destructive impulses had safely run their course (being limited in time, space, participation, audience, etc.), the same group now banded together to reassert their unity once again in the eyes of the populace at large through the duly authorized civic celebration.

What bearing does this interpretive model have on all the various calculations discussed above? Inside the walls of the *curia* while the triumph debate is still in progress, I would argue, we should bear in mind the more restrictive numbers (i.e., that less than half the commanders will get away without having to mount a serious performative case before their peers), whereas afterwards, when the success of another Roman commander goes on display through the streets of the city for all to see, it is the cumulative total of celebrations produced by the system with the aristocrats in charge that really counts (i.e., more like 70–85%). Certainty is clearly impossible, but the idea of two distinct phases with different—some might even say contradictory—emphases, each one implying its own view of the felicific calculus of triumphs, as I have just described, not only does justice to the evidence (such as it is), but also, and more important, mirrors the fundamental paradox of the Republican constitution to which this study has found reason to return again and again.[7]

7. The idea that there are two opposing trends in interactions between Roman aristocrats—one emphasizing competition and debate, the other common interest and consensus (cf. Rosenstein 1990a and 1995)—can help to explain away many paradoxes. For instance, the erroneous conclusion of Itgenshorst 2005, 112–25 (discussed above, p. 143 n. 51), that triumphs per se actually mattered less to Roman aristocrats than military success, results from focusing on the second trend while ignoring the first. Triumphs did in fact represent the pinnacle of achievement and aspiration on the competition side (hence 30.15.12 and all similar passages), and yet any *nobilis* could proudly broadcast his *res gestae* in the conventional ways, including via monuments and inscriptions, whether he had a triumph to his credit or not.

BIBLIOGRAPHY

Abbreviations of journal titles in this bibliography follow those appearing in the annual issues of *L'Année Philologique.*

Adcock, F.E. 1957. "Consular Tribunes and Their Successors." *JRS* 47: 9–14.

Afzelius, A. 1938. "Zur Definition der römischen Nobilität in der Zeit Ciceros." *C&M* 2: 40–94.

———. 1945. "Zur Definition der römischen Nobilität vor der Zeit Ciceros." *C&M* 7: 150–200.

Alcock, S.E. 2002. *Archaeologies of the Greek Past: Landscape, Monuments, and Memories.* Cambridge: Cambridge University Press.

Astin, A.E. 1989a. "Roman Government and Politics, 200–134 B.C." In *The Cambridge Ancient History,* 2nd ed., vol. 8, *Rome and the Mediterranean to 133 B.C.,* ed. A.E. Astin et al., 163–96. Cambridge: Cambridge University Press.

———. 1989b. "Sources." In *The Cambridge Ancient History,* 2nd ed., vol. 8, *Rome and the Mediterranean to 133 B.C.,* ed. A.E. Astin et al., 1–16. Cambridge: Cambridge University Press.

Badian, E. 1958. *Foreign Clientelae (264–70 B.C.).* Oxford: Oxford University Press.

———. 1966. "The Early Historians." In *Latin Historians,* ed. D.R. Dudley and T.A. Dorey, 1–38. London: Routledge and Kegan Paul.

———. 1968. "Ennius and His Friends." In *Ennius,* Entretiens sur l'Antiquité Classique 17, 149–208. Geneva: Fondation Hardt.

———. 1971. "The Family and Early Career of T. Quinctius Flamininus." *JRS* 61: 102–11.

———. 1988. "Kommentar" [on section 5, "Magistratur und Gesellschaft"]. In *Staat und Staatlichkeit in der frühen römischen Republik,* ed. W. Eder, 437–75. Stuttgart: Franz Steiner.

———. 1993. "Livy and Augustus." In *Livius: Aspekte seines Werkes,* Xenia: Konstanzer Althistorische Vorträge und Forschungen 31, ed. W. Schuller, 9–38. Constance: Universitätsverlag Konstanz.

———. 1996. "*Tribuni Plebis* and *Res Publica*." In *"Imperium sine Fine": T. Robert S. Broughton and the Roman Republic,* ed. J. Linderski, 187–213. Stuttgart: Franz Steiner.

Bandelli, G.. 1972. "I processi degli Scipioni: Le fonti." *Index* 3: 304–42.

———. 1974–75. "Il processo dell'Asiatico." *Index* 5: 93–126.

Barchiesi, A. 1997. *The Poet and the Prince: Ovid and Augustan Discourse.* Berkeley and Los Angeles: University of California Press.

Barton, C.A. 2001. *Roman Honor: The Fire in the Bones.* Berkeley and Los Angeles: University of California Press.

Bartsch, S. 1994. *Actors in the Audience: Theatricality and Doublespeak from Nero to Hadrian.* Cambridge, Mass.: Harvard University Press.

Beard, M. 1990. "Priesthood in the Roman Republic." In *Pagan Priests: Religion and Power in the Ancient World,* ed. M. Beard and J.A. North, 19–54. Ithaca: Cornell University Press.

———. 2003. "The Triumph of the Absurd: Roman Street Theater." In *Rome the Cosmopolis,* ed. C. Edwards and G. Wolf, 21–43. Cambridge: Cambridge University Press.

Beck, H. 2005. Review of *L'annalistique romaine,* vol. 3, *L'annalistique récente: L'autobiographie politique (Fragments),* by M. Chassignet. *Bryn Mawr Classical Review,* http://ccat.sas.upenn.edu/bmcr/2005/2005-05-01.html.

Bell, A. 2004. *Spectacular Power in the Greek and Roman City.* Oxford: Oxford University Press.

Bergmann, B. 1994. "The Roman House as Memory Theater: The House of the Tragic Muse." *Art Bulletin* 76: 225–56.

———. 1999. "Introduction." In *The Art of Ancient Spectacle,* Studies in the History of Art 56, ed. B. Bergmann and C. Kondoleon, 9–36. Washington, D.C.: National Gallery of Art.

Bettini, M. 1979. *Studi e note su Ennio.* Biblioteca di Studi Antichi 20. Pisa: Giardini.

Bispham, E. 2006. "Literary Sources." In *A Companion to the Roman Republic,* ed. N. Rosenstein and R. Morstein-Marx, 29–50. Malden: Blackwell.

Bleicken, J. 1981a. "Die Nobilität der römischen Republik." *Gymnasium* 88: 236–53.

———. 1981b. *Zum Begriff der römischen Amtsgewalt: Auspicium—potestas—imperium.* Göttingen.

Bloomer, W.M. 1992. *Valerius Maximus and the Rhetoric of the New Nobility.* Chapel Hill: University of North Carolina Press.

Blösel, W. 2000. "Die Geschichte des Begriffes *mos maiorum* von den Anfängen bis zu Cicero." In *Mos maiorum: Untersuchungen zu den Formen der Identitätsstiftung und Stabilisierung in der römischen Republik,* Historia Einzelschriften 141, ed. B. Linke and M. Stemmler, 25–98. Stuttgart: Franz Steiner.

Boatwright, M.T. 1984. "Tacitus on Claudius and the *Pomerium* (*Annals* 12.23.2–24)." *CJ* 80: 36–44.

———. 1986. "The Pomerial Extension of Augustus." *Historia* 35: 13–27.

Bodel, J. 1999. "Death on Display: Looking at Roman Funerals." In *The Art of Ancient Spectacle,* Studies in the History of Art 56, ed. B. Bergmann and C. Kondoleon, 259–82. Washington, D.C.: National Gallery of Art.

Bonnefond-Coudry, M. 1989. *Le sénat de la république romaine de la guerre d'Hannibal à Auguste: Pratiques délibératives et prise de décision.* Rome: École Française de Rome.

Bourdieu, P. 1977. *Outline of a Theory of Practice.* Trans. Richard Nice. Cambridge Studies in Social and Cultural Anthropology. Cambridge: Cambridge University Press. [Translated from the 1972 French edition.]

Boyancé, P. 1972. "Fulvius Nobilior et le dieu ineffable." In *Études sur la réligion romaine,* vol. 2, Collection de l'École Française de Rome 11, 229–52. Rome: École Française de Rome.

Boyce, A.A. 1942. "The Origin of *Ornamenta Triumphalia.*" *CPh* 37: 130–41.

Brennan, T.C. 1994. "M'. Curius Dentatus and the Praetor's Right to Triumph." *Historia* 43: 423–39.

———. 1996. "Triumphus in Monte Albano." In *Transitions to Empire: Essays in Greco-Roman History, 360–146 B.C., in Honor of E. Badian,* Oklahoma Series in Classical Culture 21, ed. R.W. Wallace and E.W. Harris, 315–37. Norman: University of Oklahoma Press.

———. 2000. *The Praetorship in the Roman Republic.* Oxford: Oxford University Press.

———. 2004. "Power and Process under the Republican 'Constitution.'" In *The Cambridge Companion to the Roman Republic,* ed. H.I. Flower, 31–65. Cambridge: Cambridge University Press.

Brilliant, R. 1999. "'Let the Trumpets Roar!': The Roman Triumph." In *The Art of Ancient Spectacle,* Studies in the History of Art 56, ed. B. Bergmann and C. Kondoleon, 221–30. Washington, D.C.: National Gallery of Art.

Briscoe, J. 1972. "Flamininus and Roman Politics, 200–189 B.C." *Latomus* 31: 22–53.

———. 1973. *A Commentary on Livy, Books XXXI–XXXIII.* Oxford: Oxford University Press.

———. 1981. *A Commentary on Livy, Books XXXIV–XXXVII.* Oxford: Oxford University Press.

———. 1982. "Livy and Senatorial Politics, 200–167 B.C.: The Evidence of the Fourth and Fifth Decades." *ANRW* 2.32: 1077–1121. Berlin: Walter de Gruyter.

———, ed. 1986. *Titi Livi Ab Urbe Condita, Libri XLI–XLV.* Stuttgart: Teubner.

———. 1989. "The Second Punic War." In *The Cambridge Ancient History,* 2nd ed., vol. 8, *Rome and the Mediterranean to 133 B.C.,* ed. A.E. Astin et al., 44–80. Cambridge: Cambridge University Press.

———, ed. 1991. *Titi Livi Ab Urbe Condita, Libri XXXI–XL.* Stuttgart: Teubner.

———. 1993. "Livy and Polybius." In *Livius: Aspekte seines Werkes,* Xenia: Konstanzer Althistorische Vorträge und Forschungen 31, ed. W. Schuller, 39–52. Constance: Universitätsverlag Konstanz.

Brock, R. 1995. "Versions, 'Inversions' and Evasions: Classical Historiography and the 'Published' Speech." *Papers of the Liverpool Latin Seminar* 8: 209–24.

Broughton, T.R.S. 1951. *The Magistrates of the Roman Republic.* Vol. 1, *509 B.C.–100 B.C.* Ed. P.H. De Lacy. American Philological Association Monograph 15.1. Cleveland: Case Western Reserve University Press.

———. 1991. "Candidates Defeated in Roman Elections: Some Ancient Roman 'Also-Rans.'" *Transactions of the American Philosophical Society* 81(4).

Brunt, P.A. 1971. *Italian Manpower, 225 B.C.–A.D. 14*. Oxford: Clarendon Press.

———. 2004. "*Laus Imperii*." In *Roman Imperialism: Readings and Sources*, ed. C.B. Champion, 163–85. Malden: Blackwell.

Brunt, P.A., and J.M. Moore. 1967. *Res Gestae Divi Augusti: The Achievements of the Divine Augustus*. Oxford: Oxford University Press.

Bucher, G.S. 1987. "The *Annales Maximi* in the Light of Roman Methods of Keeping Records." *AJAH* 12: 3–61.

Bunse, R. 1997. *Das römische Oberamt in der frühen Republik und das Problem der 'Konsulartribunen.'* Trier: Wissenschaftlicher Verlag Trier.

Burck, E. 1964. *Erzählungskunst des T. Livius*. Berlin: Weidmann.

———. 1971. "The Third Decade." In *Livy*, ed. T.A. Dorey, 21–46. London: Routledge and Kegan Paul.

———. 1991. "Livius und Augustus." *ICS* 16: 269–81.

Burckhardt, L. 1990. "The Political Elite of the Roman Republic." *Historia* 39: 77–99.

Cancik, H. 1969. "Zur Geschichte der Aedes (Herculis) Musarum auf dem Marsfeld." *RhM* 76: 323–28.

Castagnoli, E. 1961. "La pianta marmorea di Roma antica." *Gnomon* 33: 604–10.

Chaplin, J.D. 2000. *Livy's Exemplary History*. Oxford: Oxford University Press.

Churchill, J.B. 1999. "*Ex Qua Quod Vellent Facerent:* Roman Magistrates' Authority over *Praeda* and *Manubiae*." *TAPhA* 129: 85–116.

Cizek, E. 1992. "À propos de la poétique de l'histoire chez Tite-Live." *Latomus* 51: 355–64.

Coarelli, F. 1968. "La Porta Trionfale e la Via dei Trionfi." *DArch* 2: 55–103.

———. 1988. *Il Foro Boario dalle origini alla fine della Repubblica*. Rome: Quasar.

Coleman, K.M. 1993. "Launching into History: Aquatic Displays in the Early Empire." *JRS* 83: 48–74.

Combès, R. 1966. *Imperator: Recherches sur l'emploi et la signification du titre d'imperator dans la Rome républicaine*. Paris: Presses Universitaires de France.

Corbeill, A. 1996. *Controlling Laughter: Political Humor in the Late Roman Republic*. Princeton: Princeton University Press.

Cornell, T.J. 1986a. "The Formation of the Historical Tradition of Early Rome." In *Past Perspectives: Studies in Greek and Roman Historical Writing*, ed. I.S. Moxon et al., 67–86. Cambridge: Cambridge University Press.

———. 1986b. "The Value of the Literary Tradition Concerning Early Rome." In *Social Struggles in Archaic Rome: New Perspectives on the Conflict of the Orders*, ed. K.A. Raaflaub, 52–74. Berkeley and Los Angeles: University of California Press.

———. 1995. *The Beginnings of Rome: Italy and Rome from the Bronze Age to the Punic Wars (c. 1000–264 BC)*. London: Routledge.

Crawford, M.H. 1974. *Roman Republican Coinage*. London: Cambridge University Press.

———. 2004. "Rome and the Greek World: Economic Relationships." In *Roman Imperialism: Readings and Sources*, ed. C.B. Champion, 96–107. Malden: Blackwell.

Crowther, N. 1973. "The *Collegium Poetarum* at Rome: Fact and Conjecture." *Latomus* 32: 575–80.

D'Arms, J.H. 1999. "Performing Culture: Roman Spectacle and the Banquets of the Powerful." In *The Art of Ancient Spectacle,* Studies in the History of Art 56, ed. B. Bergmann and C. Kondoleon, 301–20. Washington, D.C.: National Gallery of Art.

David, J.-M. 2000. *La République romaine: De la deuxième guerre punique à la bataille d'Actium, 218–31.* Points Histoire, Nouvelle Histoire de l'Antiquité 7. Paris: Le Seuil.

———. 2006. "Rhetoric and Public Life." Trans. R. Morstein-Marx and R. Martz. In *A Companion to the Roman Republic,* ed. N. Rosenstein and R. Morstein-Marx, 421–38. Malden: Blackwell.

Degrassi, A. 1937. *Inscriptiones Italiae.* Vol. 13.3, *Fasti et Elogia: Elogia.* Rome: Libreria dello Stato.

———. 1947. *Inscriptiones Italiae.* Vol. 13.1, *Fasti et Elogia: Fasti Consulares et Triumphales.* Rome: Libreria dello Stato.

Deninger, J. 1985. "Livius und der Prinzipat." *Klio* 67: 265–72.

Develin, R. 1975. "*Comitia Tributa Plebis.*" *Athenaeum* 53: 302–37.

———. 1976. "C. Flaminius in 232 B.C." *AC* 45: 638–43.

———. 1977. "*Lex Curiata* and the Competence of Magistrates." *Mnemosyne* 30: 49–65.

———. 1978. "Tradition and the Development of Triumphal Regulations in Rome." *Klio* 60: 429–38.

———. 1979a. *Patterns in Office-holding, 336–49 B.C.* Collection Latomus 161. Brussels: Latomus.

———. 1979b. "The Political Position of C. Flaminius." *RhM* 122: 268–77.

———. 1980. "The Roman Command Structure and Spain, 218–190 B.C." *Klio* 62: 355–67.

———. 1985. *The Practice of Politics at Rome, 366–167 B.C.* Brussels: Latomus.

Dorey, T.A., and C.W.F. Lydall. 1972. *Livy: Book XXXIII.* London: University Tutorial Press.

Drummond, A. 1980. "Consular Tribunes in Livy and Diodorus." *Athenaeum* 58: 57–72.

Dueck, D. 2000. "Historical *Exempla* in Augustan Rome and Their Role in a Geographical Context." In *Studies in Latin Literature and Roman History* 10, Collection Latomus 254, ed. C. Deroux, 176–96. Brussels: Latomus.

Earl, D.C. 1961. *The Political Thought of Sallust.* Cambridge: Cambridge University Press.

———. 1972. "Prologue-Form in Ancient Historiography." *ANRW* 1.2: 842–56. Berlin: Walter de Gruyter.

Eck, W. 1984. "Senatorial Self-Presentation: Developments in the Augustan Period." In *Caesar Augustus: Seven Aspects,* ed. F. Millar and E. Segal, 129–67. Oxford: Clarendon Press.

———. 1999. "Kaiserliche Imperatorenakklamation und Ornamenta Triumphalia." *ZPE* 124: 223–27.

———. 2003. *The Age of Augustus.* Trans. D.L. Schneider. Malden: Blackwell.

Eckstein, A.M. 1987. *Senate and General: Individual Decision-Making and Roman Foreign Relations, 264–194 B.C.* Berkeley and Los Angeles: University of California Press.

———. 1995. *Moral Vision in the "Histories" of Polybius.* Hellenistic Culture and Society 16. Berkeley and Los Angeles: University of California Press.

———. 1997. "*Physis* and *Nomos:* Polybius, the Romans, and Cato the Elder." In *Hellenistic Constructs: Essays in Culture, History, and Historiography,* Hellenistic Culture and Society 28, ed. P. Cartledge et al., 175–98. Berkeley and Los Angeles: University of California Press.

———. 2006a. "Conceptualizing Roman Imperial Expansion under the Republic: An Introduction." In *A Companion to the Roman Republic,* ed. N. Rosenstein and R. Morstein-Marx, 567–89. Malden: Blackwell.

———. 2006b. *Mediterranean Anarchy, Interstate War, and the Rise of Rome.* Berkeley and Los Angeles: University of California Press.

Edmondson, J.C. 1999. "The Cultural Politics of Public Spectacle in Rome and the Greek East, 167–166 BCE." In *The Art of Ancient Spectacle,* Studies in the History of Art 56, ed. B. Bergmann and C. Kondoleon, 77–96. Washington, D.C.: National Gallery of Art.

Edwards, C. 1996. *Writing Rome: Textual Approaches to the City.* Cambridge: Cambridge University Press.

Ehlers, W. 1939. "Triumphus." *RE* 7A1: 493–511. Stuttgart: J.B. Metzler.

Epstein, D.F. 1987. *Personal Enmity in Roman Politics, 218–43 B.C.* London: Croom Helm.

Ernout, A. 1973. *Recueil de textes latins archaïques.* Paris: Éditions Klincksieck.

Fantham, E. 2004. "Literature in the Roman Republic." In *The Cambridge Companion to the Roman Republic,* ed. H.I. Flower, 271–93. Cambridge: Cambridge University Press.

Favro, D. 1992. "*Pater Urbis:* Augustus as City Father of Rome." *Journal of the Society for Architectural Historians* 51: 61–84.

———. 1994. "The Street Triumphant: The Urban Impact of Roman Triumphal Parades." In *Streets: Critical Perspectives on Public Space,* ed. Z. Çelik et al., 151–64. Berkeley and Los Angeles: University of California Press.

———. 1996. *The Urban Image of Augustan Rome.* Cambridge: Cambridge University Press.

———. 1999. "The City Is a Living Thing: The Performative Role of an Urban Site in Ancient Rome, the Vallis Murcia." In *The Art of Ancient Spectacle,* Studies in the History of Art 56, ed. B. Bergmann and C. Kondoleon, 205–20. Washington, D.C.: National Gallery of Art.

Fears, J.R. 1981. "The Theology of Victory at Rome: Approaches and Problems." *ANRW* 2.17.2: 736–826. Berlin: Walter de Gruyter.

Feig Vishnia, R. 1996. *State, Society and Popular Leaders in Mid-Republican Rome, 241–167 B.C.* London: Routledge.

Feldherr, A. 1997a. "*Caeci Avaritia:* Avarice, History, and Vision in Livy V." In *Studies in Latin Literature and Roman History* 8, Collection Latomus 239, ed. C. Deroux, 268–77. Brussels: Latomus.

———. 1997b. "Livy's Revolution: Civic Identity and the Creation of the *Res Publica.*" In *The Roman Cultural Revolution,* ed. T. Habinek and A. Schiesaro, 136–57. Cambridge: Cambridge University Press.

———. 1998. *Spectacle and Society in Livy's History.* Berkeley and Los Angeles: University of California Press.

Flower, H.I. 1996. *Ancestor Masks and Aristocratic Power in Roman Culture.* Oxford: Clarendon Press.

———. 2000. "The Tradition of the *Spolia Opima:* M. Claudius Marcellus and Augustus." *CJ* 19: 34–59.

———. 2004a. "Introduction." In *The Cambridge Companion to the Roman Republic,* ed. H.I. Flower, 1–11. Cambridge: Cambridge University Press.

———. 2004b. "Spectacle and Political Culture in the Roman Republic." In *The Cambridge Companion to the Roman Republic,* ed. H.I. Flower, 322–43. Cambridge: Cambridge University Press.

Fornara, C. 1983. *The Nature of History in Ancient Greece and Rome.* Berkeley and Los Angeles: University of California Press.

Forsythe, G. 1999. *Livy and Early Rome: A Study in Historical Method and Judgment.* Historia Einzelschriften 132. Stuttgart: Franz Steiner.

———. 2005. *A Critical History of Early Rome.* Berkeley and Los Angeles: University of California Press.

Fraccaro, P. 1956. *Opuscula.* Pavia: Presso la Rivista "Athenaeum."

Frier, B.W. 1999. *Libri Annales Pontificum Maximorum: The Origins of the Annalistic Tradition.* Ann Arbor: University of Michigan Press.

Gagé, M.J. 1939. "Le genre littéraire des '*Res Gestae*' triomphales et ses thèmes." *REL* 17: 33–34.

Galli, F. 1987–88. "L'iscrizione trionfale di Ti. Sempronio Gracco." *AION (filol)* 9–10: 135–38.

Geertz, C. 1973. "Deep Play: Notes on the Balinese Cockfight." In *The Interpretation of Cultures: Selected Essays,* 121–46. New York: Basic Books.

———. 1983a. "Centers, Kings, and Charisma: Symbolics of Power." In *Local Knowledge: Further Essays in Interpretive Anthropology,* 121–46. New York: Basic Books.

———.1983b. "Local Knowledge: Fact and Law in a Comparative Perspective." In *Local Knowledge: Further Essays in Interpretive Anthropology,* 167–234. New York: Basic Books.

Giovannini, A. 1983. *Consulare imperium.* Schweizerische Beiträge zur Altertumswissenschaft 16. Basel: Friedrich Reinhardt.

———. 1988. "Magistratur und Volk: Ein Beitrag zur Entstehungsgeschichte des Staatsrechts." In *Staat und Staatlichkeit in der frühen Römischen Republik,* ed. W. Eder, 406–36. Stuttgart: Franz Steiner.

Gleason, M.W. 1995. *Making Men: Sophists and Self-Presentation in Ancient Rome.* Princeton: Princeton University Press.

Goltz, A. 2000. "*Maiestas sine viribus:* Die Bedeutung der Lictoren für die Konfliktbewältigungsstrategien römischer Magistrate." In *Mos maiorum: Untersuchungen zu den Formen der Identitätsstiftung und Stabilisierung in der römischen Republik,* Historia Einzelschriften 141, ed. B. Linke and M. Stemmler, 237–68. Stuttgart: Franz Steiner.

Gowing, A.M. 2005. *Empire and Memory: The Representation of the Roman Republic in Imperial Culture.* Cambridge: Cambridge University Press.

Grainger, J.D. 1995. "The Campaign of Cn. Manlius Vulso in Asia Minor." *Anatolian Studies* 45: 23–42.

———. 2002. *The Roman War of Antiochus the Great.* Mnemosyne Supplement 239. Leiden: E.J. Brill.

Green, P. 1990. *Alexander to Actium: The Historical Evolution of the Hellenistic Age.* Hellenistic Culture and Society 1. Berkeley and Los Angeles: University of California Press.

Gruen, E.S. 1974. *The Last Generation of the Roman Republic.* Berkeley and Los Angeles: University of California Press.

———. 1978. "The Consular Elections for 216 B.C. and the Veracity of Livy." *California Studies in Classical Antiquity* 11: 61–74.

———. 1984a. *The Hellenistic World and the Coming of Rome.* 2 vols. Berkeley and Los Angeles: University of California Press.

———. 1984b. "Material Rewards and the Drive for Empire." In *The Imperialism of Mid-Republican Rome,* ed. W.V. Harris, 59–88. Rome: American Academy in Rome.

———. 1985. "The Coronation of the Diadochoi." In *The Craft of the Ancient Historian: Essays in Honor of Chester G. Starr,* ed. J. Eadie and J. Ober, 253–71. Lanham: University Press of America.

———. 1992. *Culture and National Identity in Republican Rome.* Cornell Studies in Classical Philology 52. Ithaca: Cornell University Press.

———. 1995. "The 'Fall' of the Scipios." In *Leaders and Masses in the Roman World: Studies in Honor of Zvi Yavetz,* ed. I. Malkin and Z.W. Rubinsohn, 59–90. Leiden: E.J. Brill.

———. 1996. "The Roman Oligarchy: Image and Perception." In *"Imperium sine Fine": T. Robert S. Broughton and the Roman Republic,* Historia Einzelschriften 105, ed. J. Linderski, 215–34. Stuttgart: Franz Steiner.

———. 2004. "Rome and the Greek World." In *The Cambridge Companion to the Roman Republic,* ed. H.I. Flower, 242–67. Cambridge: Cambridge University Press.

Habinek, T.N. 1998. *The Politics of Latin Literature: Writing, Identity, and Empire in Ancient Rome.* Princeton: Princeton University Press.

Hadas, M. 1940. "Livy as Scripture." *AJPh* 61: 445–57.

Hammond, N.G.L. 1967. *Epirus.* Oxford: Oxford University Press.

———. 1988. *A History of Macedonia.* Vol. 3, *336–167 B.C.* Oxford: Oxford University Press.

Harris, W.V. 1985. *War and Imperialism in Republican Rome, 327–70 B.C.* Oxford: Clarendon Press.

———. 1989. "Roman Expansion in the West." In *The Cambridge Ancient History,* 2nd ed., vol. 8, *Rome and the Mediterranean to 133 B.C.,* ed. A.E. Astin et al., 107–62. Cambridge: Cambridge University Press.

———. 1990. "On Defining the Political Culture of the Roman Republic: Some Comments on Rosenstein, Williamson, and North." *CPh* 85: 288–93.

———. 2004. "On War and Greed in the Second Century B.C." In *Roman Imperialism: Readings and Sources,* ed. C.B. Champion, 17–30. Malden: Blackwell.

Harrison, S.J. 1989. "Augustus, the Poets, and the *Spolia Opima.*" *CQ* 39: 408–14.

Hatscher, C.R. 2000. *Charisma und res publica: Max Webers Herrschaftssoziologie und die römische Republik.* Historia Einzelschriften 136. Stuttgart: Franz Steiner.

Hellegouarc'h, J. 1963. *Le vocabulaire latin des relations et des partis politiques sous la République.* Publications de la Faculté des Lettres et Sciences Humaines de l'Université de Lille 11. Paris: Les Belles Lettres.

Herman, G. 1997. "The Court Society of the Hellenistic Age." In *Hellenistic Constructs: Essays in Culture, History, and Historiography,* Hellenistic Culture and Society 28, ed. P. Cartledge et al., 199–224. Berkeley and Los Angeles: University of California Press.

von Hesberg, H. 1999. "The King on Stage." In *The Art of Ancient Spectacle,* Studies in the History of Art 56, ed. B. Bergmann and C. Kondoleon, 65–76. Washington, D.C.: National Gallery of Art.

Hickson, F.V. 1991. "Augustus *Triumphator:* Manipulation of the Triumphal Theme in the Political Program of Augustus." *Latomus* 50: 124–38.

Hickson-Hahn, F. 2000. "Pompey's '*Supplicatio Duplicata*': A Novel Form of Thanksgiving." *Phoenix* 54: 244–54.

Hölkeskamp, K.-J. 1987. *Die Entstehung der Nobilität: Studien zur sozialen und politischen Geschichte der römischen Republik im 4. Jhdt. v. Chr.* Stuttgart: Franz Steiner.

———. 1988. "Senat und Volkstribunat im frühen 3. Jh. v. Chr." In *Staat und Staatlichkeit in der frühen römischen Republik,* ed. W. Eder, 437–57. Stuttgart: Franz Steiner.

———. 1993. "Conquest, Competition and Consensus: Roman Expansion in Italy and the Rise of the *Nobilitas.*" *Historia* 42: 12–39.

———. 1996. "*Exempla* und *mos maiorum.*" In *Vergangenheit und Lebenswelt: Soziale Kommunikation, Traditionsbildung und historisches Bewußtsein,* ScriptOralia 90, ed. H.-J. Gehrke and A. Möller, 301–38. Tübingen: Gunter Narr.

———. 2000. "*Fides—deditio in fidem—dextra data et accepta:* Recht, Religion und Ritual in Rom." In *The Roman Middle Republic: Politics, Religion, and Historiography c. 400–133 B.C.,* Acta Instituti Romani Finlandiae 23, ed. C. Bruun, 223–50. Rome: Institutum Romanum Finlandiae.

———. 2001. "Capital, Comitium und Forum: Öffentliche Räume, sakrale Topographie und Erinnerungslandschaften der römischen Republik." In *Studien zu antiken Identitäten,* ed. S. Faller, 97–132. Würstburg: Ergon.

———. 2004a. *Rekonstruktionen einer Republik.* Historische Zeitscrift, Beiheft 38. Munich: R. Oldenbourg.

———. 2004b. "Under Roman Roofs: Family, House, and Household." In *The Cambridge Companion to the Roman Republic,* ed. H.I. Flower, 113–38. Cambridge: Cambridge University Press.

———. 2006. "History and Collective Memory in the Middle Republic." In *A Companion to the Roman Republic,* ed. N. Rosenstein and R. Morstein-Marx, 478–95. Malden: Blackwell.

Holliday, P.J. 1997. "Roman Triumphal Painting: Its Function, Development, and Reception." *Art Bulletin* 79: 130–47.

Hölscher, T. 1978. "Die Anfänge römischer Repräsentations-Kunst." *RhM* 85: 315–57.

———. 2001. "Das Alte vor Augen: Politische Denkmäler und öffentliches Gedächtnis im republikanischen Rom." In *Institutionalität und Symbolisierung: Verstetigungen kultureller Ordnungsmuster in Vergangenheit und Gegenwart,* ed. G. Melville, 183–211. Cologne: Böhlau.

———. 2006. "The Transformation of Victory into Power: From Event to Structure." In *Representations of War in Ancient Rome,* ed. S. Dillon and K.E. Welch, 27–48. Cambridge: Cambridge University Press.

Hopkins, K., and G. Burton. 1983. "Political Succession in the Late Republic (249–50 BC)." In *Death and Renewal,* Sociological Studies in Roman History 2, 31–119. Cambridge: Cambridge University Press.

Hoyos, D. 2001. "Generals and Annalists: Geographic and Chronological Obscurities in the Scipios' Campaigns in Spain, 218–211 B.C." *Klio* 83: 68–92.

Ingleheart, J. 2007. "Propertius 4.10 and the End of the *Aeneid:* Augustus, the *Spolia Opima* and the Right to Remain Silent." *G&R* 54: 61–81.

Itgenshorst, T. 2004. "Augustus und der republikanische Triumph: Triumphalfasten und *summi viri*–Galerie als Instrumente der imperialen Machtsicherung." *Hermes* 132: 436–58.

———. 2005. *Tota illa pompa: Der Triumph in der römischen Republik.* Hypomnemata 161. Göttingen: Vandenhoeck und Ruprecht.

Jacobsthal, P. 1943. "On Livy XXXVI, 40 (Boiian Silver)." *AJA* 47: 306–12.

Jaeger, M. 1993. "*Custodia Fidelis Memoriae:* Livy's Story of M. Manlius Capitolinus." *Latomus* 52: 350–63.

———. 1997. *Livy's Written Rome.* Ann Arbor: University of Michigan Press.

———. 2003. "Livy and the Fall of Syracuse." In *Formen römischer Geschichtsschreibung von den Anfängen bis Livius: Gattungen, Autoren, Kontexte,* ed. U. Eigler et al., 213–34. Darmstadt: Wissenschaftliche Buchgesellschaft.

Jashemski, W.M.F. 1950. *The Origins and History of the Proconsular and the Propraetorian Imperium to 27 B.C.* Chicago: University of Chicago Press.

Johnson, S.K., and R.S. Conway, eds. 1935. *Titi Livi Ab Urbe Condita, Libri XXVI–XXX.* Oxford: Clarendon Press.

Kajava, M. 1998. "Visceratio." *Arctos* 32: 109–31.

Kallet-Marx, R.M. 1995. *Hegemony to Empire: The Development of the Roman Imperium in the East from 148 to 62 B.C.* Hellenistic Culture and Society 15. Berkeley and Los Angeles: University of California Press.

Kaster, R.A. 1997. "The Shame of the Romans." *TAPhA* 127: 1–19.

Kierdorf, W. 1980. *Laudatio funebris: Interpretationen und Untersuchungen zur Entwicklung der römischen Leichenrede.* Beiträge zur Klassischen Philologie 106. Meisenheim am Glan: Hein.

———. 2002. "Anfänge und Grundlagen der römischen Geschichtsschreibung." *Klio* 84: 400–413.

Klar, L.S. 2006. "The Origin of the Roman *Scaenae Frons* and the Architecture of Triumphal Games in the Second Century B.C." In *Representations of War in Ancient Rome,* ed. S. Dillon and K.E. Welch, 162–83. Cambridge: Cambridge University Press.

Kleiner, F.S. 1989. "The Study of Roman Triumphal and Honorary Arches Fifty Years after Kähler." *Journal of Roman Archaeology,* 197–206.

Knapp, R.C. 1975. *Aspects of the Roman Experience in Iberia, 206–100 B.C.* Valladolid: Universidad de Valladolid.

Konrad, C.F. 1996. "Notes on Roman Also-Rans." In *"Imperium sine Fine": T. Robert S. Broughton and the Roman Republic,* Historia Einzelschriften 105, ed. J. Linderski, 103–43. Stuttgart: Franz Steiner.

Koortbojian, M. 2006. "The Bringer of Victory: Imagery and Institutions at the Advent of Empire." In *Representations of War in Ancient Rome,* ed. S. Dillon and K.E. Welch, 184–217. Cambridge: Cambridge University Press.

Köves-Zulauf, T. 1998. "Die Worte des Sklaven an den Triumphator." *A&A* 44: 78–96.

Kraus, C.S. 1991. Review of *Livy Book XXXVI (191 B.C.)*, by P.G. Walsh. *Bryn Mawr Classical Review*, http://ccat.sas.upenn.edu/bmcr/1991/02.06.21.html.

———. 1994. *Livy Ab Urbe Condita Book VI.* Cambridge: Cambridge University Press.

Kraus, C.S., and A.J. Woodman. 1997. *Latin Historians.* Greece & Rome New Surveys in the Classics 27. Cambridge: Cambridge University Press.

Künzl, E. 1988. *Der römische Triumph: Siegesfeiern im antiken Rom.* Munich: C.H. Beck.

Kurke, L. 1993. "The Economy of *Kudos.*" In *Cultural Poetics in Archaic Greece: Cult, Performance, Politics,* ed. C. Dougherty and L. Kurke, 131–63. Cambridge: Cambridge University Press.

Kuttner, A. 1999. "Hellenistic Images of Spectacle, from Alexander to Augustus." In *The Art of Ancient Spectacle,* Studies in the History of Art 56, ed. B. Bergmann and C. Kondoleon, 97–124. Washington, D.C.: National Gallery of Art.

———. 2004. "Roman Art during the Republic." In *The Cambridge Companion to the Roman Republic,* ed. H.I. Flower, 294–321. Cambridge: Cambridge University Press.

Laird, A. 1999. *Powers of Expression, Expressions of Power: Speech Presentation and Latin Literature.* Oxford: Oxford University Press.

Lake, A.K. 1937. "The Supplicatio and Graecus Ritus." In *Quantalcumque: Studies Presented to Kirsopp Lake by Pupils, Colleagues and Friends,* ed. R.P. Casey, S. Lake, and A.K. Lake, 243–51. London: Christophers.

Lambert, A. 1967 [1946]. "Die indirekte Rede als künstlerisches Stilmittel." In *Wege zu Livius,* ed. E. Burck, 415–29. Darmstadt: Wissenschaftliche Buchgesellschaft.

Lazenby, J.F. 1978. *Hannibal's War: A Military History of the Second Punic War.* Warminster: Aris and Phillips.

———. 2004. "Rome and Carthage." In *The Cambridge Companion to the Roman Republic,* ed. H.I. Flower, 225–41. Cambridge: Cambridge University Press.

Leeman, A.D. 1967. "Werden wir Livius gerecht? Einige Gedanken zu der Praefatio des Livius." In *Wege zu Livius,* ed. E. Burck, 200–216. Darmstadt: Wissenschaftliche Buchgesellschaft.

Leigh, M. 1995. "Wounding and Popular Rhetoric at Rome." *BICS* 40: 195–212.

Lemosse, M. 1972. "Les éléments techniques de l'ancien triomphe romain et le problème de son origine." *ANRW* 1.2: 442–53. Berlin: Walter de Gruyter.

Lendon, J.E. 1997. *Empire of Honour: The Art of Government in the Roman World.* Oxford: Clarendon Press.

Lind, L.R. 1989. "The Idea of the Republic and the Foundations of Roman Morality." In *Studies in Latin Literature and Roman History* 5, Collection Latomus 206, ed. C. Deroux, 5–34. Brussels: Latomus.

———. 1992. "The Idea of the Republic and the Foundations of Roman Morality, Second Part." In *Studies in Latin Literature and Roman History* 6, Collection Latomus 217, ed. C. Deroux, 5–40. Brussels: Latomus.

———. 1994. "Thought, Life, and Literature at Rome: The Consolidation of Culture." In *Studies in Latin Literature and Roman History* 7, Collection Latomus 227, ed. C. Deroux, 5–71. Brussels: Latomus.

Linderski, J. 1986. "The Augural Law." *ANRW* 2.16.3: 2146–2312. Berlin: Walter de Gruyter.

———. 1988. "The Auspices and the Struggle of the Orders." In *Staat und Staatlichkeit in der frühen römischen Republik,* ed. W. Eder, 34–48. Stuttgart: Franz Steiner.

———. 1990. "Roman Officers in the Year of Pydna." *AJPh* 111: 53–71.

———. 1993. "Roman Religion in Livy." In *Livius: Aspekte seines Werkes,* Xenia: Konstanzer Althistorische Vorträge und Forschungen 31, ed. W. Schuller, 53–70. Constance: Universitätsverlag Konstanz.

———. 1996. "Q. Scipio Imperator." In *"Imperium sine Fine": T. Robert S. Broughton and the Roman Republic,* ed. J. Linderski, 145–85. Stuttgart: Franz Steiner.

Linke, B. 2000. "*Religio* und *res publica:* Religiöser Glaube und gesellschaftliches Handeln im republikanischen Rom." In *Mos maiorum: Untersuchungen zu den Formen der Identitätsstiftung und Stabilisierung in der römischen Republik,* Historia Einzelschriften 141, ed. B. Linke and M. Stemmler, 269–98. Stuttgart: Franz Steiner.

Lintott, A.W. 1972. "Imperial Expansion and Moral Decline in the Roman Republic." *Historia* 21: 626–38.

———. 1999. *The Constitution of the Roman Republic.* Oxford: Clarendon Press.

Lipovsky, J. 1981. *A Historiographical Study of Livy, Books VI–X.* New York: Arno Press.

Luce, T.J. 1965. "The Dating of Livy's First Decade." *TAPhA* 96: 209–40.

———. 1977. *Livy: The Composition of His History.* Princeton: Princeton University Press.

———. 1990. "Livy, Augustus, and the Forum Augustum." In *Between Republic and Empire: Interpretations of Augustus and His Principate,* ed. K.A. Raaflaub and M. Toher, 123–38. Berkeley and Los Angeles: University of California Press.

———. 1993. "Structure in Livy's Speeches." In *Livius: Aspekte seines Werkes,* Xenia: Konstanzer Althistorische Vorträge und Forschungen 31, ed. W. Schuller, 71–88. Constance: Universitätsverlag Konstanz.

Magdelain, A. 1968. *Recherches sur l'"imperium": La loi curiate et les auspices d'investiture.* Travaux et Recherches de la Faculté de Droit et des Sciences Économiques de Paris: Série "Sciences Historiques" 12. Paris: Presses Universitaires de France.

———. 1976. "Le *pomerium* archaïque et le *mundus.*" *REL* 54: 71–109.

———. 1977. "L'inauguration de l'*urbs* et l'*imperium.*" *MEFR* 89: 11–29.

Marshall, A.J. 1984. "Symbols and Showmanship in Roman Public Life: The *Fasces.*" *Phoenix* 38: 120–41.

Martin, R. P. 1989. *The Language of Heroes: Speech and Performance in the "Iliad."* Ithaca: Cornell University Press.

Martina, M. 1979. "Ennio poeta cliens." *QFC* 2: 15–74.

———. 1981. "Aedes Herculis Musarum." *DArch,* 49–68.

Maslakov, G. 1984. "Valerius Maximus and Roman Historiography: A Study of the *Exempla* Tradition." *ANRW* 2.32.1: 437–96. Berlin: Walter de Gruyter.

McCall, J.B. 2002. *The Cavalry of the Roman Republic: Cavalry Combat and Elite Reputations in the Middle and Late Republic.* London: Routledge.

McClain, T.D. 1997. Review of *The Initiation of the Second Macedonian War: An Explication of Livy Book 31,* Historia Einzelschriften 97, by V.M. Warrior. *Bryn Mawr Classical Review,* http://ccat.sas.upenn.edu/bmcr/1997/97.04.11.html.

McCuarg, W. 1991. "The *Fasti Capitolini* and the Study of Roman Chronology in the Sixteenth Century." *Athenaeum* 49: 141–59.

McDonald, A.H. 1974. "The Roman Conquest of Cisalpine Gaul (201–191 B.C.)." *Antichthon* 8: 44–53.

McDonnell, M. 2006. "Roman Aesthetics and the Spoils of Syracuse." In *Representations of War in Ancient Rome,* ed. S. Dillon and K.E. Welch, 68–90. Cambridge: Cambridge University Press.

Meier, C. 1966. *Res publica amissa: Eine Studie zu Verfassung und Geschichte der späten römischen Republik.* Wiesbaden: Franz Steiner.

Mette, H.J. 1961. "Livius und Augustus." *Gymnasium* 68: 269–85.

Miles, G.B. 1995. *Livy: Reconstructing Early Rome.* Ithaca: Cornell University Press.

Millar, F. 1984. "The Political Character of the Classical Roman Republic." *JRS* 74: 1–19.

———. 1986. "Politics, Persuasion, and the People before the Social War." *JRS* 76: 1–11.

———. 1998. *The Crowd in Rome in the Late Republic.* Jerome Lectures 22. Ann Arbor: University of Michigan Press.

Miller, J.F. 2000. "*Triumphus in Palatio.*" *AJPh* 121: 409–22.

Minyard, J.D. 1985. *Lucretius and the Late Republic: An Essay on Roman Intellectual History.* Mnemosyne Supplement 90. Leiden: E.J. Brill.

Mitchell, R.E. 1990. *Patricians and Plebeians: The Origins of the Roman State.* Ithaca: Cornell University Press.

Moevs, M. 1981. "Le Muse di Ambracia." *BA* 12: 1–12.

Moles, J. "Livy's Preface." *PCPhS* 39: 141–68.

Mommsen, T. 1879. *Römische Forschungen.* 2 vols. Berlin: Weidmann.

———. 1887. *Römisches Staatsrecht.* 3rd ed. 3 vols. Handbuch der römischen Altertümer 1–3. Leipzig: S. Hirzel.

Moore, T.J. 1989. *Artistry and Ideology: Livy's Vocabulary of Virtue.* Altertumswissenschaft, Beiträge zur Klassischen Philologie 192. Frankfurt a./M.: Athenäums Monografien.

Morgan, L. 2000. "The Autopsy of C. Asinius Pollio." *JRS* 90: 51–69.

Morstein-Marx, R. 2004. *Mass Oratory and Political Power in the Late Roman Republic.* Cambridge: Cambridge University Press.

Mouritsen, H. 1990. "Elections, Magistrates, and the Municipal Elite." *Arctos* 24: 201–3.

———. 2001. *Plebs and Politics in the Late Roman Republic.* Cambridge: Cambridge University Press.

Münzer, F. 1912. "Furius 86 (L. Furius Purpureo)." *RE* 7.1: 362–64. Stuttgart: J.B. Metzler.

———. 1920. *Römischer Adelsparteien und Adelsfamilien.* Stuttgart: J.B. Metzler.

Musti, D. 1993. "Livio e l'archeologia delle origini." In *Livius: Aspekte seines Werkes,* Xenia: Konstanzer Althistorische Vorträge und Forschungen 31, ed. W. Schuller, 111–24. Constance: Universitätsverlag Konstanz.

Nash, E. 1968. *Pictorial Dictionary of Ancient Rome.* 2nd ed. New York: Praeger.

Nicolet, C. 1980. *The World of the Citizen in Republican Rome.* Trans. P.S. Falla. Berkeley and Los Angeles: University of California Press.

Nixon, C., and B. Saylor Rodgers. 1994. *In Praise of the Later Roman Emperors: The Panegyrici Latini.* Berkeley and Los Angeles: University of California Press.

Nodelman, S. 1975. "How to Read a Roman Portrait." *Art in America* 63: 26–33.

North, J.A. 1981. "The Development of Roman Imperialism." *JRS* 71: 1–9.

———. 1990a. "Democratic Politics in Republican Rome." *P&P* 126: 3–21.

———. 1990b. "Politics and Aristocracy in the Roman Republic." *CPh* 85: 277–87.

———. 2006. "The Constitution of the Roman Republic." In *A Companion to the Roman Republic,* ed. N. Rosenstein and R. Morstein-Marx, 256–77. Malden: Blackwell.

Northwood, S.J. 2000. "Livy and the Early Annalists." In *Studies in Latin Literature and Roman History* 10, Collection Latomus 254, ed. C. Deroux, 45–55. Brussels: Latomus.

Oakley, S.P. 1985. "Single Combat in the Roman Republic." *CQ* 35: 392–410.

———. 1997–98. *A Commentary on Livy, Books VI–X.* 2 vols. Oxford: Oxford University Press.

———. 2004. "The Early Republic." In *The Cambridge Companion to the Roman Republic,* ed. H.I. Flower, 15–30. Cambridge: Cambridge University Press.

Ogilvie, R.M. 1958. "Livy, Licinius Macer, and the *Libri Lintei.*" *JRS* 48: 41–46.

———, ed. 1974. *Titi Livi Ab Urbe Condita, Libri I–V.* Oxford: Clarendon Press.

Oppermann, H. 1967. "Die Einleitung zum Geschichtswerk des Livius." In *Wege zu Livius,* ed. E. Burck, 169–80. Darmstadt: Wissenschaftliche Buchgesellschaft.

Orlin, E. 1997. *Temples, Religion, and Politics in the Roman Republic.* Mnemosyne Supplement 164. Leiden: E.J. Brill.

———. 2000. "Why a Second Temple for Venus Erycina?" In *Studies in Latin Literature and Roman History* 10, Collection Latomus 254, ed. C. Deroux , 70–90. Brussels: Latomus.

Östenberg, I. 2003. *Staging the World: Rome and the Other in the Triumphal Procession.* Lund: Media-Tryck.

———. 2007. Review of *Tota illa pompa: Der Triumph in der römischen Republik,* by T. Itgenshorst. *Bryn Mawr Classical Review,* http://ccat.sas.upenn.edu/bmcr/2007/2007-04-37.html.

Packard, D.W. 1968. *A Concordance to Livy.* Cambridge, Mass.: Harvard University Press.

Pagnon, B. 1982. "Le récit de l'expédition de Cn. Manlius Vulso contre les Gallo-Grecs et de ses prolongements dans le livre 38 de Tite-Live." *LEC* 50: 115–28.

Palmer, R.E.A. 1970. *The Archaic Community of the Romans.* Cambridge: Cambridge University Press.

Parker, H.N. 1999. "The Observed of All Observers: Spectacle, Applause, and Cultural Poetics in the Roman Theater Audience." In *The Art of Ancient Spectacle,* Studies in the History of Art 56, ed. B. Bergmann and C. Kondoleon, 163–80. Washington, D.C.: National Gallery of Art.

Patterson, J.R. 2006. "The City of Rome." In *A Companion to the Roman Republic,* ed. N. Rosenstein and R. Morstein-Marx, 345–64. Malden: Blackwell.

Petersen, H. 1961. "Livy and Augustus." *TAPhA* 92: 440–52.

Petzold, K.-E. 1993. "Zur Geschichte der römischen Annalistik." In *Livius: Aspekte seines Werkes,* Xenia: Konstanzer Althistorische Vorträge und Forschungen 31, ed. W. Schuller, 151–88. Constance: Universitätsverlag Konstanz.

Phillips, J.E. 1974a. "Form and Language in Livy's Triumph Notices." *CPh* 69: 265–73.

———. 1974b. "Verbs Compounded with *Trans-* in Livy's Triumph Reports." *CPh* 69: 54–55.

———. 1982. "Current Research in Livy's First Decade." *ANRW* 2.30.2: 998–1057. Berlin: Walter de Gruyter.

Pinsent, J. 1975. *Military Tribunes and Plebeian Consuls: The Fasti from 444 V to 342 V.* Historia Einzelschriften 24. Stuttgart: Franz Steiner.

Plattus, A. 1983. "Passages into the City: The Interpretive Function of the Roman Triumph." *Princeton Journal* 1: 93–115.

Polo, F.P. 1995. "Procedures and Functions of Civil and Military *Contiones* in Rome." *Klio* 77: 203–16.

Potter, D. 2004. "The Roman Army and Navy." In *The Cambridge Companion to the Roman Republic,* ed. H.I. Flower, 66–88. Cambridge: Cambridge University Press.

Raaflaub, K.A. 1974. *Dignitatis contentio: Studien zur Motivation und politischen Taktik im Bürgerkrieg zwischen Caesar und Pompeius.* Vestigia: Beiträge zur alten Geschichte 20. Munich: C.H. Beck.

———. 1999. "Born to be Wolves? Origins of Roman Imperialism." In *Transitions to Empire: Essays in Greco-Roman History, 360–146 B.C., in Honor of E. Badian,* Oklahoma Series in Classical Culture 21, ed. R.W. Wallace and E.W. Harris, 273–314. Norman: University of Oklahoma Press.

———. 2006. "Between Myth and History: Rome's Rise from Village to Empire (the Eighth Century to 264)." In *A Companion to the Roman Republic,* ed. N. Rosenstein and R. Morstein-Marx, 125–46. Malden: Blackwell.

Rawson, E. 1971. "Prodigy Lists and the Use of the *Annales Maximi.*" *CQ* 21: 158–69.

———. 1989. "Roman Tradition and the Greek World." In *The Cambridge Ancient History,* 2nd ed., vol. 8, *Rome and the Mediterranean to 133 B.C.,* ed. A.E. Astin et al., 422–75. Cambridge: Cambridge University Press.

Reiter, W. 1988. *Aemilius Paullus, Conqueror of Greece.* London: Croom Helm.

Reynolds, L.D., and N.G. Wilson. 1974. *Scribes and Scholars: A Guide to the Transmission of Greek and Latin Literature.* 2nd ed. Oxford: Clarendon Press.

Rice, E.E. 1983. *The Grand Procession of Ptolemy Philadelphus.* Oxford: Oxford University Press.

Rich, J.W. 1976. *Declaring War in the Roman Republic in the Period of Transmarine Expansion.* Collection Latomus 19. Brussels: Latomus.

———. 1993. "Fear, Greed, and Glory: The Causes of Roman War-making in the Middle Republic." In *War and Society in the Roman World,* ed. J. Rich and G. Shipley, 38–68. London: Routledge.

———. 1996. "Augustus and the *Spolia Opima.*" *Chiron* 26: 85–127.

———. 1997. "Structuring Roman History: The Consular Year and the Roman Historical Tradition." *Histos,* http://www.dur.ac.uk/classics/histos/1997/rich1.html.

Richard, J.-C. 1992. "Tribuns militaires et triomphe." In *La Rome des premiers siècles: Legende et histoire (Actes de la table ronde en l'honneur de Massimo Pallottino, Paris, 3–4 mai 1991),* Biblioteca di "Studi Etruschi" 24, ed. L.S. Olschki, 235–46. Florence: Istituto Nazionale di Studi Etruschi e Italici.

Richardson, J.S. 1975. "The Triumph, the Praetors, and the Senate in the Early Second Century B.C." *JRS* 65: 50–63.

———. 1991. "*Imperium Romanum:* Empire and the Language of Power." *JRS* 81: 1–9.

Richardson, L. 1977. "Hercules Musarum and the Porticus Philippi in Rome.: *AJA* 81: 355–61.

———. 1992. *A New Topographical Dictionary of Ancient Rome.* Baltimore: The Johns Hopkins University Press.

Richter, G. 1955. "The Origin of Verism in Roman Portraits." *JRS* 45: 39–46.

Ridley, R.T. 1983. "*Falsi Triumphi, Plures Consulatus.*" *Latomus* 62: 372–82.

———. 1986. "The 'Consular Tribunate': The Testimony of Livy." *Klio* 86: 444–65.

———. 1988. "Patavinitas among the Patricians? Livy and the Conflict of the Orders." In *Staat und Staatlichkeit in der frühen römischen Republik,* ed. W. Eder, 103–38. Stuttgart: Franz Steiner.

———. 2000. "Livy and the Hannibalic War." In *The Roman Middle Republic: Politics, Religion, and Historiography c. 400–133 B.C.,* Acta Instituti Romani Finlandiae 23, ed. C. Bruun, 13–40. Rome: Institutum Romanum Finlandiae.

Rilinger, R. 1976. *Der Einfluss des Wahlleiters bei den römischen Konsulwahlen von 366 bis 50 v. Chr.* Vestigia, Beiträge zur Alten Geschichte 24. Munich: C.H. Beck.

Rohde, G. 1942. "Ovatio." *RE* 18.2: 1889–1903. Stuttgart: J.B. Metzler.

Roller, M.B. 1996. "Ethical Contradiction and the Fractured Community in Lucan's *Bellum Civile.*" *CA* 15: 319–47.

———. 2001. *Constructing Autocracy : Aristocrats and Emperors in Julio-Claudian Rome.* Princeton: Princeton University Press.

Rosenstein, N. 1990a. *Imperatores Victi: Military Defeat and Aristocratic Competition in the Middle and Late Republic.* Berkeley and Los Angeles: University of California Press.

———. 1990b. "War, Failure, and Aristocratic Competition." *CPh* 85: 255–65.

———. 1993. "Sorting Out the Lot in Republican Rome." *AJPh* 116: 43–75.

———. 1995. "Competition and Crisis in Mid-Republican Rome." *Phoenix* 47: 313–38.

———. 2006. "Aristocratic Values." In *A Companion to the Roman Republic,* ed. N. Rosenstein and R. Morstein-Marx, 365–82. Malden: Blackwell.

Rossi, A. 2000. "The Tears of Marcellus: History of a Literary Motif in Livy." *G&R* 47: 56–66.

Roth, J.P. 2006. "Siege Narrative in Livy: Representation and Reality." In *Representations of War in Ancient Rome,* ed. S. Dillon and K.E. Welch, 49–67. Cambridge: Cambridge University Press.

Rotondi, G. 1912. *Leges Publicae Populi Romani.* Milan: Società Editrice Libraria.

Rüpke, J. 1990. *Domi militiae: Die religiöse Konstruktion des Krieges in Rom.* Stuttgart: Franz Steiner.

———. 1995. "*Fasti:* Quellen oder Produkte römischer Geschichtsschreibung?" *Klio* 77: 184–202.

———. 2004. "Roman Religion." In *The Cambridge Companion to the Roman Republic,* ed. H.I. Flower, 179–95. Cambridge: Cambridge University Press.

———. 2006a. "Communicating with the Gods." In *A Companion to the Roman Republic,* ed. N. Rosenstein and R. Morstein-Marx, 215–35. Malden: Blackwell.

———. 2006b. "Triumphator and Ancestor Rituals between Symbolic Anthropology and Magic." *Numen* 53: 251–89.

Ryan, F.X. 1998. *Rank and Participation in the Roman Senate.* Stuttgart: Franz Steiner.

Sailor, D. 2006. "Dirty Linen, Fabrication, and the Authorities of Livy and Augustus." *TAPhA* 136: 329–88.

Sandberg, K. 2000. "Tribunician and Non-tribunician Legislation in Mid-Republican Rome." In *The Roman Middle Republic: Politics, Religion, and Historiography c. 400–133 B.C.,* Acta Instituti Romani Finlandiae 23, ed. C. Bruun, 121–40. Rome: Institutum Romanum Finlandiae.

Scheidel, W. 1996. "Finances, Figures and Fiction." *CQ* 46: 222–38.

Schlag, U. 1968. *Regnum in senatu: Das Wirken römischer Staatsmänner von 200 bis 191 v. Chr.* Kieler Historische Studien 4. Stuttgart: Ernst Klett.

Scott, R.T. 2000. "The Triple Arch of Augustus and the Roman Triumph." *JRS* 13: 183–91.

Scullard, H.H. 1951. *Roman Politics, 220–150 B.C.* Oxford: Oxford University Press.

———. 1970. *Scipio Africanus: Soldier and Politician.* Ithaca: Cornell University Press.

Sealey, R. 1959. "Consular Tribunes Once More." *Latomus* 18: 521–30.

Sehlmeyer, M. 1999. *Stadtrömische Ehrenstatuen der republikanischen Zeit: Historizität und Kontext von Symbolen nobilitären Standesbewußtseins.* Historia Einzelschriften 130. Stuttgart: Franz Steiner.

Shatzman, I. 1972. "The Roman General's Authority over Booty." *Historia* 21: 177–205.

Smith, R.E. 1976. "The Aristocratic Epoch in Latin Literature." In *Essays on Roman Culture: The Todd Memorial Lectures,* ed. A.J. Dunston, 187–223. Toronto: Hakkert.

Smith, R.R.R. 1988. *Hellenistic Royal Portraits.* Oxford: Clarendon Press.

Stambaugh, J.E. 1988. *The Ancient Roman City.* Baltimore: The Johns Hopkins University Press.

Staveley, E.S. 1953. "The Significance of the Consular Tribunate." *JRS* 43: 30–36.

———. 1989. "Rome and Italy in the Early Third Century." In *The Cambridge Ancient History,* 2nd ed., vol. 7.2, *The Rise of Rome to 220 B.C.,* ed. F.W. Walbank and A.E. Astin, 420–55. Cambridge: Cambridge University Press.

Stemmler, G. 2003. "Die goldene *bulla* des Triumphators: Zweifel an ihrer Historizität." *Klio* 85: 212–16.

Stemmler, M. 2000. "*Auctoritas exempli:* Zur Wechselwirkung von kanonisierten Vergangenkeitsbildern und gesellschaftlicher Gegenwart in der spätrepublikanischen Rhetorik." In *Mos maiorum: Untersuchungen zu den Formen der Iden-*

titätsstiftung und Stabilisierung in der römischen Republik, Historia Einzelschriften 141, ed. B. Linke and M. Stemmler, 141–206. Stuttgart: Franz Steiner.

Stewart, A.F. 1990. *Greek Sculpture.* 2 vols. New Haven: Yale University Press.

———. 1993. *Faces of Power: Alexander's Image and Hellenistic Politics.* Hellenistic Culture and Society 11. Berkeley and Los Angeles: University of California Press.

Stewart, R. 1998. *Public Office in Early Rome: Ritual Procedure and Political Practice.* Ann Arbor: University of Michigan Press.

Sumner, G.V. 1970. "Proconsuls and *Provinciae* in Spain, 218/7–196/5 B.C." *Arethusa* 3: 85–102.

———. 1977. "Notes on *Provinciae* in Spain (197–133 B.C.)." *CPh* 72: 126–30.

Syme, R. 1939. *The Roman Revolution.* Oxford: Oxford University Press.

———. 1959. "Livy and Augustus." *HSCPh* 64: 27–87.

Sziemler, G.J. 1972. *The Priests of the Roman Republic: A Study of Interactions between Priesthoods and Magistracies.* Collection Latomus 127. Brussels: Latomus.

Tanner, J. 2000. "Portraits, Power, and Patronage in the Late Roman Republic." *JRS* 90: 18–50.

Tatum, W.J. 2001. "The Consular Elections for 190 B.C." *Klio* 83: 388–401.

Taylor, L.R. 1966. *Roman Voting Assemblies from the Hannibalic War to the Dictatorship of Caesar.* Jerome Lectures 8. Ann Arbor: University of Michigan Press.

Thommen, L. 1995. "Les lieux de la plèbe et de ses tribuns dans la Rome républicaine." *Klio* 77: 358–70.

Thompson, E.M. 1966. *A Handbook of Greek and Latin Palaeography.* Chicago: Argonaut.

Thomsen, R. 1957. *Early Roman Coinage: A Study of the Chronology.* Vol. 1, *The Evidence.* Nationalmuseets Skrifter Arkaeologisk-Historisk Raekke 5. Copenhagen: Nationalmuseet.

Timpe, D. 1996. "*Memoria* und Geschichtsschreibung bei den Römern." In *Vergangenheit und Lebenswelt: Soziale Kommunikation, Traditionsbildung und historisches Bewußtsein,* ScriptOralia 90, ed. H.-J. Gehrke and A. Möller, 277–300. Tübingen: Gunter Narr.

Toher, M. 1990. "Augustus and the Evolution of Roman Historiography." In *Between Republic and Empire: Interpretations of Augustus and His Principate,* ed. K.A. Raaflaub and M. Toher, 139–54. Berkeley and Los Angeles: University of California Press.

Toynbee, A.J. 1965. *Hannibal's Legacy: The Hannibalic War's Effects on Roman Life.* 2 vols. London: Oxford University Press.

Tränkle, H. 1977. *Livius und Polybios.* Basel: Schwabe.

Treggiari, S. 2003. "Ancestral Virtues and Vices: Cicero on Nature, Nurture and Presentation." In *Myth, History and Culture in Republican Rome: Studies in Honour of T.P. Wiseman,* ed. D. Braund and C. Gill, 139–64. Exeter: University of Exeter Press.

Ullman, B.L. 1980. *Ancient Writing and Its Influence.* Medieval Academy Reprints for Teaching 10. Toronto: University of Toronto Press.

von Ungern-Sternberg, J. 1986. "The Formation of the 'Annalistic Tradition': The Example of the Decemvirate." In *Social Struggles in Archaic Rome: New Perspectives on the Conflict of the Orders,* ed. K.A. Raaflaub, 77–104. Berkeley and Los Angeles: University of California Press.

Van Sickle, J. 1987. "The Elogia of the Cornelii Scipiones and the Origin of the Epigram at Rome." *AJPh* 108: 41–55.

Vasaly, A. 1987. "Personality and Power: Livy's Description of the Appii Claudii in the First Pentad." *TAPhA* 117: 203–26.

Versnel, H.S. 1970. *Triumphus.* Leiden: E.J. Brill.

———. 2006. "Red (Herring?) Comments on a New Theory Concerning the Origin of the Triumph." *Numen* 53: 290–326.

Vonnegut, K. 1968. *Slaughterhouse Five.* New York: Dell.

Walbank, F.W. 1957. *A Historical Commentary on Polybius.* 3 vols. Oxford: Clarendon Press.

———. 1971. "The Fourth and Fifth Decades." In *Livy,* ed. T.A. Dorey, 47–72. London: Routledge and Kegan Paul.

Wallace-Hadrill, A. 1987. "Time for Augustus: Ovid, Augustus and the Fasti." In *Homo Viator: Classical Essays for John Bramble,* ed. M. Whitby et al., 221–30. Bristol: Bristol Classical Press.

———. 1990. "Roman Arches and Greek Honors: The Language of Power at Rome." *PCPhS* 216: 143–81.

Walsh, P.G. 1955. "Livy's Preface and the Distortion of History." *AJPh* 76: 369–83.

———. 1961. *Livy: His Historical Aims and Methods.* Cambridge: Cambridge University Press.

———. 1966. "Livy." In *Latin Historians,* ed. D.R. Dudley and T.A. Dorey, 143–58. London: Routledge and Kegan Paul.

———. 1967. "Die Vorrede des Livius und die Verzerrung der Geschichte." In *Wege zu Livius,* ed. E. Burck, 181–99. Darmstadt: Wissenschaftliche Buchgesellschaft.

———. 1974. *Livy.* Greece and Rome Surveys in the Classics 8. Oxford: Clarendon Press.

———. 1990. *Livy: Book XXXVI.* Warminster: Aris and Phillips.

———. 1992. *Livy: Book XXXVII.* Warminster: Aris and Phillips.

———. 1993. *Livy: Book XXXVIII.* Warminster: Aris and Phillips.

———. 1994. *Livy: Book XXXIX.* Warminster: Aris and Phillips.

———. 1996. *Livy: Book XL.* Warminster: Aris and Phillips.

Walter, U. 2004. *Memoria und res publica: Zur Geschichtskultur im republikanischen Rom.* Studien zur Alten Geschichte 1. Frankfurt a./M.: Antike.

Walters, C.F., and R.S. Conway, eds. 1919. *Titi Livi Ab Urbe Condita, Libri VI–X.* Oxford: Clarendon Press.

———. 1929. *Titi Livi Ab Urbe Condita, Libri XXI–XXV.* Oxford: Clarendon Press.

Warren, L.B. 1970. "Roman Triumphs and Etruscan Kings: The Changing Face of the Triumph." *JRS* 60: 49–66.

Warrior, V.M. 1990. "A Technical Meaning of *Ducere* in Roman Elections? Livy's Account of the Elections of the Consuls for 189 B.C." *RhM* 133: 144–57.

———. 1996. *The Initiation of the Second Macedonian War: An Explication of Livy Book 31.* Historia Einzelschriften 97. Stuttgart: Franz Steiner.

Welch, K.E. 2006a. "Art and Architecture in the Roman Republic." In *A Companion to the Roman Republic,* ed. N. Rosenstein and R. Morstein-Marx, 496–542. Malden: Blackwell.

———. 2006b. "*Domi Militiaeque:* Roman Domestic Aesthetics and War Booty in the Republic." In *Representations of War in Ancient Rome,* ed. S. Dillon and K.E. Welch, 91–161. Cambridge: Cambridge University Press.

———. 2006c. "Introduction." In *Representations of War in Ancient Rome,* ed. S. Dillon and K.E. Welch, 1–26. Cambridge: Cambridge University Press.

Wiedemann, T. 1996. "Single Combat and Being Roman." *AncSoc* 27: 91–103.

Williams, M.F. 2000. "Polybius on Wealth, Bribery, and the Downfall of Constitutions." *Ancient History Bulletin* 14: 131–48.

Williams, P. 2004. "The Roman Tribunate in the 'Era of Quiescence,' 287–133 BC." *Latomus* 63: 281–94.

Williamson, C. 1990. "The Roman Aristocracy and Positive Law." *CPh* 85: 266–76.

Wiseman, T.P. 1975. "The Circus Flamininus." *PBSR* 42: 1–26.

———. 1979. *Clio's Cosmetics: Three Studies in Greco-Roman Literature.* Totowa: Rowman and Littlefield.

———. 1986. "Monuments and the Roman Annalists." In *Past Perspectives: Studies in Greek and Roman Historical Writing,* ed. I.S. Moxon et al., 87–100. Cambridge: Cambridge University Press.

———. 1989. "Afterword: The Theater of Civic Life." In *Roman Public Buildings,* Exeter Studies in History 20, ed. I.M. Barton, 151–54. Exeter: University of Exeter Press.

Wistrand, E. 1987. *Felicitas imperatoria.* Studia Graeca et Latina Gothoburgensia 48. Göteborg: Acta Universitas Gothoburgensis.

Woodman, A.J. 1988. *Rhetoric in Classical Historiography: Four Studies.* London: Croom Helm.

Yakobson, A. 2006. "Popular Power in the Roman Republic." In *A Companion to the Roman Republic,* ed. N. Rosenstein and R. Morstein-Marx, 383–400. Malden: Blackwell.

Yavetz, Z. 1974. "*Existimatio* and *Fama.*" *HSCPh* 78: 34–65.

Zanker, P. 1988. *The Power of Images in the Age of Augustus.* Jerome Lectures 16. Ann Arbor: University of Michigan Press.

Ziolkowski, A. 1993. "*Urbs Direpta;* or, How the Romans Sacked Cities." In *War and Society in the Roman World,* ed. J. Rich and G. Shipley, 69–91. London: Routledge.

INDEX LOCORUM

SUPPLEMENTAL INDEX

FASTI TRIUMPHALES

References to the Fasti Triumphales appear throughout as page numbers from Degrassi's edition (*Inscriptiones Italiae* 13.1), cited as a secondary source in author/date format (e.g., Degrassi 1947). Each extant entry in the Fasti has three page numbers associated with it: a drawing of the inscription itself, the edited text on the following page, and Degrassi's historical commentary. Because each page contains a number of separate entries, the page numbers by themselves are not unique identifiers, especially when taken out of context. Here, therefore, for the benefit of readers who may wish to search for references to particular entries from the Fasti, the notices have been identified by the name of the commander and sorted chronologically, according to the dates printed in the margins of Degrassi's edition and the sequence of entries on the stone. Where segments of the inscription are missing, only Degrassi's commentary has been cited, speculating as to what the contents of the lost entries may have been. In such cases the commander's name is shown here in italics to indicate that the entry is in fact only a reconstruction and not extant. Consular colleagues in their year of office share a single entry; other triumphs that happened to fall in a given year are listed separately.

Year (B.C.)	*Commander*	*Degrassi pages*	
753	Romulus	64–65, 534	33n2, 34n4, 277n6
640–617	Ancus Marcius	64–65, 535	33n2, 277n6
598–595, 588, 585	L. Tarquinius Priscus	64–65, 535	33n2, 277n6
571, 567, 566–564	Ser. Tullius	64–65, 535	33n2, 277n6
534–510	L. Tarquinius Superbus	64–65, 535	33n2, 277n6
505	M. Valerius Volusus	64–65, 535–36	81n51
	P. Postumius Tubertus		
503	Agrippa Menenius Lenatus	65–65, 536	70n12
	P. Postumius Tubertus		
459	Q. Fabius Vibulanus	66–67, 537	81n51
	L. Cornelius Maluginensis		
449	L. Valerius Poplicola	66–67, 538	38n17
	M. Horatius Barbatus		
428	*A. Cornelius Cossus*	538	34n4
361	T. Quinctius Pennus Capitolinus	68–69, 540	81n51
	C. Sulpicius Peticus		
360	P. Poetelius Libo Visolus	68–69, 540	45n45, 81n51
	M. Fabius Ambustus		
358	C. Sulpicius Peticus	68–69, 540	81n51
	C. Plautius Proculus		
356	C. Marcius Rutilus	68–69, 540	38n19
343	M. Valerius Corvus	68–69, 541	81n51
	A. CorneliusCossus Arvina		
326	Q. Publilius Philo	70–71, 541	33n3
322	L. Fulvius Curvus	70–71, 542	81n51
	Q. Fabius Maximus Rullianus		
311	C. Iunius Bubulcus Brutus	70–71, 542	81n51
	Q. Aemilius Barbula		
309	L. Papirius Cursor	70–71, 542	81n51
	Q. Fabius Maximus Rullianus		
294	L. Postumius Megellus	72–73, 544	43n36
	M. Atilius Regulus		

Year (B.C.)	Commander	Degrassi pages	
293	Sp. Carvilius Maximus	72–73, 544	81n51
	L. Papirius Cursor		
291	Q. Fabius Maximus Gurges	72–73, 544–45	81n51
	L. Postumius Megellus		
290	*M'. Curius Dentatus*	545	81n51
	P. Cornelius Rufinus		
289 (?)	*M'. Curius Dentatus*	545	45n45
275	M'. Curius Dentatus	74–75, 546	81n51
	L. Cornelius Canina		
272	Sp. Carvilius Maximus	74–75, 546	81n51
	L. Papirius Cursor		
268	P. Sempronius Sophus	74–75, 547	81n51
	Ap. Claudius Russus		
267	M. Atilius Regulus	74–75, 547	81n51
	L. Iulius Libo		
266	D. Iunius Pera	74–75, 547	81n51
	N. Fabius Pictor		
258	C. Aquillius Florus	76–77, 548	81n51
	C. Sulpicius Paterculus		
257	A. Atilius Caiatinus	76–77, 548	81n51
	C. Atilius Regulus		
254	Ser. Fulvius Paetinus	76–77, 548	81n51
	M. Aemilius Paullus		
241	Q. Valerius Falto	76–77, 549	73n20
231	C. Papirius Maso	78–79, 449	41n39
223	C. Flaminius	78–79, 550	40n28
	P. Furius Philus		
222	M. Claudius Marcellus	78–79, 550	14n41, 34n4, 46n49, 57n16, 149n4, 150n7
219	*L. Aemilius Paullus*	550	81n51, 149n4
	M. Livius Salinator		
207	*M. Livius Salinator*	551	70n10, 149n4
	C. Claudius Nero		
200	*L. Furius Purpureo*	551	74n24, 86n12, 149n4, 188n3
197	*C. Cornelius Cethegus*	78–79, 551–52	78nn40–41, 149n4, 188n3
	Q. Minucius Rufus		
197	M. Helvius	78–79, 552	76n32
196	M. Claudius Marcellus	78–79, 552	79n44, 181n2, 188n3
196	Cn. Cornelius Blasio	78–79, 552	61n26
195	Q. Minucius Thermus	78–79, 552–53	76n33, 92n29

Year (B.C.)	*Commander*	*Degrassi pages*	
194	M. Porcius Cato	78–79, 553	62n29
191	P. Cornelius Scipio Nasica	78–79, 553	80n50, 193n11
190	*M'. Acilius Glabrio*	553	92n31
187	M. Fulvius Nobilior	80–81, 554	123n16
187	Cn. Manlius Vulso	80–81, 554	100n51, 123n16
185	*L. Manlius Acidinus*	554	91n27
184	*C. Calpurnius Piso*	554	81n51
	L. Quinctius Crispinus		
181	*L. Aemilius Paullus*	554	117n7
179	*Q. Fulvius Flaccus*	555	96n41
178	Ti. Sempronius Gracchus	80–81, 555	83n59, 97nn42 and 44
	L. Postumius Albinus		
175	M. Titinius Curvus	80–81, 555	93n33
175	M. Aemilius Lepidus	80–81, 555–56	83n59
	P. Mucius Scaevola		
167	L. Aemilius Paullus	80–81, 556	270n62
167	Cn. Octavius	80–81, 556	271n64
167	L. Anicius Gallus	80–81, 556	271n64
19	L. Cornelius Balbus	86–87, 571	5n13

GENERAL INDEX

Text	10/12 Baskerville
Display	Baskerville
Compositor	BookMatters, Berkeley
Indexer	Roberta Engleman
Printer and binder	Sheridan Books, Inc.